1996

The Role of Transportation in
the Industrial Revolution

The Role of Transportation in the Industrial Revolution

A Comparison of England and France

RICK SZOSTAK

McGill–Queen's University Press
Montreal & Kingston • London • Buffalo

© McGill-Queen's University Press 1991
ISBN 0-7735-0840-6

Legal deposit third quarter 1991
Bibliothèque nationale du Québec

Printed in Canada on acid-free paper

This book has been published with the help of a grant
from the Social Science Federation of Canada, using
funds provided by the Social Sciences and Humanities
Research Council of Canada.

Canadian Cataloguing in Publication Data

Szostak, Rick, 1959–
    The role of transportation in the Industrial Revolution
    Includes bibliographical references and index.
    ISBN 0-7735-0840-6
    1. England – Industries – History – 18th century.
    2. France – Industries – History – 18th century.
    3. Transportation – England – History – 18th century.
    4. Transportation – France – History – 18th century.
    5. England – Economic conditions – 18th century.
    5. France – Economic conditions – 18th century.
    I. Title.
    HE243.S96 1991   330.942   C91-090098-1

Typeset in Bembo 10/12 by Caractéra inc.,
Quebec City.

For my parents,
John and Lois Szostak

Contents

Tables and Figures

Preface

It is humbling to recognize the crucial role played by others in the completion of this book. This work began as a doctoral thesis at Northwestern University. Joel Mokyr supervised the thesis, was generous with his advice, and was very supportive of a project which was quite different in orientation and methodology from his own research. I cannot thank him enough. Jonathan R.T. Hughes, Charlie Calomiris, and Gerald Goldstein also served on my dissertation committee, and contributed much in the way of advice and encouragement. Lou Cain, John Lyons, and Cormac O'Grada made a number of helpful suggestions. Last but not least, I owe a debt of gratitude to my fellow graduate students. Without such friends, this project would never have been completed.

The Social Sciences and Humanities Research Council of Canada provided me with funding which allowed me to undertake several months of research in England and France, and to complete the final draft of the book. Over the last couple of years, along with the continued interest of Joel Mokyr in the project, I have benefitted from the comments of George Grantham and Michael B. Percy. Cheryle Ann Kaplan provided much-appreciated research assistance. The two anonymous referees both provided thoughtful and helpful criticism. Peter Blaney of McGill-Queen's has been a pleasure to deal with. Claire Gigantes did a masterful job of editing the manuscript. Charlene Hill typed most of the manuscript with her usual skill and speed. Maryon Buffel and Pat Gangur completed the task admirably.

I thank Elsevier Science Publishers for permission to use material previously published in the *Journal of Economic Behavior and Organization*.

I end on a personal note. I was blessed with parents who never tried to push me in any direction but were always there to support me in whatever I chose to do. This book is for them.

To these people and others must go much of the credit for all that is good in this work. Any mistakes there may be I managed all on my own.

*The Role of Transportation in
the Industrial Revolution*

Introduction

My contention in this work is that a modern system of transportation was necessary for the Industrial Revolution to occur in England. While transport is discussed in many works on the Industrial Revolution, none have provided a comprehensive discussion of the various effects of England's superior transport system on the process of industrialization; nor, especially, have they described the links between transport improvement and technological innovation. Thus, transport has not been given the prominent position it deserves in the literature on the Industrial Revolution.[1] In this introductory chapter, I first define what is meant by the terms Industrial Revolution, necessary, and modern transportation. Next, since it is important to explain at an early stage how my analysis of the eighteenth century relates to what happened before and after that period, I place this work briefly within a broader historical context. Having done that, I sketch some theoretical arguments that explain how transportation could affect the phenomena that comprise the Industrial Revolution. My work is then discussed in relation to a number of important works on the Industrial Revolution and on the role of transport in history. The chapter ends with a brief outline of the rest of the book.

The Industrial Revolution involves four phenomena: regional specialization, the emergence of new industries, an increase in the scale of production, and a dramatic increase in the rate of technological innovation. The fourth of these, as I shall show, is caused in large part by the other three. It is also the most important in the view of most historians and will be my primary focus as well. Any attempt to describe the Industrial Revolution without devoting considerable attention to the question of technological innovation would be highly suspect. The Industrial Revolution is so important, in fact, precisely because it is the starting point of a new era in which economic growth has largely been generated by persistent technological innovation. While the eighteenth century was not characterized by high growth rates in aggregate output (see below), the period saw the emergence of a new environment highly conducive to technological change, which would come to dominate the whole economy in succeeding centuries. Parker (1982) has described this as a transformation from an economy where improvements in productivity are mostly generated by expansion in trade, the spreading of fixed costs, and increasing division of labour (which he terms Smithian growth) to an economy where the engine of growth is continuous technological change (which he terms Schumpeterian growth). While technological change has occurred throughout history, the Industrial Revolution created for the first time an environment in which it could occur with such frequency as to be the major cause of economic growth. Because of the special importance of this great transformation, my analysis extends not only to the more direct effects of improved transport on technology but also to the indirect effects through regional specialization, the emergence of new industries, and increasing scale of production.

The other three factors are necessary for a balanced view of the Industrial Revolution for they are quite important in their own right, as well as being causes of technological innovation. Regional specialization has long been recognized as an integral part of the history of England during this period, and many scholars have focused on such questions as the reasons for the increasing concentration of the wool industry in Yorkshire. The emergence of new industries gets little attention in the literature as a phenomenon though some of its components, such as the emergence of machine-making firms, have been noted. The fact that the English Industrial Revolution was characterized by the increasing scale of operation of a large number of productive units is commonly recognized. The emergence of the factory during this period receives, with good reason, much attention in the literature. As with technological change, the Industrial Revolution marks the beginning of the modern era; while isolated factories had existed before, it is in late eighteenth-century England that the factory begins to emerge as a common form of industrial organization. The coincidence of dramatic changes in the rate of technological innovation and in industrial organization has unfortunately led many scholars to attribute the latter to the former. This, it will be seen, is putting the cart before the horse; the beginning of the transition from domestic production to workshop[2] production clearly predates the introduction of new technology in most industries. Rather, the new workshops played a key role in fostering the new technology that is supposed to have created them. Important in its own right, and of great importance in the emergence of new technology, the reasons for increasing scale of production will be the second major focus of this work.

The Industrial Revolution was slow relative to most political revolutions. Arguably, however, it was more important. Wrigley (1988, 2–3) has recently asserted that its intrinsic interest and importance should make it the most exciting topic in economic history. A fairly gradual transformation along the four lines outlined above ushered in the modern world of constant technological change, large factories, industrial concentration, and a variety of new industries. Viewed in this light, it becomes very difficult (and fairly unimportant) to date the Industrial Revolution exactly. It could be argued that it continues to this day, though a more appropriate view might be that by the mid–nineteenth century the revolution was over and England had entered a mature Schumpeterian world. For my purposes, fortunately, dating the endpoint is unnecessary; I focus on the initial decades of the Industrial Revolution to show why this amazing transformation began. The first workshops emerge in the 1750s and 1760s. The upsurge in technological innovation dates from the 1760s. In the latter half of the eighteenth century various industries begin to concentrate noticeably in particular regions, and important new industries emerge. Transport improvements that were put in place in the early and mid–eighteenth century can be treated as an exogenous variable (i.e. transport improvements are not themselves a result of industrialization) which both allowed and induced the Industrial Revolution.

The word necessary must be used with caution. Many things are possible in this world with varying probabilities, and only a handful of these will be observed historically. Moreover, what is impossible in one setting may be quite possible in another. Thus, there may be many paths from Smithian to Schumpeterian growth that could occur in various places, and it would be folly to maintain that any characteristic is necessary to all. However, this is not what I mean by necessary. I mean simply that on the path which England followed, a modern transportation system was necessary for the achievement of Schumpeterian growth. I would claim further that this broad path was the only likely one to be followed in that time and place, and that similar paths also requiring modern transport were followed by the other early industrializers in their turn. I should emphasize that necessary in no way implies sufficient. "Nothing is ever so simple that a single explanation will adequately explain it" (Scitovsky 1986). The Industrial Revolution was a complex phenomenon and to attribute sufficiency to any one development would be ludicrous. Modern transportation creates an opportunity for industrial expansion. Realistically, the creation of opportunities is not enough; the economy must possess agents able and willing to take advantage of them.

I can now briefly describe what I mean by modern transportation. To many people the era of modern transportation began with the railway. Yet, as the work of Fogel and others has indicated, the importance so often attributed to railways was greatly exaggerated. These authors have shown that a combination of water and road transport could largely match the capacity of the railways with only a small loss in output. Thus, modern transport can safely be said to have begun when an extensive and reliable system which could move bulk goods at low cost or high-value goods at high speed came into existence. This could be accomplished only with a combination of land and water transport in the pre-railway era. On land, it required roads which could support wheeled traffic year-round such that a regular professional carrying system could develop. On water, it required an extensive network of canals, navigable rivers, and coastal shipping which could move bulky goods throughout a particular region. It is this early modern transport system – the combination of an extensive network of waterways and of suitable roads – which was necessary for the English Industrial Revolution. At the start of the next chapter, I shall describe in greater detail the particular roles played by land and water transport.

LOOKING BEYOND THE EIGHTEENTH CENTURY

This work is concerned with how improvements in transport aided the progress of four other phenomena: regional specialization, the emergence of new industries, an increase in the scale of production and an increased rate of technological innovation. It would be misleading to act as if none of these five phenomena had a previous history. Other attempts to understand why the Industrial Revolution occurred when and where it did have always, at least implicitly, recognized that there were significant changes in the preceding centuries. The next chapter will show that the process of transport improvement can be traced back for centuries. Doing so is essential to the argument that improved transport was a cause rather than a result of industrialization. Certainly, as discussed below, the process of industrialization, once begun, created pressures for even better transport services. But this does not mean that the line of causation always runs in that direction. Showing that improvements in transport were the result of a centuries-long process that began well before the Industrial Revolution, and that what I call early modern transport was largely in place before the Industrial Revolution began, does not prove that transport "caused" the Industrial Revolution (see the discussion of Crafts, below). It is, though, a necessary first step to be able to use improved transport as an exogenous variable in my model. Claiming that improved transport is exogenous in this sense should not be taken to mean that England's transport system was some kind of gift from the gods. The Smithian growth process has a natural tendency to generate pressures for improved transport, since Smithian growth relies on expanding trade links. However, a number of constraints – social, political, geographical, and technological – work against this tendency. If these constraints are overpowering, they can cause an economy to stagnate or even decline. The next chapter alludes to ways in which England was able to overcome these constraints. If the reader, once convinced of the importance of transportation in the Industrial Revolution, wanted to go a step beyond the question, "Why England First?," he or she would wonder why these constraints were overcome in England before they could be overcome in other countries. I shall return to this question at the end of chapter 2.

Both large-scale production and technological innovation had occurred in the past. I would argue, however, that the "factories" that are observed in previous periods in various parts of Europe were of a quite different type. They tended to be government owned or subsidized. They specialized in the production of luxuries for the court or of military hardware. Their advantage over less organized production was in terms of quality rather than quantity. Government patronage tended to make them relatively unconcerned with the cost of production. As Borchardt says, "The success or failure of the proto-industries did not depend primarily on their technological performance but on the skill of the entrepreneur in procuring courtly extravagance or the compulsory recruitment of labour" (1975, 88). Obviously, enterprises such as these are of a much different type than modern factories, and the incentives to innovate are not there.[3] Thus, the large-scale enterprises which we see emerging during the eighteenth century really were a new phenomenon for, with a couple of exceptions, it was the first time production had been organized in this manner by private individuals in response to market forces.

Technological innovation was not a new phenomenon, either. What was new was the rate of innovation. It would be convenient for my purpose if the rate of technological innovation through history showed a constant or gently rising trend to about the mideighteenth century, at which point the rate of technological innovation became much higher. When Lilley attempted to plot the relative invention rate from 5500 B.C. to modern times (1965), he found that there had been pronounced secular fluctuations before 1700. While there is much to quibble about in

Lilley's measures, it would seem that dramatic upturns in the rate of technological innovation were not new. Still, never before had such upturns been strong enough for innovation to become the major source of economic growth. More troubling is the impression that the upward trend in the rate of innovation had earlier beginnings than the eighteenth century. There is no denying that the seventeenth century did see higher rates of innovative activity than immediately previous centuries. When discussing particular industries, I will sometimes refer to inventions made during the seventeenth or early eighteenth centuries. This does not diminish the fact that the relative rate of invention quadrupled during the eighteenth century (Lilley 1965); it is in the eighteenth century that the big transformation occurred.[4] One should not ascribe undue importance to earlier changes in the seventeenth. In Court's words, "Seventeenth century England took important steps toward an industrial future; steps so varied and interesting that they may tempt us into supposing them to have been more important than they actually were" (Court 1946, 87).

Having discussed the historical antecedents of both workshops and technological innovation, it is necessary to digress and consider the relationship between the two. It is often asserted that "factories" emerged in response to the requirements of new power-driven machinery. To be sure, the later development of such machines did accelerate the shift toward centralized production. However, the earliest workshops relied on the same technology that had been used in cottages for centuries. Berg (1985) provides numerous examples of workshops using old technology. Usher noted in 1920 that "the tendency to associate factories with establishments using power machinery tends to distract attention from factories that were not based on any tools or mechanism other than the old hand machines" (Cohen 1981, 24). Bladen, Thomas, and McKendrick all provide evidence that during the eighteenth century workshops emerged in the pottery industry without power-using machinery or a central power source (Cohen 1981, 29). Some of the most famous works of the late eighteenth century used no new technology. "What then of Gott's great factory at Bean Ing? Could it not show new machinery, even if not power, applied to the weaving and finishing of cloth? The answer must be that in neither branch did it dispense with the traditional hand processes" (Crump 1929, 25-6). This is not an isolated case in the woolen industry. "While it has been suggested that there was no great advantage from the factory system over cottage industry until power was available to work machinery at high speed, there does appear to be considerable evidence of a transference of some elements of the wool textile industry from domestic manufacture to specifically constructed or converted buildings before the application of mechanical power" (Jenkins 1982, 51).

Certainly, as new technology was developed in the Industrial Revolution, it made factory organization seem more attractive and hastened the adoption of this organizational form. Nevertheless, it is very important to recognize that many eighteenth-century "factories" used old cottage technology exclusively, and to realize especially that this was certainly the case for the earliest workshops which predated the new power technology. First, this forces one to look for other causes of the rise of the factory. Second, it allows workshops to be treated as a source of technological innovation. Rather than factories being a response to new technology, this new technology is to some degree a result of the creation of a new method of organization suited to new technology. Simply put, people are much likelier to develop technology suited only to factories after factories have come into being.

Various authors have tried to explain the rise of centralized workplaces using old technology. Landes (1986) has tried to salvage the technological argument by claiming that the centralization of wool spinning and weaving was a response to technological change in the preparatory and finishing stages. This tenuous connection can hardly explain the occurrence of the same phenomenon in a variety of industries at the same time. Marglin (1974) argued that factories were introduced to allow employers to exploit workers more (Marglin is discussed in detail in Landes 1986). Oliver Williamson (1980) maintained that factories were inherently more efficient than domestic production. One major failing of these, and other, explanations is that they cannot explain the timing of the event. Why do bosses only begin to exploit workers in this way after 1750? Why was the most efficient form of organization not adopted centuries earlier? The explanation offered here can account for the timing (see also Szostak 1989). The emergence of the earliest workshops is a direct result of the impressive improvements to England's transport system in the early eighteenth century.

I should also briefly relate my analysis to the post-eighteenth-century world. I argue that due to its superior system of transportation, England was able to enter into a new era of industrialization fuelled by improvements in technology. This would create pressures for further transport improvements. The most prominent result of this pressure was the development of railways. Countries that would undergo an industrial revolution after England used extensive railway systems. There has been much discussion in the literature of the importance of railways in these countries (see below). For my present purpose, it is necessary only to recognize that debate about whether particular countries needed railways, or could have industrialized with only roads and canals, has tended to detract from the more fundamental question of whether transport improvements of any kind were necessary. By developing improvements in road transport (MacAdam and Telford techniques of roadbuilding, improvements in carriage design), water transport (steamboats etc.), and railways during the eighteenth and early nineteenth centuries, England made it considerably easier for other countries to develop modern transport systems. This was one way in which later developers were indebted to England.

More importantly, the various industrial innovations that occurred during the Industrial Revolution could be transferred easily to other countries, and most nineteenth century industrial revolutions were fuelled to a large extent by technology borrowed from England. Moreover, the process of Schumpeterian growth, once established, seems to be self-perpetuating. That is, once technological innovation starts to occur at a rapid rate, effort is continually expended toward even further innovations, and this process of growth continues. Thus, much of modern industrial history can be traced back to the English Industrial Revolution; hence explaining how the English Industrial Revolution got started is essential to an understanding of the history of the modern developed world.[5]

Such an understanding might also contain some lessons which can be applied to less developed countries today. There are many countries whose current systems of transportation are much poorer than those of eighteenth-century England. An improved understanding of the role of transport in the eighteenth century may provide insight into the problems of modern less developed countries.

THE EFFECTS OF TRANSPORTATION ON THE ENGLISH ECONOMY

I shall now look at five theoretical arguments showing how modern transportation could have an impact on the four phenomena I describe as characterizing the Industrial Revolution. Throughout, the emphasis is on how the choices faced by individual agents were altered by transport improvements. First, I argue that improved transport widened the market facing most producers. I show that a firm facing a wider market is more likely to increase its scale of operation, and that, since some regions could come to dominate the national market at the expense of others, market widening would lead to greater regional specialization. The second argument concerns a change in the methods of distribution which occurred in the eighteenth century. As well as aiding the process of market widening, this change allowed producers greater freedom and induced them to standardize their output, both of which results were conducive to an increased scale of operation.

On the input side of a firm, the third argument concerns the importance of increasing speed and reliability of transport. I compare domestic and workshop production to show that such improvements in transport would favour the latter for a number of reasons. In this discussion, the transition to workshop production is not treated merely as a special case of increasing scale of production. That is, rather than arguing simply that there is some level of output at which it becomes advantageous to switch from one mode of production to another, I discuss ways in which transport improvements made the workshop a relatively more attractive method of production than domestic production.

The fourth argument concerns the effects of lowering the cost of obtaining raw materials. I indicate that a wider range of raw materials was more necessary than is often realized. Clearly, as the cost of obtaining raw materials falls, the cost of the final good falls. Thus, it is possible to shift the supply curve without any change in the methods of production and widen the market intensively by moving along the existing demand curve. The greater availability of raw materials was the main inducement for the emergence of a number of new industries, though the availability of a wider market was also important.

Much of the impact of transport on technology is felt indirectly through the other phenomena. The fifth argument outlines the process of technological innovation, and shows how these indirect effects arise through the various other phenomena discussed in the first four sections. In the sixth section, the various relationships between improved transport and the four phenomena which make up the Industrial Revolution are outlined diagrammatically, and a few additional lines of causation are described.

Increase in Market Size

Adam Smith suggested the first causal link over two centuries ago. Lower transport costs mean wider markets which allow firms to operate on a larger scale.[6] Even under the conditions of monopolistic competition which characterized most English industry of the time, it is a straightforward result that market widening will cause firms to face a more elastic demand curve and induce them to expand production. Habakkuk (1955, 153) and Mantoux (1961, 41) are among those who have noted the beneficial impact of market extension in England. Conversely, Fohlen, describing France, says that the narrowness of the internal French market made mass production impossible (1975, 38).

Communities that were more than eight kilometres from navigable water were effectively cut off from access to markets (Meuvret 1988, 3:48).

It should be recognized in particular that transport improvements had the effect of introducing an ever widening percentage of the English population into the national marketplace. As McKendrick noted, it is often forgotten that the Industrial Revolution was founded on the sale of humble products to very large markets (1982, 53). In 1766, Whitworth wrote a passage which would fit comfortably into the modern development literature:

It is an undoubted certainty that all passage and communications bring trade into a country, and into those parts where not the least idea of traffic, among the inhabitants ever went further, or was brought to a higher pitch, than a coat to cover them, and bread to satisfy their hunger; these are the people who will soon feel the great advantage from inland navigation, who have hitherto been bred up for no other use than to feed themselves, and I may number them as some millions that have thus been buried alive, as it were, from the public service; what advantage will not accrue to this nation when so many millions will be allured out into the world of men, robust by nature, and become useful to the state, by the temptation of gain. (2–3)

Notwithstanding all of the above, it is a mistake to ascribe too central a role to the market-widening effects of transport improvements in the emergence of workshops. There are, after all, examples of very large putting-out firms throughout western Europe employing thousands of workers in their own homes. Thus, size of market does not appear to be the binding constraint preventing firms from moving toward workshop production.[7] Clearly, a market large enough to absorb the output of a small workshop is necessary before this form of production can emerge. However, it is in no way a sufficient condition, and one must look to other causal links for a more powerful explanation of the emergence of workshops in the eighteenth century. In some product lines, market widening may have been of crucial importance during this period, while in others the necessary market had perhaps existed for some time.[8]

While the role of market widening in the emergence of workshops can be questioned, it is clear that it played a key role in the process of regional specialization. Whereas previously high-cost producers had been able to maintain a hold on local markets due to the heavy expense of importing goods from elsewhere, now it was increasingly possible for low-cost regions to export their produce throughout the kingdom. It will be seen below that writers in both the primary and secondary literature attribute particular cases of regions losing or gaining particular industries to peculiar local causes. To be sure, there are numerous reasons why particular areas had advantages in particular lines of production. However, the overriding reason for the concentration of various industries in particular regions during the eighteenth century is the drop in transport costs.[9] Indeed, it would be an incredible coincidence were the same process to be observed in many branches of the textile, iron, pottery, and other industries without there being some common cause.

Along with increasing regional specialization comes increasing division of labour. As Smith noted, the production of large amounts of a particular product in a narrow geographical area allows for labour to become increasingly specialized. Marglin (1974) and Williamson (1980) have questioned the role of division of labour in increasing productivity. However, despite the simplicity of the tasks, workers must have had a comparative advantage in one task. Moreover, some of the gains from practice would have been lost had the worker performed a variety of tasks. Training costs must also have been lower where each worker mastered only one task. The fact that increasing division of labour is seen in a wide range of industries in the late eighteenth century is the best evidence that there were significant gains in productivity from this source. For my purposes, this has two important effects. Division of labour requires that semi-finished work be moved from one worker to another at many stages of production. Moreover, it becomes ever more costly to evaluate each worker's performance by looking only at output; hence the incentive to supervise the worker's labour is increased. Both of these factors contribute to making the workshop mode of production seem more attractive. It will also be seen that the division of labour into small tasks facilitates in a number of ways the development of new technology.

Change in the Methods of Distribution

In the mid-eighteenth century, improved transport brought about a change in the methods of distribution, which in turn created a need for a standardized product that could only be produced in factories. In the early part of the century, the most common method of sale for merchants and producers was to load all of their products on packhorses and travel through the countryside selling their wares at fairs and markets, and to shopkeepers. These merchants are not to be confused with small pedlars selling small items to the common man. They could have from one to several dozen horses. The major figures of the day were forced to act in this way. Abraham Darby I took some months off every year to travel to the fairs to sell his wares. Thomas Walker described the travelling merchant of the early eighteenth century: "He was exposed to the vicissitudes of the weather, to great labour and fatigue, and to constant danger ... Business carried on in this manner required a combination of personal attention, courage and physical strength not to be hoped for in a deputy" (Pratt 1912, 92).

Nonetheless, the modern reader may have difficulty imagining why entrepreneurs could not all send trusted managers in their stead. We have become accustomed to the modern corporate environment in which trusted, salaried assistants are the rule rather than the exception. We all too easily make the mistake of assuming that things have always been thus. Yet Pollard has convincingly shown that the modern manager was a creation of the nineteenth century. Adam Smith and other people of the time readily agreed that salaried managers could not administer honestly or well anything but the most routine and easily checked business (see Pollard 1965, 4–12). "In practice the trust in managers was limited for before the end of the [eighteenth] century the Peels were demanding bonds of up to £500 from recruits to the ranks of their financial management" (Chapman 1981, 72). The Crowleys developed a cumbersome system of committees at their ironworks in an attempt to reduce dishonesty and neglect to a minimum (Flinn 1957, xix). There are two ways of dealing with the agency problem. Agents can develop reputations for honesty which they see as necessary for their continued employment. Or, the agent can be put under some obligation to perform his functions well. Otherwise, means must be devised whereby the activities of the agent can be closely monitored. None of these solutions is costless. Moreover, they cannot be developed instantaneously. Practicable ways of surmounting the agency problem largely awaited the nineteenth century, when firm size grew, and methods of distribution, accounting practices, and a host of other factors became more modern. In the eighteenth century, an individual entrepreneur had no body of reputable agents to draw upon. Forms of partnership were such that none but trusted family and friends would be joined in business. Methods of monitoring agents were not readily available. It is not surprising, then, that entrepreneurs, faced with an inefficient method of distribution, felt it necessary to devote considerable time and effort to selling their own goods.

In the late eighteenth century, firms no longer sold their goods in this manner. They sent out travelling salesmen with samples and received orders from customers which they dispatched by road carrier. Aikin (1795) recalled that the shift from going out with pack-horses to going out with samples occurred in the Lancashire textile industry between 1730 and 1770. Abraham Darby's descendants were still visiting fairs in 1745, but were sending out agents in 1760 (Raistrick 1970).

Timmins noted that in the brass trades, patterns and sample books were unknown before 1760 (cited in McKendrick 1982, 67). Examples of the same transformation can be found in many industries in the same period.[10]

But how is this transformation tied to improved transport? Aikin recognized at the time that it was a result of the turnpike roads becoming good enough to accommodate regular wagon traffic. With the expansion of wheeled traffic came the development of regular carrier services throughout the kingdom.[11] Only then was it possible for producers to send their goods in response to orders rather than having to deliver them personally. That is, until a reliable system emerged by which producers could send orders and receive payment, they were forced to take their products on the road themselves and deal with the various buyers face to face. Once a system developed that circumvented this inefficient form of distribution, it was in the interest of producers to change their techniques of distribution. The best evidence of this shift in the relative costs of the two methods of distribution is the fact that so many producers switched in the same period (the decrease in relative costs would partly occur at the buying end for the buyers no longer had to travel to fairs to make their purchases, either). This could be expected to lead to an increase in total tonnage shipped. The more important result for my purposes, though, is that in order to take advantage of this new transport service, producers needed a much more highly standardized product (if this involved an increase in costs, the relative shift in transport costs would have to be great enough to outweigh the increase). This was practically impossible to achieve using the domestic system. Only in a factory setting with supervised workmen, on machinery which could produce a high output of even quality, was this possible. Nussbaum points out that a putting-out entrepreneur with a hundred weavers could not supply as uniform a product as an entrepreneur with a factory (1968, 229). Thus, improvements in the transport system provided not just an opportunity for factory production, but a need for it as well.

The effect on the use of the entrepreneur's time should be noted as well. Certainly, some putters-out hired others to take their goods around to fairs for them, but most found it to their advantage to do it themselves. As Walker's description of the travelling merchant showed, the sale of goods in this manner was not something for which a deputy could easily be found. Thus, most small entrepreneurs of the time spent up to three or four months a year on the road. This is a fact of some importance. The entrepreneur could not develop an enterprise which required constant supervision if he had to be absent for a good part of the year. As long as he was forced to devote so much time and energy to marketing his output, he was liable to concentrate more on getting a high profit per unit than on improving his method of production, and increasing productivity and output.

The other means by which final goods reached the consumer in the early eighteenth century was through London wholesalers. Local chapmen or shopkeepers, wishing to carry a wide variety of goods, would be prevented by poor transport services from establishing trade links with producers of these various goods. Thus, they relied on an inefficient method whereby London-based middlemen would collect a variety of goods from numerous producers and then supply the local retailers with all their needs. By mid-century, improvements in transport were leading to the replacement of this system by direct sales from producer to retailer. By eliminating the middleman, the cost of distribution naturally decreased.[12] While this transition does not have the same dramatic impact with respect to standardization and the use of the entrepreneur's time, it does share a market-widening role with the transition from sales by packhorse. That is, a drop in the cost of distribution will have a similar effect to a drop in the cost of transport itself.[13]

Effects of Increased Speed and Reliability

Reliability and speed are also of great importance. Chandler, studying the transformation of the nineteenth century American economy, says much that is applicable to the eighteenth century English economy. I quote at length:

But of far more importance to the expansion of the factory system was the reliability and speed of the new transportation and communication. Without a steady all-weather flow of goods into and out of their establishments, manufacturers would have had difficulty in maintaining a permanent working force and in keeping their expensive machinery and equipment operating profitably. Moreover, the marketing revolution based on the railroad and telegraph, by permitting manufacturers to sell directly to wholesalers, reduced requirements for working capital and the risk of having unsold goods for long periods of time in the hands of commission merchants. Reduced risks and lower credit costs encouraged further investment in plant machinery and other fixed capital. (1977, 245)

In the modern day, we can recognize how dependent our modern industries are on modern transport and communication. The Industrial Revolution was the starting point of modern industrial production and it required what I call early modern transport. Regular delivery and supply of raw materials and finished goods has been a necessary component of the industrial tradition from the beginning. Delays in the delivery of raw materials made it difficult to achieve continuity in employment of labour and capital, and this inhibited the development of large-scale units (Ashton 1966, 13–14). To some extent, the problem could be mitigated by the holding of large inventories. However, this would require the transfer of considerable capital from profitable employment in the process of production. Further, holding inventories could not prevent substantial losses through delays in getting finished goods to market. It must be remembered that circulating capital was much more important than fixed capital in this period.[14] Thus, losses suffered through irregular delivery on both the input and output sides could have a severe effect on the profitability of the firm. As English transport improved, the size of necessary inventory holdings dropped markedly.[15] As well, to the extent that it was impossible to cover for all of the effects of slow and unreliable transport, the degree of risk associated with investment would also be diminished.

By this line of reasoning, domestic production can be viewed as having a relative adantage over the factory system in that it seemed to suffer less from such costs. I would argue that the domestic system was simply better able to withstand the effects of slowness and irregularity than the factory system. Domestic production involved less investment in fixed capital than factory production. The buildings owned by putters-out were generally of a type that could be put to many uses. Further, the putting-out entrepreneurs usually engaged in more than one form of enterprise, so they could to some extent transfer their resources from one endeavour to another. Berg has noted that one advantage of the domestic system was the ease with which capital could be transferred from one industry to another (1985, 42). Moreover, the entrepreneur did not need to employ his workers as regularly as the factory owner. When times were bad, he would simply put out less (Rule 1981, 49). Clearly, if he was unable to get his supplies on time, he had the same option. In Medick's words, "The merchant-manufacturer has no fixed capital. The cottage workers are his machines. He can leave them unemployed whenever he wants without losing a penny" (in Kriedte 1981, 53). Also, the rural weaver or spinner often owned a small plot of land and could transfer his time to some sort of agricultural work which would yield a positive marginal product. The factory owner, on the other hand, needed to maintain a steady supply of labour, and his workers often had less recourse to favourable alternatives. Thus, the domestic system of production was much more flexible and therefore better able to cope with a relatively unreliable system of transport.[16]

As transport services became more regular, this relative advantage of domestic industry would disappear and the transition to factory production become more likely.

An important element in the increasing reliability of transport was the growing professionalism of the transport industry. Many transport services had long been provided by, for example, farmers during the off-season. The farmer with a cart or wagon would often sell his services as a carrier when he did not need his cart for agricultural work. If the opportunity cost of labour was low for the farmer, he could charge a lower fee than a professional full-time carrier. In this narrow sense, the part-time carrier might seem superior to the professional. However, the part-time carrier did not run a regularly scheduled service, and was apt to be unobtainable at any price during the busy periods of the agricultural cycle (Braudel gives examples of how transport services could grind to a halt for weeks during harvest). Further, as carrying was only an income supplement, the part-time carrier did not stand to gain as much by maintaining a reputation for either reliability or honesty as the professional. The characteristics of reliability, regularity, and trustworthiness, were of great importance to the industrial producer. In fact, in the middle of the century professional land carriers became the means by which producers received payments for the orders they had sent out. A part-time irregular carrier could not perform this task without introducing substantial delays and risks. A similar though less dramatic transformation to regular and reliable service took place in water transport as well, with the same benefits.

Increased speed of transport would have two positive effects on reliability. First, if delivery was delayed by some freak accident, the receiver could quickly send an order for and receive replacements. Second, the less time an order spent *en route*, the less vulnerable it was to robbery, pilfering or water damage. It would also make possible higher rates of stock turnover. This would be especially important at a time when merchants were moving from emphasis on profit per unit to concentration on total profit.[17] As speed of transport increased, a given level of output could be financed with less capital. Speed of passenger movement was also critical. It is noteworthy that British travellers came increasingly to criticize the trekschuit (canal barges) of the Netherlands for its slowness during the eighteenth century (de Vries 1981). Clearly, speed was becoming of greater and greater importance.

While talking of speed, the effects of the seasons on transport should be noted. English winters, mild in some years, could in others cause canals and rivers to be frozen for months. Alternatively, heavy winter rains could cause considerable flooding, which would impede river traffic as much as ice. The impact on water transport made land transport even more essential during the winter. However, heavy rains could make poorly constructed roads impassable.[18] Thus, it was only with the coming of early modern transport – which involved the completion of a road network that could be used year-round – that an industrial producer could be sure both of receiving supplies regularly and of getting his output to market during the winter months. This was especially important as winter was the period in which most industrial production was undertaken.[19] As the Industrial Revolution progressed and workers became totally divorced from the land, the level of production became relatively constant throughout the year. In the early stages, though, even factories lost workers during parts of the summer when various crops needed planting or harvesting. As noted earlier, since circulating capital was so important, delays in receiving payment for goods produced could dramatically reduce the profitability of a firm. It is easy to see how important it was that the early factory be able to market the goods it produced during the winter.

The advent of year-round reliable transport can be tied to the decline in the commercial importance of fairs. As Chartres (1977a) notes, in the era before 1750 fairs were becoming the social events they are taken for today, and had ceased to be the main avenue through which producer and retailer met. The emerging small retail shop was becoming the chief avenue of distribution. Chartres claims that such shops were widely dispersed by 1700, even outside the larger towns. This process of dispersion continued through the eighteenth century. On the wholesaling side, professional middlemen arose who provided a more direct link between producer and retailer; these, as we have seen, were in turn superceded by even more direct links between producer and consumer. This transformation had many causes. John (1943) notes correctly that the movement from fairs to shops represents a shift from intermittent spending on industrial goods to regular consumption of such goods. Rising incomes allowed consumers to purchase more often, instead of waiting until just after the harvest had been sold. However, in order for exchanges to occur throughout the year, they must be supplied throughout the year.[20] Improvements in forms of transport that enabled produce to be moved year-round must have played a significant role in this transformation. Otherwise, links between producer and retailer would have remained as tenuous as in the days when such transactions took place at fairs.

To summarize, I have maintained that the factory system had less flexibility than the domestic system. Therefore, a factory owner could be hurt more by a transport system which was slow, unpredictable, unprofessional, and potentially unusable for lengthy periods in the winter. Thus, the likelihood of a transfer to workshop production would increase as the transport system improved.

The Ability to Obtain Raw Materials
More Cheaply

The economic value of an industrial raw material in its natural state will obviously depend upon its quality or grade, its transportability, and its accessibility to transport facilities, to other raw materials, and to markets. For these reasons, investment in cheap transport is often more important than the possession of high-grade minerals for a region's successful industrialization, since it makes possible either the opening up of local resource supplies or the importation of raw materials from elsewhere. (Kenwood 1982, 112)

Histories of industrialization all too often concentrate on the existence of raw materials without paying much attention to their accessibility.[21] Clearly, the first duty of a transport system is to provide access to various materials. Once one recognizes that raw materials are not naturally placed in the most advantageous sites, the theoretical link between improved transport, the increased scale of industry, and the emergence of new industries becomes obvious. Decreased transport costs serve to shift the supply curve down and thus cause increased production (or production for the first time) of the affected good.[22]

Along with this direct effect of increased production, greater access to raw materials had a further effect in encouraging the transition to workshop production. Manufacturers who had previously relied on only one or two materials close at hand now began to use a wider range of materials to make superior products.[23] One of the advantages of workshop production was that it removed the need to deliver raw materials to scattered workers. One of the major disadvantages of domestic production was the pilfering of materials by unsupervised workers. Pilfering was monitored in domestic manufacture by comparing the amount of material supplied with the amount of output produced. As the number of materials increased, such monitoring became more difficult. Thus, with respect to both delivery and pilfering, the relative advantage of workshop production grew as access to a variety of raw materials improved.

In later chapters I will give examples of manufacturers increasing the number of materials used in the late eighteenth century – potters using a variety of clays and glazes, bucklemakers using many materials to decorate their product, and so on. I will also describe cases in which transport improvements had quite dramatic effects on the price of materials. Before moving on, it is worth noting here that coal and iron, probably the two most important inputs of the Industrial Revolution, were both bulky goods for which transport costs were generally a high proportion of delivered price, and both needed to be transported great distances.[24]

Technological Innovation

The first task is to overcome the unnecessarily sharp distinction drawn by Schumpeter (1939) between "innovation" and "invention". The occurrence of clusters of innovation was essential to his explanation of business cycles, and thus he was forced to describe an artificial separation between invention and innovation. Rosenberg has commented that this line of argument, which came to dominate discussions of technology, has obscured the continuous nature of the process of innovation (1976, 77). Most eighteenth-century innovations followed directly from inventions that had been induced by economic phenomena.[25] It is best, then, when examining the eighteenth century, to look at one process of technological innovation, and ignore the distinction between invention and innovation.

There were, to be sure, some eighteenth-century innovations which drew on much earlier, or foreign, inventions. This has led some to argue that the Industrial Revolution was largely the story of the application of a backlog of technology. However, such innovations are the exception rather than the rule.[26] Perhaps one of the more important insights in Gilfillan's (1935) pioneering work on technology is that no rule applies to all inventions. As various innovations are described in later chapters, it will be seen that the most important were based on technology developed in eighteenth-century England. Thus, it would be incorrect to treat the Industrial Revolution as some sort of super-Schumpeterian upswing in the business cycle, in which a readily available supply of technology was suddenly put to commercial use. Instead, the existence of a few innovations based on borrowed technology should merely be taken as evidence of economic forces operating in England which provided opportunities for the use of new technology. If new technology could not be borrowed from foreign lands or from the past, there would be pressure to develop it. Most of the innovations introduced during the early Industrial Revolution could not be borrowed, and had to be developed within England. This point is important not only for a proper understanding of the English Industrial Revolution but also for a proper view of the later transmission of the Industrial Revolution to other lands.

It will be seen below that because it is so difficult to explain the emergence of a technological innovation, many authors have come to view the phenomenon as exogenous. It is my contention that they have mistaken stochastic – that is, that innovations will only occur with some probability in any particular setting – for exogenous. Even the most favourable environment cannot elicit a particular innovation with certainty, while a most inhospitable environment might witness an innovation through extreme good fortune. Thus, explaining any one innovation becomes impossible because we cannot know whether it was the result of certain conditions being in place, or whether it was a chance discovery occuring in spite of the environment. We can try to explain why a particular innovation occurred in a particular time and place, but we are always open to the claim that it was mere chance.

This seemingly hopeless situation is mitigated by two factors. First, while we might not be able to say anything about one innovation, we can say something about a cluster of innovations.[27] The probability of a number of innovations emerging at the same time in an environment unconducive to innovation is exceedingly low. Thus, when, as in the Industrial Revolution, we see a dramatic increase in the rate of technological innovation, we can be reasonably certain that it is the result of a change in the environment, and we can proceed to analyse the factors which were changing during that period to see which of them could elicit this wave of innovation. There are those who would argue, however, that there were still only one or two pivotal innovations in the Industrial Revolution, and that everything else followed naturally.[28] It will gradually become clear as I discuss various industries that this is an oversimplification, and that the Industrial Revolution was characterized by a large number of innovations in virtually every industry, with no one breakthrough having caused the rest.

Second, and even more important, it must be recognized that innovations are not just one-shot acts of genius, but a process usually involving a number of people over a lengthy period of time.[29] Usher (1954) recognized this decades ago. He divided the process of innovation into four steps. The first is called "perception of the problem." Not only must some unfulfilled want be recognized but people must decide that it is worth expending effort to fulfill the want. This step contains the challenge and response argument, which is classically used to describe the pressures to improve spinning technology once great strides were made in weaving. In Usher's framework, it assumes its proper place as part of a bigger picture.

The second step is "setting the stage." Usher argues that a number of disparate ideas must be brought together in the creation of a new idea. "Invention is a new combination of the prior art" (Gilfillan 1935, 6). The various elements necessary to the new innovation must come together in someone's mind. Implicitly, Usher is recognizing that the onward march of technology occurs in small steps rather than giant leaps. One way in which the stage can be set is through a process of trial and error. A prospective inventor could keep trying to accomplish something by making minor adjustments until, hopefully, a successful method emerges.

Once the stage is set, Usher proceeds directly to the "act of insight." It is this step that gets the most attention, though the others are of equal importance. As Basalla has noted (1988, 24), this is the stage where psychological factors are likely to be more important than economic factors. The act of insight does not result automatically in a workable innovation. Instead, a period of "critical revision" is necessary before the innovation becomes economically feasible. "Good ideas usually acquire significance only when they are refined and elaborated and have gone through what is often an exhaustive process of patient modification and revision" (Rosenberg 1976, 80). If someone or some group of people were not willing to put forth the necessary effort to revise an innovation, it would have no effect on the methods of production.

Using Usher's framework, one is better equipped to analyse the process of technological innovation. Usher notes that the traditional concentration on individual inventors rests on the mistaken assumption that an achievement can be identified with a particular person at a given moment. Instead of concentrating on the third step, one must look at the other three. "It is not necessary to explain the final act of insight; the task now consists in explaining how the stage is set to suggest the solution of the perceived problem" (Usher 1954, 78). In what follows, I will analyse the effect of various forces on the first, second, and fourth stages. It must also be borne in mind that this four-step process does not occur in a vacuum. Any one process of innovation will aid and be aided by others in many ways. One innovation could lead to the perception of new problems, be essential to setting the stage for another innovation, and be necessary for the critical revision of still another (this interrelatedness should not be confused with the Crafts idea that a couple of inventions triggered everything else). Without Wilkinson's boring machine, the Watt steam engine was impossible. Thus, an analysis of any one process of innovation must be broad. "In historical analysis, it would be unusual not to find that several strategic inventions were involved in any achievement of large social importance" (Usher 1954, 69). Since technology develops through physical artifacts, innovations of little importance in their own right can play a key role in fostering other innovations (Basalla 1988, 30).

Even Usher's framework does not allow us to pinpoint exactly why a particular innovation occurred at a particular moment. "The succession of events is orderly and logical" but the intervals between stages are indeterminate (Usher 1954, 79). Innovation is still a stochastic process, and the exact period of time in which an innovation is realized is not predetermined. No one person is essential to a particular process of innovation, but one person can cause a result to be discovered earlier than it would be otherwise. There must, of necessity, be some fuzziness in tracing the history of an innovation because there are no reules describing the speed with which the four stages occur. What one can do is describe the forces which affected the first, second, and fourth stages of a particular process. It is now possible to look at some theoretical links between these three stages and the phenomena outlined earlier.[30]

Various factors will increase the possibility that a particular problem will be recognized. As entrepreneurs are freed from the necessity of devoting most of their time to the actual sale of their output, they are able to pay more attention to the process of production. Not only are they more likely to see problems, but they are also likelier to see them as worth solving because they know they will be able to supervise the changes that such solutions involve. As passenger transport becomes cheaper, quicker, and more reliable, information flows will improve so that a particular problem will be recognized by a much wider group of people. Increasing regional specialization will also tend to enhance interest in particular problems, for as an industry comes to dominate a particular area, its needs, and the gains that would accrue if those needs were satisfied, would become obvious to all those nearby. The problems which faced producers would be common topics of conversation.[31] Access to a wider market could spur efforts to expand output.[32]

Still more important is the increasing division of labour and increasing scale of production which characterize the period under study. Once a skilled task is broken down into a number of smaller parts, it is much easier to see how these tasks can be mechanized. Moreover, the productivity gain from mechanizing a particular task is greater when each worker performs one task than when each performs fifteen tasks. In Gilfillan's words, "the more monotonous and stupid the job, the nigher it has been brought to abolition" (1935, 50). Mechanization, as the process of replacing human hands with machinery, proceeds best when the work of human hands has become simple and easily duplicated.[33] One major source of new technology was the emergence of specialized machine-making firms – a particularly important case of division of labour.

As production gathered in workshops, improvements became much easier to visualize. Once a number of looms had been collected in one place, for example, the idea of connecting and powering them would naturally occur (Wadsworth 1965). Also, as David (1975) notes, it may only be worthwhile to replace direct labour with indirect labour if output is large. That is, to borrow from Allyn Young, it does not pay to make a hammer to hit one nail (David 1975, 6). This point must be emphasized. It is far less likely that any kind of factory or power-driven machinery would be developed at a time when production occurs only in cottages. Once certain occupations are gathered in workshops, however, the potential advantages of hooking machines together or powering them become readily observable.[34]

The second stage in the process of innovation is affected by an even greater number of factors. This stage clearly benefits from the increased ability of entrepreneurs to devote their time to innovation. Increased regional specialization allows different potential innovators to discuss a problem and trade ideas until a solution is arrived at. Increased interregional information flows serve the same end.[35] They could also provide increased knowledge of developments in other industries which would be of use locally.[36] Division of labour allows greater knowledge of particular processes. Increasing scale of production not only makes the course of change more obvious but allows for increased experimentation. Thus, one could experiment and fail, and still survive. The interplay between workers and supervisors could be a valuable source of innovation (Landes 1986, 615). In a centralized workshop, merchant-manufacturers observed the production process, which was performed out of sight under the domestic system (Deane 1984, 130–1). Pollard notes that experiments could more easily be undertaken in a centralized manufacture "as the master disposed of relatively large resources," and where improvements would be employed on a larger scale (1965, 34). The emergence of new industries would be especially important here. New industries could bring forth new ways of doing things, providing a necessary input into the process of innovation in an older industry. For example, the rolling mills developed to serve the emerging tinplate industry played a major role in the improvement of ironmaking technology later in the eighteenth century.

Some comment should be made on the role of science in the development of eighteenth-century technology. With very few exceptions, all that technology gained from science during this period was the scientific method. The inventions of the early Industrial Revolution were not sophisticated inventions that broke through a critical technological barrier (Lilley 1976, 195). Instead, they were simply new devices which, rather than requiring brilliant flights of thought, took hours and even years of painstaking effort, and often considerable expense as well. Even Musson and Robinson, who favour a strong connection between science and technology, admit that "Probably most of the achievements of the early Industrial Revolution were similarly products of practical empiricism" (1969, 72). They cite contemporary craftsmen who bemoaned the fact that it was science which was indebted to common craftsmen rather than the other way around (82–3). While they do find some innovations in which science had a hand, their own evidence indicates that, at least in the crucial early years of the Industrial Revolution, it did not play a critical role. Despite their efforts, all that Musson and Robinson have shown is that early industrialists, scientists, and entrepreneurs had more social contact with each other than had been thought (Gould 1972, 335).[37] To the extent that science was used, it fits into the framework used here. Musson notes two facts: there were substantial opportunities for self-education, and there were greater opportunities for applying scientific knowledge in England than elsewhere. It is unnecessary, then, to devise bizarre theories that English science was more advanced (France, after all, was the centre of the eighteenth-century scientific world), or that English science was somehow more practical than science elsewhere.[38] Indeed, Rees felt that it was French science that had the practical bent: "In France, more than in any other country, men of science have been consulted in matters of public concern, and the reputation of Lavoisier caused him to be applied to, in 1776, to superintend the manufacture of gunpowder, by the enlightened Minister Turgot" ("Lavoisier" 1802-20). If English science was more often applied to practical problems than in other countries, the explanation is simple. English people would see problems as more worth solving and would thus be willing to expend the necessary effort on self-education to set the stage properly for the solution to be found. It should not be surprising that scientific knowledge that was available throughout Europe would see its first practical application in England where the environment was conducive to such a development.

The fourth stage, critical revision, is subject to the same forces that affect stage two, though to a different degree. I need not review these forces here. What should be emphasized is the importance of having strong economic incentives to achieve a technological advance. Critical revision in particular can involve a great deal of expense, for it often requires that working models of the innovation be used in production while major changes are made. Crawshay spent four years at his ironworks in Wales revising Cort's puddling and rolling process, and naturally incurred considerable expense in doing so. If people are either unwilling or unable to suffer such losses, innovations will never become usable. In this regard, it should be noted that any economic factors which cause increased demand for the output of a producer could be instrumental in encouraging that producer's willingness to bear the cost of innovation. Factors which make industries more profitable could also lead to increased experimentation (especially at a time of poorly developed capital markets). In Deane's words, "Most innovations require a period of development before they are certain of success and most eighteenth century manufacturers were too poor to face a potentially long period of loss or nil return" (1965, 123). Rosenberg describes how expectations of extra-high profits could lead to increased innovative activity (1976, 124). Griliches, in his classic study of the development of hybrid corn, found that the development of strains suitable to particular areas was largely guided by the expected payoff (1957, 515). While the cost of deriving an innovation would remain the same, the expected return would increase. To the extent that new technology required extensive modifications to existing plant, the construction of new plants as markets widen could be of great importance. Each new plant would try to improve on the last. Thus, "the annual gain of productivity due to embodied technical progress will tend to be all the greater the larger the number of new plants constructed each year" (Kaldor 1972, 1243). It is essential that the reader keep in mind the role of economic forces in bringing forth a successful technological innovation.[39]

Associated with critical revision is the diffusion of an innovation through an industry. As I am concerned with technological innovation because of its ability to transform methods of production, I am also interested in the forces that influence the spread of an innovation. The emergence of workshop production, to the extent that it involved the use of similar production processes across firms, was very important in this respect because it allowed other firms easily to adapt innovations introduced by any one firm. As with the act of critical revision itself, an expanding market also served to hasten the spread of an innovation by causing the emergence of new productive units. Since adapting an innovation often involves replacing old capital equipment with new, the emergence of new firms could help to speed up the process of diffusion.

Deane notes that it could take decades for an innovation to spread across eighteenth-century England (though she seems to underestimate the extent of English integration during this period), but far less time if an industry was concentrated in one county (1965, 91–2). Clearly, the degree of regional specialization affected the rate at which an innovation spread. So did improved flows of information between productive units. It must be remembered that the transfer of technology during this period generally required personal inspection; mailing blueprints would not suffice.[40] Innumerable minor innovations of which we know nothing had a greater overall impact on productivity than the few major innovations which are talked about in the history books. As these innovations were more quickly transmitted from one enterprise to another, they could more easily be built upon to make further advances. Enos looked at the twentieth-century petroleum refining industry and found that minor improvements had increased productivity more than major changes in technology (1962, 302). If this is the case in modern industry where major changes in technology have become common, one would expect that it would hold true in the eighteenth century as well.

While discussing the importance of minor innovations, mention should be made of the role of learning by doing. Many minor changes in production techniques were devised by employees. If these were not transmitted from firm to firm quickly, firms could develop different production practices. David has noted that if firms have developed different practices a new technique will not have the same advantages for all, and thus the process of diffusion could be slowed significantly (1975, 4). Regional specialization and improved flows of information, to the extent that they caused minor changes in technique to be transmitted between firms, would increase the potential gain from further innovation, and would make it easier to transmit major technological advances in the future.

Nothing has been said thus far about whether inventors might want to keep their inventions to themselves. Undoubtedly many wished to do so. Chapman (1979, 38–9) has even suggested that one of the reasons for early factories was to protect innovations. However, in England, due to the great interaction between producers, these attempts at secrecy were scarcely ever successful.[41] This perhaps explains the great degree of cooperation observed between English producers in innovative efforts (e.g. using coke in forges). In France, secrecy remains a pervasive force throughout the eighteenth century. The interaction necessary for developing and spreading new inventions (even those imported from England) was lacking.

Putting it All Together

Figure 1 represents diagrammatically the five arguments outlined above. The main purpose of this diagram is to indicate the interrelatedness of the processes I have described. Imagine a particular entrepreneur who is contemplating gathering his workers into a workshop. He faces pressures to standardize his output. He has more time to devote to supervising a centralized workplace. He can count on reliable transport services to deliver a variety of supplies when he needs them. He faces a wider market because he can now acquire inputs and distribute outputs more cheaply. While no one of these forces might be sufficient to induce the entrepreneur to change his method of production, their combined effect could be quite persuasive.

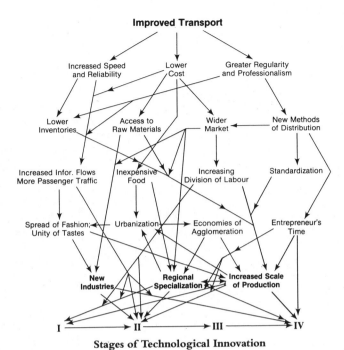

Figure 1: The Model

The story does not end there. There are other results of improved transport not yet discussed which will affect the entrepreneur. The first of these is signified on the diagram by "Inexpensive Food" but should really be seen in the broader context of a number of agricultural improvements wrought by improved transport. One such improvement was the increased use of fertilizers such as lime, as well as new tools and machines. In addition, agricultural producers, like their industrial counterparts, were freed from the necessity of serving only local markets and could sell their output widely. Ironically, transport improvements were often opposed by local landowners who feared a loss of monopoly power, but these landowners generally found that instead of losing their local markets, they gained from increased access to other markets. While improved techniques were the key to increased agricultural productivity before 1700, in the eighteenth and nineteenth centuries market integration and regional specialization were most important. There also appears to have been a connection between transport improvements and enclosures.[42] While the impact of transport on agriculture merits a great deal of study, it is quite beyond the scope of this work. There are three points which are worth mentioning here, though. First, the widespread notion that only some small areas of England participated in the Industrial Revolution is overstated. In order for some regions to specialize in industrial production, others – in addition to providing a national market for industrial goods – had to specialize in agriculture and produce a surplus to feed the industrial workers. In other words, improvements in agricultural production and distribution were necessary for increased regional specialization in industrial production.[43] Second, the literature on any industry discloses a number of cases, especially early in the eighteenth century, where employers themselves had to import food from other regions to feed their workers. Thus, an entrepreneur considering an expansion in scale would need to take into account the availability of food for the increased work force.[44] While perhaps not a major consideration, it is another way in which improved transport could induce a change in scale.

The third effect of inexpensive food is that it fosters the growth of industrial towns (along with inexpensive coal, building materials, etc.). Any modern discussion of European urbanization during the eighteenth century must take as its starting point the work of Jan De Vries (1983, 126–40). His concern is to show how the growth of any one European town should be looked at in terms of forces acting on cities throughout Europe. The growth or decline of a city can only be fully understood by reference to its role in a system of European cities. Yet De Vries recognizes that the history of a particular city is a result of both international and intranational forces, and the former can be hard to trace when the focus shifts to a particular city. De Vries' figures show that the experience of English towns during the eighteenth century was radically different from that of the rest of Europe. Of all European cities with a population over 20,000 in 1800, nineteen of them had seen their population double over the previous fifty years. Eleven of these were in England, one in Scotland, and none in France. De Vries divided cities into groups by population: those between 10,000 and 20,000, between 20,000 and 40,000, between 40,000 and 80,000, and so on. Only eight cities in all of Europe moved up by two categories between 1750 and 1800; six of these were in England while none were in France. Even in the period 1700–50, England contributed two of the four cities which moved up at least two categories while France contributed none. While the late eighteenth century was characterized by the growth of cities throughout Europe, it is clear that England experienced a much greater degree of urbanization than other countries. And it must be emphasized that growth in other English towns was even more remarkable than the great expansion of London during this period.

Improved transport was not the only factor that encouraged English urbanization during the eighteenth century, but it would appear to be of great importance. Much of the urbanization in England occurred as small local market towns lost business to larger centres. Chalkin states, "In some areas, there was a tendency for the bigger market towns or regional cities to increase in importance at the expense of the smaller towns as better communications rendered the greater trading facilities of the larger centres more attractive" (1974, 30). Corfield makes a similar point: "Trade concentrated in the established urban markets in the most accessible towns, especially as improvements in transport and communications reduced travel times and correspondingly increased mean distance travelled" (1982, 20). Not surprisingly, then, as means of communication improved, a number of very small trading centres were replaced by large provincial towns.[45] A number of these eighteenth-century marketing centres developed as industrial centres by extension of their commercial activities (Corfield, 22). The rise of major industrial centres generally followed improvements in transport. Leeds' role as the main centre of West Yorkshire was a result of the Aire and Calder Navigation of which it was the western terminus, and the turnpike system of the 1740s which connected it to other towns; the expansion of Leicester and Nottingham later in the century can also be tied to canals (Chalkin, 39–41). The populations of England's major ports also expanded considerably. "Undeniably, a considerable amount of the eighteenth century port expansion was promoted by the growth of inland trade" (Corfield, 34). The growth of Liverpool and Hull, among other centres, was in large part due to the extension of canal systems (Chalkin, 50). Even the growth of resort centres such as Bath can to some extent be attributed to improved transport which allowed the whole nation easy access to these resorts (see Corfield, 54–61). In sum, then, it appears that transport improvements during the eighteenth century were a major factor in the growth of towns.

The growth in provincial towns was of considerable importance. The seeming dominance of the English economy by London tends to divert attention from these other centres. However, it must be remembered that the provincial towns taken together had a population equal to that of London by 1750 and had double London's population by 1800 (Corfield, 11). The effects of this growth are many. It has been suggested that life in towns served to overcome the existence of backward bending supply curves for labour (Corfield, 84). Moreover, town life served as the purveyor of a new consumer ethos; indeed, this was the essence of contemporary criticism of these centres (Corfield, 97). Town growth was also essential to the expansion in scale of industries whose output was not easily transported, such as the building[46] or brewing industries. Here, however, I concentrate on industries that needed a national market; for my purposes, the most important effect of urbanization is the creation of economies of agglomeration. "External economies for industrial growth were provided by the towns' reservoir of labour, their provision of specialist services [such as banking, insurance, law, and education], and their access to the communications network" (Corfield, 97). Concentration of an industry in a particular town leads to the creation of service industries and infrastructure tailored to the needs of that particular industry.[47] Also, a pool of labour with training in that particular industry will be formed. As factory production requires both a steady supply of full-time labour and a greater investment in physical capital, it can incur major cost savings in an environment where these external economies can be gained. To the extent, then, that transport improvements allowed production to concentrate in one area, they helped create an overall environment conducive to large-scale production.[48] By increasing the advantages that an industry possesses in that area, agglomerative economies also hasten the process of regional specialization. Thus, the processes of regional specialization and increasing scale of production, once set in motion, are self-perpetuating. Moreover, these two phenomena reinforce each other. As industry becomes more concentrated in one area, it is easier to expand the scale of production, and as scale of production increases it is likely to lead to greater regional concentration.

Another result of transport improvements, as shown in Figure 1, is increased information flows. I have alluded to the improvements in the transmission of information which accompanied improvements in the flow of goods. In the early eighteenth century few people travelled. By the later eighteenth century, travel for pleasure had become much more common. People of the day often commented on this great change.[49] One can well imagine how increased comfort, speed, and reliability of coach services, coupled with much lower costs, could elicit such a response. The growth in pleasure traffic made it easier for entrepreneurs to visit each other's establishments and trade advice on methods of production. The speed and reliability of postal delivery improved at the same time. One of the main results of this transition is that market information was more readily transmitted throughout the country; hence entrepreneurs could react more quickly to gluts or shortages. Increased access to information of this sort might also have encouraged producers to favour a production mode that allowed them to react quickly to market forces. It also, of course, played an essential role in the development and transmission of technology.[50]

The increase in information flows, aided by increased urbanization, created national fashion trends. Previously, provincial tastes differed markedly from each other and from London fashion, and tended to change gradually if at all. With improved transport, London fashion came to dominance.[51] This not only meant a more unified market but a market throughout which tastes could shift suddenly. Thus, it had two effects. The first was a simple market-widening effect as tastes became more widespread. One result of this was the emergence of new fashion-conscious industries. Second, producers wanted to be able to react quickly to changes in taste. Using the domestic system of production, one could never be sure when the finished good would be ready, so that quick adjustment to please tastes was impossible. Pollard describes how masters would not know within a fortnight when weavers would be finished with a piece of work (1965, 33). If workers were gathered in a workshop, changes could be made immediately. All too often history deals with aggregates like "textiles" or "iron," and neglects the fact that individual producers produced much more narrowly defined goods. Thus, forces which act only at this disaggregated level are all too readily ignored. The Industrial Revolution is, however, the story of numerous decisions made by individual entrepreneurs, all of whom were conscious of the need to satisfy tastes. The need to adjust quickly to changes in taste provided an important incentive to adopt new methods of production in many industries.

LITERATURE REVIEW

There is a vast literature on the various sorts of transport which existed during the eighteenth century. Many turnpikes, canals, and rivers have been studied in detail by scholars. Yet these studies generally make no attempt to indicate how developments in transport affected the wider world. In the preface to *Transport in the Industrial Revolution* (1983, x), Aldcroft and Freeman state, "Our final regrets must be for the limited attention it has been possible to give to the transport/economy theme. If any single criticism can be levelled at the literature of British transport history, it is surely the deficient space accorded to this all-important relationship." On the other hand, general economic histories of the period make only passing mention of the role of transportation. Some choose to ignore it while others note its importance without going into any detail on how, exactly, transportation had an impact.[52] Thus, my work can be seen as connecting two distinct bodies of literature – one on transportation and one on the Industrial Revolution. I cannot relate this work to similar works, for there are none. Instead, I discuss its relationship to a few classic works on the Industrial Revolution and the role of transportation in general. I shall not rehash the entire literature on the Industrial Revolution. The introduction to Mokyr (1985) provides a concise but thorough survey of potential causal factors, along with the shortcomings of each. While nothing herein precludes the operation of cultural forces, the underlying premise of this work is that, at least in their economic attitudes, the English were little different from the French. I will show that the environments in which they operated were sufficiently different to account for the quite different results observed on opposite sides of the Channel. When differences in attitude are discerned, I shall endeavour to show that these, in their turn, are due to the different environments which result from the different transport systems.

O'Brien and Keyder, and Roehl: Was England First?

O'Brien and Keyder (1978) have argued against the common view that French economic development lagged far behind that of England. They base their argument on two points: that growth in per-capita income from 1780 to 1914 was not radically different in the two countries, and that labour productivity appears to be similar in many industries that operated in both France and England. On the first point, it should be noted that population grew much faster in England than in France over this period, so in aggregate terms the English economy did perform much better. On the second point, Crafts (1984) has shown that estimates of French labour force sizes are often too low and therefore that estimates of labour productivity are generally too high. O'Brien and Keyder can be criticized on a number of points (see Crafts 1984). It is not necessary to go into detail here. They recognize that England had a much lower proportion of its labour force in agriculture than France, produced a wider range of industrial goods, and was much more urbanized; that English producers faced a wider market than their French counterparts (while these authors place undue emphasis on the role of English foreign trade, they also recognize that local French markets were protected from internal competition by the relatively high cost of transport in France before the coming of railways), and enjoyed greater "opportunities for the production and sale of standardized manufactured goods on a large scale" (O'Brien and Keyder, 1978, 191). They note that domestic industry was able to compete successfully with factories much longer in France than in England because of the narrowness of the French market. They also recognize that "there must have been inefficiency in French industry that stemmed from lags in the adoption of British technology, as well as failure to copy British forms and scale of business organization" (O'Brien and Keyder, 192). Thus, O'Brien and Keyder are not denying the English Industrial Revolution as defined here occurred long before France experienced the same phenomenon. Their work should not be taken as an argument that England was not the first nation to experience an Industrial Revolution. Rather, they are making the point that there is more than one way to advance from a pre-industrial state to a modern industrial state, and that France followed a different route than England. They are less than convincing in this task. Their work suggests that previous scholars may have overemphasized the degree to which France lagged behind England. Some of their empirical work does indicate that French development was not as "retarded" as many have thought (though the comparison of English and French transport systems in the next chapter shows that, even in her most advanced regions, France's transport services were still far inferior to those of England). Nor do they offer any explanation of how else the French economy might have developed if not by following the English model.

Roehl (1976) made many of the same points as O'Brien and Keyder, though in a different way. As Locke (1981, 418) has pointed out, Roehl's analysis rests on a confusion between the terms economic growth, defined by North and Thomas as a long-run increase in per-capita income, and industrialization, defined by Rostow as a systematic, regular, and progressive application of science and technology to the production of goods and services. That France had respectable rates of growth in the eighteenth and nineteenth centuries is certainly interesting and worthy of analysis. It does not, however, detract from the English achievement of an Industrial Revolution. As mentioned before, the English Industrial Revolution ushered in a period of steadily increasing productivity. Though Roehl tries to argue that France followed a different path, even he recognizes that France had to borrow technology from England in those industries that were of primary importance: iron, textiles, and steam engines. Roehl refers to McCloy's study (1952) of French eighteenth-century inventions to show that France was not technologically inferior. Yet McCloy's work shows that French inventions were heavily concentrated in the scientific, medical, and military fields. "Eighteenth century France had some excellent technicians in fields like shipbuilding, ordnance, and public works, not to mention many marvellous craftsmen, but their talent was not applied to the improvement of industrial techniques" (Crouzet 1967, 156). It is inventions which increase productivity that I am concerned with, and in these England had a clear advantage.

As Locke points out, the Northian idea that growth is more important than industrialization may be a useful guide when analysing previous periods in which technology was relatively stagnant. However, in looking at the modern era, it is clear that industrialization should be the dominant focus (Locke 1981, 422–3). Nor should the assertion that France lagged behind England in terms of industrialization be dismissed as a fiction of modern historians as Roehl suggests. "References to this backwardness fill the memoirs, letters, books, brochures, parliamentary minutes, and governmental reports produced by contemporaries throughout the eventful nineteenth century" (Locke 1981, 421). Frenchmen of the time were well aware that something of great importance had begun in England. Throughout the nineteenth century, they would devote considerable energy to catching up.

The distinction between industrialization and growth is especially important given the focus of much modern research – notably various works by Crafts and Williamson – on the macroeconomic history of eighteenth- and nineteenth-century England. These works, while at odds on many points, do agree that dramatic growth in per-capita output did not occur until decades into the nineteenth century. Concentration on growth, then, would make it difficult to ascribe unusual importance to the last half of the eighteenth century. In terms of industrialization, though, this is far from the case. One would not have expected the new factories and innovations to have a large immediate effect on aggregate output. As mentioned earlier, the Industrial Revolution was initiated by some hundreds of individuals. At first, of necessity, these individuals comprised an extremely small proportion of the national economy. Diffusion of any innovation, even in a conducive environment, occurs slowly at first until the original scepticism has been overcome. Thus, it is not surprising that it is some decades after the beginning of the revolution before Gross National Product figures show the effects.[53] The dramatic growth in per-capita incomes witnessed in England and elsewhere since that time is still owed to the various phenomena which characterize the Industrial Revolution.[54] Botham and Hunt (1987) have recently found that real wages did rise in North Staffordshire (the Potteries) from 1760. They suggest that the same result could be found for the other regions in which industry was concentrated. National averages mask the fact that a crucial breakthrough occurred in late eighteenth-century England. It is correct, therefore, to focus on that period. That is when the Industrial Revolution began, ushering in a new era of economic growth.

The Crafts Critique

Crafts (1977) suggested that the question "Why England First?" could not be answered. His argument rested on two points, one correct and deserving of note, the other quite mistaken. Crafts' first point is that since there was only one historical occurrence of the English Industrial Revolution, one cannot simply look at differences between pre-industrial England and the European continent, and treat any differences as causal factors. Just because England had more (or less, or better, or worse) of "X" does not mean that "X" caused the Industrial Revolution. "X" may have had no effect on the Industrial Revolution, or may even have had a negative effect. By making this valuable point, Crafts correctly brought into focus a weakness in much historical work on the causes of the Industrial Revolution.

In this work, showing that England possessed the best transport system in the world is only the first step. I proceed to develop a model of the effect of transport on the phenomena that comprise the Industrial Revolution, and then show how the course of eighteenth-century English industrial history can be explained in terms of the model. By doing this it becomes possible to make a concrete statement about the role of transport. While necessity cannot be proven, it can be shown convincingly in the end that transport improvements were of considerable importance in bringing about the Industrial Revolution.

This brings us to Crafts' second point. Not only does he feel that changes in technology were the whole story but he also thinks that there were two pivotal inventions – Hargreave's spinning jenny and Arkwright's water frame – from which everything else followed. From this mistaken premise he goes on to say that, given the stochastic nature of invention, we cannot be sure from two key technological changes whether England's was the most suitable environment or whether she just got lucky. If the concept of the Industrial Revolution is expanded to include various innovations of a relatively independent nature, this problem dissolves. My exploration of particular industries will show that each experienced technological innovation during the same period.[55] Sullivan (1989), whose examination of English patent data shows an acceleration in the rate of activity beginning somewhere between 1757 and 1762 (which cannot be attributed to any change in patenting rules or regulations), finds that this increased activity is spread across a wide range of industries. While there is some interrelatedness between innovations in different industries, it is simplistic to argue that any one or two caused all the rest. Moreover, it will be seen that there are signs of change from mid-century on in most industries, decades before the appearance of the two inventions which Crafts claimed started the ball rolling (1764 for the spinning jenny and 1769 for the water frame). However, there is an even more telling argument against the Crafts idea. If, in fact, the Industrial Revolution was the result of the chance occurrence of two inventions, one would expect that other countries would have been able to borrow these inventions and start their own industrial revolution at the same time as England. For example, if France in fact possessed a more conducive environment for technological innovation, she should have been able to borrow the jenny and water frame from "lucky" England and leapfrog past her rival right at the start of the Industrial Revolution. The fact that it is decades before any other country follows in England's footsteps is powerful evidence that there is something more complex going on than the mere occurrence of two easily duplicated inventions.[56]

To support his contention that only a couple of innovations made the Industrial Revolution, Crafts argues that growth in productivity was only high in a couple of industries. However, he himself has admitted that sectoral productivity estimates are highly unreliable thanks to poor wage and price data; hence the conjecture that technological progress was not widespread, while plausible, remains unproven (1987, 252–5). De Long (1986) has argued that productivity growth in other sectors could not have been as low as Crafts suggests. I will provide throughout examples of technological innovation across a wide range of English industry. While this cannot solve the productivity question – we do not know the effect of particular innovations – it will show that innovative effort was indeed widespread in eighteenth-century England.

It is best, then, to treat the Industrial Revolution as first of all a story of simultaneous technological advance on many fronts. Nor can the phenomena of regional specialization, emergence of new industries, and increasing scale of production be ignored. Since one can reasonably attempt to explain why these four broad phenomena occurred, and if it can be shown that improved transport was of major importance in bringing them about, it can be stated that transport was an important cause of the Industrial Revolution.

Technology as Exogenous

Implicitly, many modern economic historians have treated technological change as an exogenous shock to the English economy. Finding no easy way to explain the rise in the rate of technological innovation, they treat it instead as an explanatory variable. The most obvious example is Gaski (1982), and his article will be used here as an example of how such thinking can warp our perception of history. Gaski begins by positing a number of possible "necessary" pre-conditions for the Industrial Revolution: optimal population size, improvements in agricultural productivity, capital formation, large markets, natural resources, and favourable social and political attitudes. He argues, however, that none of these could be sufficient in themselves, in part because they can be observed in other situations where industrialization did not occur. He devotes special attention to the role of large market demand, stating that it can bring about all of the other necessary conditions. While it is thus almost established as a sufficient condition it falls short because, according to Gaski, it (and by extension the other conditions which it brings about) could not generate technological innovation. Gaski then claims that since nothing can be seen as having caused technological innovation, and since innovation can be visualized as bringing about the other necessary conditions (invoking Say's Law in the process), innovation itself must be the sought-after cause of the Industrial Revolution. "Technological innovation ... thus appears to be the kind of 'God-given' factor capable of inducing the other conditions necessary for industrialization" (232).

If increases in the rate of technological innovation could not, in fact, be explained by any other phenomena, one would have to regard it as exogenous, hence the only possible cause of the Industrial Revolution. However, once it is recognized that technological innovation is subject to a number of forces, Gaski's whole argument collapses. One sees how important it is to develop a model that explains how certain factors could lead to an increase in the rate of technological innovation, and then how various innovative processes could be attributed to economic forces. Otherwise, one can say very little about the cause of the Industrial Revolution.[57]

Mokyr: Demand vs. Supply
in the Industrial Revolution

Much more sophisticated is Mokyr's examination (1977) of the roles of demand and supply in the Industrial Revolution. His major thrust is that the Industrial Revolution cannot be explained by shifts in aggregate demand. He discusses various supposed causes of increased aggregate demand in England, and finds that arguments relying on increases in population, foreign trade, or agricultural productivity do not bear close theoretical or empirical scrutiny. Thus, the only possible cause of increased aggregate demand would be an increase in aggregate income which in turn must be due to a previous increase in non-agricultural aggregate supply. Given that there is no way to explain a dramatic shift in aggregate demand without reference to a previous increase in aggregate supply, the question of whether an increase in demand could induce a shift in the supply function is unimportant.[58] If there is an increase in output, then, the initial cause must be sought on the supply side, as there could not be a significant exogenous shift in demand. It would seem, therefore, that the causes of the Industrial Revolution must be sought in such supply-side factors as technological change, capital accumulation, and improvements in organization and attitudes (Mokyr 1977, 989).

Mokyr's article, like Crafts', serves a valuable purpose in showing how misguided much of the scholarly work on the Industrial Revolution has been. Many scholars have attempted to explain the Industrial Revolution in terms of shifts in aggregate demand without being able to explain satisfactorily where this dramatic increase in demand came from. As various industries are examined, Mokyr's analysis will prove valuable in refuting the many claims that increases in the output of a number of different goods resulted from an increase in aggregate demand.

However, while Mokyr's article does call into question a number of poorly-formulated arguments on the demand side, it overstates the case for a supply-generated Industrial Revolution. The problem with his analysis is that it focuses on the macroeconomic level whereas the Industrial Revolution was basically a microeconomic phenomenon. While a sizeable shift in demand cannot be explained at the aggregate level, it is quite possible to explain shifts in the demand facing an individual producer, and the story of the Industrial Revolution is really the story of numerous decisions made by a relatively small number of producers.

It is difficult to explain a simultaneous shift in the demand curves facing producers by any means other than through a reduction in transport costs. Thus, transport improvements become the only plausible way of mounting a demand-side argument at the microeconomic level to explain a phenomenon as widespread as the Industrial Revolution (though one could still think of a drop in transport costs as a supply-side change). This book, therefore, does not serve merely to emphasize the importance of transportation. It becomes the only reasonable way of explaining the Industrial Revolution in terms of something other than shifts in the supply curve due to something like an exogenous increase in the rate of technological innovation.

The Evolutionary Approach

Numerous writers (for example Goodman 1988; Gutmann 1988) have in recent years attempted to downplay the importance of the Industrial Revolution. "Industrial Europe in 1914 was the product of many centuries of interacting forces which together constituted a single process of industrialization. It is hoped that this book has finally obviated the notion of the Industrial Revolution, which in the past has misdirected the thoughts of historians" (Goodman 1988, 203). The premise is that, by showing that important and even necessary changes occurred in the preceding centuries, the Industrial Revolution becomes at best inevitable and at worst irrelevant. Gutmann emphasizes the necessity of the previous victory of rural industry over urban artisan production. Implicitly, at least, most writers on the Industrial Revolution have recognized that it could not have occurred earlier than it did. However, it is a giant step from this to inevitability. Gutmann must maintain that cottage production was inherently inefficient (1988, 215, 218). If so, why did it last so long? How could generations pass before the inevitable centralization of workers occurred? The history of the world contains many examples of centuries of growth and structural change leading only to stagnation (see Jones 1988). Wrigley (1988) has suggested that the types of change occurring before the eighteenth century could not overcome the problem of diminishing returns, and only the switch to inorganic materials during the Industrial Revolution – which he views as far from inevitable – made possible the dramatic increase in per-capita income in the nineteenth century.

It is frustrating that we are still so far from understanding the causes of the major transitions within modern economic history. However, one should not take the easy way out and deny their existence. The main purpose of economic history must be to understand why economic growth and change occur more rapidly in some times and places than in others. Two facts are unavoidable: that the nineteenth century witnessed previously unheard of economic growth, and that England was clearly decades ahead of the rest of Europe in terms of the changes that comprise the Industrial Revolution. It must be proved, not simply asserted, that the Industrial Revolution was inevitable. England's dominant role must still be emphasized. My premise is that the changes seen in the sixteenth and seventeenth centuries would not necessarily have led to an industrial revolution. Had the obstacles to transport improvements not been overcome, Europe's destiny might have been stagnation and decay.

Fogel on the Role of Railways

No examination of the role of transport systems in any historical setting can ignore Fogel's (1964) path-breaking work on nineteenth-century American railways. Fogel painstakingly attempted to estimate what the annual cost to the American economy would have been if railways had not existed. Doing so required years of data collection and estimation of the costs of transport by the roads and canals that could have been built instead of railways. The end result was that the loss of railways would have cost the American economy an estimated five per cent of its annual output at most. This fairly low, though not insignificant, result seemed to quash the (admittedly exaggerated) myths about the essential role railways had played in American economic development. Since it has served to convince many people that transport systems were far less important than they actually were, it is necessary to look critically at Fogel's analysis.

One of the problems with an opus of this sort is that the end result is difficult to refute because of the sheer volume of work that went into producing it. At every step in designing his counterfactual world without railways, Fogel had to make a number of assumptions. No economic historian would be happy with all of his assumptions, and a good many have found some of them to be highly questionable. Yet, without duplicating the bulk of Fogel's labours, it is difficult to show how alterations in any set of assumptions would affect the end result. In other words, the very size of the undertaking serves to guarantee it some success.

As I am not concerned with railways, I need not discuss the particular attacks levelled against some of Fogel's assumptions. There are three points, however, which need to be discussed here. The most obvious point is that Fogel compared an economy possessing railways to an economy possessing good roads and canals, whereas I speak of the gains accruing through the establishment of good systems of road and water transport. The fact that the transition from roads and canals to railways may not have been as important as was once thought does not diminish the importance of the establishment of a system of roads and canals in the first place. Fogel himself recognized this, stating in his conclusion that, "While cheap inland transportation was a necessary condition for economic growth, satisfaction of this condition did not entail a specific form of transport." As mentioned earlier, the controversy over the role of railways has distracted attention from the importance of rivers, canals, coastal shipping, and roads. A year-round network of both road and water transport is called early modern transport here because I believe it is the establishment of such a system that marks the greatest transformation in the English transport sector. It is precisely because roads and canals and rivers are able to transport goods so efficiently that Fogel is able to obtain such a low estimate for the gain from railways.[59] Social savings for eighteenth-century road and water improvements would be significantly higher than for nineteenth-century railways.[60] I have described elsewhere (1991) the role played by road and water transport in early nineteenth-century American industrialization.

America did not possess a complete network of roads and canals before the coming of railways. Fogel has to hypothesize the construction of numerous roads and canals (not to mention overestimate the capacity of existing roads and canals). This brings me to the second point. Transport systems do not just happen. Railways were important not just because they represented cost savings over alternative forms of transportation but also because of their aura of romance and excitement, which prompted a much higher rate of investment in transport than would otherwise have occurred. Transport, by its very nature, produces a much larger social than private gain, since it is impossible to charge each user the total value of the transport services he receives. Though many early railways lost money, they still provided a net social gain to the economy. In estimating this gain, one cannot blindly assume that road and canal improvements would have occurred in place of railway construction. Thus, when considering the impact of railways, it must be remembered that investment in transport does not naturally occur just because it is socially beneficial. It is important to keep this in mind as I try to describe why England was the first country in the world to develop an early modern transport system. Many other countries may have stood to gain as much or more by such an undertaking but only England developed the means of achieving it.

The third point is the most fundamental. Fogel's analysis is completely static. The effect of removing the railways is to increase the cost and reduce the speed of transport. The effect of reduction in speed is an increase in the size of inventories. The possibility that this change in transport might have caused some businesses to cut back production, which would in turn have had further repercussions on the rest of the economy, is not discussed. Though Fogel expends great effort in estimating the importance of backward linkages, especially railway demand for iron, he does not consider at all the important matter of forward linkages. In a work of this type, it would be virtually impossible to do so. As Fishlow (1972) says, "The magnitude of such indirect effects is virtually impossible to calculate in a dynamic process in which transport innovation was but one important element. Nevertheless, they should not be forgotten."[61] Fogel seems to assume that demand was almost entirely inelastic so that the increase in transport costs had no effect on the quantity demanded (see David 1975, 300–1). Thus, he is able to ignore the negative effect on productivity of decreased demand for the output of firms operating with increasing returns to scale. I will leave the question of how much this distorts Fogel's analysis of nineteenth-century America to other scholars. Clearly, however, it would be ludicrous to examine the Industrial Revolution as defined here without considering the indirect effect of transport improvements. That is why this work proceeds so differently from Fogel's work and other similar works on the role of railways. My main concern is the effect of changes in transport services upon the decisions made by individual firms. Rather than try to come up with one number that represents the effect of transport improvement, one must look at different industries in turn and see how transport improvements affected their development.

North and Transaction Costs

It is also important to relate this work to Douglass North's work on transaction costs. When looking at changes that took place over millennia, it is necessary to overlook some detail, but important phenomena can easily be ignored in the process. While in some of his earlier work North does mention transportation, in his 1981 book, *Structure and Change in Economic History*, he speaks of transaction costs only in terms of the costs of measuring the dimensions of the good or service transacted and of enforcing the terms of exchange. Such costs are important to North's attempt to explain what he calls the "second economic revolution" in terms of institutional changes. While he recognizes the central importance of improvements in facilities for internal trade in generating economic development, he ignores the most important component of the cost of trading most goods – the cost of moving those goods from one place to another.

There is a special irony here, for the main theme of North's work is that economic growth follows from the creation of institutions that strengthen individual property rights. Yet, as the next chapter will show, the English system of transport in the late eighteenth century would not have been possible had the English government not given private turnpike, river improvement, and canal companies the right to force landowners to sell them land. The central government's exercise of eminent domain on such a large scale would be seen by many as the antithesis of the protection of property rights.

Foreign Trade

By concentrating on the internal transport networks of England and France, this work focuses on internal rather than external trade. I am in agreement with most of the modern literature and at least some contemporary writing in recognizing that it was the internal market that was of primary importance during this period. There had been a certain tendency in the literature to try to attribute a major role in the Industrial Revolution to English foreign trade. This tendency arose partly because international trade leaves better records for the historian than internal trade. Moreover, contemporary writers – especially those of a mercantilist bent – tended to devote more of their energy to discussing foreign trade.[62] Even some industrialists, such as Boulton and Wedgewood, spoke of their need for foreign markets, though they sold the bulk of their output within England.

It is now commonly recognized that the links between foreign trade and industrialization are weak. To be sure, an autarkic England would have had to devote rather more of its resources to agriculture and rather less to industry, at least for part of the period under study (Crafts 1985, ch. 6). In addition, certain necessary raw materials such as cotton had to be imported. However, for all goods with a large output home consumption remained higher than foreign consumption throughout the eighteenth century.[63] In the nineteenth century, the foreign market would come to be of central importance to some industries such as cotton, but during the period I am looking at this is not the case.[64] Changes in the magnitude of English foreign trade do not precede changes in industrial output but rather follow them. Thus, it appears that increased foreign trade, rather than inducing industrialization, was itself largely a result of industrialization. One suggested link between trade and industrialization was that profits from trade funded the new industrial establishments. However, a very small proportion of investment in English industry came from this source (see Crafts 1985, 125). So while foreign trade undoubtedly had positive effects on the English economy, and while some key materials were imported, it does not appear that it can be given an important causal role in the Industrial Revolution.

On the other hand, development of the internal transport system had an important role to play in fostering foreign trade. Industry rarely locates right on the coast so that it can freely import raw materials and export final goods. The simple point that inland industry requires the use of roads, rivers, and canals to communicate with other countries is too easily overlooked by concentrating on ocean shipping.[65] For example, though Sheffield relied heavily on imports of Swedish iron, it is clear that the growth of the town depended largely on improvements in the Don Navigation which allowed increased access to this imported material (see chapter 3).

PLAN OF WORK

In the rest of this book, I shall compare eighteenth-century England and France to show that England was able to industrialize because of her superior transport system while France lagged behind. Comparisons of different countries or regions are too little used in economic history. One could look only at England and describe how industrialization was dependent on previous transport improvements. However, there are dangers in analysis of that sort. While the very complexity of the Industrial Revolution allows for the possibility of explanation, the fact that such an event occurred only once makes any attempt at analysis difficult. The task is made easier, and more convincing, by looking at France as well, and showing that the lack of adequate transport facilities made it impossible for France to industrialize at the same time as England. As François Crouzet wrote, "A systematic comparison of the eighteenth century English economy with that of another country – and France as the leading continental power of the time seems the obvious choice – should bring out more clearly what factors were peculiar to England and might therefore have determined what is a unique phenomenon, the English Industrial Revolution of the eighteenth century" (1967, 139). Moreover, looking at France provides a benchmark against which to judge England. While the events of the eighteenth century were truly revolutionary, it is difficult for a modern-day scholar to appreciate the significance of particular transformations without reference to a country in which the same changes did not occur.

My first task, then, is to compare English and French transport systems in the late eighteenth century. The second chapter begins by describing the roles played by different forms of transport in eighteenth-century England, showing that both modern road and water transport systems were necessary for industrialization to begin. Different elements of the English and French transport systems are then compared to show that England's was superior in every way, and to try to provide some insight into the further question of why England developed such a system. In particular, it will be shown that the process of transport improvement started centuries before the Industrial Revolution, and was largely in place before industrialization began.

In order to see the dynamic effects of improved transport, the best method is to analyse the course of development of various eighteenth-century industries in terms of the model outlined above. Arguably, the most important industry in the Industrial Revolution was iron. Chapter 3 examines the English iron industry and those industries closely associated with it. Chapter 4 focuses on the French iron industry. Iron was one of the most talked about industries of the period, and it underwent dramatic changes in output, scale, location, and technology during the Industrial Revolution. Wrigley (1988) has argued that the shift from organic materials such as wood to inorganic materials such as coal and iron was one of the main achievements of the Industrial Revolution as well as the key to England's ability to overcome the law of diminishing returns and achieve unprecedented income growth. Thus, it is especially important to be able to explain the changes which occur in the coal and iron sectors.

While looking at the iron industry in both countries, I concentrate on how the decisions of individual entrepreneurs were affected by the quality of available transport services. Naturally, I am especially interested in the course of technological innovation. With respect to England, I show first that eighteenth-century innovations were induced by economic forces and that the processes of innovation can be described in terms of Usher's framework. For innovations introduced during the second half of the century, the next task is to show how each stage in the process of innovation was related to the various phenomena affected by transport improvements. When looking at France, I describe the relative lack of technological innovation, and explain that this was a natural outcome of the decentralized, small-scale industry which characterized eighteenth-century France because of its poor transport system.

The fifth and sixth chapters deal with the English and French textiles industries. As the relative importance of cotton, wool, linen, and silk was different in the two countries, it seemed best to look at all four, though somewhat greater emphasis is placed on cotton. One of the advantages of looking at all four is that one can see how widespread technological innovation truly was in the late eighteenth century. It is important for my purposes to show there were a large number of innovations in a variety of English industries during this period, and I try to cover all important innovations in the chapters on England. I also describe the interaction of ideas involved in the major innovations. By the end of the book, the reader should be persuaded that the late eighteenth century was a period of greatly heightened innovative effort in England, and that there was a good reason for this.

The notion that the whole story of the Industrial Revolution is to be found in iron and cotton is encouraged by the concentration of research in these areas. To dispel this notion one must look elsewhere. Despite the relative paucity of information on other industries, I turn in chapter 7 to the rest of eighteenth-century industry, and especially to the English and French pottery industries. Here again England pulls far ahead of France both technologically and organizationally, and transport will be shown as the key to these changes in English industry.

Throughout the discussion of French industry, I will emphasize the extent to which France was already behind England in 1789. I will not enter into the interesting question of how much of French backwardness in 1815 can be blamed on political upheaval in the years following 1789. The essential point is that France was already decades behind at the time

of the French Revolution, after which various governments all supported efforts to borrow English technology.[66] While the French Revolution may have slowed the responses of French industry, it cannot
alone explain why England was first or why England was so far ahead
technologically and organizationally at the start of the nineteenth century.

CHAPTER TWO

English and French Transport Compared

The main purpose of this chapter is to show that England in the late eighteenth century possessed a far better transport system than France. Since France is considered to have been England's closest rival at the time, the implication is that England had the best transport system in Europe, and thus the world. As I will be comparing both road and water transport facilities, I shall first establish that before the coming of the railway, road and water transport systems served different purposes and were both needed by industrialists. A brief survey of the rest of the world will show that no other country could possibly have rivalled England in terms of either water or land transport.

My comparison of English and French transportation focuses on length and quality of waterways and roads, speed of travel, reliability and professionalism, ability to transmit information, and cost of transport. I also look at other indicators of transport quality: traffic, regional specialization, and methods of distribution. Since France displayed great regional diversity in both transport and industrialization, I will look briefly at northeastern France to see how it compares with the rest of France on the one hand, and with England on the other.

I shall not delve deeply into the historical development of English and French transport systems. A number of detailed studies are listed in the bibliography for the interested reader. However, I do consider the historical question of why England developed such a superior system, since the question will naturally be asked by those who accept the main thesis of this work.

THE NEED FOR BOTH ROAD AND WATER TRANSPORT

With the advent of the railway, the world acquired a form of transport that could handle low-cost, high-bulk goods and high-cost, low-bulk goods with speed and reliability. Moreover, this form of transport could be extended almost anywhere. In the pre-railway era, however, the various advantages of transportation services were distributed quite unevenly between the alternative modes of transport. As these advantages were in some cases quite pronounced, the idea that different types of transport were necessary is compelling. This becomes especially clear with regard to the two major divisions of water and land. While it was physically possible to move coal by packhorse from Newcastle to London, the cost would have been prohibitive. "The demand for transport services follows a complex pattern, set ultimately by the needs of the traffic to be conveyed – its bulk, value, urgency, ease of handling, risk. The services have, therefore, to be equally complex, some catering for the bulk, low priority traffic at a cheap rate, others meeting more specialized needs at appropriately higher prices" (Chartres 1983, 81). In later chapters, as I discuss the impact of improved transport on the process of industrialization, it will be seen that emerging factories needed both road and water transport.

The main advantage of water transport and especially coastal shipping lies in its ability to ship bulk goods at a lower cost per ton-mile than road transport. While estimates vary, this ratio of costs was rarely above 1:2. For example, Jackman (1916) analyses eight routes for which he can find both water and land rates during the period 1780–1800, and finds that land transport was between three and four times as expensive (1916, Appendix 8). Pratt also finds ratios of between 1:3 and 1:4 when he calculates the cost of goods transport from Liverpool and Manchester to selected places in 1777 (1912, 178). Bagwell, looking at a somewhat later period, still finds no instance where canal carriage cost above half the cost of road (1974, 19). Willan compares a number of different routes and finds that road transport ranges from being twice to twelve times as costly as river transport (1964, 119–21). Letaconneux (1908–09) cites a couple of instances where French land transport cost twice or five times what water transport cost. Meuvret (1988, v.3, 53–7) finds similar results for late seventeenth-century France. It was generally on small rivers or on the upper reaches of large rivers that river costs came closest to land transport costs. Willan notes further that land carriers themselves never denied that water transport was universally less expensive. Given this cost differential, and given the importance of lower transport costs in this analysis, it is clear that improvements in water transport will play an important role.[1]

The disadvantages of water transport are many. Most obviously, it cannot by its nature go everywhere. Even in England, some tracts of land could never feasibly be served by water. Willan has performed an exercise in which he outlines the area within fifteen miles of a navigable river at various times. While the area not served in this manner shrinks considerably over time, there are still areas left unserved. If a similar exercise were done after the canal era, there would still be untouched areas, especially in the hillier regions. By nature, then, water transport cannot get finished goods to diverse markets (Freeman 1980, 18–19). While canals might be sufficient for moving a bulky raw material from Point A to Point B, road transport would have to play some part in moving the finished good to consumers who were not located on waterways.

Road transport is also much faster than any type of water transport. Coastal shipping could be very fast, but it was subject to the vagaries of the winds; it could take months to complete the Newcastle–London trip. In fact, even though coastal shipping was less expensive, passenger traffic almost always went by road to avoid delays. River boats relying on sails were even slower than their coastal counterparts. Canal barges could not be pulled as fast as a wagon and the inevitable delays at locks could only widen the margin. Thus, road transport had an advantage throughout the period in transporting goods for which speed was more important than cost. Numerous high-cost, low-bulk goods fell into this group, including many finished products and some raw materials. Even raw materials normally transported by water might be transported by road if an entrepreneur needed supplies in a hurry to keep his factory running, and if water transport was unable to deliver the goods as expected.

This is one way in which road transport has an edge in terms of reliability. There are others. The possibilities of delay or damage were far smaller than on water. During times of war, insurance costs could actually make land transport cheaper (Turnbull 1982, 62). During the eighteenth century when wars were common, the dangers of piracy must have far outweighed the dangers of highwaymen. Wars frequently drove trade inland, in part because sailors would stop work to avoid press gangs (Turnbull 1979, 58).[2] Further, while mud could slow down a man or horse, it could not bring them to a halt like a calm at sea or a frozen (or waterless) river or canal.[3] Given enough effort a wagon stuck in the mud can be pulled out, but a ship wrecked on the rocks is gone forever. Also, the defects of road transport were easier to overcome. A good road can be used all year while even the best of canals can be closed due to ice in winter, flood in autumn, or drought in summer (both French and English waterways suffered from flooding and drought, as will be seen). The best of sailing ships can still be stopped for weeks if the wind dies, or if storms force ships to hide in ports. In winter especially, winds were liable to delay French coasting vessels so much that land transport was preferred (Price 1983, 32). Small ports on the English east coast often served as harbours of refuge for coasting vessels and were given parliamentary authority to levy duty on coal shipped from northern ports as a result (Jackson 1983, 198).

The size of boats and barges, while lowering costs, also presents disadvantages. For small consignments, the cost differential between road and water transport would be reduced, and possibly eliminated. "The high cost and high loading factor of the typical canal boat rendered it an unwieldy unit of transport outside of categories of goods which easily lent themselves to bulk consignments" (Turnbull 1979, 87). By the same token, road transport can be more regular, for it takes comparatively little to fill up a wagon. On routes with a low density of traffic, frequency of service will be inversely related to the size of the transport unit. Often, then, road transport will be more readily available (Turnbull, 62). Again, boats take much longer to load and unload than a wagon or pack-horse, and this can cause considerable delay. Not surprisingly, road transport was generally used to move finished goods from producer to consumer. Add to this the damage caused in transit by water and rats: a Yorkshire clothier remarked in 1720 that "The clothiers of Yorkshire would rather give double the price for land carriage than have their wool brought by sea where it receives much damage" (in Albert 1967, 6). For these reasons, the output of the two most important industries of the English Industrial Revolution, textiles and small metal wares, were usually shipped by land.

Further, road transport was inherently more flexible. A given road could support a large number of wagons while a canal could easily become congested as long lines of barges waited to get through a lock. This was indeed the fate of many eighteenth-century canals. Also, while all boats need some type of docking facility, a wagon can be loaded or unloaded anywhere. On top of this, horses and wagons used for agricultural work could be shifted to transport services in times of great demand, while the short-run supply of boats and barges was much more limited. Due to their speed of travel and their extension throughout the land (and their various advantages in transport of finished goods), land carriers came to provide an essential link between producer and consumer. They became both the means of payment and a conduit for the exchange of information. It is difficult to imagine water transport fulfilling such a role.

It should be clear, then, that both water and land transport were of vital importance. I have discussed the comparative advantages of road transport at length because of the widespread view that road transport in this period was inferior to water transport. Whereas most textbooks tend to deprecate the quality, efficiency, and significance of road transport in the early modern period, it was the basis of most trades in England except the coastal mineral trade (Chartres 1977a, 29). Daniel Defoe called road carriage the very medium of England's inland trade (in Chartres 1977b). A more romantic view came from Daniel Bourn in 1763: "Nothing merits the regard of a nation more, not anything abounds more to its honour or gives it such grace and beauty, so facilitates its commerce, or affords such ease and pleasure to its inhabitants as good roads" (Bourn 1763, 1).[4]

COMPARISON WITH THE REST OF THE WORLD

For the most part, the difference between English transportation and transportation elsewhere was so great as to require only slight mention. Outside of Europe, only China requires much examination. The New World was only just shaking off colonial status and was some decades behind in the construction of transportation (see Szostak 1991, for a discussion of the American case). The bulk of its land mass was still underpopulated. Australia was in a similar position. The rain forests and deserts alone would have precluded the development of a good system of transport in Africa.[5] Most of south and southeast Asia had only rudimentary transport links. In China, however, there was a network both of waterways and roads[6], though these were designed for administrative rather than economic purposes. It would seem on cursory examination that the roads were designed for travel on foot or horseback, and were incapable of supporting substantial wheeled traffic. Tales abound of Chinese roads turned to mud after rain. One may also question the ability of the waterways to provide quick or reliable service. It would be interesting to expand the scope of this work to include the whole world, and analyze why transport did or did not develop in various areas. Geography looms large in some areas while historical considerations are dominant elsewhere. In this way, one could move beyond the question, "Why England first in Europe?" to the broader, "Why Europe first?" For now, however, one must be satisfied with the fact that the best transportation system in the eighteenth century[7] was within Europe, and focus solely on that continent.

Within Europe, it is still possible to eliminate contenders on the basis of circumstantial evidence. In eastern Europe, the only decent transport links were those used for export.[8] Cursory examination shows that Spain, Portugal, Italy, and Scandinavia could not compare with England. There is evidence that Spain, for example, had some of the same problems as France, only to a greater degree. The government devoted itself to building a set of roads which went in straight lines from Madrid to port cities, and these had little economic impact. Carting was done only part-time by farmers. Expensive canal schemes were embarked upon with little effect (Ringrose 1970, ch. 1). The German areas suffered from political fragmentation. This not only meant that there were substantial tolls and tariffs to be dealt with in transporting goods and people (a point I will return to) but that the development of "through" transportation was severely limited – each state built only for its own small needs. And most states were not generally interested in transport improvements. Germany's first stone road was built in Bavaria in 1753. Prussia did not get her first until 1788 (Clough 1946, 444). A humourous writer of the late eighteenth century recommended a journey over north German roads as the best way next to marriage of learning patience (Birnie 1933, 33). In what is now the Netherlands, of course, there was very good water transport.[9] However, the roads there were bad, even by continental standards (De Vries 1981, 61). During the Napoleonic period, it was recognized that the southern and eastern parts of the country were poorly served by transport infrastructure of both types (Buyst 1990, 73). And the national market was in any case small compared to either England or France. Belgium also possessed a small national market. Its condition with respect to inland waterways was much worse than that of the Netherlands. Belgium possessed few good roads and these were mostly in Flanders. Most road travel occurred on narrow and tortuous country roads. Nevertheless, Voltaire in 1750 claimed that Belgium and France possessed the best roads in Europe[10] (Dechesne 1932). There is disagreement among contemporaries on the state of eighteenth-century Irish roads. Arthur Young, whose impressions of French roads I will discuss later, felt that Irish roads were better than English, while Bush, visiting Ireland in 1764, found them "good for riding but by no means equal to the English for a carriage" (O'Brien 1977, 361). As the Irish roads were maintained on the initiative of the country gentry, it would seem likely that any apparent superiority of Irish roads would be due to the light traffic which they received (Young himself claimed that the state of Irish roads was due to the use only of one-horse carts; see O'Brien 1977, 361). In terms of waterways, though considerable funds were expended over the eighteenth century, the canals were next to useless largely because of government corruption, and attempts at river improvement met the same fate (O'Brien 1977, 362–4).[11] My main focus of concern, then, must be France.

ENGLISH AND FRENCH TRANSPORT

Waterways: Length and Quality.

One might think that length of navigable waterway would make an easy point of comparison. However, navigability is not a simple binary concept; rather, there is a continuum of degree of navigability. Willan (1964) surveyed extensive archival materials to determine which stretches of English waterway were navigable in the seventeenth and eighteenth centuries. Turnbull has recently argued (1987) that Willan exaggerated the extent of navigability of some English rivers at that time. If one accepts Willan's figures, England possessed 1100 km of navigable river in 1660, and 1900 km in 1725 (1964, 133). By 1830, a date for which the figures are more certain, England possessed 3400 km of navigable river and 3200 km of canal. (Clough 1946, 446). France in 1837 had less than 9000 km of navigable river, only a slight improvement over the 8000 km she possessed in 1700; she had 930 km of canal on the eve of the Revolution and had extended this total to 3500 km by the mid-nineteenth century (Dunham 1955, 30). France, then, with almost four times the land area of England, possessed less than double the navigable waterway in the mid-nineteenth century. A more telling comparison is the proportion of land within, say, twenty-five kilometres of a navigable waterway. Phillips' map (1975) of English inland navigation shows that only parts of central Wales and northern England lie a great distance from navigable water. Leon (1976) provides a map of French waterways on the eve of the Revolution. Not only in the south-centre of the country, but in the southeast, southwest, northwest, north-centre, and east, there are vast tracts of land with no easy access to water transport. About one third of France was over twenty-five kilometres from the nearest navigable waterway.

While I am concerned with the eighteenth century, I have relied somewhat on figures from the nineteenth century because of their greater accuracy. In this, I follow authors such as Lepetit (1984) and Meuvret (1988). Given that there is some dispute over the level of achievement in the early eighteenth century, it is worthwhile to examine the course of later transport improvements. There is perhaps no better evidence of the superiority of the eighteenth-century English network than the amount of work which remained to be done in France.

Nineteenth-century France, under the Becquey Plan, saw considerable investment in canals and some in rivers. Wolkowitsch (1960, 35) notes that the considerable efforts toward canal construction and river improvement in the nineteenth century were a sign that insufficient work had been done previously. Efforts to improve French waterways in the eighteenth century had generally come up short. Hundreds of projects had been proposed, and work had begun on a number of them, but only a handful had been completed by the time of the Revolution.[12] The Ancien Régime, despite its general neglect of waterways, had planned canals linking the Rhône and Rhine, Loire and Yonne, Saône and Yonne, Saône and Loire, the upper and lower Loire, and the Somme and Oise.[13] However, none of these projects were completed and most barely got underway. The Canal du Centre was almost finished but it was so shallow, narrow, and poorly dug that it needed to be almost entirely rebuilt (Dunham 1955, 30). The Revolutionary and Imperial periods saw little more than the completion of some earlier projects like the Canal du Centre. The task of giving France a network of inland waterways was left to the Restoration. At the time of the Restoration, 3000 km of projected canals were unfinished, and 10,000 km more were desired (Clapham 1921, 105).[14] Even if Willan's claims were exaggerated, the record of English efforts at river improvement in the eighteenth century would appear to be far superior.[15] Then, after the completion of the Sankey Brook Navigation and the Duke of Bridgwater's canal, a network of canals was quickly constructed. The Mersey and Severn Rivers were linked by canal in 1772, the Trent and Mersey in 1777, and the Thames and Severn in 1789. These canals and others linked the major industrial areas of England with each other and with the largest markets. While most canal traffic was local, it was possible to move bulky goods at low cost throughout most of England. All that was needed in the nineteenth century was improved trans-Pennine links. Basically, nineteenth-century English canal investment was of an intensive rather than extensive nature,[16] as the network of waterways was already in place. In comparing England and France, then, it is apparent that England paid considerable attention to improvement of waterways in the seventeenth and eighteenth centuries, and thus did not need to devote much energy to extending this network in the nineteenth century, whereas France, having neglected waterways throughout the seventeenth and eighteenth centuries, was forced to expend a good deal of energy on them in the nineteenth century.

In addition to length of waterway, the further consideration of quality tips the balance even more heavily toward England. English river improvements proceeded in a logical and orderly fashion from the late sixteenth century on. First, rivers were dredged, banks reinforced, river courses straightened, and water level controlled with the use of sluices and staunches (Bagwell 1974, 13). Before the English embarked on the centuries-long task of extending waterways, they strove to improve the quality of navigation on rivers that were already navigable.[17] Over the next centuries, these efforts were continued on both old and new rivers. While the system thus created was far from perfect, it was far superior to the system in France. The Loire, the most heavily used river in France, was littered with sandbars and suffered from an irregular flow. As late as 1787, it could take as much as eight months to reach Nevers from Nantes, using the Loire. The upstream trip was so dangerous that only the cheapest of goods were sent (Letaconneux 1908–09, 283).[18] And above Roanne, the river could only be used during flood. The Seine, with its slow and meandering course, was almost unusable with a sail. Moreover, though perhaps the best of French rivers, it still had shoals, rapids, weirs, islands, and sandbars (Dunham 1955, 38). Arthur Young, taking a ride on the Seine, said that it "was rougher than I thought a river could be" (1900, 115–16). Michel Chevalier, in 1838, complained that it was in the same shape as when Julius Caesar saw it (Clapham 1921, 109). The Rhône suffered from torrential floods which made upstream traffic difficult, along with sandbars, rapids, and weirs (Price 1981, 13).[19] In fact, most French rivers, the Somme, Seine, Marne, and Mayenne among them, had rapids which required considerable extra effort to get through. And French river beds, notably the Garonne, were littered with wood and rocks which for the most part were not removed (Letaconneux 1908–09, 38).[20] Accidents were frequent. "Careless maintenance heightened the risks of capsizing, a perpetual menace on the rivers" (Kaplan 1984, 84–5).[21] Towpaths along French rivers were often interrupted as well (Leon 1976, 174). To be sure, English rivers were not free of obstacles, but on the main rivers most of the problems with sandbars, or rocks, or man-made obstacles like weirs, had been taken care of over the years. Say (1852, v.1, 327) was sure that the circuitous course, rapids, currents, and water level problems of French rivers could be fixed by man.

The matter of irregular flow – flood or drought – was not entirely within man's control. The English, by straightening and widening channels, were able to reduce the dangers somewhat, but there was little that could be done in the face of drought or, for that matter, ice. English rivers, one might think, would have suffered as much from these problems as French, perhaps more so with ice. Yet English rivers seem to have fared reasonably well. On the other hand, "Most French rivers, especially the Loire and Garonne, are irregular in flow; others, like the Rhône, are torrential, and many are shallow" (Dunham 1955, 28).[22] When navigation on the Severn was halted once or twice because of drought in the late eighteenth century, it was considered quite strange. Many French rivers, especially those in the Mediterranean region, suffered regularly and severely from drought. The Allier was closed 180 to 200 days a year (Wolkowitsch 1960, 35). The Loire could be navigated with certainty between Tours and Orleans only six months a year; navigation on the Rhône, even in the 1830s, was interrupted three to four months a year due to high or low water (Price 1983, 29,31). Ice was a problem in northern England; the Aire was frozen for four months in the unusually cold winter of 1740–41. On the whole, though, ice was a problem only on some waterways, and affected river or canal traffic for only a few weeks each year. And French rivers and canals, especially at higher altitudes, faced ice problems as well.[23] The Rhône–Rhine canal, when completed in the nineteenth century, was closed for three months in winter (Price 1983, 31). Predictably, the nature of French rivers, draining large areas of high elevation, seems to have made them more susceptible to flooding. In fact, the key geographical difference between the two countries appears to be that England, being flatter, tended to have slower rivers with more gradual slopes. English rivers were navigable in both directions, while upstream travel on many French rivers was extremely difficult. On the upper Seine and other rivers, boats were often dismantled and sold at the end of their downstream journey, as the return trip was too difficult. On still other rivers, the trip could be made but not with a full load.

On the whole, most English and French waterways would rate poorly by today's standards. Yet by the standards of the day, the superiority of English waterways is clear. Voyages were both slower and less reliable in France. Water transport in France was so slow that contemporaries often commented on it. Wine from Orléans or Beaujolais could take two months to reach Paris, and often spoiled on the way (Letaconneux 1908–09, 290). No river travel in England could take anywhere near as long as the eight-month upstream trip to Nevers on the Loire, nor was English river travel subject to anything like the time variations encountered in France.[24] The trip from Roanne to Briare varied between six to twenty days there and nine to twenty-five back. Meuvret (1988, v.3, 79) has noted that the delays and risks associated with high or low water could significantly increase the price of final goods.

Along with their superior quality, English waterways also formed a more cohesive network than French waterways. All navigable portions of English rivers flow into the sea, so that river navigation always connected with coastal shipping (discussed below). The various difficulties of French rivers, especially the existence of rapids, meant that many navigable portions of rivers were unconnected with other rivers or the sea. Moreover, English canals were built to connect navigable rivers. River improvement was considered unimportant in eighteenth-century France and left to local initiative, while canals were given serious attention (Petot 1958, 326). In 1838, Michel Chevalier complained that many canals then existing or under construction lost much of their value by linking rivers that were imperfectly navigable. The Becquey Plan in the 1820s recognized that for canals to get traffic, the rivers they connected needed to be improved. Still, by mid-century the French network was not comparable to England's, or even to Germany's (Léon 1976, 250). Even when waterways were linked, the use of different types of boat on each necessitated costly trans-shipment (Meuvret 1988, v.3, 78). In eighteenth-century England every mile of navigable waterway was connected in some way with every other, while many French waterways were not integrated into a national network at all and thus served only local needs.

The problems of French river transport were exacerbated by the institutional setup. Whereas everybody was free to provide transport services on English rivers, the French government granted monopolies to groups of boatmen over certain stretches of French rivers. As boatmen could only work on a particular stretch of river, goods often had to be trans-shipped many times on a long trip. This naturally added to the delay and uncertainty of river traffic. As well as raising the price of carriage, this system encouraged pilfering to such an extent that merchants came to include "la perte assurée" when calculating cost of transport. Clearly, as bad as French rivers were to start with, such a practice would only make them even less appealing as a means of transport.[25]

Along with its advantage in inland waterways, England also had a considerable advantage in coastal shipping. It was recognized in the seventeenth century that England had more coastline per square mile of land (estimated figures are England south of Firth of Forth one mile of coastline per fifty-five square miles, France one mile of coastline per 134 square miles) than any other country in Europe, and that this advantage was important (Willan 1964, 4). Not only did England have a relatively long coastline, but it was more indented than that of France and contained many large natural harbours. The French coastline was, as Dunham put it, "on the whole too straight." It contained a number of small harbours but "few natural ports able to hold large ships or handle any great volume of trade" (Dunham 1955, 4). Beyond the gifts of nature, the English put greater effort into improving their port facilities during the century.[26] The expansion of English ports was encouraged by the fact that internal transport improvements were exposing them to a larger hinterland.[27] The north coast of France was especially hard hit by the absence of major port facilities in the eighteenth century. Rouen, which was to become France's main harbour, required extensive excavation as well as improvements to the lower Seine, none of which had been contemplated by 1800 (Dunham 1955, 4). Arthur Young, travelling in northern France in 1787, noted that England had a naval advantage in that she possessed much better port facilities on the English Channel than did France.[28] England was blessed with good ports almost all along her coast. Thus, not only did England's system of inland navigation connect with the coast at many points, but it connected with a coast that was admirably suited for use as a means of transport. With the improvements to port facilities on the one hand, and considerable expansion of her coasting fleet on the other, England at the time of the Industrial Revolution possessed an overwhelming advantage over France in coastal shipping.[29] This is not to say that France was totally without good harbours. Some of these, like Brest and Dunkirk, were poorly connected with inland areas. Others, such as Bordeaux, were in the least important areas economically. England's major ports – Liverpool, Hull, Bristol, Newcastle – gave admirable access to England's industrial heartland, and were aided by a number of river systems which flowed from the heartland to those ports. In France, the best ports and longest rivers were generally not in those areas best suited to industrialization. In sum, France had a relatively poor system of inland waterways in terms of length, quality, and cohesion,[30] and a relatively poor position in coastal shipping as well, and the water transport resources which France did possess tended not to be in the regions where they were most needed.

Road Quality and Length

The term "road" can encompass anything from a modern super-highway to a mere path through the wilderness. I am concerned here only with roads of minimal quality capable of supporting year-round wheeled traffic.[31] A packhorse could generally carry less than one fifth of what a horse could pull in a wagon on a decent road, and was ill-suited for items of extreme weight or bulk.[32] Moreover, though one does see organized packhorse carrying services in some parts of the world, the organization of an integrated network of road-carriers seems to have been largely dependent on the construction of roads capable of supporting wheeled traffic (see Aikin 1795, for example). It is important to make this distinction at the outset since the characteristics required of a road for use by wagons are quite different from those required for travel on horseback.

The eighteenth century witnessed serious efforts to improve roads in both England and France, but these efforts took quite different forms. In England, after centuries of attempts to induce local parishes, on the one hand, to take better care of roads using statute labour, and on the other, to induce road users to do less damage to road surfaces, the decision was made to set up turnpike trusts. Tolls would be collected from road users and the funds used for road maintenance, in many cases to build new roads that would be shorter or less steep. The first turnpikes were introduced in the seventeenth century, while in the first half of the eighteenth a network of turnpike roads was established linking virtually all towns in England.[33] In France, however, road construction and maintenance were largely in the hands of the central government's Corps des Ingénieurs des Ponts et Chaussées. Juggling political, military, and economic needs, the government concentrated on a system of spokes emanating from Paris toward France's frontiers and other major cities. It is indeed difficult to measure the economic importance of French roads designed for non-economic purposes as they "largely ran indifferent to the local population and its activities" (Pollard 1981, 125). In a few cases, local intendants or Estates-General would construct and maintain other roads on their own initiative.

The French network of royal roads, with a few roads leading from Paris, could hardly compare with the network of turnpikes in England (Pawson 1977, maps the network at various dates). By 1770, only in pockets of East Anglia and the north could an Englishman find himself more than twenty kilometres from a turnpike. Of course, roads other than "spokes" in France received some attention. More importantly, the mere fact that roads are drawn on a map does not necessarily mean that the roads are good. Nevertheless, Pawson's work is valuable in that it attacks the old myth, so often repeated in the literature, that English turnpike trusts, as creatures of local initiative, were scattered around the country haphazardly and did not, as late as 1800, form a cohesive network. Albert (1967) has shown that turnpikes tended to be created where they were most needed – where the traffic was heaviest and roads poorest.[34] Thus, English turnpikes, even in the first half of the eighteenth century, did connect with each other and form a network throughout the country.

How, though, were these roads constructed? It is important to realize that both French and English engineers knew how to make good roads. It is a common misperception that methods of proper road construction only became available late in the eighteenth century with the work of Telford and MacAdam in England and Trésaguet in France. However, the principles of modern road construction had long been known. A good road requires a solid base which is protected by a layer of loose stone. Drainage is necessary for the base will shift or sag in places if it gets wet. Drainage is ensured by making the road surface convex. The ditches must be wide and capable of carrying the water away. The innovation of Telford and Trésaguet was to use a base of large pointed stones carefully emplaced by hand. McAdam's innovation was that by using the correct type and shape of broken stone, a layer could be formed on top of the road through which water could not pass. These, clearly, are refinements of the general principles outlined above. During the eighteenth century, the general principles of road making were widely known and applied. While the Webbs may rejoice in examples of bizarre styles of road construction, most "engineers" hired by turnpikes were knowledgeable of these principles (though the unpaid parish surveyor was quite often unaware of what he was trying to achieve). Naturally, the engineers of the French Ponts et Chaussées were at least as well informed. With the proper resources, both could build roads of high quality. The innovations of Telford, Trésaguet, and MacAdam served to create roads that were somewhat easier to maintain. In what follows, care must be taken to distinguish between construction and mainte-nance. A perfectly constructed eighteenth-century road could soon become impassable if not properly maintained, while a road which was regularly maintained could remain usable even if imperfectly con-structed.

The quality of roads can best be measured by contemporary com-ment. In the early eighteenth century, with the turnpike era only a couple of decades old, Defoe said, "The benefit of the turnpikes appears now to be so great and the people in all places begin to be so sensible of it, that it is incredible what effect it has already had upon trade in the countries where the roads are completely finished" (1748). Through-out the eighteenth century, English writers echo these sentiments. Sir Henry Parnell said, "It is therefore to the turnpike system of manage-ment that England is indebted to her superiority over other countries with respect to roads" (in Webbs 1963, 145).[35] Still more telling, visitors from the Continent heap praise upon English roads. A German writer in 1782 exclaimed that the roads near London were incomparable (Greg-ory 1938, 196). French visitors themselves commented favourably on English roads. De Saussure, in the late eighteenth century, said, "The high roads of England ... are magnificent, being wide, smooth, and well kept, rounded in the shape of an ass's back" (1902, 146–47). Baron Dupin, visiting England in the early nineteenth century, stated that while the best of French roads were as good as those of England, the average English road was better than the generality of French roads (Clapham 1921, 75). The most careful observer of late eighteenth-century English roads was Arthur Young. Gay, systematically analysing Young's comments on roads in his *Northern Tour*, found that he rated seventy-five per cent of turnpikes as good or medium and forty per cent of other roads the same. Young's *Tours* have often been cited by authors lambasting English roads, for he could be very colourful on the subject of roads that did not meet his standards. Yet, looking at the numbers, it is clear that Young undoubtedly came to view good roads as the norm in England and might thus be expected to describe at length those below par. It would appear, then, that turnpike trusts did a good job of constructing and maintaining roads. It is also noteworthy that nearly half of the non-piked roads were considered good. While turn-pike roads are the main subject of this inquiry, linking as they did almost all commercially important centres, it should be recognized that they comprised less than one fifth of total road mileage at the end of the eighteenth century. The fact that other roads were in decent shape is probably the result of two factors. First, by drawing through traffic off local roads, turnpikes made them easier to maintain.[36] Second, parishes had begun to replace statute labour with taxes and paid labour. At least in their ledgers, statute labour was commuted to money terms from the seventeenth century on (Ginarlis 1971, 125). Statute labour had always proved poor for mending roads (as will be shown below for France). Reluctant and uneducated in the art of road making, statute labourers could also be called upon only once or twice a year. Paid workers would not only be better motivated and educated but could repair the road as needed.

As Baron Dupin's remarks suggest, commentary on the French road system might be expected to vary depending on whether the traveller took the few "spokes" deemed important by the government or not. In fact, the only commonly cited favourable view of French roads comes from Arthur Young, who journeyed to France in 1787, 1788, and 1789. As Dunham said of early nineteenth-century France, for readers of Young "It is an unpleasant surprise to find that most contemporary and many modern writers were loud in their complaints of the bad conditions of French roads – that they were badly built, or badly maintained, that there were extensive gaps where they were almost impassable, and that the cost of travelling on them was high" (1955, 14). This echoes Sée, who noted that while Young admitted the beauty of the roads, they were poorly maintained and there were many complaints about their condition (Sée 1939, 295). It must be asked why Young's comments on French roads are so different from most other commentary. First, Young spent most of his time in France on the main roads, or in areas, such as Languedoc or the north, which for many reasons[37] had above average roads. Second, he travelled generally in summer (complaining often of the heat in the south), and thus would have seen the roads at their best, in dry weather after the spring work of the corvée. Third, and perhaps most important, his first two trips to France were spent largely on horseback, and this could well have made him think the roads better than they really were. Thus, it is not surprising that while Young compliments the roads of northern France, the English traveller Swinburne finds the roads of Picardy almost impassable in a coach during the reign of Louis XVI (Trenard 1950, 105). Nevertheless, even Young found French roads to criticize, though not as many as he complimented. Journeying from Toulouse toward the Pyrenees, he says, "The road now is bad all the way" (Young 1900, 34). Of an entire region in western France he says, "Poitou, from what I have seen of it, is an unimproved, poor, and ugly country. It seems to want communications, demand, and activity of all kinds" (Young, 72). Near Auvergnac in the northwest, he comments, "A fortuitous jumble of rocks and steeps could scarcely form a worse road than these five miles ... Such a road, leading to several villages and one of the first noblemen of the province, shows what the state of society must be – no communication – no neighbour-hood – no temptation to the expenses which flow from society" (130). The road was hard to pass by horse and must have been impossible by wagon. On 3 August 1789, Young informs us that he has left the great Lyons road near Chagnic. On 4 August he writes, "By a miserable country most of the way and through hideous roads to Autun" (226–7). Later in the same trip, unwittingly taking a road that is only half finished, his horse loses its footing and horse and chaise almost fall off a precipice (245–6). Still later, he notes that "The country to Marseilles is all mountainous ... and much of the road is left in a scandalous condition, for one of the greatest in France, not wide enough at places for two carriages to pass with convenience" (259). Clearly, Young had trouble not only when he left the main road but sometimes on major roads as well. It is unfortunate that his itinerary and mode of travel in France were so different from his travels in England; otherwise his accounts could be compared systematically. As it is, one must rely on various other accounts of French roads, and they are generally derog-atory.

Young was not alone in finding gaps in major roads. Royal routes were often mediocre, narrow, and poorly finished; breaks in their surface which would snap the axles of wagons were frequent (Léon 1976, 174). A contemporary informs us that "The highway between Troyes and Paris, consisted, between Coubert and Brie, only of a ballast bed of stones so soft that they are immediately crushed and flattened out ... it is simply mud in winter and dust in summer" (Fohlen 1975, 39–40). As late as 1836 the royal road network was still incomplete (Lepetit 1984, 101). Gaps on highways through mountains were especially common (see Cavailles [1946, 161] for a description of gaps in the system). Nor was Young's experience of two carriages being unable to pass unusual. Many part-time carters pulled heavy wagons with only one horse, and were thus capable of creating traffic jams (Girard 1965, 219). And those were the main roads. Cavailles discusses the vast commentary on local French roads echoing the same idea: villages were isolated, roads were in a poor state, either poorly laid out or completely absent, bridges in ruin. He notes that the number of accounts and their geographical dis-persion prove the universality of the problem (1946, 118–19).[38] Purely local roads, when built, were generally designed to please the local seigneur. Interestingly, there seems to have been considerable local objection to paying for roads used by others and a desire to have roads paid for by the road users (Petot 1958, 331–3). Intermediate roads, unless looked on kindly by local authorities, were generally ignored by the central government. They often followed lengthy ancient routes, rather than the short cuts taken by the royal roads. The construction and maintenance of cross-routes formed a major task for the nineteenth century (Clout 1977, 464). In 1800, villages at a distance from major capitals or market centres had to rely on footpaths which were usually unsuitable for wheels and muddy when wet, with planks serving as bridges. Often, landowners bordering the road were responsible for maintenance and they had neither the means nor desire to build good roads (Price 1981, 6).

The foregoing does not mean that French roads had not improved considerably over the course of the eighteenth century. Early eighteenth-century French roads had been worse. It is clear that around 1700 the roads were in a deplorable state (Meuvret 1988, v.3, 64). Even the royal roads were irregularly maintained. Noblemen's carriages were accompanied by footmen to prop them up over rough parts of road and right them if overturned (Birnie 1933, 33). Alsace had not a single paved road, roads in Auvergne were unsuited to wheeled traffic, and Limousin exported no wine as it had no roads (Pounds 1979, 273). Progress was certainly made during the eighteenth century in France. It was simply made more slowly than in England.[39] Most significantly, progress was spotty. Only a few roads benefitted, and even the royal roads, despite important achievements in the second half of the century, "exemplified both poor surfaces and spatial incompleteness" (Clout 1977, 463–4). The completion of a network of all-weather roads for use by carts throughout France was to be a nineteenth-century goal (Price 1983, 257).

One of the failings of the French system was that it tended to emphasize construction over maintenance. To be sure, English turnpike trusts all borrowed heavily at the start for construction purposes, and many had to devote most or all of their earnings to paying off this debt. In general, though, there were revenues from the tolls which could be applied to regular maintenance, and all turnpikes had surveyors to regularly inspect the road and report needed repairs.[40] With French roads, one of the purposes in construction was to make a monument to the French crown (D'Haussez 1828, 19–23). Thus, while funds were lavished on expensive road construction projects, comparatively little was left for maintenance. "The government made considerable efforts to build new roads, but tended to allow existing roads to fall into disrepair and to remain subject to seasonal accidents that made them impassable up to half the year" (Kaplan 1984, 83–4). Roads were only repaired when they had deteriorated severely and complaints were loud (Cavailles 1946, 163–4). Moreover, because of the sheer expense of French construction, only a few roads could be dealt with (Dunham 1955, 15). Many roads that were much admired when first built would soon decay without proper maintenance.[41] The new roads of Languedoc which Young complimented so heavily were virtually unrecognizable a few years later (Cavailles 1946, 164). Thus, improvements to roads often failed to change transport conditions fundamentally (Price 1981, 5). During the Restoration, L. Navier was sent to England to study English roads. He echoes much of what has been said here, noting that English roads were much better maintained but not as well laid out as French roads, and commenting that French roads were a monument to strong central administration (Cavailles 1946, 165).

One of the contributing factors in the poor maintenance of French roads was the use of the corvée. Extended to all of France in 1738, at a time when England was steadily moving away from the use of statute labour, it required all men aged sixteen to sixty to work thirty days a year on the roads. Though localities were allowed to tax instead, the corvée was generally kept until 1787. As mentioned above, not only were forced labourers unwilling and unknowledgeable, but they could only be called forth at certain times of the year. As a result, French roads were at best repaired twice a year. Although there were exceptions, corvée labour generally resulted in poor roads which degraded rapidly and would become impassable over the course of the winter. Areas which replaced the corvée with taxes after 1760 generally got better roads, for those paid to fix roads did better than those forced to do so, and such areas were more likely to adopt better methods of road making (Cavailles 1946, 87–90). Habits of inspection matched those of maintenance. Though Trésaguet insisted that roads should be regularly inspected, it was only after the Restoration that the position of Road Patrolman was established to ensure regular inspection (Dunham 1955, 16).

There were further problems, for French road makers often did not seem to have the interests of road users in mind. It has been noted that they favoured wide soft shoulders and deep ditches which made it difficult for vehicles to pass, and would likely have created massive traffic jams had French roads received more traffic. More seriously, French road designers, motivated by political and administrative needs[42] rather than economic, and more concerned with movements of messengers on horseback than with the needs of carriers, seem to have thought map and ruler the only tools necessary for picking a route between two points. They built straight line roads, no matter what obstacles lay in the way; hence portions of many French roads were extremely steep. This made life difficult for travellers, and almost impossible for wagons. Undernourished French animals were not strong enough to pull wagons up slopes of more than 15 per cent, and had serious difficulty with much smaller gradients (Price 1981, 3). Not surprisingly, many roads, especially in upland areas, were only used by packhorses.

Along with its inferiority in road surfaces, France also lagged in construction of bridges. In England, one of the first effects of pressure for improved road transport was the building of bridges in the seventeenth century (Chartres 1977a, 40–9). Justices of the peace spent vast sums widening, repairing and rebuilding medieval bridges in the late seventeenth and eighteenth centuries; stone bridges which could support heavy wagons replaced wooden ones (Hey 1980, 75–9). In the eighteenth century there were a number of bridge trusts. Only the widest rivers or most minor roads were left without bridges. In France, bridges were rare (Leon 1976, 174). One is struck, reading Young's *Travels in France*, by the number of times he is forced to ford streams or take ferries. The Ponts et Chaussées tended to favour big bridge projects and ignore crying needs on a smaller scale. One of the main routes from Bordeaux to Toulouse required a number of bridges, but none were built during the eighteenth century, and thus ferries were still used (Cavailles 1946, 11). Between 1815 and 1848, over 500 bridges were built or repaired in France. Again, perhaps the best evidence of the poverty of eighteenth-century road transport is the amount of work that remained for the nineteenth.

The above discussion gives a better relative impression of English and French road systems than any comparison of numbers, but it is still useful to attempt to quantify the amount of good road in each country. This, however, is difficult to do in the absence of frequent commentary on the state of every road in each country. The fact that money was spent on a road does not mean that the road was necessarily made passable. Even if it were, it could soon become impassable. Simply looking at figures of the amount of road worked on, without reference to how successful such efforts were, will give an inflated total of good road. Thus, comments that Trudaine was able to construct 40,000 km of road relying on corvée work (Rousseau 1961, 158), or that 25,000 km were constructed or improved during 1740–80 (Price 1981, 5), give an exaggerated impression of usable road mileage in late eighteenth-century France. On the other hand, Sée's estimate, echoed by Braudel (1973, 424), that France on the eve of the French Revolution had 12,000 km of completed road and 12,000 km more under construction, may well be too low.

We know that, in general, only royal highways of the first grade were of high quality, and even they were not without fault. Yet, even in 1837, after years of expansion by the Restoration government, only four per cent of French roads were royal highways[43] and only three quarters of these were in good condition (Clout 1977, 446). At that date, there were an equal number of departmental highways, but in pre-Revolutionary days the performance of provincial Estates or intendants in constructing additional roads was very spotty.[44] In 1815, there were 17,000 km of royal routes, of which thousands were unusable (Trenard 1950, 118; he notes only 14,288 km that were usable in 1824). It is difficult to backcast these figures, for the Imperial period saw immense road construction projects in some areas while other roads were destroyed by war or lack of maintenance. It seems likely, though, that the net effect was negative. Thus, if one took this figure, and added a few thousand kilometres for Napoleonic destruction and pre-revolutionary efforts of enlightened provinces, one could arrive at a figure of about 20–25,000 km of good road in France at the time of the Revolution. While only the roughest of estimates, this does have the virtue of splitting the high and low estimates from above. If Lepetit is correct in hypothesizing that the road network of 1820 is similar to that of the Ancien Regime, this may be an overestimate (1984, 72–3).

English totals are somewhat easier to arrive at. In 1770, England possessed virtually 15,000 miles (24,000 km) of turnpike road. Previous discussion has shown that the vast majority of English turnpike roads were of good quality, while a respectable proportion of non-turnpike roads were good as well. Thus, using the figure for turnpikes is likely to understate the total amount of good English road (if Gay's analysis of Young's *Northern Tour* were widely applicable, one would understate by more than a factor of two). Using this figure, the result remains that England had as much good road as France, despite being only slightly more than one quarter the size. Even if one were to use the most advantageous figures for France and the least advantageous for England, England can still claim a much higher ratio of good roads per square mile than France.

Speed of Road Transport

There are two reasons for being interested in the speed of road transport. First, the speed at which vehicles are able to travel is a good indicator of the quality of the roads over which they travel. Second, speed of travel, as discussed in the first chapter, is itself an important characteristic of a transport system. "Transport is the necessary finishing point for business. The faster it goes, the better it is for business" (Braudel 1982, 349). Simon Vorontsov, the Russian ambassador to London, remarked in 1801 that the rise of English prosperity was due to "the multiplication by five in fifty years of the speed of circulation" (Braudel 1982, 349). Industrialists must be able to obtain quickly both market information and raw materials, hence my interest in both passenger and freight traffic. In practice, though, speed of freight transport is harder both to estimate and interpret.[45] I will concentrate here on the speed of stagecoach travel. It would appear that if English coaches proved faster than French, the comparison of freight transport rates would be even more favourable to England. English professional carriers, organized as a network, were able to change horses many times on long routes. French *roulagers* in the eighteenth century used the same horses for the whole trip (Cavailles 1946, 149). After Turgot, French coaches had frequent relay stations, often every four miles (Rousseau 1961, 233). Thus, in addition to the problems of poor road surfaces that plagued French coaches, French freight traffic faced the additional problem of horse fatigue.

In France, "L'Indicateur Fidèle," published in 1764–65, 1780, and 1785, described routes, and gave times of departure and arrival for meals and sleep. Though these schedules were only tentative, agents were expected to keep to them unless delayed by an accident or something unavoidable (Arbellot 1973, 786). The poor state of French roads did cause frequent accidents and detours, so much so that being late was almost usual (Letaconneux 1908–09, 11). Thus, the figures from the schedule can be taken as a reasonable indicator of the speed travelled at the best of times, but are somewhat misleading as an indicator of average speed.

For England, comprehensive timetables are unavailable for the late eighteenth century, but enough fragmentary evidence exists to give a good idea of travel times on English roads. While early eighteenth-century English timetables were often unreliable, late-century timetables are known to have been accurate, with coaches generally keeping to schedule – in itself an indicator of improved reliability of English road transport (Gregory 1938, 194–95). The longest list of coaching times is still contained in the Appendix to Jackman's classic work. In Table 1 are reproduced Jackman's travel times for trips of at least one day from the 1760s and 1780s. These can easily be compared to travel times from France for the years 1765 and 1785 in Table 2. I compare only longer trips because estimates of miles per day are more accurate than estimates of miles per hour on longer trips. Coaches would generally stop at some specific inn if at all possible, and schedules would presumably be set to allow this. The number of miles that a coach travels in a day obviously depends on the length of time it travels as well as speed. Yet the ability to travel at times when the light is poor – early morning and late evening – is dependent, of course, on the quality of road. One would not want to venture out in the dark on a road full of rocks or potholes (England and France naturally get different amounts

Table 1
Speed of Coach Travel on English Roads, 1760s and 1780s

Year	Route	Days	Km/Day
1760	Manchester–London	3	108
1760–61	London–Leeds	3–4	76–101
1760	London–Sheffield	3	81
1760	Birmingham–Bristol	2	69
1761	London–York	3–4	81–108
1761	Newcastle–London	5	93
1763	Newcastle–Edinburgh	2	84
1764	York–Newcastle	1	145
1764	Leeds–London	4	76
1764	Shrewsbury–London	2	127
1765	Newcastle–London	3	155
1766	Liverpool–London	2–3	112–69
1769	Leeds–London	2.5	122
1780	Birmingham–Manchester	1	137
1780–81	Stroudwater–London	1–2	89–177
1781	Liverpool–London	2	169
1782	Chester–London	2–2.5	116–45
1782, 1784	London–Bristol	1	193
1783	Bristol–Birmingham	1	138
1784, 1789	Bath–London	1–2	89–177
1785–86	London–Chester	2	145
1785	Chester–Holyhead	1.25	77
1785	Newcastle–London	under 2	over 233
1787	London–Manchester	1	314
1788	Birmingham–Manchester	1–2	89–177

Note: Some of these routes were served only during the summer.
Source: Jackman 1916, 685–7, 690–3.

of daylight at different times of year). The measure of kilometres per day tends to yield underestimates of speed since part days tend to be counted as whole. That is, a coach leaving in the afternoon and arriving the next noon may be considered to have taken two days. Naturally, this bias will be smaller the more days a trip takes. Thus, France, with greater distances and longer trips, will tend to suffer less from this than England.

A cursory comparison shows that England has much quicker stage-coach service in both time periods than France. In the 1760s, most French coaches travelled at 40 to 55 km/day, with a few outliers managing 80 to 130 km/day. In England, most coaches travelled 80 to 130 km/day, with top speeds of over 160 km/day. In the 1780s, most French travel ran to between 80 and 130 km/day, with some services as low as 43 km/day and others as high as 163 km/day. England at the same time had most services at 110 to 180 km/day, while the important

Table 2
Speed of Coach Travel on French Roads, 1765 and 1785

Route	1765			1785		
	Vehicle	Days	Km/Day	Vehicle	Days	Km/Day
Paris–Angers	Messag.	6.5	49	Dilig.	3	106
Angers–Nantes	?	1.5	60		1.5	60
Paris–Rennes	Carrosse	8	43	Dilig.	3	115
Paris Blaye	Carrosse	13.5	40			
Paris–Bordeaux				Dilig.	5.5	103
Paris–Toulouse	Messag.	15.5	44	Dilig.	7.5	91
Paris–Lyon	Dilig.	5	94	Dilig.	5	94
Paris–Strasbourg	Carrosse	11.5	42	Dilig.	4.5	109
Paris–Metz	Carrosse	7.5	43	Dilig.	3	108
Paris–Besançon	Carrosse					
– three changes	or Coche	7	57			
– direct				Dilig.	4	101
Besançon–Bale	Dilig.	3	50	Dilig.	3	50
Paris–Sedan	Coche	5.5	47	Dilig.	2	129
Paris–Reims	Dilig.	2	82	Dilig.	1	165
Paris–Laon	Carrosse	3	42	Dilig.	1	127
Paris–Bale	Carrosse					
– two changes	or Coche	10	49	Dilig.	5	98
Bale–Strasbourg	Dilig.	1	129	Dilig.	1	129
Paris–Lille	Dilig.	2	117	Dilig.	2	117
Paris–Valenciennes	Dilig.	2	101	Dilig.	2	101
Paris–Dunkerque	Dilig.	3	103	Dilig.	3	103
Paris–Arras	Carrosse	4	44	Carrosse	4	44
Paris–St.-Quentin	Carrosse	3	46	Dilig.	1	139
Paris–Caen	Coche	5	45	Dilig.	2	113
Caen–Cherbourg	Coche	2.5	47	Dilig.	1.5	80
Caen–Coutances	Coche	1.5	56	Coche	1.5	56
Paris–Rouen by						
Mantes	Carrosse	2.5	54	Dilig.	1	135
Pontoise	Coche	1	125	Coche	1	125
Rouen–Dieppe	Coche	1	58	Dilig.	.5	116
Paris–Beauvais	Coche	1	76	Dilig.	1	76
Paris–Amiens	Carrosse	2.5	52	Dilig.	1	130
Lyon–Marseille						
– change	Coche	7	48			
– direct				Dilig.	3	112
Paris–La Rochelle	Carrosse	10	47	Carrosse	5	94
Paris–Dunkerque						
by Abbeville				Dilig.	4	79
Paris–Clermont-Ferrand				Carrosse	4	97

Source: Arbellot 1973, 790, from L'Indicateur Fidèle ou Guide des Voyageurs, Paris, Michel et Desnos, 1765, 1785.

London–Manchester route records an amazing rate of 255 km/day, nearly twice the speed of the fastest French service. This evidence, not surprisingly, confirms the view of contemporaries that travel by coach in England was much faster than anywhere else (see, for example, Add Ms. 27828, 17). While these speeds are hardly striking by the standards of our day, the modern reader can perhaps still empathize with the impressions of Carl Moritz when he visited England in 1782:

From Oxford to Birmingham is sixty-two miles; but all that was to be seen between the two places was entirely lost to me, for I was again mewed up in a post-coach, and driven along with such velocity from one place to another, that I seemed to myself as doing nothing less than travelling ... The journey from Northampton to London I can hardly call a journey, but rather a perpetual motion, or removal from one place to another in a closed box. (In Pawson 1977, 287)

Care must be taken, though, in using these results to infer something about the relative quality of roads. Since speeds of more than a couple of miles per hour require a greater expenditure of horse energy per ton-mile, regardless of road surface, it is possible that high speeds tell us more about the traffic than the roads. Pawson, comparing the reduction in English travel times over the period 1660–1840 with the formation of turnpike trusts, has shown that the increase in speed was largely dependant on road improvement (1977, 287–92). In France, however, the improvement in travel times between 1765 and 1785 resulted from Turgot's 1775 reforms which replaced slow, poorly suspended coaches or carrosses with the superior diligences and established frequent relays for horses on many routes. Routes which had diligences already in 1765 show little improvement in speed in 1785, while those which saw a change in type of carriage often show dramatic improvement. It would seem, therefore, that from the 1765 figures one can say little of certainty about the relative quality of French roads. By 1785, though, it appears that coach and horse should receive less of the blame for the difference between English and French travel times.[46] It is possible, as well, that differences in institutional structure could explain some of the discrepancy in travel time. Competitive coaching firms in England had an economic incentive to travel as fast as possible, which the French monopoly may have lacked. Yet, Turgot clearly felt that speed of communication was of great importance, and wanted diligences to travel as fast as possible. Thus, it would seem that the figures from the 1780s do provide evidence that English roads were better than French roads at the time. For such a comparison, top speeds may be more illuminating than averages, and the fact that the fastest English coach was twice as fast as the best France had to offer is convincing evidence that English roads were better.

Moreover, the reader must keep in mind that I have been comparing speeds on the main roads in each country.[47] It was earlier conceded that the best French roads were as good as the best in England, but that the average French road was considerably worse than the average English road. Now there is evidence that even the best of French roads in 1780 could not compare with those of England.

Reliability and Professionalism

It has been seen that French road travel was not only slower but also less reliable than English road travel. Moreover, French merchants were often unable to obtain carrying services at all since carting was done on a part-time basis by farmers. Professional carrying was virtually unknown in seventeenth-century France, and was still only emerging in the early nineteenth century (Meuvret 1988, v.3, 63). Even intendants were not immune. In 1771, Intendant Bonneville of the Faucigny, trying to get rye for bread, reported that "we are at the height of harvest and without seriously hindering it cannot have as many local carts as we would like." A steelmaster's factor complains during the Empire that "the ploughs [i.e., the ploughing season] have completely prevented the carters from working" (Braudel 1982, 352–3). "Thus, the activity of the industrial establishments was dependent on the fluctuations of agriculture, and the conditions of transport acted as a brake to the whole economic life of the country" (Girard 1965, 220).

In England, the situation was quite different. With the improvements in turnpikes had come an increasing degree of professionalism in English carrying services. Early on, a legal distinction was drawn between private and common carriers. While the former behaved much like the *roulagers*, the latter needed the resources to withstand liability and were allowed to form networks. They established regular routes with set times of departure, as opposed to private carriers who needed to establish personal relationships with a few customers. As discussed in the first chapter, by about the middle of the eighteenth century a network of carriers had come in to being which not only provided a regular, reliable conduit for goods to be sent to and from almost anywhere in England (see Hey 1980, 211), but also provided for the return of payment.[48] Braudel marvels at the records of Kent of Kirkby Stephen in England (described by Willan), an inland shopkeeper of the late eighteenth century who was able to receive supplies from throughout the island by road carriers who handled bills of exchange (1982, 65–7). Connections were considerably more tenuous in France.

The French situation was exacerbated once again by the institutional structure. The royal monopoly on passenger transport was also a monopoly on the carriage of goods of less than fifty livres on the routes served by the Messageries, and heavy fines were imposed on *roulagers* who broke this rule. The rule was especially harmful to merchants in the early eighteenth century when many of those granted the monopoly over a particular route abused the privilege. Even after the government took over in 1775, the rates charged for carriage were considerably higher than *roulagers* would have charged (see Letaconneux 1908–09, 118–20). The Messageries were never given a total monopoly over all goods carriage (they were briefly given a quasi-monopoly from 1778–84 which drastically reduced the number of private carriers) because merchants complained loudly that they charged five to six times as much when given the chance (Braudel 1982, 354). Not only was this practice harmful to the users of road transport, but it severely hampered the evolution of professional carrying services by taking away the most lucrative cargo. And it was not the only restriction placed on private carters. *Roulagers* were forbidden to have regular departure days. Thus, they were actually prevented by law from forming regular transport links between various centres.

Information Flows, the Post Office, and Passenger Service

As already noted, transportation is important not only for the movement of goods but for the movement of information as well.[49] It is worth considering briefly the degree to which the English and French transport systems facilitated the movement of information. As road transport improved over the course of the eighteenth century, England became unified in the sense that information of all types flowed freely from one part of the country to another. France moved in the same direction, but at the end of the century information of all types was very slow to move from one area to another. There is no better proof of this than the travels of Young in France before and during the French Revolution. He is constantly amazed at his inability, while in other parts of the country, to get accurate reports of what is transpiring in Paris. He goes so far as to suggest that the Revolution would not have turned out as it did had nobles been able to get a better idea of what was happening elsewhere in the country. He describes how much easier it is to learn of English news while in England:

That universal circulation of intelligence, which in England transmits the least vibration of feeling or alarm, with electric sensibility, from one end of the kingdom to another, and which unites in bands of connection men of similar interests and situations, has no existence in France. (1900, 216)

While part of the problem in France was the lack of newspapers, a larger part was due to inefficient postal services and poor passenger transport. These I will discuss in turn.

The French postal service suffered from many problems throughout most of the eighteenth century. It was poorly organized and had too few offices (Sée 1939, 298). It only existed on a few routes, and was subject to considerable abuse by those holding a monopoly on a particular route. The latter problem was alleviated, though not eliminated, as the state gradually took greater control.[50] However, the difficulty of routes remained. Letters between nearby towns were often carried through Paris, or some other large centre like Lyons, with great loss of time, because of a shortage of routes (Letaconneux 1908–09, 104). The route from Bordeaux through Nantes to Brest did not receive postal service until the eve of the Revolution (Cavailles 1946, 161). French postal services at the time of the Revolution covered only a few routes, and even on these the service was slow and irregular. Many towns had no post office at all (Leon 1970, 177–8). The situation in England was much better. The first cross-post in England was introduced in 1696, so that letters would not all have to go through London. By 1721, when Ralph Allen first leased the cross- and by-posts, he was able to provide thrice-weekly service to "all the country," except the east and southwest which were served daily. Daily service spread to the rest of the country through the century. It became increasingly common to use the post office to send light goods like lace or diamonds, as well as patterns and samples (Moffit 1925, 243–6). Defoe, early in the century, described a postal route from Exeter along the Severn to Liverpool, then east through Yorkshire to Hull. This route alone would knit together the major industrial areas of England. At the time of the Industrial Revolution, England was already blessed with the best post office anywhere.

Information travels not only by letter but through the movement of people. It has been seen that travel became common in England as English transport became quicker, cheaper, more reliable, and more comfortable. The author of "Country Manners in the Present Age" remarked in 1761 that while there was at that time a great deal of travel in England, half a century earlier a trip into the country was considered almost as great an undertaking as a trip to the Indies (cited in Pratt 1912, 96).[51] No such transformation in travel occurred in France. French stagecoaches were not only much slower than their English counterparts; they were also less comfortable. Young, who commonly travelled by coach in England, detested French diligences. Taking one from Calais to Paris, he remarked, "This is the first French diligence I have been in and shall be the last. They are detestable" (1900, 151). Louis XVIII, returning from England to Paris in 1818, noted that English coaches were much better than the public carriages from Calais to Paris and throughout France. In that year, better diligences were introduced in France (Rousseau 1961, 234). On top of discomfort, French passenger service also suffered from infrequent departures. Though there was some improvement during the eighteenth century, many routes in 1800 only had one or two departures a week, though others like Paris to Lyons or Paris to Bordeaux had four or five per week (Letaconneux 1908–09, 102). And this was only on the main routes. There was no service at all on most crossroads. Young, noting the absence of coach service between Marseilles and Toulon, and Nice and Italy, remarked, "Such great cities in France have not the hundredth part of the connection and communication with each other that much inferior places enjoy with us, a sure proof of their deficiency in consumption, activity, and animation" (1900, 266). The government monopolized passenger service and was only interested in routes important to the administration. Merchants were forced to purchase their own horses and vehicles in order to visit smaller towns (Letaconneux 1908–09, 103–4). Renting was no trivial matter, as Young discovered to his chagrin. In Cannes, a fair-sized town even at the time, there was neither post-house, carriage, horse, nor mule to let. Young was forced to walk to the next town, with his possessions loaded on the back of an ass belonging to a woman headed in that direction (1900, 271). On another occasion, Young marvelled at his inability to rent a post-chaise in Mirepoix, a town of 15,000, as he could have done in any English town one tenth the size (1900, 56). Clearly, the flow of information in France was far more constrained than in England. Smaller towns were especially hard hit, being unconnected to the rest of their province or kingdom (Letaconneux 1908–09, 104).

Cost of Transport

Comparisons of transport costs are very difficult. In England, there are very good sources on costs of land transport and reasonably representative statistics of water transport rates. In France, however, extreme regional variations in the costs of transport render the available fragments of evidence highly suspect.[52] Road transport costs varied widely between regions and over time, and depended on whether a return cargo was available or not. Costs were much higher in winter because the days were shorter, the main roads difficult, and crossroads impassable (Letaconneux 1908–09, 108–9). Matters were even worse on water. "It is almost impossible to determine the exact rates charged, because few writers use the same measurements of volume or distance and few distinguish between navigation dues and the actual cost of hauling the boat" (Dunham 1955, 42).

To venture into a comparison of the fragmentary evidence we have for France with English costs would not be worthwhile at this point. Examples of high French transport costs will crop up in the discussion of French industries, below. There is considerable evidence that people of the time recognized that English transport was less expensive. After all, one of the chief assumptions underlying Becquey's plan to improve French transport in the early nineteenth century was that England had benefitted greatly from low-cost transport, the lack of which formed the chief bottleneck of France's economic system.

But English transport had to be less expensive, at least in the sense that I am concerned with. I have claimed that the impetus for industrialization came from the home market. Thus, when talking of transport costs, I am concerned with the cost of transport relative to other prices in the economy (wages, food prices, etc., were higher in England than in France). That is, I am concerned with the relative costs of transport and production: the real domestic cost of transport. I shall look at road transport first. The cost of supplying road transport services is the cost of building and repairing a wagon, feeding the horses, and paying the going wage to the carter. Given that English roads allowed English carters to carry heavier loads per horse and travel faster, the real cost per ton-mile of providing transportation must have been lower in England than in France.[53] One might argue that turnpike tolls inflate the English figure, but turnpikes would not have been used if the tolls were not more than compensated for by savings in time and effort.[54] In France, however, the carter through most of the eighteenth century faced unavoidable tolls and internal tariffs that had nothing to do with the state of the road.[55] Though progress was made through the century, some customs barriers between French provinces remained until 1790. The only factor that could cause a higher real price to be paid by the English for road carriage is that professional carriers had to cover fixed as well as variable costs, while part-time carters who needed horse and wagon for agricultural work in any case were only concerned with covering variable cost. However, the discussion of professionalism above showed that, in fact, this difference was an advantage for the English.

The same argument applies to water transport, for French water transport was generally slower than English. Moreover, as already noted, many French rivers could be navigated in one direction only, which further added to costs. In the case of river transport, various non-economic factors tipped the balance even more heavily toward England. As Braudel notes, costs of transport by river in England were just economic costs, while in France, in addition to tolls,[56] there were government-set tariffs and carrying conditions, loading by order, and government-granted monopolies (1982, 359–60). As previously shown, monopolistic boatmen not only raised prices but made pilfering endemic. If a merchant decided to send an agent along with his cargo to prevent such losses, the agent either became an accomplice or was tossed overboard (Letaconneux 1908–09, 287).[57] All in all, French water transport, as with road transport, had to be relatively much more expensive than its English counterpart.

Other Indicators: Traffic, Regional Specialization, and Methods of Distribution

There are other characteristics of the French and English economies which reveal something about the state of transport in the two countries. One of these is traffic. The degree to which roads or rivers are used is, of course, a function of demand as well as supply, and thus does not unequivocally give us an indication of quality of transport. It is still worth looking at, though. English travellers were often struck by the lack of traffic on French roads. This is a constant refrain in Young's book. Each time he arrives in or leaves Paris, he notes how little traffic there is, at one point mentioning that he has not met one tenth of what he would meet near London at the same hour (1900, 16). He also frequently bemoans the poor quality of French inns, noting that the lack of high-quality French inns must reflect the lack of traffic on French roads. As for rivers, the Loire and Seine were fairly busy, but traffic on other rivers was generally scarce and irregular. To some degree, this comparative lack of traffic may have been due to demand-side considerations (discussed later), but to a larger degree it must have resulted from the fact that "Commercial exchanges over defective networks of communications were difficult and expensive, being rendered even more unattractive by the internal dues and tolls that existed prior to 1789" (Clout 1977, 450).

The degree of regional specialization provides another indication of the quality of transport. I will in later chapters discuss the fact that French industry was much less concentrated than that of England in the later eighteenth century. "Spatial dispersion, smallness of scale, integration with other sectors of the local economy, and use of local sources of energy, and usually of raw materials, were critical themes in the industrial geography of France prior to the age of the steam engine and the economic territorial unity that accompanied it" (Clout 1977, 450).[58]

For present purposes, it is better to look at agriculture because it avoids the problem of disentangling cause and effect between the Industrial Revolution and the so-called Transport Revolution. That is, the fact that people claim that improvements in transport were a result rather than a cause of industrialization makes it difficult to draw conclusions about the state of transport from differences in industrial structure. Agricultural analysis is free of this difficulty, for nobody has claimed that transport improvements were a result of agricultural specialization. Causation is only expected to run in one direction.

In England, there was a notable degree of regional specialization in agriculture, rooted in the seventeenth century (see Pawson 1977, ch. 2). As turnpike roads further improved road transport during the eighteenth century, dramatic changes occurred in agricultural production in those areas served by the new roads. By the end of the century, agricultural prices virtually throughout England depended somewhat on the London market. In France, the situation appears to have been worse, though scholarly opinion is divided. Roehl has argued that France did possess a national market, at least for grain, by the end of the eighteenth century; he cites as evidence a decrease in the number of food riots and the fact that grain prices tended to move in concert in different regions (1976, 263–4). He goes on to complain that while agriculture was improving in some regions of France during this period, scholars always focus on the regions where this was not the case. Price (1983), though, has devoted a whole book to describing how local subsistence crises disappeared from France only in the mid-nineteenth century as a result of the transport improvements of the time. The fact that grain prices appear to move together in different regions is to a large extent the result of shared monetary trends rather than market integration.[59] And the fact that some regions may have shown signs of the same changes that occurred in England while others did not is in itself an indication that vast areas of France had not felt the beneficial effects of improved transport links. Price describes France as possessing two types of regions: continental interiors where agriculture was autarkic and inward looking,[60] and other areas on the coast or along navigable rivers where communications and exchange were more highly developed (1981, 1). Areas which by geographical or historical accident were blessed with good transport links connecting them to major markets would give evidence of agricultural specialization and trade. Other areas not so blessed would languish in a state of self-sufficiency. The difference between England and France in the late eighteenth century was not that France was formed entirely of small, self-sufficient units while England was one big market. The difference, though major, was one of degree. Almost all of England was connected by good transport links to form a unified market with a great degree of regional specialization. In France, vast areas were virtually unconnected with the rest of the economy, and agricultural production was generally for local consumption.[61] France achieved a unified national market in the 1860s at the earliest, after much work had been done on roads, canals, and railways (Fohlen 1975, 46–7, or Price 1983).[62]

It has already been noted that one of the natural results of improvements in transportation is the replacement of indirect means of exchange, such as fairs, with direct means. Thus, a faster decline in fairs in one country indicates that it has benefitted from greater improvements in transport. In England during the eighteenth century fairs lost their economic importance and became the carnivals we know them as today. The writer of the "Historical Account of Sturbridge and Bury Fairs" noted that fairs were still of great commercial importance in parts of the continent where transport links were poor. The great Stourbridge Fair, however, had been in decline for twenty years due to the increased number of carriages, easy communications with cities and manufacturing towns, new canals, and riders receiving orders direct from manufacturers (cited in Moffit 1925, 222–5). The last was, of course, of crucial importance, for the story of eighteenth-century English commerce is the replacement of various indirect means of distribution by direct movement from producer to retailer.

To be sure, there was a decline in the number of French fairs as well during the eighteenth century. This was often accompanied by a growth in size, though, and fairs remained the most important opportunity for commerce until the early nineteenth century (Price 1981, 28–30). "Travelling salesmen and fairs provided an important means for supplying the needs of the peasants and townfolk which could not be satisfied from local production, in the absence of a more permanent network of distribution. There were signs, toward the end of the century, that distribution was improving ... The continued vitality of fairs having a regional or even a national or international significance, testifies to the development of commerce, but also to the fact that it was still not backed up by an adequate system of transport, distribution, and credit, which, as it came, would make them superfluous" (Kemp 1971, 53). The great Beaucaire fair, for example, declined only in the nineteenth century as roads and railways made more direct transactions possible (Price 1981, 29). As one might expect, the history of French fairs varied widely from area to area. Fairs declined in large cities where goods could be bought in shops. "There was nevertheless no lack of fairs in France," for they remained strong in mostly rural areas (Pounds 1979, 290).[63]

A CLOSER LOOK AT
NORTHEASTERN FRANCE

I have concentrated so far on showing that English transport was much better overall than French transport. However, France's superior size and the spottiness of French transport together suggest that some region of France may have possessed much better transport services than the country as a whole, and might be comparable to England. The area to the northeast of Berry[64] is similar in size to England and is thought to have possessed the best transport system in France at that time. Parts of this area were also the first in France to industrialize. Lepetit's study of French transport in the nineteenth century indicates that in the period after 1820, the northeastern quarter of France did indeed possess a much better transport network than the rest of the country (1984, 52–3, 64–5).

In Berry itself, the first half of the eighteenth century saw very little accomplished; there were some repairs to existing bridges and roads but virtually no new creations (Jenn 1980, 219). Later eighteenth–century intendants were interested in transport improvements, in large part because there was no connection between Bas-Berry and Bourges; the mode of finance, small sums allotted, use of corvée, and reliance on workhouses ensured that the roads stayed in poor shape (Jenn 1980, 219). Nothing was done to the waterways.[65] The Canal du Berry had been much talked of in the eighteenth century but was only completed decades into the nineteenth. Thus, Berry had both poor internal communications and poor connections with the rest of France.

In Burgundy, the local Estates devoted considerable attention to roads and bridges during the eighteenth century (Kleinclausz 1976, 315–16). Nevertheless, a great many roads needed to be constructed in the nineteenth century; only then was the isolation of mountain regions ended and villages connected with the outside world (Levesque 1965, 359). The area saw efforts toward the completion of a number of canals, but there was unwillingness on the part of locals to support these projects. "It is not enough to organize projects; they must be completed" (Kleinclausz 1976, 318). The Canal du Centre was only achieved in 1793, the Canal du Bourgogne[66] and the Rhône-Rhine in the 1830s. Navigation on the Yonne and Loire remained subject to seasonal fluctuations, though the Saône was progressively improved in the nineteenth century and became a magnificent river for transport (Levesque 1965, 359).

The central part of the region was traversed by a number of rivers, but their full potential for navigation was not realized. The Seine had been extended from Mery to Troyes in the seventeenth century, but the navigation was under royal control and, due to inadequate maintenance, became unnavigable from 1720 (Peuchet 1807, "Aube").[67] The Aube was navigable for some distance but had dangerous rapids which required a lateral canal (Peuchet, "Marne"). It was recommended in 1780 that the Aube be improved so that Paris could obtain more wood from the region (F12 653) but nothing was accomplished. The Marne navigation could easily have been extended to the great benefit of the department of Marne and Haut-Marne (Peuchet, "Haut-Marne"). The Haut-Marne, as the source of rivers flowing in many directions, was the subject of many canal suggestions. But nothing came of them.[68] In the Aisne, the Marne suffered from low water in some seasons, "but it is possible, at little cost to overcome this inconvenience" (Peuchet, "Aisne").[69] The Aisne itself was potentially navigable throughout that department but was actually navigable only to Pontavaire. The Oise was only navigable from Chaumy but could easily have been extended to Hirson (Peuchet, "Oise").

The late completion of the Rhône–Rhine Canal had even more severe consequences for Franche-Comté. The province had only one port in the eighteenth century, through which virtually all of its commerce had to pass. Without the canal, Franche-Comté remained poorly attached to the rest of the country, an enclave frontier province (Brelot 1977, 380). In the nineteenth century, much bridge building had to be done, and many steep ramps had to be reduced to allow rapid travel and the carriage of bulky goods (Brelot 1977, 383). Great effort was required for local road improvement in the nineteenth century, a matter of great importance in a rural area like Franche-Comté.

Alsace in the eighteenth century was the site of much road building (Livet 1970, 322). The first priority was connection with Paris for political and military reasons. Corvée labour was relied on for most of the century (Livet 1977, 322). Leuillot describes in detail the sorry state of transport in early nineteenth-century Alsace but attributes it to the Revolution (1959, 205). It would appear, though, that Alsace in the eighteenth century relied on the same inadequate methods of transport improvement as the rest of France, so much of the blame for the poor state of nineteenth-century communications must lie in the pre-Revolutionary period.[70]

Lorraine also suffered from neglect. De Verzemous, a government official, wrote glowingly of the gains which could be obtained by both Lorraine and Alsace if improvements were made to the navigation of the Moselle or Sarre rivers (F12 1512B). Yet in the nineteenth century, Boucqeau noted that the navigation of the Moselle could easily be improved by clearing rocks and improving the haulage path (an XII, 6). He also noted that narrowing the channel would make the river navigable at low water, and complained that sinuosity added fifty per cent to the length of the journey. Peuchet ("Moselle") also spoke of the need for a haulage path on the Moselle, and suggested that the Sarre could be rendered navigable by clearing the river bed in a handful of places, building a haulage path, and clearing some sandbars.

Even near Paris, there were many difficulties with transport. "Complaints about roads in the Brie, both those leading to Paris and those linking the various parts of the region, persisted throughout the century ... The roads in the Beauce inspired similar criticism" (Kaplan 1984, 83). A number of canals were proposed for the Paris area in the eighteenth century, but special interests were able to persuade the government not to support them (Kaplan 1984, 86). The lack of success near Paris is especially significant given the great importance attached to the provisioning of that city by the government.[71] Not only were there great difficulties in obtaining supplies from the south and east, but Paris lacked the same easy access to the sea which London possessed. There were proposals to make the Seine capable of bearing ocean-going vessels to Paris (Noël de la Morinière, an VII) but these were not acted upon. Even for river boats the lower Seine presented many problems in the way of rocks and shifting sandbars and a sinuous course.[72] Apart from the Seine, there was no navigation at all in the Seine-Inférieure, making it difficult for local producers to reach even the Paris market.[73]

The Nord (the departments of Nord and Pas de Calais) was perhaps the best situated of all French regions to develop a modern transport network. For military reasons, France had often concentrated on roads connecting Paris with the frontiers of France. A desire to assimilate Flanders had also spurred road improvements in the area (Trenard 1950, 107). Moreover, the land was generally flat, and thus conducive to the building of roads for both political and economic reasons. Though the military and the Ponts et Chaussées often argued about road placement in the area, the net effect of their interest was highly positive (Thbaut 1961, 154). One indicator of the superiority of northern roads is that larger wagons tended to be used more there than elsewhere (Price 1981, 3). The flat land also gave the region a number of navigable rivers and was conducive to the building of canals.[74]

Nevertheless, the communication network of the area left much to be desired.[75] Until the nineteenth century, regional commerce was hurt by poor transport. The road from Dunkirk to Calais was declared unusable in 1777 (Coornaert 1970, 239). In the valley of the Lys, roads were difficult for wagon traffic for most of the year (Coornaert 1970, 239). The Nord had a denser transport network than elsewhere in France, but many routes were still not properly maintained. "The Nord Department had one sixth of all the improved river and canal mileage at the beginning of the nineteenth century, but most of the waterways were adapted to serving a local, rural economy" (Geiger 1974, 194). They were best suited for movement over small distances by tiny boats. The Escaut suffered from silting and flooding, and great loops which doubled the distance travelled; boats foundered every couple of years, impeding navigation until the wreck was cleared. "Although the Escaut was well supplied with water in comparison with many other French rivers, it was nevertheless impassable at certain seasons of the year" (Geiger 1974, 180).

The Nord's internal problems were matched externally. Throughout the eighteenth century, there was speculation about the completion of a canal to link the area with the Seine-Oise basin, but only in the nineteenth century was the St-Quentin canal completed, giving the region access by water to Paris. The coastal position of the region should have proved an advantage. Yet its hinterland was poorly connected with its ports. Not only were road links to Dunkirk questionable, but "as late as 1835 navigation between Dunkirk and the French interior was closed entirely for eight months, and Lille had to obtain by road the foreign raw materials its industrialists imported at Dunkirk" (Geiger 1974, 195). The port itself was in poor shape, and in any case the rest of the north coast of France was poorly suited to handling the coasting trade.

The northeast of France, and especially the Nord, did possess a better than average transport system by French standards. Yet not even in the Nord could it compare to English transport. Its facilities for coasting, inland waterways, and roads were all less developed than in England. While northeastern France might be much more capable of industrializing than the rest of France, it was not capable of achieving an industrial revolution as in England.

WHY?

The basic theme of this work is that England had the Industrial Revolution because she had the best system of transportation in the world. If this thesis is accepted, it naturally gives rise to the question, "Why did England develop such a system of transportation before anybody else?" It is not my purpose here to provide the definitive answer to that question. However, my description of English and French transportation has touched on historical matters a number of times, and a brief discussion of why England succeeded and France did not may serve to cast light on the subject.

The first task, one of crucial importance, is to dispel the myth that transport improvements were a result rather than a cause of the Industrial Revolution. The myth stands if one dates the onset of modern transportation from the coming of the railway and steamship, for these clearly were results of the Industrial Revolution. Yet, it must be recognized that "The economic takeoff of the eighteenth century in fact coincided with the peak achieved by traditional methods of circulation" (Braudel 1982, 349). The Industrial Revolution had its genesis in an era of horse and sail, and was well under way long before the coming of the railway and steamship which only it could create. I do not deny that industrialization, once begun, created a demand for even better transportation. All I claim is that a network of waterways and roads, usable in all but the most extreme weather conditions, had to be in place before the Industrial Revolution could begin. The timing of events supports this conclusion. The Industrial Revolution is commonly thought to have had its beginnings between the years 1760 and 1780. Thanks to centuries of attempts at road improvements, a system of good turnpike roads had been established through almost all England by 1750. The mideighteenth century is also the point at which a hundred years of river improvements, which had doubled the length of navigable waterway, gave way to the construction of canals[76] which, within a couple of decades, had forged the basic links necessary for England to possess a national network of inland waterways connecting her major industrial areas and markets. "What we see in the fifty years from 1770 was the culmination of a long, at times uneven but nevertheless perceptible movement toward greater efficiency, both in terms of basic infrastructure (the provision of networks and services) and in the institutional framework within which that infrastructure fell ... The picture of transport development is characterized not by phases of concentrated radical change, so much as a flowering of past efforts to upgrade and improve, the final working out of a continuous process of refinement and readjustment" (Freeman 1983, 3–4). The fact that both road and water transport systems were largely in place before the Industrial Revolution was underway, and that both were the result of centuries of effort, is convincing proof that this transport system was not itself a result of industrialization. One can move on to other possibilities.

Perhaps the easiest way to answer the question of why adoption of improved transport was not more widespread is to note how extremely expensive it was. Heaton has stated that transport improvements, because of their great expense, required a good deal of state intervention, much more than was necessary in industry (1948, 515).[77] While the English case disproves the idea that state intervention was necessary, it is still true that the creation of an early modern transport system involved an incredible mobilization of resources for the time. Thus, it should not be considered surprising that only one country was able to put forth the necessary effort.

In the first chapter I described how the Smithian growth process has a natural tendency to bring about transport improvements, but there are a number of obstacles which can prevent this. A lengthier theoretical discussion may be helpful here. Smithian growth means increasing trade, which means increasing use of the existing transportation system. This will cause both increasing congestion and increasing cost of maintenance. This, in turn, will cause attempts to expand and upgrade the system. It will also, in conjunction with an increasing desire for less expensive and speedier transport, lead to some search for technological improvements. The various constraints that the economy faces will determine what, if any, improvements are made in the system. If substantial improvement is made, an opportunity is created for the emergence of the process of Schumpeterian growth. On the other hand, if the transport system is not substantially improved, the transfer to Schumpeterian growth is cut off and the economy is forced to rely on continued Smithian growth which may at some point give way to stagnation or decay. If one accepts the verdict of much recent scholarship that England was not radically more advanced than France, then there are three areas of inquiry one should pursue – technological capabilities, geographical advantages, and socio-political factors. To the extent that England was farther along in the process of Smithian growth, this could explain part of her success. Still, Smithian growth alone would not lead to significant transport improvements.

One factor that can be ruled out is the possibility that England possessed some technological advantage over France. It has already been established that both countries possessed the same knowledge of the art of road making. In terms of canals, it would appear that any advantage lay with the French. France had, after all, built the Languedoc canal during the seventeenth century, a major technological achievement that Young still marvelled at a century later. Since the technology of river improvement is generally similar, it would appear that France had no initial disadvantage in this respect, though England after centuries of effort may have developed some special expertise in dredging.

Geography seems to have worked to England's advantage, though not overwhelmingly. Both England and France were blessed with numerous navigable rivers. While England had done much to extend her river system, France had not. As already noted, France did face somewhat greater problems in terms of rapids than England. Canal building is not easy anywhere. Opinion on French opportunities varies; Dunham notes that French watersheds are high and numerous and the distance between rivers great (1955, 48), while Pounds argues that French canal building was aided by gentle relief and interpenetrating river basins (1979, 299).[79] It is clear, however, that the failure of eighteenth-century canal building schemes was not due to geography, though geography may have placed an important cap on how far successful canal construction could proceed in France.[80] England itself, while possessing some areas quite suited to canal construction, was on the whole poorly suited for canals, as the land was uneven and the supply of water limited. "Thus if England, the first large consumer of coal, was also the first country to possess, as early as the end of the eighteenth century, an important network of canals, it was largely a result of historical factors rather than natural endowment" (Girard 1965, 222). In terms of roads, French mountains were certainly a major obstacle to road construction in central and southeastern France. However, the north and northeastern plains were admirably suited to road construction. England had its own problems. Clay soils and frequent rain conspired to keep roads throughout central England a muddy mess, unless they were carefully constructed and maintained. In both countries, materials for road construction were not readily available in some areas. In England, this situation was ameliorated as river and canal improvements made it easier to move building materials from one region to another. England's biggest overall advantage was her superior facilities for coastal shipping. One must recall that England not only had relatively more coastline than France but her coastline was much better endowed with natural harbours. Coastal shipping was the base from which other transport services grew. A much deeper historical analysis would be necessary to see to what degree England's superiority in transportation was owed to what contemporaries referred to as "the river 'round England."

Much of the explanation, it appears, must fall to social or political factors. Little light can be shed on the former.[81] There is an obvious avenue for research, however. In the eighteenth century, a number of canal schemes were proposed in France – much as they were during the English canal boom – but nothing came of them. Some of these schemes involved private capital while others were to be totally government funded. The reasons for government failure will be discussed below.[82] It would be interesting, though, to know more about the relative lack of private interest in canals. Again, in the nineteenth century, a cornerstone of the Becquey plan was that private capital would be unavailable for most canal projects. How much was simply due to government determination to supervise French transport? Or, conversely, is it attributable to the (alleged) conservatism of French businessmen, the differences in capital markets between the two countries, or differences in internal trade patterns? Further research is necessary.

To my mind, the most convincing explanation is an institutional one. France failed where England succeeded because decision making was too centralized in France. Transport networks must serve a variety of needs and the concentration of power in a few hands in France inevitably led to the formation of a system that served political and military needs but not economic ones. Business interests were generally ignored in France in both the planning and operation of canals (Dunham 1955, 44–5). Thus, canals, even in the nineteenth century, were not built in the most important places – if they were built at all. As Young says of the Canal du Centre, "it is a truly useful undertaking, and therefore left undone" (1900, 226). As discussed earlier, moreover, France paid little attention to necessary river improvements, while favouring more expensive canal construction. In terms of roads, the French spent huge amounts on a few roads while ignoring the rest. As Cavailles notes, the roads Young speaks so highly of were new roads, created not by need but by government decision, unmindful of the needs of the populace, and favouring towns over countryside (1946, 167). The huge budget of the Ponts et Chausées was often squandered on ostentatious display.[83] This is in marked contrast to England where thousands of turnpike trusts each applied relatively small sums of money to the proper maintenance of small sections of road.[84] And English canals, according to Girard, were, "even more than the English road system, built by local initiative responding to local needs" (1965, 222). Not only did local initiative increase the likelihood of good projects being undertaken but it meant that maintenance would be undertaken as required. French roads, as shown, suffered from irregular maintenance.[85]

I stated earlier that sheer expense is the simplest answer to the question of why transport improvements do not naturally arise where needed. The French approach exacerbated this problem in two ways. First, an insistence on central government control ensured that almost all of the funding had to come from the public treasury. The English government could not afford to improve the rivers and roads, and build the canals at its own expense; neither could the French government (see Becquey 1818, 15; Meuvret 1988, v.3, 71). The French government's determination to run the show[86] meant that there could never be sufficient funds for all of the worthwhile undertakings. While not ensuring that all projects were undertaken where the social benefit exceeded social cost, the English method of making users pay was for that time a much better device for improving the transport network than relying on bureaucratic decision. The French government had many expenses and was thus often forced to cut back on projects of great utility (Becquey 1820, 13). During the American War of Independance – a period when canal building continued in England – the French government found itself unable to deliver sufficient funds to its canal projects; the Picardy canal, for one, was forgotten until the Peace of 1781 ("Opinion," an X, 10). Yet, not until the end of the century did the government consider the option of charging tolls to pay for construction and maintenance. The same debate about the propriety of tolls which had occurred in England a century earlier occupied the minds of Revolutionary legislators.[87] Without extensive private investment or toll revenues, the French government in the eighteenth century could not afford improvements on the same scale as those being achieved across the Channel.

The second problem with the French approach was that inefficient bureaucracy often led to seriously inflated construction costs. It might seem at first glance that the existence of a trained corps of engineers in the Ponts et Chaussées would give France an edge in both road and water improvement. Yet it appears that England was better served by a group of independent engineers who could be hired by trusts or companies. English engineers were responsible for their own actions, like doctors and lawyers, while their French counterparts were part of a faceless bureaucracy (Say 1852, 318). Construction and maintenance in England were monitored closely by locally based authorities. Expenses in France were imperfectly controlled from Paris. Lequinio, surveying Ancien Regime canal efforts, asserted that private companies would have been much more careful with their funds and cited a number of government projects which had proved much more expensive than predicted (an I, 61–3).[88]

French bureaucracy, by favouring ostentatious display, discouraging private investment, ignoring tolls, and allowing waste, did much to slow the pace of French transport improvements. It also had the usual characteristic of bureaucracy in being slow to act. The simplest project had to pass through layers of red tape before being engineered, a process which could take years (D'Haussez 1828, 6, 23). In England, local authorities could respond quickly to local needs.

It must not be forgotten how unique the English Private Bill was. No other legislature in the world possessed such a device. Local transport needs could be brought up before the national government, and a bill passed which would set up the legal framework in which work could be undertaken. While the cost of getting such a bill passed was far from trivial, there was at least an established procedure which could be followed by people in all localities. The ability to collect tolls not only gave locals the necessary cashflow to undertake the work, but also reduced their reluctance to maintain routes largely used by others. In France, the institutional set-up by which people could have undertaken local transport improvements was lacking. Not only were there no Private Bills; the Estates General was called for the first time during the eighteenth century in 1789. The government bureaucracy was unlikely to pay much heed to the suggestions of locals, or to allow local interests to acquire control of any part of the transport network.

Not only did Private Bills set up the trusts which would undertake the work but they also set up a system whereby landowners could be forced to sell their land. In modern times, it is recognized that transport improvements require exercise of the power of eminent domain. Otherwise, every landowner along the route will have an incentive to charge an exorbitant price for his land. The eighteenth century was no different, for the building of canals as well as the straightening of roads and rivers and the extension of navigability to previously unnavigable rivers required that particular parcels of land be obtained. In England, all the road, river, and canal Acts provided for the same system of arbitration when landowner and trust could not agree on a price for land.[89] While the boards that made such decisions were heavily weighted with landowners, Ward (1974) has shown that, on the whole, the trusts were able to obtain land at reasonable prices (it could be argued that landowners in England were more supportive of transport improvements than those elsewhere). In France, there was no general rule for the expropriation of land, each case was decided individually, and in some cases a very high price seems to have been exacted (Petot 1958, 208–11). Again, it would appear that the English political and legal framework was much more conducive to transport improvements than that of France. The French king was hesitant to use his powers of expropriation, and no framework was set up to adjudicate arguments over the value of land until the next century.[90]

In sum, the most compelling explanation for English transport superiority is an institutional one. Local interests in England could obtain the rights to charge tolls and expropriate land to perform necessary work, and local control helped to control costs. The French bureaucracy could not (would not, in the case of tolls) raise enough money, had misplaced priorities and a flair for monument building, did not minimize costs, and was hampered in obtaining land. The result, it will be seen, was that England was ready for an Industrial Revolution; France was not.

CHAPTER THREE

The English Iron Industry

Iron, as a producer goods industry, needs special treatment; proper coverage requires that one looks at the uses to which iron was put. This is especially important because the output of the eighteenth-century iron industry went for quite different uses than those associated with the modern iron industry. This chapter will begin with a brief overview of the iron industry and those trades closely allied with it. A pictorial description of the iron and allied trades is provided on the following page. To avoid clutter, the various other raw materials required for these processes of production are listed at the bottom of that diagram.

The first operation is the smelting of iron ore to produce pig iron. This act was performed in a furnace using either charcoal or coal as a fuel, and with the addition of a flux such as limestone to draw some of the impurities from the ore. From the furnace, pig iron could be used for two purposes. It could in molten form be cast to produce a variety of cast-iron goods. More commonly, it was taken to a forge where it was converted to wrought iron and formed into bars. Pig iron (or cast iron) has a carbon content of four per cent while wrought iron has virtually no carbon content. A low carbon content makes iron very malleable and thus capable of being hammered into different shapes. However, low carbon content makes it difficult for the final good to keep an edge. Therefore, for cutting tools, steel, which has a two per cent carbon content, was preferred. One might think that steel would be made by drawing off half the carbon from pig iron, but the technology of the day required that steel be created by adding carbon to wrought iron. Due to the expense of steel making, edge tools were generally made with a thin strip of steel attached to an iron body.

In what follows, I will treat the operations of furnace and forge as being the iron industry. Everything else that uses pig or wrought iron

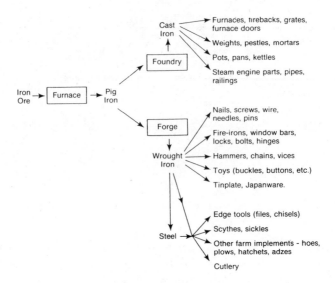

Figure 2: The Eighteenth Century Iron Industry and the Uses of Its Output
Other raw materials used included charcoal, coal, tin, zinc, brass, copper, clay,
limestone, brick, pitch, resin, oil, acids, paints, varnishes, stone, timber, gold, silver.

as an input will be termed the metal trades, in part to draw attention
to the fact that a variety of other metals were required for many of
these trades. While such a division is artificial, it is appropriate to my
concern with how the production of pig and wrought iron were affected
by changes in the trades that used them.

The poor records left by most inland trade of this period make it
impossible to estimate what proportion of iron output went to the various trades. It will be instructive, then, as I list the metal trades, to
discuss the uses for the final goods. The largest source of demand for
iron was undoubtedly the nail trade. At a time when most structures
were made of wood, nails of various sizes were always needed. Needles
were especially important since everyone made their own clothes. Wire
was needed, among other things, to make cards for carding cotton and
wool. Agriculture was a major user of metal ware. Scythe and sickle
making were trades of great importance. Other agricultural tools
included shovels, adzes, hoes, axes, and, of course, plows. Some steel
was required for most of these implements. There were also special
trades to provide buckles and other metal parts for saddlery, not to
mention horseshoes. Most households needed a number of metal products, including fire-irons, locks, and hinges. Those who wished not to

eat with their hands needed cutlery. More important was the craftsmen's need for tools: chisels, files, hammers, vices, pliers, gauges, etc. In this day of precision machinery, it is easy to forget the variety of tools needed by earlier workers. For example, virtually all craftsmen in all industries needed at least one file. Many of these implements required some steel as well.

In addition to these traditional trades, a number of new trades emerged during the eighteenth century. These trades in general served less utilitarian desires. Tinplate, as one would expect, was iron plate coated with tin, and then formed into various shapes. Japanware also involved the coating of iron with something both more attractive and more water resistant. In this case it was different types of varnish, in an attempt to imitate East Indian woodwork (hence the name). The best known of the new trades was the toy trade which produced buttons and buckles (of great importance in the days before zippers and shoe-laces), and other small pieces.

The foundry trade came to produce a greater variety of goods during the eighteenth century as well. At the start of the century, it produced furnaces, firebacks, and furnace grates and doors. It was also responsible for some smaller items such as weights, pestles and mortars. It came to replace other metals in the production of cooking vessels such as pots and pans. As the century wore on, it increasingly produced steam engine parts and pipes for the expanding towns.

Having sketched the uses of iron in the eighteenth century, I shall examine the impact of the various theories developed in the first chapter on the iron industry. The effects of a wider market would first be felt in the metal trades and would be fed back to the iron industry if the metal trades responded in a way that increased their demand for iron. Improved methods of distribution would have their main direct effect on the output of the metal trades, but would also have an effect on the iron industry's sales of iron to metalworkers. Increased reliability of transport would allow and encourage producers in all industries to expand their scale of production. A greater availability of various raw materials would have a significant impact on both the iron industry and the metal trades. As these various forces had their effects, they would create an environment more conducive to technological innovation in both the metal trades and the iron industry.

In what follows, I will first look at the metal trades. It will be seen that they were exposed to new methods of distribution (and a need for standardization) and a wider market, and that they needed and received more reliable transport, as well as greater access to a wide variety of raw materials. Then, I will look at the responses of the metal trades to these forces, focusing in turn upon the division of labour, the move toward workshop production, mechanization, and the establishment of intermediate industries between the iron industry and some of the metal trades. I then look at both the output and scale of operation of the iron industry and show that the metal trades encouraged and allowed the changes I describe, along with direct effects of improved transport. Shifting to the input side of the iron industry, I discuss first how changes in transport caused coal to become much cheaper, and then how the iron industry needed a number of other raw materials which it was better able to obtain as the century wore on. I then look at the technological reactions of the iron industry to all of these forces, discussing the introduction of coke to both furnace and forge, along with a couple of other important innovations. This is followed by a brief discussion of the importance of changes in the iron industry for the wider economy. One of the major impacts of improvements in the quality and quantity of iron output was the ability to produce better steam engines, and the chapter finishes with a discussion of the roles of both the transport system and the iron industry in fostering the development of steam engines during the century. As the discussion is necessarily somewhat disjointed, I provide a brief summary at the end.

THE METAL TRADES

Methods of Distribution

The easiest task is to show that the changes in methods of distribution outlined in the first chapter did in fact occur in the metal trades. I cited the Darbys as an example and it will be useful to expand on their story here. The early development of Coalbrookdale was based on the Darbys' salesmanship at fairs and markets through much of England, where they established the personal contact between producer and consumer crucial to the company's success (Raistrick 1970, 2). Abraham Darby I spent three or more months of the year on various trips, visiting markets as well as customers in their shops and houses.[1] The company did sell large amounts of goods to a family firm in Bristol (most likely for export) with which Darby had personal ties, but aside from this and three more minor wholesale arrangements, the company relied on retail sales at fairs, which comprised the bulk of its sales. As transport improved, the company was able to build upon the personal ties it had formed and send shipments directly to its consumers. Fairs came to be a place where orders were taken and payments settled, rather than a place where goods actually changed hands. At mid–century, the Darbys began to send travellers (salesmen) to the fairs and through the country to take orders which would later be dispatched by barge or carrier. The need for face-to-face contact between producer and consumer had vanished. As it became possible to transport small consignments inexpensively, the company could rely on salesmen with samples to sell its product. To serve various markets more quickly the company established warehouses in London and Liverpool as well as Bristol. As the company steadily expanded into the steam engine business, it used commission agents in the northeast to obtain orders from local mines and industries. These orders could be quickly transmitted by carrier to the foundry, and the goods dispatched by water to the purchaser, with payment returned by carrier as well.

The cast iron trade is, of course, a very special case within the metal trades. Most metal workers operated on a much smaller scale in the early eighteenth century. The Midlands metal trades were largely organized on a putting-out basis. The same people who provided manufacturers with raw material would travel through Oxfordshire, East Anglia, or the southeast, visiting the major fairs and markets of the area. Often, they would leave their goods with local chapmen, who would travel about the local area selling the wares and meet with the Midlands chapmen on their next trip to settle accounts (Rowlands 1975, ch. 1, 94). Rowlands describes the route of one Birmingham man who travelled in the 1720s through Lincolnshire, Leicestershire, Northamptonshire, Rutland, and Huntingdonshire, averaging thirty miles a day on horseback, delivering goods, taking orders, and collecting payment (95). Hey describes a Sheffield-based ironmonger serving Lancashire, Cheshire, Yorkshire, and Derbyshire with nails, and thus not competing with Midlands ironmongers. To quote Lloyd, "For the most part, craftsmen had to rely on the visits of the travelling chapman, who appeared with his packhorses from time to time, bartered for or bought such goods as he required, and then went his way" (1913, 327–30).[2] In the later eighteenth century, these travellers were gradually replaced by direct sales in both the West Midlands and Sheffield trades.[3] Similar changes were going on in the Lancashire tool trade. Peter Stubs, the filemaker, at first dealt with a number of factors in various regions who took his files around. As the century wore on, Stubs came to deal directly with the customers of these factors. He was better able to send small parcels to particular customers (he used the Post Office at least once in 1776) and was able to send these long distances (Ashton 1939, 6). He could also obtain better information on market conditions in various parts of England. He was able to travel quickly through the country to gather information. Thus, he could do without the factors and establish trade links with consumers throughout the country. In all regions, then, as the century wore on, indirect methods of sale through horseback travellers were replaced by direct sales. Manufacturers no longer needed to spend months on the road, but would instead communicate with their customers by mail or through salesmen, and dispatch their goods by carrier.

Travelling chapmen were not the only means by which goods reached customers in the early eighteenth century. London wholesalers played a major role in supplying much of England with metal ware. Since they were able to receive bulk supplies from a number of different sources, these wholesalers were able to supply regional ironmongers or shopkeepers (a class of people which was continually growing) with a variety of goods. Rowlands notes that the local retailer needed to stock a great variety of nails, locks, and harness parts (and many other goods as well), and this must have perpetuated the practise of dealing with the London wholesalers who could supply all of these needs (1975, 94). I would argue further that it was poor transport links which, by making it difficult for a small retailer to deal with a large number of suppliers, forced him to deal with one supplier who could supply all his needs (though dealing also, perhaps, with chapmen who called at his house with advantageous prices on particular items). As transport links developed, the local retailer was better able to deal with a number of suppliers. Indeed, by mid-century, London wholesalers were circulating price lists for all the goods they dealt in, and thus competing with each other as well as with Midlands ironmongers on every product line. The Sheffield cutlery trades had also been forced to deal with London wholesalers. These, operating through factors in Sheffield, seem to have been able to depress prices through their control of the market (Lloyd 1913, 327–30).[4] Transport was so poor that Sheffield masters did not regularly visit markets until near mid-century. Gradually, Sheffield merchants began to establish trading ties. "Long before 1800, some Sheffield manufacturers had become substantial merchants and they greatly extended the trade relations of Sheffield" (Lloyd 1913, 329).

Thus, as the eighteenth century wore on, both the chapmen and the London wholesalers lost business to direct sales from producer to consumer. In the first chapter I discussed the probable effects of such a change. As merchant manufacturers were allowed to spend less time actually selling their goods, they could turn more of their attention to production. As middlemen were eliminated from the system, the actual cost of distribution decreased and this helped to widen the market. More importantly, as information flows improved and retailers became able to deal with a number of suppliers, the suppliers were forced to abandon the old way of doing business which concentrated on high profits per item and concentrate instead on higher output and lower cost. This spur to mass production is matched by the fact that the new method of sale using samples or catalogues required the production of a standardized good. Since the matter of standardization is so important to my theory, I will look next at the degree to which the metal trades responded by standardizing their output.

Standardization would naturally occur in some trades before others. In 1729, London wholesalers printed lists of prices they were willing to pay for 25 different types of nail, indicating that the output of the industry was already fairly standardized by that time (Rowlands 1975, 80). By the 1750s, producers of more ornamental metal wares were issuing pattern books to attract the consumer's attention (Rowlands, 152). This trend to standardization would be expected to yield changes in both technology and organization. For the moment, a couple of examples will suffice. In the japanware trade, the need to produce a standardized product both allowed and required the introduction of stamping and pressing machinery. The use of such machinery, along with the need to supervise workers (in part to maintain standardized output) were the causes of the rise of large establishments in the japan trade (Court 1938, 235). Perhaps the best example of the need for standardization is the integrated works of the Crowleys in the northeast. This early forerunner of large-scale production in the iron industry was largely set up in order to achieve standardization and high quality. In the conclusion to his study of the Crowleys, Flinn writes, "The main incentive to break away from the traditional pattern lay in the need to standardize the product by absolute control over the product employed. There were endless possibilities of adulteration of the product and the clandestine use of inferior metal, while the geographical dispersion of thousands of domestic workers rendered standardization an impossible achievement. In order to control the raw material employed by domestic workers, and to supervise and standardize their work, it was essential to bring them together into a single industrial unit" (1962 253-4). I shall return to this matter below.

It should be noted that standardization did not come at the cost of fashion. I showed earlier how improved transport helped lead to national fashions which could change very rapidly. While clearly not a concern in the nail trade, many other metal trades had to be fashion conscious. The pattern books mentioned before would contain a wide variety of patterns which would be changed with the fashions (sometimes causing changes in fashion). This need to cater to people's tastes made worker supervision even more important. The fact that these tastes could change made industry even more sensitive to reliable transport, while encouraging methods of production which were less time-consuming so that changes in tastes could be quickly responded to.

Evidence Of Market Widening

In order to show that the market was widening in the eighteenth century, one would need evidence that particular goods from particular areas were circulated within a particular region in 1700, a larger region in 1750, and an even larger region in 1800. Unfortunately, as Hey says about the Sheffield trades, "The evidence for domestic sales is scrappy" (1972, 51). I have already noted that the greater availability of data on foreign trade has encouraged historians to underestimate the importance of the home market. The same paucity of data makes it extremely difficult to detail the expansion of the geographical market any producer deals with. There is some mention of people establishing relations in areas of the country with which they had not been in contact before. For example, in the cast iron trade, ironfounders ceased to deal with isolated regional markets but sold instead on a national basis (Hyde 1977, 129). Such evidence, however, is fragmentary.

The fact that contemporaries like Adam Smith spoke at great length about the impact of a widening market indicates that the process must have been observable to those present at the time. Yet it seems that the existing evidence has generally been interpreted to mean something else. Jones, in his study of the West Midlands needle trades, cleverly deduces that there was a substantial increase in needle sales in the 1730s and 1740s, but then suggests that this stemmed from a macroeconomic increase in demand rooted in a series of good harvests (1978, 368). Hey notes the expansion during the seventeenth and eighteenth centuries of the Sheffield cutlery trades, but attributes this to foreign markets and an increase in household demand.[5] It was suggested in the first chapter that those who argue that increased supply during the Industrial Revolution was a result of increased demand must be able to explain how this increased demand could occur without an earlier increase in supply. The only way that one could explain an increase in the demand facing particular producers without resorting to a previous increase in incomes (which would require an increase in output) would be to describe a widening of the market which allowed those producers to reach more distant customers. Thus, a dramatic increase in the demand for needles in certain West Midlands towns, or cutlery in Sheffield, or a variety of other metal goods in various localities, suggests that these localities have gained access to markets which they could not previously penetrate.[6] The result should be increasing regional specialization. When the needle and cutlery manufactures in other localities begin to die out, one is surely observing a classic case of market widening whereby a lower-cost locale is able to take over the markets of other producers. This phenomenon could also be explained without recourse to decreasing transport costs by positing shifts in the relative costs of production in different localities (due perhaps to changes in organization of production or technology), but a country-wide improvement in transport can explain this phenomenon, while any other explanation depending on relative cost changes requires a second level of explanation as to why some regions developed while others did not. When the same process is observed in all industries, it becomes very difficult to explain why relative costs were shifting in all of them, let alone find evidence of such shifts. Likewise, it would be difficult to imagine a shift in tastes that could explain a significant increase in demand over such a range of industries. On the other hand, I have already provided solid evidence that the cost of transportation did decrease over the course of the eighteenth century. Thus, while the evidence may not be conclusive, it does point strongly toward the existence of much wider markets by the end of the century.

The Need For Reliable Transport

The metal trades were as dependent as any other industry on the reliability of the transport services they used. Rowlands describes how frequent delays in delivery caused a considerable amount of extra clerical work (delays might be caused by frost, flood, difficulty with carriers and boatmen, boats sinking, wagons overturning, and the pressing of boatmen for the navy and landsmen for the army). These delays required that a note be sent by separate means to announce that goods were on their way and a note sent back announcing their arrival. Such precautions were necessary not only to ensure that the goods arrived but that the carrier did not pilfer any *en route*, and that the rate he charged the receiver of the goods was the same as that agreed to by the sender. This contrasts sharply with the later eighteenth century when a professional network of carriers could be entrusted to ship goods quickly and reliably throughout the country. Uncertainty of delivery of both inputs and output could make it very risky for a large scale operation with high fixed costs to operate. It would need to hold very large inventories, both of raw materials at the factory and of finished goods near the market (the Darbys, as previously noted, needed to build a number of warehouses to supply their widening market). The earliest successful large-scale operation in the metal trades was the Crowley's integrated works. The Crowleys served the London market from their factory in the northeast. The irregularity of supply they encountered with coastal shipping, coupled with irregular demand from the navy, forced the Crowleys to keep huge inventories in their London warehouses (Flinn 1962, 151). At the time, land transport over such a distance was not a feasible alternative. On the input side, the Crowleys were of course aided by the presence of ironworks and metal manufacture on the same site. In his conclusion, Flinn hypothesizes that the reason nobody copied the ideas of the Crowleys for over half a century was that there were no other men of Crowley's calibre (1962, 254). It seems unlikely that one man would so tower above all of his peers. It is more likely that conditions simply were not conducive to the establishment of other such enterprises at that time. Due to naval contracts and a reputation for quality, the Crowleys could weather interruptions in trade which would threaten other businesses. As transport services improved, more opportunities would arise for larger scale enterprise, and others would come forward to apply the lessons of the Crowley works. In the meantime, industry would remain small and flexible, producing no more than could surely be sold and ordering supplies as needed. This could of course make it difficult for those who might use the outputs of one industry as inputs. Peter Stubs needed steel from Sheffield, but Sheffield steelmakers kept very low inventories. This, in conjunction with poor transport links, meant that it could take weeks or even months to fill an order (Ashton 1939, 37). Thus, one sees a vicious circle between industries reinforcing the effects of poor transport. Only an improvement in the reliability of transport could allow the metal trades together to enter a new era.

Before leaving this section, I should comment on the flow of information as well as the flow of goods. I mentioned before that the first result of road improvements in the early eighteenth century was an increase in the speed and frequency of postal delivery and stagecoach transport. Thus, even at this time Crowley could have a letter transmitted from London to the northeast in three days. Such a quick link between market and manufacture was necessary for the running of the Crowley enterprise. It would become even more important as the century wore on and many trades had to adjust swiftly to changes in taste. While less observable than flows in goods, information flows were essential to early modern industry, and it is difficult to imagine any large enterprise surviving unless closely tied to market information.

The Need For Different Raw Materials

In the introduction to this chapter, I indicated that the English iron industry used a wide variety of raw materials. The need to obtain a wide variety of materials in substantial amounts from different geographic regions was a severe impediment to the development of many of the metal trades before low-cost efficient transport was available.[7] The tinplate industry had to transport tin from Cornwall to South Wales (or the West Midlands) to combine it with local iron and coal or charcoal. While much of the journey was done by ship via the Bristol channel, it also required the forging of links between the coast and the hinterlands of Cornwall and South Wales. The picture was further complicated by the fact that different types of iron were used in South Wales, from the Midlands, the Forest of Dean, Lancashire, and even America and Sweden (though relative prices were the main determinant of which iron was bought).

Many trades followed the practice of using different types of iron; thus even trades which did not seem to require a large number of raw materials might regularly require iron from diverse locations. Most notable were the scythe makers, cutlers, and edgetool makers who needed both iron and steel to work with. The brass industry needed a number of raw materials as well. Zinc and copper were both found in Cornwall but not the coal needed for smelting, and it took twenty-five tons of coal to smelt one ton of zinc. Further, the smelting process required clay pots which could only be made from Stourbridge clay. Thus, before any goods requiring both iron and brass could be produced, a number of bulky materials would have to be transported over long distances. Along with those trades which grew as the raw materials they required became more accessible, there were others which expanded their use of various raw materials as these became more available. Rowlands notes that buckle makers, who in the seventeenth century worked with iron and a little tin, were by 1760 using copper, brass, and zinc, and were using glass jewels and alloys imitating gold and silver for decorations (1975, 132).

The most dramatic change, though, was the number of new industries that emerged in the early or mid-eighteenth century and which required a number of raw materials. These trades were more ornamental than the traditional metal trades, and thus benefitted from the existence of national fashion trends. The toy trade is first heard of in Birmingham in 1714. Among the raw materials used in the toy trade were iron, copper, brass, zinc, and small quantities of gold and silver.[8] By the middle of the century, metal japanware was also being manufactured. Japanning required a variety of oils, resins, and dyes, some produced in England and others imported (Rowlands 1975, 134–6).

The story does not end there, however. Trinder describes attempts, some successful, to obtain useful by-products such as oil, tar, and pitch during the coking process in the 1780s and 1790s in Shropshire (1973, 93–5). One can easily imagine that new industries such as japanning would spur a search for new sources of these materials. In less dramatic ways, such as opening up new mines, one can imagine other reactions to the emergence or growth of industries requiring diverse raw materials. As sources of raw materials are developed, their increased availability (which will be accompanied by lower prices if there are any economies of scale in either production or distribution) will act as a spur to other industries that can use those materials. Thus, improved transport sets off a self-reinforcing chain of events leading to increased use of raw materials previously difficult to obtain. In the metal trades, this process was at work in the development of various industries which play a significant role in what follows.

The Reaction of the Metal Trades

The metal trades adjusted in many ways to the possession of a much more efficient system of distribution, a wider market, more reliable means of obtaining inputs and delivering outputs, and better access to a variety of raw material supplies. The most widespread effect was increased division of labour. Those tasks which require the most supervision are the first to be transferred to workshops. In general, tasks requiring the least skill are the easiest to mechanize. While the chain of causation is not always the same, in what follows I will first look at the increasing division of labour, then the introduction of workshops, and finally at mechanization. I will show that there were a number of innovations in the metal trades, though they are less well known than the major innovations in the iron industry. Some tasks which had applications to more than one trade were affected more strongly than the various trades and were among the first to be mechanized. These grew into intermediate industries and were possibly the most important transformation undergone by the metal trades. As such, they will be discussed last.

Increasing Division of Labor.   On the face of it, many of the metal trades may seem so simple as to have provided little scope for division. The basic nail or pin or needle might seem to require very little effort to those who have never made one. Adam Smith knew better, of course: he described many steps into which pin making could be divided and showed how, with different hands applied to each task, output could be greatly increased (Smith 1776, 4). Even Smith, though, did not describe the full nature of the pin-making process. Rather than recovering the ground he trod, one can look instead at the needle trade, for which a very complete description exists, showing that needle manufacture involved about fifteen distinct steps. As briefly as possible, these were: drawing wire to correct thickness; cutting wire into pieces of correct length, flattening one end of pieces on anvil; making the eye with two punches; removing roughness around the eye by cutting a groove with a file; rounding the head with a file; forcing the point with a file; hardening by heating and dropping in cold water, straightening again (if necessary) with hammer and anvil; changing to steel if iron was used originally, scouring with sand and soap (by kicking around in bags, originally); rubbing to produce a shine; washing; and packing (Donald 1971, 12). If something as simple as the needle could take so many steps, the other metal trades must also have been susceptible to a great degree of division of labour. The reader could also note in passing the number of different iron or steel tools – files, hammers, anvils, cutting tools – which this one trade required.

Not only did substantial scope for division of labour exist in the metal trades, but various trades did indeed take advantage of the new situation and divide labour among their workers over the course of the eighteenth century. Certainly, this occurred in the needle trade. In the village of Crendon, where earlier in the century one worker would perform most or all of the required tasks, they had by 1798 constructed two-way cupboards between cottages so that the workers could specialize in one task and pass the work on to the next worker in the chain. As the eighteenth century wore on, the gun trade was increasingly divided into a number of smaller trades. Not only did the manufacture of different parts of the gun become more specialized but the various tasks involved in making each piece came to be done by specialized workers.[9] A look at Stubs' file-making workshop of the late eighteenth century shows the work divided into a number of different tasks performed by different workers (Ashton 1939, 4–5). Lord Shelburne, visiting a button maker in 1776, stated, "A button passes through fifty hands and each hand perhaps passes a thousand in a day" (Court 1946, 96). White argues that from the beginning, the metal button trade could only be organized on a highly specialized basis because of the various processes which needed to be mastered (1977, 69). Thus, he implicitly argues that metal buttons could only replace cloth buttons after the market had been widened to a point capable of supporting a substantial division of labour.

The reader is referred to any of the classic works on the metal trades for further evidence of increasing division of labour. Rolt, in his book on the tool industry, states (somewhat simplistically) that all the metal trades went through three phases, of which increasing division of labour was the first, followed by the introduction of specialized tools and then powerdriven mills (1968, 56–7). Court, the historian of the West Midland trades, describes how growing division of labour from the seventeenth century through the eighteenth increased output through the enhanced skill of human hands and tools (1946, 93). Lloyd, the first modern chronicler of the Sheffield cutlery trades, states that "The restriction of the typical operative to a specialized process gradually became effective during the eighteenth century, though there were important exceptions" (1913, 178). A perusal of these works or of many others on the metal trades will turn up a number of examples of increased division of labour.

The Transition to Workshops.   To argue that division of labour led naturally to workshops is to trivialize the historical process. It was in most cases a necessary condition but never a sufficient condition. The workshop environment will be more advantageous if the work process has been broken down into small, easily monitored operations.[10] Operations that require the least skill are in general the most amenable to the workshop environment. Highly skilled tasks are more difficult to supervise and fewer advantages accrue from supervising the highly skilled worker. The skilled nature of needle making may be the reason why the Crendon needle trade was still being pursued in various cottages in 1796. The relative skill level of a task is not, however, the sole determinant of whether it will be organized in a workshop. A need to overcome pilfering or shoddy workmanship was also important, as was the desire to obtain higher quality output or more standardized output than could be achieved outside of a workshop. I will present many examples of workshops that were set up to meet these ends.

First it must be shown that there was a dramatic increase in the number of workshops during the late eighteenth century. The fact that workshops began to emerge in great number during the century is so well documented that a few references to the literature should suffice. Rowlands describes how workers came to be hired for full-time employment in workshops with their tools supplied for them during the second half of the eighteenth century, and in fact goes on to cite the provision by employers of buildings, equipment, and tools on an unprecedented scale as a reason for their attempts to seek out new markets and new methods of production (1975, 157–85). As already noted, the button trade moved directly to workshop production, but it was not the only new trade to do so. The japanning industry also started out as workshop production and was transformed into factory industry before dying in the nineteenth century (Gibbs 1953, 222). Even some of the industries that are commonly used as examples of continued domestic production also moved toward workshops. Hey cites cryptic references to a "nail manufactury" by the ironmonger Spencer (c. 1740) which seem to indicate the existence of a workshop employing a number of people (1972, 45). Pollard affirms that Spencer had gathered his nailworkers together to ensure quality production (1965, 33). Berg notes that Taylor of Birmingham had 600 employees in 1759, though some may have been outworkers, that Soho had 800 to 1,000 by 1770, but that the most common method of production in Birmingham was the medium-sized workshop of forty to one hundred workers. "[I]n general, the variety and extent of machinery and tools in use in the toy trades belie any simplistic notion of garret run or family production as the rule" (1981, 290, 301). Further, not only did workshops come into existence, but many of them significantly expanded their output over the century. Gibbs describes a tinplate works that went from producing fifty to sixty boxes per month in 1758 to 200 per month in 1764 to between 14,000 and 20,000 per year in 1799 (Gibbs 1951, 123–7). The question, then, is not, "Were there workshops?" but, "Why were there workshops?" After discussing the correct answers to this question, I will briefly consider some of the incorrect answers.

The key to the emergence of workshops was the possibility of supervision which these allowed. One factor enhancing the attractiveness of supervision was increasing division of labour. A highly skilled craftsman performing various functions needed little supervision.[11] When production was broken into its constituent parts, two problems would arise: it would be necessary to ensure a smooth flow of material from one worker to another, and it would be increasingly difficult to measure the productivity of individual workers by monitoring output alone. The solution to these problems lay in gathering workers together and supervising their actions.

Division of labour was only one reason for the increased attractiveness of workshops. Rowlands attributes the tendency to gather workmen to four factors: the variety and expense of raw materials, the use of dangerous chemicals, the need for supervised heating of certain materials, and the need to respond to fashion with planned production (1975, 155). The second and third apply only to a limited number of industries and require little further discussion, except to note that they both fit the idea of an increased need for supervision. The first of Rowlands' explanations deserves further examination. As trade links lengthened and the scale of commercial operation expanded, it became even more difficult to control pilfering or the substitution of substandard material for good. These problems had long plagued domestic production, and even if they had not been of growing importance (in part due to the variety and expense of raw materials which Rowlands mentions), they would have provided great incentive to move to a workshop environment as it became economically feasible to do so. As the number of required raw materials began to rise for many products, the problem of carrying a variety of often bulky supplies to dispersed cottage workers would in itself motivate putting-out entrepreneurs to collect their workers in a centralized place.

Rowlands' fourth point indicates an even greater incentive to embrace workshop production: the need to ensure a high-quality product and to respond to changes in fashion. As the methods of distribution shifted away from face-to-face contacts, it became more difficult to police the quality of merchandise procured. Court notes that in a few industries, manufacturers brought workers together at first to maintain the quality on which their sales depended (1946, 87).[12] Hey describes the problems of a nail merchant in 1741–42 whose customers complain that they are receiving nails without heads or points, and who has great difficulty in convincing any particular nailmaker that he might suffer as a result (1972, 47-8). Rowlands notes that the Foleys almost lost a naval contract over the same problem with nails and also describes a locksmith sending locks without the keys to open them (1975, 82). In a previous era, when the merchant would collect nails from each nailmaker and deliver them to buyers at fairs and markets, such behaviour would have been detected and dealt with more easily. Yet, even as the ability to guarantee quality in domestic production declined, the necessity of doing so rose. This need was especially acute in the newer trades which produced ornaments rather than necessities, and was another reason why such trades tended to be workshop oriented from the start. These were also the trades which had most to respond to changes in fashion and thus had a further incentive to organize production into workshops. These new industries must be viewed as special cases of a larger process in which division of labour, the move to workshops, and new technology had to occur together. The older trades were far from immune to these forces, however. They were especially affected by the need to standarize their product in order to take advantage of new distribution methods.

Mechanization in Workshops. In the metal trades as elsewhere, the earliest workshops emerge before the application of power or the introduction of new machinery.[13] As I will be discussing the mechanical devices that grew out of workshops below, no more needs to be said now. As for the matter of power, Court describes a Birmingham mansion surrounded by a moat which was purchased and transformed into a metal workshop (1938, 136). Clearly, the need for power could not have been the driving force behind the acquisition of the mansion, nor was it for most other workshops of the period. Most metal trades had little need for power until machines were developed, and this, it will be seen, occurred after the transition to workshops.

The metal trades were quite technologically innovative in the late eighteenth century. They do not produce any one innovation as famous as coke-smelting or puddling and rolling, but they do produce a number of innovations suited to the needs of the various trades.[14] As Berg remarked, the development of hand tools and small machinery is just as notable as later steam-powered machines (1981, 177), though historians have tended to concentrate on the latter.[15] Marx wrote of the metal workshops of the late eighteenth century: "this workshop, the production of the division of labour in manufacture produced in its turn machines" (in Berg 1981, 265). After a lengthy examination of the Birmingham metal trades, Berg concluded, "These industries really were the locus of Nathan Rosenberg's 'continuum of small improvements' or anonymous technical change" (1981, 265).

Many of these inventions have been long forgotten,[16] and those which are remembered are too numerous to list here. In the button trade, for example, White notes that nearly every year brought a new patent (1977, 76). Rees describes innovations not only in button making but also for making nails by machine (patented in 1790) making lead pipes by drawing them through rollers (a 1790 Wilkinson patent based on a 1728 French idea), and producing locks that were much more difficult to pick.[17] The list goes on and on; the heightened degree of technological innovation in the late eighteenth century metal trades is clear.[18] There were, moreover, some innovations of wide applicability. While a machine capable of punching eyes in needles with only passive human assistance was not yet a possibility, improvements in drilling equipment became widespread during the second half of the century (Jones 1978, 365). The most important of the new innovations were machines for stamping and pressing. Lady Shelburne was impressed by the use of such machinery while visiting a Birmingham japanware works in 1766. Only the existence of a wide market demanding a standardized output could make the advent of such machinery feasible.[19] Introduced originally in the larger workshops, stamping and pressing machines came to be used widely in both large and small workshops. While output figures are unavailable, one can imagine how greatly such machinery would affect the output, quality, and cost of production of a variety of metal wares, yet such machines gain little attention in the history of technology of the period. As Court notes, "The revolution produced before the age of steam by comparatively simple unexciting pieces of mechanism such as the stamp are not often recognized." (1938, 244).[20]

Intermediate Industries.   While numerous small innovations in the metal trades were probably ignored by contemporaries and historians alike, the emerging intermediate industries were too large to be missed. It may seem difficult to imagine that at the start of the eighteenth century the domestic nailmaker received his raw material in large bars and had to turn these bars into nail rods himself. As the nail trade became more localized, it became easier for ironmakers to service the needs of the nail trade. The obvious response was the slitting mill where the iron bars were reheated and cut into rods the diameter of nails. The advantages of performing this operation on a large scale rather than at the nailmaker's hearth are too obvious to require much discussion. The same is true for the wire works which developed somewhat later in the century to service needlemakers, cardmakers, and others. The technology involved in a slitting mill was nothing new and that involved in a wire works only slightly more complex.[21] They were relatively simple responses to new conditions in the metal trades. Along with the effect of greatly improving the overall productivity of the trades they supplied, they served to centralize the demand for iron from the nail, needle and other trades.

Another intermediate industry that developed during the century was the rolling mill. Rolling mills had been in existence for decades before Cort applied the technology to the process of ironmaking. The idea of a rolling mill can be traced at least to da Vinci, and rolling mills for lead, tin, and copper existed in the seventeenth century. The first rolling mill for iron seems to have been erected in the 1690s in Pontypool. Many minor adjustments were needed before the rolling mill could be successful. It was an important innovation, though, for not only did it eliminate the laborious and costly job of hammering iron plate by hand, but it was capable of producing smoother surfaces than could be achieved by hammering. One of the major beneficiaries of the use of the rolling mill was the tinplate trade. It is not clear exactly when during the early eighteenth century the rolling mill was applied to tinplate, but the pre-eminence of the English tinplate industry in the second half of the century is attributable to the superiority of rolled plate over hammered plate. The main advance in rolling technology during the early eighteenth century was a system of adjustable rollers so that plates of various thicknesses could be produced.[22] While an apparently simple improvement, the equipment of the day made adjustable precision difficult to achieve. The rolling mill, like the slitting mill, served to lower the cost of production of the trades it served and to centralize the demand of these trades for iron. Further, it improved the quality of the product and thus increased the effective demand for the output of the trades it served. Finally, the ability to produce plates of any desired width was to prove very important in the history of technology for Cort's puddling and rolling process required this capability.[23] I will return to this matter when I discuss Cort's invention later.

Though technically not a new industry, the improvements in steel production deserve to be discussed here as well. In the early 1700s, not only did English iron make steel of very poor quality, but metalworkers preferred steel from foreign lands to English steel made from foreign iron. As the production of metalware increased, there was naturally an increased effort to produce better quality steel in England. The English had been producing steel by the cementation process (borrowed from Germany) since the seventeenth century. During the early eighteenth century, steelmaking spread from Stourbridge to Birmingham, Sheffield, and Newcastle, to meet increased demand. Since foreign iron was necessary for good steelmaking (until into the nineteenth century), the Sheffield steel industry would have been severely hampered but for the completion of the Don navigation of 1726–33 (Flinn and Birch 1954, 173). Instead, it was in Sheffield that new methods of steelmaking would be developed.

It was Benjamin Huntsman, a watchmaker desiring better steel to make springs with, who devised a method of making better steel. It involved the reheating of blister steel (wrought iron with carbon added) in clay pots. By trial and error, over a period of three years, Huntsman achieved a result which possessed the exact carbon content desired (though, as with many inventors of the period, Huntsman had no idea why the steel he produced was so superior).[24] He produced only small amounts for five years (possibly a period of critical revision) before setting up on a commercial scale in 1751. The secret to the Huntsman process was clay pots strong enough to withstand considerable heat (Flinn and Birch 1954, 171), which Huntsman could obtain from Stourbridge or Holland.[25] One must be careful not to overemphasize Huntsman's role. "It seems that the increased access to both raw materials and home and overseas markets for finished steel afforded by transport developments must be considered as one of the most important factors in the rise of the Sheffield steel industry" (Flinn and Birch 1954, 175). Huntsman was not the only one to respond to this new environment by experimenting; he was just the first to succeed.[26] The Sheffield steel industry was to remain a fairly small scale operation through the century, but nevertheless the industry produced a large amount of high-quality steel (there were eleven steelmakers in Sheffield by 1787). This enabled many metalworkers to produce a much higher quality product and thus more readily sell their output. Since metalworkers required both iron and steel in their work, it also created an increased demand for iron.

THE IRON INDUSTRY

Iron Output and the Role of the Metal Trades

There are many different estimates of the output of the English iron industry during the eighteenth century. These estimates have tended to converge to the point where, for my purposes, any modern estimates would serve. The estimates made by Riden in 1977 draw upon the previous work of Hammersley and Hyde. These figures show a slight, though unsteady, increase in output during the first half of the eighteenth century (in contrast to the many assertions by previous authors that the industry was in a state of decline). Riden graphs his data and notes that there is an important turning point at mid-century. From 1570 to 1750, the increase in iron output was about four per cent per decade, but this rises to sixty per cent per decade from 1750 to 1860.

Historians have paid considerably more attention to the growth rate of iron industry output than to the question of what this increased output was used for, as if the answer were self-evident. In this section, I will first discuss various uses for which iron could have been produced, and show that none of these alternatives could have absorbed the increased output. Then, I will turn to the role of the metal trades in inducing the increase in output.

Riden deals with two possible explanations himself. Citing Schumpeter's "Overseas Trade Statistics," he notes that both before and after 1750, home demand was more important than exports, and that the impact of war on the industry was less than he expected (Riden 1977, 458). I would argue, with Hyde, that quite apart from the numbers, neither the foreign nor military markets were capable of inducing a sustained increase in iron output. Both markets were too volatile and uncertain. Cule (1938–40) describes how foreigners refused to pay for goods received from Boulton and there was little Boulton could do to make them pay. Any ironmaker daring to face the foreign market could find himself in such a situation. The spectacular call for arms during wars could certainly create a boom in profits for ironmakers, but the periods between wars could ruin an entrepreneur who built to meet war demand. The growth in output of the iron industry was inextricably tied to a growth in the scale of ironworks, and such growth could not be based on the untrustworthy foreign and military markets. Instead, a solid dependable base of home civilian industries recording (in aggregate) steady growth through the period was required.

Within the home market, the iron industry did begin to produce goods more like those we associate with today's iron industry – steam engines and machinery. Recent scholarship has shown that the number of steam engines produced during the eighteenth century was much greater than previously thought. Nevertheless, they still only number in the 1000 to 2000 range. Most of these were of Savary or Newcomen design, and required very little iron in their construction. Von Tunzelman has calculated that, even in the late 1790s when construction of Boulton and Watt engines was at its peak, their consumption of iron was under one quarter of one per cent of annual output of cast iron and one fifth of one per cent of wrought iron (1978, 103–4). Iron machinery came into wide use very late in the century, and thus could not have caused the dramatic increase in output from mid-century on. These new uses of iron, then, are simply not capable of absorbing enough iron output to induce substantial changes in the iron industry as a whole during the eighteenth century. As I will show later, they were more the result of changes in the iron industry than causes of change.

Two other possible sources of increased demand are of special interest here. One is a direct backward linkage effect of improving transport. Increasing road use meant a greater need for iron tires and horseshoes. Birch cites this as a significant source of demand (1967, 15), though it is not capable of causing a sixty per cent per decade increase in output. More important is the increasing urbanization of the period (the impact of transport on urbanization was discussed in the first chapter). This created a demand not only for building materials such as nails, but also increasingly for iron pipes to provide water for the growing towns.

Taken together, these other sources of demand cannot explain the course of development of the eighteenth-century iron industry. One must look to the metal trades, then, for their ability both to induce and absorb substantial increases in output. By now, it should come as no surprise that the metal trades were to play such a role. By increasing the division of labour, moving from domestic production to workshops, and mechanizing where possible, they were able to lower their costs while increasing their quality. In this way, they were able to greatly increase their output and, by extension, their demand for iron. It is important to be clear that the increased volume of sales in the metal trades came from shifts in the supply curve rather than the demand curve. Hey states that it was greater demand for all sorts of metalware that stimulated the need for inventions and larger iron and steel works (presumably in the interest of attaining higher iron output; 1972, 50). He gets half the story right, in recognizing that it is the metal trades to which the changes in the iron industry should be attributed. He makes the mistake, though, of treating these trades as a mere conduit through which derived demand is transmitted to the iron industry. Earlier, I discussed the fact that one cannot speak of a significant increase in economy-wide demand without conjuring up a previous increase in real income. Unless there was a dramatic shift in tastes toward iron (a dubious possibility given that increased demand is cited by historians of all industries of the time), the explanation for the increase in output of the metal trades must come from within the metal trades themselves, in their ability to lower the price and improve the quality of the traditional trades, and introduce a broad range of new goods to the market.

I have, of course, been looking only at the output side of the iron industry. Some would argue that it was not an increase in demand for iron but the elimination of supply constraints which led to the increase in output. Later in this chapter, when I discuss the coal industry, I will show that the common assertion that England was running out of wood in the early eighteenth century is grossly exaggerated. In fact, it appears that it was demand, not supply, that was highly inelastic at that time. Ashton describes how the arrival of a fairly small shipment of Russian iron caused a substantial drop in price (1951, 104). This would indicate that a shift in the demand curve was necessary for the iron industry to expand significantly. The demand for iron probably became more elastic through the century as the new, more ornamental, metal trades emerged, since (other things being equal) derived demand for an input will be more elastic if demand for the final good is more elastic. None of this says, however, that the supply side was not important. England could (and did) always import iron from other countries such as Sweden and Russia. Increased demand could merely have been transferred abroad had the iron industry not responded to various forces by increasing its productivity and quality.[27] The technological responses of the iron industry will be discussed later (though I shall note in passing that many prominent innovators, such as Darby and Walker, began their careers in the metal trades). Much of the increased productivity in the iron industry arose from operating at a larger scale, and I will turn to this question shortly. First, however, I shall look briefly at the demand for cast iron goods.

The cast iron industry played a central role in the story of coke-smelting, so it deserves some special attention. There are no good figures for the output of the cast iron sector. "Contemporaries generally thought of the iron industry in terms of the output of bar iron and tended to ignore the very small foundry trade" (Riden 1977, 445). We do know, however, that the Darbys greatly expanded their capacity, and faced increasing competition as the century wore on. Some of this increased output went for steam engine cylinders or pipes for the growing towns. Of greater importance was the fact that the industry expanded into production of a wide range of goods. No longer did it produce just firebacks, and a small number of cooking utensils. Court attributes this to the use of coke fuel which allowed the casting of thinner pieces (1938, 182). It will be seen that this type of production only emerged when individual foundries faced a wide enough market to make the mass production of pots, pans, and so on profitable.[28] As producers ceased to face small regional markets, the cast iron industry was able to produce a wider range of goods (see Hyde 1977, 129–30). In this way, ironfounders were able to take over markets in which they had previously been unable to compete – such as replacing copper pots and pans – and the cast iron industry greatly expanded.

The Scale of Operation of the Iron Industry

The changes in scale that occurred during the eighteenth century will be outlined during the discussion of technological changes. Here, I consider how changes in the metal trades (and in transportation) allowed and encouraged increases in scale. Suffice it to say that the charcoal furnaces of 1700 could justifiably be termed domestic production (Raistrick 1970, 1) while the large industrial units of 1800 are more like our modern iron industry. Using Riden's figures (1977), the average output of 1700 charcoal furnaces was about 300 tons per year while an 1800 coke furnace averaged about 1000 tons per year. I should first note that there was a change in the method of distributing iron to the metal trades, similar to that which occurred in the distribution of metalware to consumers. In the early eighteenth century, most iron bars were sold through a large body of ironmongers, many of whom dealt only with a handful of metal workers (Rowlands 1975, 69). The trade depended on face-to-face meetings between these ironmongers and their customers. In the later eighteenth century, direct sales from forge to metal worker became increasingly common.

This process of change was, of course, aided by the changes in the metal trades discussed above. The fact that workers came to be collected in workshops made it easier to deliver iron to the workplace. Increasing regional specialization among the metal trades also encouraged the construction of large ironworks.[29] As productivity rose thanks to division of labour and mechanization, larger orders could be placed on a regular basis. As intermediate industries interposed themselves between the iron producers and the metal trades, they were able to place large orders regularly with particular ironmasters, whereas the trades they served would otherwise have irregularly purchased small quantities from a variety of producers. Thus, the ironmasters were able to move from selling most of their output on an intermittent basis to a number of small merchants who visited their establishments, to selling larger amounts regularly and directly to the larger industrial units that were emerging in the metal trades. Clearly, improving the level of output of furnace and forge would become a far more attractive and attainable objective.

Naturally, demand conditions were not the only stimulus to increased scale of operation (or increased output) in the iron industry. Large-scale ironworks were dependent on regular supplies of raw materials.[30] Consideration must be given to the input side of the iron industry as well.

I will first look in detail at the effects of improved transport on the coal industry, which was to become the main source of fuel for the iron industry during the eighteenth century.

Coal and Transport.   Estimates differ for the output of the coal industry during the seventeenth, eighteenth, and nineteenth centuries. One of the earliest estimates was made by J.U. Nef (1932). Nef was trying to show that the Industrial Revolution was not an eighteenth-century occurrence but a phenomenon of the sixteenth and seventeenth centuries. Accordingly, he developed estimates showing a fifteeenfold to nineteenfold increase in coal output in the period from 1563 to 1684. Nef's estimates, in fact, show that rates of increase in coal output were higher in both the seventeenth and nineteenth centuries than in the eighteenth. Coleman (1977) has criticized the statistical bases used by Nef. Nef had used data from single years which may or may not have been typical of the eras they are supposed to represent; Kerridge (1977) in his comment on Coleman's book, asserts that the years Nef has data for were typical, and his estimates valid. Coleman, using averages of data for a number of years between 1590 and 1690, finds that only a threefold increase in output occurred during that period. Kerridge argues that even if Coleman is correct, Nef could still be correct overall if a sixfold increase in output occurred between 1563 and 1590. Of course, astonishing rates of increase can always be found if the base one starts from is small enough. The end result was that by 1700 only a relatively small coal industry existed in England. All of the major coalfields had been discovered, but it was really only in the northeastern coalfields which served London by coastal shipping that the industry was large and competitive. The rest of the English coal deposits, lacking the same access to good transport that the northeast possessed, served only small local areas and thus tended to operate on a small scale. This picture would change dramatically during the eighteenth century.

The best sources of data for the period come from collieries, such as those in Northumberland and Durham, which sold most of their output by sea. Fewer records survive of the output of inland coalfields. Yet the share of these inland coalfields in total English output was to rise considerably during the century. Using the northeastern coalfields as a proxy for overall English production will therefore result in underestimation of the rate of increase for the industry as a whole. Realizing this, Flinn develops separate estimates for the various regional coalfields. Then, the totals for the various coalfields can be added to form national output figures (1984, 26). Starting from just under three million tons in 1700, output rose by 1.13 per cent per year to 1750 (5.2 million), and by about 2.4 per cent per year through to 1800 (over 15 million).

The growth rate was even higher in the first fifteen years of the nineteenth century – 2.65 per cent, after which it dropped to 2.09 per cent from 1815 to 1830. Nevertheless, the fivefold increase in coal output over the eighteenth century must be seen as a dramatic change. As Flinn notes, no other industry provides us with such high rates of growth over this whole period (Flinn, 28).

Some of the increased output was due to expansion in the northeastern coalfields – from 1.29 million tons in 1700 to 4.45 million in 1800 – an increase of 3.5 times. At the same time, the share of the northeast in national coal output dropped from 43.2 per cent to 29.6 per cent. Clearly, even more dramatic changes occurred elsewhere. Output in the West Midlands expanded five times (510,000 to 2.55 million), in the East Midlands ten times (75,000 to 750,000), in Lancashire seventeen times (80,000 to 1.4 million), and in South Wales twenty-one times (80,000 to 1.7 million), though again, the base from which all but the West Midlands began was quite small.

To sum up this picture of the coal industry, the eighteenth century appears to have seen an impressive increase in output. While this was in part due to increased production in those coalfields which were already of considerable importance in 1700, it was more a story of rapid exploitation of internal coalfields.[31] Such a change must be bound up with the dramatic improvements in internal transport occurring during the eighteenth century. This was, indeed, the opinion of Flinn who noted "above all" the importance of transport in changing the relative shares of coalmining by region (Flinn, 28), and that "In [some] coalfields, including those in which production grew rapidly, like South Wales, the East and West Midlands, Lancashire and Yorkshire, the creation of water transport facilities was crucial" (Flinn, 447). Before discussing the central role of transport improvements in the growth of the inland coal trade, I must do away with a couple of fallacious arguments often used to explain the increase in coal output.

The first argument is that England was running out of trees, and thus was forced to use increasing amounts of coal fuel for various purposes. In fact, many historians have gone so far as to treat the wood shortage itself as a major cause of the Industrial Revolution. The perversity of attributing economic growth to shortages of a particular raw material must seem attractive to a number of scholars, for the alleged tree shortage in eighteenth-century England is one of the greatest exaggerations in historiography (see Evans 1982, for the opposing argument). As much of the discussion about the limited supply of wood has centred on the role of the iron industry, it will suit my purpose to concentrate on the iron industry's use of wood. First, it should be noted that the best charcoal comes from trees that are between fifteen and twenty years old, while builders of both ships and houses required wood from much older trees. In some places, ironmasters and shipbuilders had a symbiotic relationship where the ironmasters cut down a number of young trees, allowing the others to grow taller and larger. In most cases, though, ironmasters regularly harvested and replanted woods surrounding their ironworks in a fifteen- to twenty-year rotation (see Flinn 1984, 452). In the long run, then, an ironworks would cause no decrease in the amount of woodland unless it failed to ensure that any wood it cut down was replaced (and it was in the long-term interest of the ironmaster to look after nearby woodlands, for charcoal would break up and become useless if transported far). Therefore, a static iron industry should have no effect on the amount of forested land. This is an important point – it is not the cutting of wood but the failure to replant that decreases the supply of wood over time. Only as woodland is encroached on for agricultural uses, or as towns spread into surrounding forests, will the number of trees decrease. Neither of these processes occurred in the eighteenth century at a rate fast enough to imperil England's overall reserves of forest.[32]

Even a growing iron industry will not affect the amount of forest if there are unused tracts available to set up ironworks in, and there is considerable evidence that unused woodland could be found in many areas. In 1750, the tanners of Sheffield, Doncaster, Gloucester, and Southwark petitioned Parliament to restrict imports of foreign iron because this would diminish the local use of timber and thus the supply of bark which they used in their work (Lloyd 1913, 75). This suggests that the local iron industry was not constrained by the amount of available wood.[33] Nevertheless, one might expect that as demand for wood increased from a variety of sources including the iron industry itself, the price of wood would tend to rise. This seems to have generated much of the confusion about the wood situation. People have observed an upwardly sloping supply curve, and supposed instead that this curve was vertical and, worse yet, that it was shifting to the left over time. There is no denying that wood was scarce in the economic sense, but this does not mean that England was running out.[34] Further, if a shortage of wood were to spur an increase in coal output, it would do so through an increase in the price of coal. Yet, as will be seen, the price of inland coal tended to drop during the century in many areas. Those who switched from wood to coal were simply reacting to a change in relative prices. Shifts in relative prices occur all the time in history. They need not, and should not, elicit the tales of doom that have been applied to the English wood supply.

So much for the wood shortage. Another oft-cited explanation for increased coal output is improved technology. Before the work of Flinn, it was generally accepted that there had been relatively little technological change in eighteenth-century coal mining, as Flinn himself recognized (1984, 3). This accorded well with the idea that technological change occurred only in iron and cotton. However, one would expect that as early eighteenth-century transport improvements dramatically changed market access for inland coalfields, which greatly expanded in number and scale, there would be a technological response.[35] Moreover, mineowners, facing similar pressures to increase output while maintaining or reducing costs, could increasingly interact and discuss improvements.

Flinn describes a number of technological innovations. Explosives were introduced early in the eighteenth century, though the safety fuse awaited the nineteenth. Improved methods of lining shafts and supporting roofs emerged. Longwall mining, capable of extracting a greater proportion of the available coal, replaced the old bord and pillar method in coalfield after coalfield.[36] Underground transport was improved with the successive adoption of wheels, wooden rails, and iron rails, and sometimes canals. As mines went deeper, better methods of pumping and winding were developed – most notably using the steam engine. Some success was achieved in ventilation, though mechanical ventilation was a nineteenth-century innovation. Though the eighteenth century perhaps sees no one outstanding innovation, it clearly sees a number of improvements in technology (see Flinn, 70–140). Flinn concludes that technological change allowed mining output to increase without a rise in costs (Flinn, 447–8).[37] As output increased, mines were forced to go deeper and thus suffered greater problems of pumping, winding, and ventilation. On the other hand, there do appear to have been some economies of scale in coal mining,[38] and the point has been made that changes in scale cannot be discussed without reference to market demand. Once again, one must look to the role of transport improvements for an understanding of the causes of the great increase in scale and output of the coal industry. As Flinn himself recognized, "the most restrictive bottleneck in the business of British mining in early eighteenth century Britain was not merely getting coal to the pithead, but transporting it from the pithead to the ultimate consumer" (1984, 445).

"Coal is, of all commodities in general use, the one least valuable in proportion to its bulk. Costs of transport are inevitably a primary problem in its marketing" (Nef 1932, 78).[39] In fact, the cost of transporting coal even a small distance could be greater than the cost of mining it. The costs for working coal in various collieries on a Glamorgan estate, and transporting coal from those collieries to the dock in 1733 (a wey was about five tons at the time) are shown in table 3. Even the cost of

Table 3
The Cost of Working vs Carrying Coal on a Glamorgan
Estate

Cost of Working (wey)	Cost of Carriage (wey)
10s	3s
6s	5s, 6d
5s	8s
8s, 10d	3s
7s, 11d	4s, 2d
8s, 4d	3s, 4d

Source: John 1943, 93.

transporting coal across an estate could outweigh the cost of mining the coal in the first place, and these figures do not include the cost of further transporting the coal to the final consumer. It was generally assumed during the eighteenth century that the price of coal doubled if carried ten miles by land, though it could be carried twenty times as far by water at the same cost (Flinn 1984, 146). It should not be surprising, then, that many of the transport improvements of the time were designed with the object of obtaining cheap coal. Pratt (1912) estimated that over half the canal acts passed in the second half of the century were aimed mainly at coal carriage. Coal, because of its extremely low value/bulk ratio, was more strongly affected by lowered transport costs than other goods.

There is no use in trying to describe an overall national trend in coal prices because movements in coal prices were so dependent on a particular transport improvement joining a particular market to a particular coalfield. I shall look instead at a few examples. When, in 1767, a canal was completed connecting the Wednesbury coalfields and Birmingham, the price of coal nearly halved from 13s per ton to 7s per ton (Hutton 1791, 266). The Bridgwater canal caused coal prices in Manchester to drop by half.[40] The city of Northampton devoted considerable attention to attempts to obtain cheaper coal by improving transport in the region. In 1750, they were paying 30d per hundred weight (cwt) for coal that cost only 4d per cwt at the pithead in Warwickshire. By making the Nene navigable in 1761, they were able to obtain Newcastle coal for 14d per bushel (approximately 21d per cwt). This was still much higher than the cost of coal for those near inland collieries. When the Grand Junction Canal was completed to within four miles of town, Northampton residents were able to obtain coal at the canal bank for 10.5 to 12.5d per cwt (Hatley, 1980–81, 210–17). Improvement of water transport were not the only way to lower the cost of coal. It is important to realize that coal could be, and was, carried distances of thirty miles or so by land if water transport was unavailable. For example, Griffin (1978) notes that a number of Leicester collieries did quite well from 1790–1830 even though their only outlet to market was the turnpike road. Flinn gives examples of roads being used to carry coal as far as eighteen miles, in the absence of water transport (1984, 147–8). Coal was carried westward into the Peak District by packhorse before turnpikes but by wagon after the construction of turnpikes (Hey 1980, 124–5). It is not surprising, then, that the authors of *A Case Relating To An Intended Road From Nottinghamshire*, could claim in 1764 that improving the road could cause the price of coal to drop by half. The hundreds of river improvements and canals and thousands of turnpike roads of the eighteenth century resulted in a tremendous and widespread drop in the price of coal within those regions which possessed workable coalfields (the regions referred to in this chapter – the West Midlands, South Lancashire, and South Yorkshire – all had coal).

The areas that did not benefit were not only those, such as the West Country, far removed from inland coalfields[41] but all those areas which had previously been served by coastal shipping, as well. There were no duties on inland coal, whereas the coastal coal trade had long been a substantial source of government revenues. In fact, even after London was connected by canal to much cheaper inland coal, restrictions and tolls were imposed to keep the Durham-Northumberland monopoly of the London coal trade intact. It was not until well into the nineteenth century that London was able to obtain coal as cheaply as other centres. Perhaps it is for this reason that chroniclers of the coal industry have so largely ignored the dramatic decreases in price paid by coal users in the industrial heartland of England.

The drop in the price of coal did not result solely from reductions in transport cost.[42] Turnbull (1988) has noted that canals allowed increased exploitation of the best seams, and thus led to a reduction in the costs of mining coal as well. A further indirect effect was the breakdown of monopoly power through the destruction of collusive arrangements (collusive agreements were probably much more common in the eighteenth century than they are today). The effects of collusion are difficult to quantify. Hausman has recently shown that the net effect in the Newcastle-London trade was much lower (six to eight per cent) than had previously been thought (though collusion can all too easily occur without public knowledge, and the misclassification of some years as non-collusive could severely bias the result). Even this number is not insignificant. In any case, collusion was much easier to sustain in the smaller inland coalfields where only a handful of small producers would operate. Thus, Duckham (1970) speaks of a Glasgow cartel in 1776 causing the price of coal to rise from 2s6d to 3s. Further, there were many areas served only by one colliery, and one would expect such monopolies to charge more and produce less than they would in a competitive market. As transport costs fell, consumers would be able to obtain coal from a larger number of suppliers, making it more difficult for producers to collude or exercise monopoly power. In Warwickshire, Court describes how a group of colliery owners who colluded in dealing with local markets opposed canal plans which would have introduced Staffordshire coal into their area.[43] While it is difficult to estimate exactly how important the effects of collusion were in any given area, much less throughout England, it should be clear that any decrease in transport costs could lead to an even greater decrease in the delivered cost of coal.

Other Raw Materials Used in Ironmaking. Along with fuel of some type, the other major raw material of the iron industry was, naturally, ironstone. It might be thought that the iron industry would locate itself near sources of this bulky material, so that transport problems would not be severe. However, there were other factors influencing the location of the iron industry: the need to be near supplies of fuel, the need for water power until steam engines came to be used as a source of power in the later part of the century, and a desire to be near markets. These factors ensured that furnaces were often located some distance from the source of ironstone. Still, Johnson, in a study of the location of ironworks, found only one furnace more than eight or nine miles from an ore supply in 1717 (1951, 169). As the century wore on and progressively less desirable sources of power and fuel were used, the situation may have worsened. Even if a furnace were located near a source of ironstone, it might require more supplies than could readily be obtained there. The Carron ironworks in the northeast needed to import ironstone from Cumberland. More importantly, the manufacture of good quality iron, given the technology of the time, required the mixture of different ores. Forges which relied on only one ore source would almost certainly produce poor quality iron.[44] All of the Sheffield metalworkers except the nailworkers complained of low quality iron which was produced from the local ores and pressed for imports of higher quality ore (Hey 1972, 15). The mixture of different ores occurred sometimes at the furnace, but often at the forge. Many forges received pig iron from a wide range of furnaces. Trinder (1973, 16) states that "One of the characteristics of the charcoal iron trade was the transport of semi-finished iron over very long distances." He gives examples of a Shropshire forge using pig iron from the Forest of Dean, and of a forge in Monmouthshire getting some of its pig iron from furnaces in East

Shropshire. He later describes movements of pig iron to forges in North Wales as well (Trinder, 81). Hyde noted that there was substantial interregional trade in pig iron due to differences in phosphorus content (1977, 17), while Johnson notes that a number of forges blended high and low quality ores for intermediate uses (1951, 176). It is clear, then, that iron ore, in unfinished and semi-finished states, had to be transported considerable distances.

Iron and fuel were not the only raw materials required in large amounts by the iron industry. The furnaces were substantial structures built almost entirely of brick. Far from being a one-shot capital expense, the heat of the smelting process required that the inside bricks be replaced yearly. In complaining about a proposed tax on bricks in 1784, John Wilkinson, William Reynolds, and the Earl of Dudley claimed that they used a million bricks a year, though a significant proportion of these may have been needed for associated mining concerns (Trinder 1973, 98). Clay pots were essential to the forging process. As the heat levels employed in these processes increased, special clays that could take the higher temperatures were required. Stourbridge clay came to be used throughout England, as it was capable of withstanding higher temperatures than any other clay. Limestone was essential to smelting for it was used as a flux to draw the impurities from the ore. This ingredient was so important that canals were constructed in Shropshire to connect ironworks with sources of limestone (Trinder 1973, 96–8).[45] Clearly, the iron industry could benefit from improved transport of a number of materials.[46]

Before moving on, I should emphasize that the iron industry benefitted not just from lower costs of transporting these various materials but from increased reliability of transport services as well. It has already been noted how important it is that supplies arrive on time if one is running a large-scale enterprise, and this applies to the iron industry no less than any other. "In the early eighteenth century, a barge load of pig iron would probably last a charcoal forge for a month or more, and a year's supply could be delivered in a few weeks of favourable water. By the late 1790s, a number of Black Country forges and foundries depended on regular week-by-week supplies of very large quantities of Shropshire iron" (Trinder 1973, 115).[47] When a freak drought stopped ships on the Severn near the end of the century, Boulton and Watt were able to obtain their iron supplies by land. The ability of furnaces and forges to get their supplies when they needed them rather than have to hold substantial inventories was of great importance to the iron industry, and an important factor in inducing the industry to increase its scale of operation.

Changing Technology in The Iron Industry

I can now turn to the process of innovation in the iron industry during the eighteenth century. Of necessity I shall concentrate only on the most important innovations. However, one should not lose sight of the growing number of experiments that were made as the century wore on.[48] It is also important to recognize that even after an "innovation" had been devised, numerous minor innovations were required before the original innovation could become workable. "There was usually a time lag, often substantial, between the initial innovation and the beginning of widespread adoption. This lag or gestation period existed because most of the new techniques were really clusters of interdependent innovations that developed over time" (Hyde 1977, 193). With this proviso in mind, I shall turn now to the role of Abraham Darby I. While the innovation of coke-smelting occurs too early to be attributed to the transport changes I have described, it is useful to show that the innovation was less revolutionary than is often claimed, and then to consider the role of transport improvements in its diffusion.

Abraham Darby and Coke-Smelting.   Abraham Darby I is a well-known figure in the history of iron industry technology. He was the first person to succeed (at least commercially) in casting iron goods using sand rather than loam for the mould. The use of sand was borrowed from the brass trade, though it had previously been known in the iron trade. However, Darby was the first to cast bigbellied pots successfully (Raistrick 1970, 101–2). While this may seem a minor improvement, the change allowed Darby to gain a wide market for his ironware and thus become the first ironmaster who could devote the entire output of a furnace to the foundry trade. For reasons yet to be discussed, is enabled him to use coke as a fuel in his furnace, an option that was not available to those involved in wrought iron production at the time.

Since the iron industry's switch from charcoal to coke in the later eighteenth century has received so much attention, it is not surprising that Darby's much earlier use of coke (starting from about 1709) has been hailed as revolutionary. It is important to put this in perspective. First, it is not all that difficult to make iron with coke as a fuel. It had been done before. The trick was to make good-quality iron using coke. Coke-smelted pig iron would have a high silicon content, which means that it would need further refining (desiliconizing) before fining (decarburizing) could be successful: because of the order of oxidation of metalloids, the silicon must be removed before the carbon can be removed. In early eighteenth-century forges, fining and pounding into bar form were the two functions performed, and so even if charcoal fuel were used in the forge, coke-smelted pig would yield a final product with a high carbon content. This would make it very brittle and exceedingly difficult to work with. On the other hand, brittleness is not a handicap for the founder who obtains his output by pouring molten iron into a mould. Further, coke was capable of yielding higher temperatures and thus a more fluid molten iron more suitable for casting (especially the casting of thin pieces). Clearly, Darby was in a very different position than other ironmakers of that era, and it is not that surprising that he should be the first to use coke as a fuel for smelting (see Hyde, 1977).

It is far from clear, in fact, that Darby did anything new. Coal was used as a fuel in the saltmaking, tar-distilling, glassmaking, and brick and pipe industries of Shropshire at the time, and had been used in smelting lead, copper, and tin since the 1690s at least. More importantly, coke had long been used in malting, a trade with which Darby had had a long association (Trinder 1973, 22). The original furnace used by Darby was a decades-old charcoal furnace to which he does not seem to have made major adjustments. Some contend that Darby, through use of improved bellows, was able to achieve a hotter blast than others, but there is no evidence to support this claim (Mott 1936, 20). Indeed, there is no solid evidence for any conjecture that Darby had done something new. Once one recognizes that Darby was producing iron for a different reason than any of his forerunners or contemporaries, it can be seen that he was able to adapt existing technology to produce goods which had never been produced on that scale before. In this he was aided by at least one fortuitous circumstance. Shropshire coal has a much lower sulphur content than most other English coal; hence Darby's output would have fewer impurities than if he had started up elsewhere in England.

It would appear, then, that the historical significance of Darby's use of coke has been highly overrated. Still, one should be careful not to err in the opposite direction and understate its importance. All inventions are, after all, merely the bringing together of disparate pieces of information to produce something that has never existed before. As I will soon show, this small step set off a chain reaction that led to a shift throughout the iron industry toward the use of coke as a fuel over the next century. While Darby's innovation does not in itself tie in strongly with my arguments about the role of transportation (though one should note that his furnace was situated on the banks of the Severn which was, at the time, the busiest river in England), the link between the later adoption of coke-smelting and transport improvements will become clear.

Historians have been puzzled by the fact that coke-smelting was not quickly adopted by other ironmasters, and many have hypothesized that the Darbys managed to keep it a secret for the next half century.[49] The answer, however, lies in the fact that only ironfounders would be interested in Darby's method. Darby had a partial interest in two furnaces (Vale Royal and Dolgelly) as well as friends who owned a furnace in Furness, and we know that Darby's technology was available to these three furnaces from an early date (Raistrick 1970, 40). However, the first two declined to use it because of extensive local supplies of wood, and the third because its output went to nailmakers who would refuse coke-smelted wrought iron. As long as wood was comparatively cheap, there was no incentive for those in the wrought iron trade to attempt the switch to coal.

The early expansion of the use of coke comes through its increasing use in the foundry trade. It was noted earlier that the ability to expand their geographical market size enabled founders to produce a wider range of goods, and that the total number of ironfounders increased as a result. While this trend gained momentum after mid-century, it could also be observed earlier. Trinder lists six furnaces that used coke as a fuel in the forty years after Darby started to use it (1973, 24). As the cast iron trade expanded in this manner, the use of coke-smelting naturally spread. This spread might have occurred with no noticeable effect but for the important fact that founders from time to time would sell small quantities of coke-pig to other forges. Hammersley argues that coke-smelting furnaces were bound to produce more iron than could easily be cast (1975, 85), but this seems to be an exaggeration. More likely, the furnaces, if run as efficiently as possible, would yield a steady output of pig iron through most or all of the year, while the attached foundry would cut or expand production as the demand for various products shifted. Thus, on an irregular basis, ironmasters could find themselves with excess supplies of pig iron, which they would sell to forgemasters when they could. Whatever the reason, there was a trade in coke-pig between founders and forgemasters throughout the century. The Darbys seem not to have had any excess pig iron as long as they only operated one furnace, but once they expanded to two they sold a good deal of coke-pig to various forges. Some of this pig was dispatched to the Leighton furnace to be sent with Leighton pig to the forges it supplied (Trinder 1973, 29). The Darbys also had their own forge which, though supplied with charcoal pig from various other furnaces, also received some of their own coke-pig.

This might seem surprising given that coke-pig was unsuitable for the making of wrought iron. However, as shown earlier, there was a substantial trade in pig iron, with forges blending pigs of varying qualities to produce the desired output. This is where coke-pig fits in. While unsuitable for wrought iron on its own, it could be mixed with charcoal iron to make a wrought iron of intermediate malleability. Of course, the price would have to be right in order to interest forgemasters in such pig iron. I discussed earlier how and why the relative cost of coal, as opposed to charcoal, dropped through the century. This would naturally increase the attractiveness of coke-pig. As the commodity became cheaper, more forgemasters would be willing to purchase it; hence more people would be interested in producing it. One of the earliest technological reactions to the increased use of coke was to improve methods of coke making. The beehive oven was in use from the 1750s and Wilkinson developed improvements in the heaping process in 1768. These improvements made coke even less expensive, and even more attractive as a fuel.[50]

Still, there was a limit to the amount of coke-pig that could be absorbed in the wrought iron trade until new technology was introduced improving the quality of coke-pig. Complaints about wrought iron made from coke-pig continued until late in the century. The 1774 *Report to the Mining Board* stated that coal-smelted iron was poor for wrought iron making unless mixed in small quantities with better iron. By mid-century, however, relative price changes had made coke-pig a very attractive input, spurring efforts to improve the quality of coke-pig. Since these efforts naturally coincided with attempts to introduce coke to the fining stage, I will discuss the two together.

Cort and the Introduction of Coke Fuel Throughout the Ironmaking Process.
Ashton noted long ago that Cort's invention was more important than Darby's for two reasons. First, more fuel was used in the fining process than in smelting. Second, until coke was introduced to fining, it had only been smelted for use in ironfounding. With his second point, he hits on something important which scholars both before and after him have tended to miss. The cluster of innovations that is associated with the name Cort (though many others were involved) not only introduced coke to the fining process but allowed it to be used throughout the smelting industry. The solution to the problem of coke-pig was to be found not in the furnace but in the forge.

There are those who wrongly assume that the increased use of coke-pig in forges in the 1750s indicates an improvement in quality. Raistrick, for example, points to the annual sale after 1754 of hundreds of tons of Coalbrookdale coke-pig to various forges, and attributes it to improvements made in the smelting process by the Darbys (if the Darbys did achieve some improvement, it is not known how it was accomplished. Some fortuitous combination of ore and fuel may have allowed them to improve quality to some extent). One can see, though, that hundreds of tons per year, however impressive, could still be a small proportion of the inputs of a large number of forges, in which case the phenomenon could easily be explained by the shift in relative prices. The 1774 *Mining Board* report cited earlier indicates that no dramatic improvement in the quality of coke-pig had occurred to that point.

The best description of the process leading up to Cort's patent is found in Morton and Mutton (1967), and I borrow heavily from them in what follows. They recognize that the switch to coke in forges came about for economic reasons, and that "The difficult technical problems were gradually resolved by a process of trial and error" (722). Attempts were first made to transform ore directly to bar. It was soon recognized that a number of distinct processes were necessary.

By 1761, as a result of many efforts, the use of reverberatory furnaces was firmly established. Different fluxes were being used. While the problem of silicon content had not been solved, it was being tackled properly. In 1766, the Cranages at Coalbrookdale were able to make good wrought iron from scrap metal by puddling. Since scrap metal would have a low silicon content, they did not tackle the major obstacle to coke-fining, but their experiment does indicate that some form of puddling was in use decades before the Cort patent. In 1773, Jesson and Wright separated the refining process from the others, and developed the stamping and potting process, which involved the heating of broken pieces of pig iron in clay pots. Onions improved on these ideas ten years later. It is not clear how close to the puddling process Onions came. In 1784, Cort consolidated the ideas of those who had gone before him, and added rollers.[51] The rollers used by Cort were based on rollers patented in 1766 for making bolts, rod, and wire, and this patent in turn must have owed much to the rolling technology developed earlier in the century for making iron plate. It would not be wrong to say that Cort simply combined a number of innovations developed by others; Cort himself readily acknowledged that his methods were not fundamentally new (Rowland 1974, 21).

As one would expect, the puddling and rolling process went through a period of critical revision. It needed many minor improvements before it was commercially viable (Hyde 1977, ch. 5). One of the earliest proponents of the process was Crawshay and it took him four years at Cyfarthfa before he was commercially successful.[52] This limited the spread of the innovation in the early years. Also, because of the fees charged by Cort, many relied on the stamping and potting method which, while less efficient, was also a viable method of producing wrought iron. As both these methods involved a separate refining stage, they served to remove the technological barrier to coke-smelting, and thus allowed increased use of coke in smelting as well.

The process of innovation, thus, was clearly not the work of one man but the result of efforts by many men over many decades. Such a sustained effort did not occur accidentally. The effect of relative price shifts is only part of the story. The process could only occur if information flowed freely from one inventor to another. Wood and Guest in South Wales knew the results of the Cranages' experiments at Coalbrookdale within ten days (Morton and Mutton 1967, 724). Also, South Wales could not have played a major role in the spread of Cort's innovation had good transport not given the area access to a national market, for there was little local demand. Further, one of the major advantages of puddling and rolling was that it was capable of producing a homogeneous output; the emergence of new methods of distribution would create a great incentive to produce such an output. Finally, one must note the important effect of increased demand for iron due to the expansion of the metal trades. This also fostered inventive activity. Since the expansion of the iron industry was one of the causes of higher wood prices, it must have become increasingly obvious, as demand for iron rose, that a switch to coke would be highly advantageous. More importantly, innovations would spread much more easily in a growing industry than in a stagnant one, since new ironworks could be built to embody the latest technology, while using new technology would involve costly renovations in existing ironworks.[53] Beyond that, growing industries are much more likely to attract the attention of inventors in the first place, since the expected return on invention will be higher. Thus, the increased demand for iron from the metal trades during the later eighteenth century can be seen both as having caused increased interest in the creation of this new technology, and having hastened the spread of the innovation through the country.

Other Innovations in the Iron Industry and the Scale of Operation.   While I have devoted considerable space to the introduction of coke as a fuel to the iron industry, one must be careful not to give it too much importance. Hyde notes that there is a vast difference between the charcoal and coal eras in the scale of operation, the required level of investment, and the form of power used (1977, 118). He is certainly correct, but correlation must not be mistaken for causation. Darby's success indicates that coke did not require furnaces larger than those commonly used in the English charcoal iron industry, though the use of coke may have encouraged the use of larger furnaces.[54] Nor were the innovations which came to characterize the later eighteenth century impossible to achieve with charcoal. Large charcoal furnaces were constructed through the nineteenth century in North America, and in the twentieth century in

Australia. There is no obvious, direct relationship between the use of coke and the scale of operation or the introduction of other innovations. It may be that coke fuel made some of these innovations easier, but with only one historical observation one cannot be sure.

The use of coke does seem to have encouraged certain innovations. The bellows used in furnaces were much improved during the eighteenth century. Bellows are necessary to maintain a certain atmospheric pressure within the furnace. With charcoal fuel, the required atmospheric pressure was only ½ lbf per sq.in. while with coke fuel atmospheric pressure should be at least 1¼ to 1¾ lbf per sq.in. It can readily be seen that the switch to coke fuel would provide an incentive for the development of improved blowing systems. It is not surprising, then, that the first known improvement is the introduction of wooden bellows at Coalbrookdale in 1742–44 to replace the old leather ones used by the Darbys. After mid-century, the effort to develop improved bellows intensified. In 1757, John Wilkinson came up with a new iron blowing machine (based on a patent taken out by his father) which was to be the basis for blowing machines throughout the century.[55] In apparent response to the requirements of the new fuel, new bellows were developed which not only met this need but facilitated the operation of much larger furnaces.

The other notable change in iron technology was the introduction of steam power. The development of the Watt steam engine, as I argue below, was dependent on previous improvements in the iron industry. In the last decades of the century, the steam engine in turn became an important part of many ironworks. The Newcomen steam engine had been used since the 1740s for pumping water into reservoirs above the water wheel that operated the bellows. With the development of new bellows and better steam engines, it became possible to create a much stronger blast by applying steam power directly to the blowing engine. Steam engines also allowed the mechanization of many parts of the forging process. By removing the necessity of locating near water power, they enabled ironworks to locate in new areas and concentrate all stages of the operation on one site.[56] The application of steam power to the iron industry allowed the industry to produce goods much more cheaply than before, and more cheaply than other countries could.

Thus, the increasing scale of operation in the iron industry was due only in small part to the switch from charcoal to coke. Of greater importance were improved blowing machines operated by steam engines. As these came into use, furnace owners were able to increase the size of their furnace. As already noted, improvements in bellows were related to the increased use of coke as a fuel. In a later section, I will show how the development of steam engines fits into the story. It is important to recognize that while these innovations facilitated the increase in scale, they in no way made it necessary. It would be incorrect to view large-scale ironworks as responses to the demands of new technology. To reiterate an earlier point, many changes in the metal trades and in transportation both encouraged and allowed increases in scale. It should also be noted that an innovation of this type is much more likely to spread in an industry that is facing a steadily increasing demand. Hyde notes that the expanding demand for iron accelerated the diffusion of all innovations, and hypothesizes that such a process may be a necessary element in any radical departure from previous practice (1977, 199). As new furnaces and forges are built to meet increased demand, they will naturally imitate the most productive technology available. The more ironworks there are operating with new technology, the likelier it is that further improvements will be made. If demand for iron had been stagnant, the adoption of new techniques would have been greatly slowed.

Effects of Increased and Improved Iron Output

The nexus between the users of iron and the iron industry runs, of course, two ways. The metal trades induced a number of changes within the iron industry, which responded by improving quality and lowering price. This induced further changes in the metal trades, and also allowed new uses to develop for iron. The iron industry had an importance far beyond the level of its output because it provided the raw material for the tools and machines that all workmen needed. As the quality of iron improved, it became possible to construct much better tools.[57] Lower prices further encouraged experimentation with tools. Rolt describes how dramatic the impact of new tool design can be:[58]

In machine tool history, one reason why an evolutionary process which now seems obvious to us was not obvious to the pioneer tool-makers is the remarkable propagating power of tools. One man constructs a new or improved tool in order to solve a particular problem, but others speedily discover that this same tool makes practicable inventions such as its inventor never dreamed of. (1968, 12)

The most important of the new tools were those that could be called machines. The Industrial Revolution is, after all, in large part a story of machines replacing human labour. As iron became better and cheaper, much that had previously been constructed of wood could be made of iron. Moreover, machines that were impossible to construct of any other material now became feasible. The introduction of iron machinery in the later eighteenth century played a major role in the development of other industries.[59] I have already noted that machines of this type were introduced into the metal trades. By 1799, visitors would remark that the entire Caerleon tinplate millworks was made of iron (Gibbs 1951, 123).[60] Developments in the iron industry were not the only cause of this shift to machinery. Improvements in transport were important, as well. First, before a machine-producing industry could be developed it had to be possible to move heavy objects to various centres of industry. Second, purchasing such machinery would only be profitable if the machinery could be used continually:

A machine tool is an expensive item of equipment. It represents an investment of capital which can only be justified if its capacity for greater productivity can be fully exploited. This condition cannot be met unless the flow of raw materials to the machine and of finished product away from it can be cheaply and reliably maintained by an efficient transport system. (Rolt 1968, 40)

Speaking of transportation, it was from the iron industry that the next great innovations in transport were to come. John Wilkinson, the ironmaster, began experimenting with iron boats in the middle of the century. Railways had their beginnings at the same time. While the modern railway is a creation of the nineteenth century, iron rails were used at mines and a variety of other settings during the later eighteenth century, both above and below ground. They were introduced by Reynolds at Coalbrookdale in 1767 because the price of iron was low and he wanted some useful place to store his inventory. As the price of iron dropped through the century, the idea caught on throughout the country. Naturally, improvements were made in rail design as its use increased. Thus, the way was paved for the introduction of the railroad in the early nineteenth century.

STEAM ENGINES

Before discussing the development of steam engines and the role of transport therein, it is important to address another myth pervading eighteenth-century history: the myth that England was running out of water power. Pelham (1963) argues that the rotative steam engine was developed because of a severe shortage of water power in the Birmingham area. Yet he notes that Birmingham manufacturers made little use of the rotative engine once it was introduced. He also notes that the best sites for water power in the area were occupied by corn mills. It would seem that if demand for water power was great, one or two of these sites might have been obtained for the right price. Or other, less desirable, sites might have been landscaped to provide water power. As with the alleged wood shortage discussed earlier, an upward-sloping supply curve has been confused with a vertical curve. Certainly the most desirable sources of water power would be used first. As demand for water power increased, people would either have to buy out existing mills or move to less attractive sites. Many sites could be landscaped to provide water power, though this would be less desirable than having a natural waterfall to place a wheel under (see Trinder 1973, for a discussion of the landscaping required to provide power to the Darbys' Horsehay works). Roepke (1956) notes that England possessed innumerable small streams which could be used for water power, so that constraints on industrial use of water power could not have been that severe. The cotton industry relied primarily on water power until well after 1815, as "Quite a small river, stream, or reservoir was sufficient to work a number of water wheels ... In Keighley in 1815 there were 30 mills upon one little brook" (Edwards 1967, 208).

The foregoing does not mean that steam engines had no advantages over water power. As the cost of water power increased, steam would become increasingly attractive. Moreover, water power was erratic. In 1733, the output of the Darby furnaces was greatly reduced by low water levels. Still, one could use a Savary or Newcomen engine to pump water back above the water wheel, as the Darbys did in the 1740s; hence it was unnecessary to run equipment directly with a rotative steam engine. The big advantage of steam was that it allowed freedom in the choice of location. Thus, while England was not in dire need of another source of power, the steam engine did play a major role in the development of English industry, at least in the nineteenth century.

The Newcomen Engine

The Newcomen engine was the first real steam engine, as the so-called Savary engine was really only a pump. Still, the Newcomen engine should not be viewed as a break with the technological past, for Newcomen owed a great deal to previous attempts at achieving steam power (though it is not clear whether Newcomen knew of Savary's machine).[61] Both Savary and Newcomen were motivated by the need to improve the drainage of mines. Although there were alternatives such as digging adits (drainage tunnels) in hilly terrain, the demand for pumping machines steadily increased as miners dug more deeply (it would be interesting to estimate how much more slowly English industry might have grown in the absence of improved drainage techniques). Beyond noting that Newcomen was not the only one experimenting with steam engines at the time, and that he succeeded with a little luck only after many years of experimentation,[62] I will not spend time on the actual invention since it occurred so early in the eighteenth century. I am more concerned with its development over time, and the extent to which later inventions were dependent upon it.

The Newcomen engine was designed in such a way that it could be put together by local craftsmen. Early engines were made of brass, copper, lead, and wood. This was largely because transport services were still too poor for the various parts to be mass-produced at some central location and shipped throughout the country. Naturally, a machine put together by local craftsmen could not meet high standards of engineering. Cylinders tended to be very rough and the pistons were packed with watered hemp to create a seal. Thus, the early engines were far from efficient, but even if more efficient engines had been designed they would have been impossible to produce commercially. 1725 marked the introduction of smoothly bored iron cylinders, which could withstand greater heat than brass cylinders. With the development of boring machines, iron came to be used in virtually all cylinders, though other materials were still used for other parts.

Major advances were made in boring techniques during the eighteenth century. Once the production of cylinders became centralized, it was only natural that attempts would be made to create better cylinders. The Darbys developed a simple boring machine, consisting of a long rod anchored on one end, which was capable of boring a fairly round hole but not a straight hole, as there was nothing to keep the cutting edge at a steady height. Wilkinson developed two new boring machines in 1774 and 1781. The first owed a great deal to technology developed for the boring of cannon. The second was specially designed for steam engine cylinders, which were open at both ends. Whereas all previous boring machines had remained stationary while the cylinder turned, Wilkinson's second machine kept the cylinder stationary while the borer turned, and was able to produce much better cylinders.

Raistrick notes that improvements in casting and boring cylinders seem to have been the only technological change that affected the Newcomen engine in the six decades after its introduction (1970, 148).[63] This is not surprising given that most other engine parts continued to be made on site by unskilled craftsmen. As better cylinders were produced, not only did the Newcomen engine become more efficient in its fuel use; it also became more regular in its operation. Thus, it was possible to use the Newcomen engine for purposes other than pumping. In the words of Musson and Robinson:

It is impossible not to be impressed by the great variety of functions which were being performed by Savary and Newcomen engines in Lancashire. At first they were used for pumping water from coal pits or for waterworks, and then for the motive power of overshot water wheels. Engines of this last kind, and atmospheric engines adapted to a crank and fly wheel, were used, along with pirated Boulton and Watt engines, for many industrial purposes: for winding coal, blowing furnaces, driving boring engines and lathes, milling corn, driving carding and spinning machines, grinding materials in dye works, turning rollers in calico-printing and calendaring works and squeezers and washers on bleach fields. (1959, 439)

Not only was the Newcomen engine a precursor to the Watt engine; it was also a substitute for the Watt engine.

The Watt Engines

The most important thing to realize about the Watt engine is that it was impossible to build one successfully until the 1770s. Where the Newcomen engine was designed to be built by local craftsmen on site, the Watt engine could not be built in such a manner. The various parts of the machine had to be finely engineered at a central manufactory and sent to the purchaser.[64] Thus, both improvements in transport and in the ability of the iron industry to produce an output meeting high engineering standards were required. Wilkinson could not have supplied all England with engine parts in 1700 as he did in 1790.[65] Nor could any ironmaster have produced the parts needed for the engine in the early eighteenth century. The most important improvement in iron technology in this regard was the boring machine. Watt could not successfully construct a large engine of his type until Wilkinson developed his improved boring machine. While the standards of engineering required for a Watt engine may seem low by modern standards (Watt was elated that Wilkinson's borer was precise to within a coin-width), they were much higher than could be achieved in the early eighteenth century.[66] It is sensible, therefore, to get away from the idea that England had been waiting since the time of Newcomen for some genius to make the next technological leap forward. Rather, one should realize that the Newcomen engine was the best possible at the time. Once conditions changed so that a better engine was possible, it did not take long for such an engine to appear.[67]

One would expect that the problem of high fuel consumption with the relatively inefficient Newcomen engine would spur inventive activity. As long as the engine was used largely for coal mining, the problem of coal use was not too severe (coal mines were to use Newcomen engines rather than the more expensive Watt engines throughout the century). The expanding output of Cornish tin and copper mining in a region devoid of coal was of great importance to Boulton and Watt in the early days of production (Roll 1968, 67). The increasing scale of industrial establishments also provided an incentive for the development of improved steam engines.[68] The later eighteenth century witnessed numerous efforts to create new engines.

Watt was the first to succeed. As with other inventions, the perfection of the Watt steam engine took many years and required considerable funds. In 1768, Watt was heavily in debt due to costly experimentation.[69] Boulton then undertook to help with the financing; for years Watt had to be provided with materials and assistants (Roll 1968, 26). Smeaton, on inspecting the Watt steam engine, "doubted the practicability of getting the different parts executed with the requisite precision"; the commercial introduction of the engine required that workmen be trained to produce the necessary parts.[70] When ready for market, Boulton and Watt had to suffer additional financial outlays to entice the first sceptical buyers to make this major investment (Stuart 1825, 124). All told, it was estimated that some £50,000 were invested by Boulton and Watt before they began to turn a profit.[71] In any case, it should be clear that an immense collective effort was required to produce the Watt engine.

And then, of course, the fears of the earliest buyers were confirmed by the fact that the first engines did not work very well. The engine installed at Coalbrookdale had to be modified many times during the 1780s. One of the exigencies of the sales of the earliest engine was that Watt himself or one of the firm engineers had frequently to visit the various engines to deal with breakdowns. One may conclude, given the difficulty of finding competent engineers, that diffusion of the Watt engine would have been much slower, and might even have stalled, had speed of travel been at 1700 levels.[72] Gradually over time these engineers were able to tinker with the engine and make it less subject to breakdown.

It is possible that without Watt, England would have fared nearly as well. Von Tunzelman estimated the social savings from Watt steam engines in 1800 as .1 per cent of national income (1978, ch.6), though estimates decades into the nineteenth century are higher. Not only was the Newcomen engine a possible (though less efficient and reliable) substitute for the Watt engine in all its uses, but there is good reason to believe that others would have succeeded in Watt's stead. The last decades of the eighteenth century saw the introduction of a rash of new engine designs.

Some, admittedly, were simply attempts to evade Watt's patent. Others, however, were quite different designs. It is instructive to look at a breakdown of the types of engines in existence in England at the end of the eighteenth century (from Kanefsky 1980; estimates based on 2191 engines):

Newcomen pump	42.7%
rotary	3.9%
Watt pump	7.4%
rotary	14.4%
Pirate Watt	2.9%
Savary	1.5%
Various other	4.5%
No data	22.7%

Since the data on Watt engines are much better than data on any other engines, one would assume that the 22.7 per cent for which there are no data would most likely be of the Newcomen type, though some would belong to the "various other" category. The most glaring result of this table is that Newcomen engines comprise the majority (probably about two thirds) of all engines. Clearly, most people stayed with Newcomen engines for a long time after the Watt engine was introduced. It is also interesting that there were almost one fourth as many engines of other types as there were Watt engines. It is not our place here to discuss in any detail the designs of these engines. At least one, the Heslop engine, may have been more efficient than the Watt engine (Raistrick 1970, 156). Others, such as the Hornblower[73] and Bull engines, were significant improvements which ran into problems with Watt's patent (Rowland 1974, 33). Together, they indicate that there were a substantial number of inventors capable of producing workable steam engines at the time. As Watt's patent lasted twenty-five years, and legally precluded any unlicenced use of some basic elements of steam engine technology of the time, such as the separate condenser, it is even possible that his net effect on steam engine development was negative.[74]

Right at the end of the eighteenth century, Trevithick began experimenting with engines that used steam to provide the power for piston movement. All previous engines, including Watt's, merely used condensation of steam to create a vacuum below the piston, and relied on the atmosphere to provide the power stroke. Steam engine development in the nineteenth century was to follow the lines of Trevithick's development. This naturally required even higher standards of engineering (because of the higher pressures involved) than the Watt engine.[75] It is worth noting here that the future course of engine development would follow quite a different line than the Watt engine.

I have been talking mainly about the original Watt engine here, but what I have said applies as well to the rotative engine developed later by Watt. It was, in fact, attempts to make the Newcomen and other engines capable of rotary power that spurred Watt to design a rotative engine. Rotary power had been applied to Newcomen engines from 1779 by Wasborough, but Boulton and Watt would not license him to use his patented invention with their engine (Roll 1968, 108). Therefore, for use with his engine, Watt had to develop sun and planet gears, with the help of William Murdock (according to Smiles). For many purposes which did not require great regularity, the less expensive Newcomen engine was preferred, though for tasks requiring a regular motion the Watt engine was far superior.

SUMMARY

The metal trades did benefit from all of the transport-induced changes outlined in the first chapter. They enjoyed a more modern system of transportation, penetrated wider markets, needed and received more reliable transport services which allowed them to operate on a larger scale, and gained much greater access to a wide variety of raw materials. They responded to this burgeoning environment with increasing division of labour, centralization of production in workshops, and the introduction of numerous technological innovations. Many of these innovations were too minor to receive much attention, but some, like stamping machinery, were of great importance. Perhaps the most important innovation was the emergence of intermediate industries. These technological advances were not great leaps forward but fairly straightforward reactions to new opportunities. Taken together, the changes had three major results. First, by lowering costs of production, the metal trades were able greatly to expand sales, and thus their demand for iron. Second, concentrating production within regions and workshops and establishing intermediate industries centralized the demand for iron, so that individual ironmasters could establish regular deliveries to producers who required large amounts of iron. Third, some of the technological innovations in the metal trades, such as the rolling mill, were prerequisites for certain technological changes within the iron industry.

There was a dramatic increase in iron output in the second half of the eighteenth century. Only the metal trades were capable of encouraging and absorbing this increased output. Two minor sources of increased demand for iron were improved transport (iron tires, horseshoes) and increased urbanization (nails and pipes). There was also an increase in the scale of operation of the iron industry. In addition to the effects of the metal trades discussed earlier, the increase in scale was aided by improved methods of distributing iron to the metal trades.

Transport improvements led to a large drop in the price of coal for inland users, partly because of a decrease in collusion or monopoly power. Contrary to the myth that England was running out of wood, the transition from one fuel to another can be seen as a reaction to changing relative prices. The iron industry required various other raw materials as well, including different types of ore, and thus stood to benefit considerably as access to such materials was improved. Moreover, the iron industry needed and received more reliable transport services before it could increase its scale of operation.

The history of the iron industry has all too often been viewed as just a story of new technology. Instead, it should be viewed essentially as a tale of transport-induced changes. Once the impacts of improved transport on both the output and input sides of the industry are understood, it is possible to explain the technological history of the industry. Darby's use of coke was not revolutionary; it was the application of old technology to a new product. The spread of coke-smelting in the early years was totally dependent on the growth in the cast iron trade. As founders came to deal with a national market, they were able to produce a wider variety of goods and thus greatly increase their output. Small quantities of coke-pig were sold to forgemasters throughout the early eighteenth century.

As the relative price of coal versus charcoal dropped, increasing efforts were made to use coke as a fuel in both furnace and forge. Decades of work by many men yielded a couple of methods of doing so, of which the most famous was Cort's puddling and rolling process. Cort himself recognized that he had not done anything more than synthesize a number of existing ideas (one of which, the adjustable roller, owes a great deal to technology developed in the metal trades). Since innovations of any sort are more likely to occur in a growing industry, and will also spread faster once discovered, the increased demand for iron from the metal trades played an unseen role in fostering these developments.

Other important innovations were also instrumental in encouraging and allowing the increase in scale. Much better bellows were introduced, in part because of the need for a stronger blast in coke furnaces. Steam engines came to play a major role in both furnace and forge. Neither innovation, however, can be said to have forced the iron industry to increase in scale. Rather, they allowed the industry to expand in response to increased and more centralized demand from the metal trades, and cheaper and more reliable transport.

Changes within the iron industry were of tremendous importance. They allowed the production of more and better tools and machinery, a development that would eventually affect every other industry. These (and other backward linkage effects which I have not discussed) will come up again as I look at other industries. Improvements in iron production were also to play a major role in later transport developments (iron boats, railroads) that fall largely outside the scope of this study.

Changes in the iron industry had an important impact on the development of steam engines. The Newcomen engine was the most efficient possible in the early eighteenth century, given the relatively backward state of the iron industry and the transport system. Improvements in the casting and boring of cylinders enhanced the quality of the Newcomen engine and paved the way for later engines. It would have been impossible to construct the Watt engine commercially until the 1770s. There were many others working on improved steam engines in the late eighteenth century, and some of them were successful. Moreover, the Newcomen engine could perform almost all of the functions performed by the Watt engine (adequate sources of water power were also still available to English industry). Further, many hands and considerable funds were involved in the development of the Watt engine, which was also subject to a period of lengthy critical revision. Thus, it should be treated just like any other invention, as the net result of many people's efforts to improve steam engine design. And these efforts could only be successful after a number of developments had taken place in both the transport sector and the iron industry.

CHAPTER FOUR

The French Iron Industry

Historians in general, and economic historians no less, tend to pay more attention to history's success stories than to her failures. In part, this is because it is generally easier to answer the question, "Why?" than the question, "Why not?" The French iron industry during the eighteenth century was relatively stagnant compared to that of England. My task, then, is to show that the poor quality of the French transport system prevented the French iron industry from developing as the English industry did. I argue that if France, like England, had possessed an early modern transport system, her iron industry could have developed in the same ways. This does not necessarily mean that it would have done so – I claim only that transport was a necessary, not a sufficient, condition.

Clearly, the backward French transport system described in chapter 2 did have a negative effect on the French iron industry. Rioux (1971, 58–9) felt that there were many partial explanations of English success, "but it is the enlargement of the English market which played the determining role." While he overemphasizes the importance of higher per-capita incomes in creating this larger market, he does capture the great importance of large market size in economic development. "It is necessary then to furnish standardized quality products; a division of labour occurs, along with concentration of work to better supervise the regularity and continuity of production of each worker." Almost two centuries earlier, Guiraudet (1802) had puzzled over ways to improve the state of the French iron manufacture. His first suggestion involved improvements to transport facilities to expose French producers to a larger market. To recover lost foreign markets, "it is necessary to open canals if one wishes to return life to the manufacture and commerce of iron" (Guiraudet, 26). Internally, he questioned the recent decision to impose tolls on roads. "Tolls, this false imitation of the English, are incompatible with all sorts of commerce for a people who, having but few navigable rivers, and almost no canals, are forced to move their goods by land over a large continent" (Guiraudet, 26). The high cost of bulk transit would naturally affect the movement of raw materials to an even greater extent than the movement of the finished good.[1] Moreover, the iron industry, like others, would be hurt not only by the high cost of transport but also by the slowness and unreliability of the system. "The slowness and uncertainty of transport required that, to assure the regularity of manufacture, large inventories be held, at the same time that the irregularity of sales forced the accumulation of stocks of semi-finished and finished goods" (Léon 1976, 539). The waste of capital in high inventory holdings made the process of capital accumulation much more difficult. Clearly, the negative impacts one might expect from poor transport were there to some degree. In what follows, I will look in greater detail at particular aspects of the French iron industry, following a similar order to that used for the English industry, to see how important these negative impacts were.

Discussion of the English industry began with an outline of the uses to which iron was put in the eighteenth century, and the changes in the English metal trades which had profound feedback effects on the iron industry itself. Excepting the metal trades that emerged during the eighteenth century in England, the French iron industry supplied much the same industries as its English counterpart, though perhaps in different proportions. However, the French metal trades did not undergo the same transformation that occurred in England. In the eighteenth century the metal trades remained regionally diffuse. They were to concentrate on French coalfields in the nineteenth century, more than half a century after the same transformation had occurred in England; this "would have been impossible without improved means of transport" (Pounds 1957a, 114–15). Naturally, there was far less division of labour than in England.[2] Nor was there a great degree of industrial concentration. In the last decades of the eighteenth century, a number of Englishmen moved to France to attempt to set up large-scale engineering works of the type that had emerged in England (Henderson, 1956). However, even with the transplantation of English entrepreneurs, little was achieved until the nineteenth century. Not surprisingly, small-scale dispersed production saw little technological innovation. As early as 1756, a French hardware manufacturer attributed English superiority to worker concentration, and the use of powered machinery such as rolling mills (Harris 1986, 15).

In the important area of machine making, France lagged far behind England. In fact, in the early nineteenth century, "French metals, metal products and machinery were of poorer quality or higher price than those available in Belgium" (Geiger 1974, 138). The machinery developed for use in the English metal trades was almost unknown in France. In 1777–78 the French government commissioned Alcock to look into rolling and slitting mills in England, as well as ornamental hardware (Harris, 1986). In 1795, the government offered a reward of 500 livres for the "invention" of a suitable rolling mill (Woronoff 1984, 365), of which there were only two in existence before the Revolution. There were only three or four plants using stamps, punches, and similar machines to make metal goods; these were unable to compete with England after the treaty of 1786 (Gille n.d., 99–100). The production of agricultural implements was very backward, as well. At the time of the Revolution, France had agricultural implements of very poor quality (Tresse 1955). Good scythes had to be imported from other countries, not only because of an inability to make good steel, but also because of an inability to attach the blade properly to the handle (Tresse 1955). By 1794, France was importing 100,000 scythes per year (Woronoff 1984, 361–5). In England, the metal trades acquired the ability over the eighteenth century to produce better quality goods at lower cost. The same was not achieved in France.

While histories of English industry have paid little attention to the advances within the metal trades, the French were certainly aware at the time that their metal trades were falling behind. "It was for hardware that the use of machines gave the best results. The example of England indicated one more time the route to follow" (Ballot 1923, 482). The French government throughout the second half of the century attempted to establish Birmingham industry on French soil. Spies were sent to England to learn the secrets of English manufacture.[3] English workers were enticed to France. The result was a couple of "modern" establishments with some English connection, but in many regions of France the English machines remained unknown (see Ballot, 482–8). "It is remarkable in a country in the front rank as an industrial power, and manifesting so much encouragement and special favour toward those bringing in British processes, that such great difficulty was encountered in assimilating them" (Harris 1978, 199). That the circumstances of French industry were not at all conducive to organizational or technological change seems clear from the minimal impact these government-induced enclaves had on the rest of the industry.

The inability to make steel of high quality was a major failing of the French metal trades.[4] A certain amount of steel was required to make a wide range of metalware; if quality steel could not be created the market for all these goods would be severely limited. It was recognized that various French industries suffered because of the poor quality of French files (Harris, 1978). I need not rehash the development of crucible steelmaking in England. France was not only unable to develop good steelmaking techniques; it was also unable to copy this technology after it had been developed in England.[5] Even in the early nineteenth century, the use of Huntsman's method was unheard of across the Channel (Dunham 1955, 132–3). Indeed, once again, the French government supported many efforts to use English technology.[6] These proved fruitless. The willingness to experiment in France (without government aid) was negligible. Even the centuries-old cementation method was only introduced experimentally in 1770. Good-quality steel was imported from Germany or England; steel for agricultural implements was made locally by crude methods. Due largely to its small scale, the French steel industry developed very slowly during the eighteenth and early nineteenth centuries. In addition, geographical dispersion meant that cross-fertilization of ideas between steelmakers was negligible.

One of the problems faced by the French steel industry was the quality of French ores, which were ill-suited to steelmaking given the technology of the time. It must be remembered, though, that the English steel industry was forced to rely on Swedish ores. Few areas in Europe had ore capable of making good-quality steel. Both France and England had to rely on imported ore from Sweden or Russia.[7] The simple fact that a necessary raw material had to be imported does not mean that the quality of inland transport was of no importance. Sheffield would not have developed as a steelmaking centre had transport improvements not connected it with Hull. In France, as I have said, ports were poorly connected with the areas that were destined to industrialize. Thus, while imported ore might be brought to French and English coasts for the same cost, French steelmakers located inland would be unable to obtain this raw material as easily as their English counterparts.[8] Moreover, as noted earlier, the real secret to the success of the Sheffield steel industry was its access to clay from the other side of England. Harris (1986) recognizes inappropriate clay as one of the major problems confronting French steelmakers. French ironmasters would have had considerable difficulty in obtaining clay from other parts of France. And once they had gained access to raw materials, they would have had difficulty exploiting a large market. The site for the royal work at Amboise was selected because of the local supply of charcoal and coal. With no local market to serve, the output was all sold at Nantes (F12 656).

The metal trades, then, were unable to benefit the French iron industry as they had benefitted the English. In the last chapter, it was seen that military demand was too unstable to account for the development of the English iron industry. The necessary ingredient was a steady, growing demand from the metal trades, and this France lacked. Demand for iron remained feeble and diffuse. The only clients for a sizeable quantity of iron were the state and the construction industry; at the slightest crisis both could withdraw their demand and iron production would suddenly decrease (Gille n.d., 124). Fluctuating military procurements could not guarantee a stable level of demand for French iron (Price 1981, 110). Bamford describes in detail how one French ironmaster who relied on naval contracts was faced with severe fluctuations in demand, problems with payment, and hostility toward innovation (1988, 118,177). As long as French transport remained backward, French metal trades were liable to remain small, regionally dispersed and technologically backward. This meant that there was little incentive or opportunity for the French iron industry to increase its scale or output.

CHARCOAL

I turn now from the demand for iron to the supply of combustibles by which iron ore could be transformed. With one exception, all furnaces in France used charcoal throughout the eighteenth century, so I shall focus on the charcoal supply first. As noted in the previous chapter, both contemporary and modern writers have exaggerated the "wood shortage" in England. It is noteworthy that there were similar complaints in eighteenth-century France that the country was running out of wood.[9] An upward trend in wood prices triggered extensive lobbying in the late eighteenth century to restrict ironworks, which were viewed as the main cause; local governments considered forcing them to use coal (Woronoff 1984, 227–37, 332). The elders of Cosne-sur-Loire complained bitterly in 1764 that the local ironworks was using all of the local wood, leaving local bakers with no firewood (Bamford 1988, 109). Pounds (1957a, 32–3) speaks of a shortage of fuel throughout the country and is surprised that successful attempts at using coke did not result. Gille speaks of a growing crisis in wood supply. In Dauphiné the wood supply had been an issue since the fourteenth century, as it was everywhere in varying degrees from the sixteenth century on. In Franche-Comté trees as young as seven to nine years old were cut even though the best age for charcoal was fifteen to twenty years (Gille n.d., 67). In France, the problem was exacerbated by a poor system of forest management. In some regions, ironworks were unable to obtain all of the wood they needed; local governments often reacted to the wood shortage by restricting the activities of local ironmasters (Gille n.d., 71,77).[10] Clearly, England was not unique in the problems it had with its wood supply during the eighteenth century. England's problems may have been slightly worse than elsewhere but the problem was shared throughout Europe. If the fact that wood was a limited resource under pressure from various sources had indeed been behind the development of the use of coke in the English iron industry, the same result should have occurred elsewhere.

Of course, as shown, the reports of the death of England's wood supply were greatly exaggerated, and the same is true of France. Wood prices rose on the whole in France as in England, a predictable result when demand increases for a good with an upwardly sloping supply curve.[11] Some regions of France did face real problems. In general, though, France appears to have been in a somewhat better position than England. Fohlen goes so far as to complain that "wood was abundant and relatively inexpensive" (1970, 211). It does appear that the supply of wood was ample in most areas until the expansion of the French iron industry in the early nineteenth century (Dunham 1955, 86). Of course, if the French iron industry had expanded in the eighteenth century, wood resources would have found themselves under much greater pressure. Léon notes that the price of wood doubled in 1819–37 along with metallurgy consumption (1976, 551).

The possession of somewhat greater wood supplies should have placed the French iron industry at an advantage relative to the English industry. The use of charcoal did not necessarily limit the scale of operation of an ironworks. In the twentieth century, large, charcoal-using ironworks have been built. Doing so, however, requires good transport links that allow the ironworks access to a wide market as well as to a large area of forest from which the necessary charcoal can be obtained. As I have shown, the French transport system was at its worst off the routes between major cities. Those areas most suitable for charcoal ironworks were the most poorly served.[12]

Even if French charcoal ironworks had been able to expand, there is a limit to the amount of industrial concentration that can be achieved based on charcoal. At some point, the use of coal becomes necessary to achieve the type of concentration that characterized the Industrial Revolution. Still, access to abundant supplies of charcoal should have been beneficial by taking some of the pressure off of coal supplies. Nevertheless, charcoal alone was not enough, and one must look now at French coal resources and try to answer the question of why coal was not used to any significant degree by the eighteenth-century French iron industry.

Coal Quality

A constant theme running through the economic history of Europe is that the paucity of its coal resources accounts in large part for the relatively slow industrialization of France. In this section, I will endeavour to show that, at least as far as the eighteenth century is concerned, it was problems with transportation, rather than any problems with the coal resources themselves, that prevented coal from playing a major role in the development of the French iron industry. Before outlining the ways in which poor transport hindered the the the use of coal, it is necessary to consider the quality of French coal.

Contemporaries, especially during the Revolutionary and Imperial periods, often complained that French coal was of inferior quality to that of England.[13] Yet, as Geiger notes, "the very inaccessibility of English coal made it seem more desirable" (1974, 219). Even in earlier periods when importation of English coal was common, it was mainly used in coastal areas, and vast areas of inland France would have been ignorant of the exact qualities of English coal. Government tests in the early nineteenth century, though one might question their reliability, showed Anzin coal to be equal to that of Belgium or England, even though Frenchmen thought Anzin coal to be inferior (Geiger 1974, 220). Part of the problem with French coal was the lack of competition between French coal mines as a result of poor internal transport links. Many mines did not use the best veins available, coal was poorly cut, and it was mixed with coal dust (Dunham 1955, 94). Not surprisingly, the coalfields credited with the best coal were precisely those which had the best transport links (Pounds 1957a, 84). The inability to obtain coal from more than one source hid from contemporaries an advantage possessed by France which has been noted by many writers: France had many varieties of coal. Had it been possible to move this coal about easily, it should have been possible to achieve the right mixture for most industrial operations. Instead, local industrialists often had to rely at most on one viable source of coal.

The most damning criticism of French coal is that it was ill-suited for conversion to coke.[14] In large part, this is due to the fact that France adopted coke very slowly. However, as I will show, the explanation for the slow adoption of coke lies elsewhere than in the quality of French coal. When France finally achieved a modern transport network, it found that its coal could be used for coking purposes. It must be remembered that the widespread use of coke in England occurred only after modifications had been made to English forges. Isolated French furnaces would not have been able to switch to coke with positive results unless there were associated forges geared to the refining of coke-pig.

As the French began to use coke in the nineteenth century, they developed different means of turning coal into coke than the English. These means were better suited to continental coal (Pounds 1957a, 110).[15] In turn, continental methods of making coke amazed Englishmen in the nineteenth century and appear to have been unsuitable for use with English coal (Jordan, 1878). As France first began to use coke, it naturally borrowed English coke-making technology. When this proved unsuitable for use with French coal, the suspicion naturally arose that the problem lay with French coal. If history had been reversed and the use of coke developed first in France, the opposite would have happened and English coal would have proved unsuitable for coking using French technology.

It should also be remembered that in the early days of coke use, the technology was somewhat more flexible and could more easily accommodate differences in ore and coal quality. If the other conditions necessary for the establishment of a coke-based iron industry had been in place in the eighteenth century, French coal would have proven equal to the task. The first successful use of coke on the continent was in Upper Silesia in the 1790s. "It is a fact of considerable interest that this earliest successful use of coke for smelting took place on a coalfield that has never been considered a source of good coking coal" (Pounds 1957a, 107).

Coal Location

The second major complaint about French coal is that it was poorly located. To be sure, the English iron industry did have an advantage in that coal and iron tended to occur together in England. Yet this advantage should not be exaggerated. In England, as earlier described, coal was often transported great distances by both road and water. Moreover, there was a considerable trade in both iron ore and pig iron throughout England. In France, the distance separating coal and iron was often not great; there simply were not the necessary transport links between the two.[16]

Dunham makes the point that French coal was not ideally located, but largely because of the underdevelopment of French transport links. "In most cases it was far from any useful deposits of iron or, if not far away in actual distance, was so in effect because of the lack of cheap means of transportation" (1955, 91–2). The Loire area was the most like England in possessing nearby deposits of coal and iron; the first large establishments were there (Gille 1969, 48). The Le Creusot ironworks, the only works in France to smelt with coke during the eighteenth century, had both coal and iron close at hand. It was able to operate only because of the construction of the Canal du Centre which gave it access to both raw materials and markets.[17] Elsewhere, ores along the Rhône could be smelted using coal from the Rive de Gier (Pounds

1957a, 165). Fifty miles to the north of the Commentry coalfield lay the ore deposits of Bourges, Nevers, and St-Asand. "The linking of the Commentry coal and the ore of Berry was held up by the inadequacy of the means of transport" (Pounds 1957a, 158–60). The completion of the Canal du Berry in the nineteenth century allowed the movement of coal in one direction and ore in the other (Gille 1969, 149). Though the Berry iron industry was to decline in the nineteenth century as its ore supplies diminished, it could have been a viable area for a coke-based iron industry in the eighteenth century had the Canal du Berry been built a few decades earlier.

The ores of Hainaut were situated near both French and Belgian coalfields. "The local reserves of iron seemed sufficient in the nineteenth century to justify the building of new furnaces" (Pounds 1957a, 175). In the eighteenth century, though, no new furnaces were built even though this was the only ore deposit near the great northern coalfield. "The only iron ore deposits were at Trelon near Mauberges in the Avesnes area and isolated from the Anzin coalfield by the lack of water transport" (Geiger 1974, 211).[18] It was actually easier to obtain Lorraine ore than that of Hainaut.

And last but not least, there is the area that would eventually dominate the French iron industry: Lorraine. The Lorraine area had both ore and coal, though there were complaints about the quality of both. There were two types of ore in Lorraine, a limited supply of *fer fort* which was of good quality for ironmaking, and *minette* which occurred in more than one form and was less valuable due to a high phosphorus content (though it would become the basis of the local iron industry after the introduction of the Gilchrist-Thomas method in the late nineteenth century). The two ores were generally mixed to provide an adequate, easily obtainable supply to local furnaces. The de Wendels at Hayange took advantage of a location where both ore and coal were close at hand, and by 1825 they were able to produce 3000 tons of coke-pig (Fohlen 1970, 212). By the mid-nineteenth century, the Lorraine area was in an enviable position since its ironworks had access to both coal and charcoal as well as different types of ore to mix (Prêcheur 1959, 152).

The problem of the eighteenth-century iron industry, then, was not that coal was located too far from the ore, but that insufficient transport links rendered it nearly impossible in most cases for the two to be brought together. I will discuss below the difficulties of moving ore. Here, it is necessary to describe the difficulties of moving coal from mines. East arrived at the conclusion that it was difficulties with transport that prevented France from using coal to supply her industrial needs:

But above all, in addition to its shortcomings in quality and quantity, French coal suffered severely from the high cost and inefficiency of inland transport. On the one hand, a multiplicity of internal customs and dues of various kinds had to be paid at points along the roads and rivers; on the other the provincial roads were bad and carriage by pack animals and wagon was slow and costly. Even the rivers and canals were burdened by tolls and the exactions of organized boatmen; moreover they were rendered difficult owing to the seasonal variations in their regimes. (1935, 395–6)

Examples abound throughout France of coal mines facing severe difficulties in getting their coal to market.[19] Rouff devotes a few pages to the difficulties faced by individual coal mines; most often, mine owners were forced to use pack-mules to get their coal to the main routes (1922, 368–74). The great Loire coalfield, near both the Loire and Rhône rivers, would seem to be well located. However, the upper reaches of the Loire were rocky and the flow of water irregular. Even with the completion of canals linking the Loire and Seine, the route to the north remained long, slow, and expensive (Dunham 1955, 98). On the other side of the coalfield, a canal was built to connect the Saône and Rhône but it was shallow and had many locks (Dunham 1955, 99). The Blanzy coalfield was also inadequately connected by waterway to major markets. The production of the northern part of the basin was almost all consumed locally; the full resources of the basin were neither fully explored nor adequately used (Dunham 1955, 99). Woronoff (1984, 334) lists a number of coalfields too far from markets to be exploited, and notes that this is why canals were at the centre of the question of commerce in coal.

The northern coalfield of France was in the best position with respect to transport. It was indeed the superiority of its transport links, rather than the resources for mining, which gave the northern coalfield an advantage over other French coalfields (Gillet 1969, 186). Yet even on the northern coalfield the difficulties in transporting coal to market were severe. Geiger (1974, 162–84) describes in detail the problems faced by the Anzin Company in the nineteenth century. The Escaut and its tributaries gave Anzin potential access to the Nord and Pas de Calais as well as to a large part of Belgium. However, there had been virtually no river improvements on the Escaut. The river was full of curves, boulders, sandbars, shifting channels, and towpaths difficult for men and impossible for horses, and subject to freezing in winter, floods in spring, and drought in summer. Local canals had similar problems; many suffered from a deficiency of water and there were frequent traffic jams at locks as the water built up. "Transport by water was very slow, routes were indirect and long, costs were relatively high, and the quantity of goods carried was strictly limited" (Geiger, 166). Another of Anzin's problems was the monopoly power exercised by the corporation of boatmen on the river, which kept prices artificially high.[20] The towmen also colluded to keep prices high, and their power could not be broken until the towpaths were widened to allow horses in the nineteenth century. The early nineteenth century saw the completion of important canal schemes. The Sensée canal gave better access to the English Channel. The long-awaited St-Quentin canal gave Anzin coal access to the Seine-Oise basin. Road transport in the area was also highly problematic at the start of the nineteenth century. Spring thaws and rains caused local authorities to declare roads closed for long periods, and travel was difficult at best.

Naturally, the difficulties of transport translated into high costs. The cost of coal was often many times higher at the point of consumption than at the pithead.[21] In the early nineteenth century, the cost of coal in Paris was often ten times what it was in the Loire (Dunham 1955, 95). In 1829, the cost of transporting Anzin coal to Paris was about four times the cost of extraction (Geiger 1974, 247). Even though Anzin pits were generally within three miles of the river, it cost one third the cost of extraction just to get this coal to the river (Geiger 1974, 169). In 1830, coal which cost 15 fr per ton at the pithead in the Loire sold for 45 to 55 fr per ton in Mulhouse, while Saar coal, which cost 9 fr per ton at the pithead sold for 50 to 60 (Fohlen 1975, 51). In 1838, Belgian coal costing 8 fr per ton at the pit cost 37 in Charleville, 45 in Sedan, 50 in Rethel, 65 in Reims, and 87.5 in the Haute-Marne, its furthest point of penetration (Price 1981, 122). Given the improved state of transport in the early nineteenth century, the situation in the eighteenth must have been even worse. It was not to last forever, though. After the completion of the Rhône-Rhine canal in 1833, Mulhouse was able to obtain Loire coal for 12 fr per ton (Fohlen 1966, 144). The cost of coal transport decreased markedly, chiefly through the improvement of waterways (Dunham 1955, 100). The poor quality of the French transport system raised the price of coal exorbitantly, and later improvements in the system were able to bring the price of coal down considerably.

Coal Output

This leads naturally to the output of the French coal industry. Was the French coal industry capable of supplying the needs of a French industrial revolution? To be sure, the French coal industry never competed with the English in terms of output. Throughout the early nineteenth century, English production was ten times that of France (Fohlen 1966, 141).[22] However, France probably produced more than the rest of continental Europe during the eighteenth century (Pounds 1957a, 82). Nevertheless, throughout both centuries, France consumed more than she produced and had to import the difference. This does not mean, though, that France was incapable of supplying its own needs. The heavy imports in the (eighteenth and) early nineteenth centuries were a direct result of poor transport in the interior; it was easier for northern France to obtain English coal than to get French coal (Fohlen 1966, 142). Given the sad state of French transport and the easy access to coal not only from England but also from Belgium, Luxembourg, and Germany, it is not surprising that French imports were high. This does not mean that French coal mines could not have done the job if given the chance.

The French coal supply was capable of great expansion during the period I am interested in. French coal production was to grow steadily: .23 million metric tons were produced in 1789, .8 million in 1811, 2 million in 1830–34, 5.3 million in 1850–54, 10 million in 1860–64, and 15.4 million in 1870–74 (Fohlen 1975, 51, and Price 1981, 123–4). Of course, the reasons why France was able to increase its coal output so dramatically in the nineteenth century are many and varied, and it would be folly to maintain that just because it could be done in the nineteenth century it could also be done in the eighteenth. Yet a major factor contributing to the growth of output in the nineteenth century was the improvement of transport services. Even in the early part of the century, "A closer study of the cost of carrying coal shows that transportation was the most serious problem of all and served more than any other factor to keep up the price and restrict the consumption" (Dunham 1955, 98). The sales of the Anzin coal company doubled during the Restoration. Most of this occurred during the 1820s and was due to improved transport which widened their market (Geiger 1974, 223).

The French transport system had paralysed the exploitation of coal resources during the eighteenth century (Rouff 1922, 384). The negligible development of coal mining before 1815 can be attributed to two factors, according to Dunham: the unavailability of proper means of transport, and insufficient demand (1955, 91). Naturally, however, the quantity demanded would depend on the price, and the high transport costs incurred by coal would make the demand for coal seem much smaller than it otherwise would. L. Cordier in 1814 was confident that France could supply its own needs for coal (though he may not have foreseen all of the uses to which coal would be put during the next years); the only problem he foresaw was difficulty with the transport system (Pounds 1957a, 140). Certainly, nobody could argue that northern France did not have its own supply of coal, but even there, in the nineteenth century, prohibitive carting costs and waterways that did not reach all of the many industrial centres severely restricted the use of coal (Dunham 1955, 93). I have already discussed the problems faced by coalmine owners in getting their output to market. There is further evidence that these mines could have expanded their output greatly had better transport services been available. One strand of evidence is the efforts put into transport improvements in their areas by the owners of coal mines. In England, industrialists of various sorts often took an interest in local turnpike trusts or river or canal companies. In general, though, they did not have to make heavy financial investments. In France, this was not the case. The Anzin company was constantly hampered by the backwardness of the transport system. It participated directly in schemes to improve and extend the network of waterways over which its coal moved to market; in 1827, the company had nearly a one-quarter interest in the St-Quentin canal (Geiger 1974, 162,190). Anzin also needed to build local roads to connect it with the river, and it even built a bridge over the Escaut; the cost of road building, though much lower than the cost of opening a new pit, must have been substantial (Geiger 1974, 168). Heavy investments in transport by the owners of coal mines were common (see Rouff 1922, 368–72). It was also quite common for mine owners to build businesses near the pithead so that they would have some outlet for their coal; De Solage, for example, built a glassworks at Carnaux because transport costs rendered him unable to compete with English coal in Bordeaux (Rouff 1922, 368).

This is not to say that French coal did not present some extraction problems. Many French coal seams were thin, deep, and twisted, and many mines suffered from water problems. These problems should not be exaggerated. The extraction costs for St Etienne and Blanzy were similar to those for Newcastle and lower than those for Lancashire, though the coalfields of northern France were much more expensive (Dunham 1955, 95–6). On the whole, French extraction costs were probably somewhat higher than in England, though there was considerable variation among coalfields. Nevertheless, it was transport, not extraction, that was the dominant cause of the high cost of coal to consumers. The Anzin company had some of the greatest extraction difficulties in the country (see Geiger 1974, 160), but the cost of transport to Paris was still four times the cost of extraction. Moreover, high extraction costs in France were by no means entirely due to the quality and location of coal seams. The insufficient transport network forced many mines to operate below their minimum efficient scale and thus caused average costs to be higher than they could have been. Anzin also suffered from the poor quality of French machinery (Geiger 1974, 141). Even more important was the difficulty it faced in getting wood for propping. There were ample supplies in the Avesnes district, but "lack of water communications and poor roads between the two limited the access of the Avesnes timber to the dense industrial and agricultural population around Valenciennes" (Geiger 1974, 142). To be sure, the northern coalfield faced greater difficulties in this respect than other French coalfields, but it is instructive to see that extraction costs were far from being independent of transport costs.

I noted earlier that in the early part of the eighteenth century, collusion or the exercise of monopoly power raised the price and restricted the output of English coal, but that as the English system of transportation improved over the course of the century, the market for coal became increasingly competitive. In France, not surprisingly, competition among coalfields remained rare throughout the eighteenth century. It was really only in the next century that the small mines of the Centre began to face competition from the bigger mines in the Nord (Price 1981, 122). Though there were exceptions, France, even in the early nineteenth century, was divided into non-competing regions for coal (Dunham 1955, 98). Due to poor transport, then, French coal prices were higher and output lower than they might have been.

To sum up the discussion of coal, it was the poor French system of transport that made eighteenth-century French coal reserves appear to be of poor quality, poorly located, and insufficient. If France had possessed better transport facilities, she would have found that her coal reserves were more than sufficient to see her through the early stages of an industrial revolution.

IRON ORE

Any difficulties that France might have had with its coal supply were absent when it came to iron ore. France possessed nearly half of western Europe's ore reserves, and many times more than Germany or England.[23] Not only was France blessed with an abundant supply of ore, but it was generally of good quality (Dunham 1955, 120–1). Woronoff (1984) finds that on average French ore had a forty-five per cent metallic content. And it was easily mined. Ore near the surface formed the basis of French ironmaking (Woronoff 1984, 204). Galleries were used in Lorraine, and about half of the ore mined in Dauphiné was underground, but almost all other iron in France was strip-mined (Gille n.d., 76). Since mining was generally possible on the surface, little capital was required for plant and equipment. As a result, ore mined in France was one third to one half as expensive as that in England (Dunham 1955, 122). Costs of mining in French Lorraine were low compared to those in Germany, as well (Pounds 1957a, 190).

To be sure, much of this ore was found in small, scattered deposits. However, there was one major exception: in Lorraine France possessed the most valuable deposits in Europe. I mentioned earlier that Lorraine contained two types of ore which could be mixed. The most common was *minette* which had a high phosphorus content. It must not be thought, however, that Lorraine had to wait for the development of methods for the use of highly phosphoric ore in the later nineteenth century before the area became suitable for ironworks. First, in the eighteenth and early nineteenth centuries Lorraine had an abundance of *fer fort*. The Lorraine iron industry, with the exception of Hayange and Moyeuvre which used some *minette*, relied on *fer fort* (Prêcheur 1959, 151). However, the *minette* ore also played a role. The ore of the northern part of the *minette* field was calcareous, and thus useful for fluxing. It was often used for founding as well, and could be puddled and used to make agricultural implements; the southern *minette* was needed to make a liquid slag (Pounds 1957a, 189–91). *Minette* was indeed used considerably before the invention of the Gilchrist-Thomas method.[24] Lorraine possessed an abundance of *fer fort* with which substantial quantities of *minette* could be mixed to good effect. Therefore, there is no question that the Lorraine field was capable of supporting a massive iron industry given the right conditions. What was needed was an ability to bring together the various types of ore with the other necessary raw materials. It was transport difficulties that kept the Lorraine iron field, and indeed the French iron industry as a whole, from being all that it could be. If one remembers the amount of mixing that occurred in the English industry, it should be apparent that the scattered nature of France's other deposits need not have inhibited the large-scale production of quality iron. High costs of transport meant that only local ore was used by most ironmasters.[25]

Dunham, after noting that French ore could be mined for one third to one half the cost of English ore, goes on to say that by the time it reached the foundry, it cost as much or more (1955, 122). While Dunham speaks of the legal difficulties of transporting iron, one can see the signs of an inadequate transport network hindering the development of the French iron industry. Indeed, examples abound of the difficulties of getting ore to furnace or forge. The Intendant of Bordeaux complained in 1772 that pack-mules and asses were needed for the two lieues between the mines near Excedeuil and the forges near Thiviers (Gille n.d., 104–5). Woronoff (1984, 252–4), after discussing the sorry state of French rural roads, notes that the location of mines, forests, and works meant that pack-mules, and even men in some especially treacherous places, were often required; he notes that over 400 mules were required to do the work of thirty wagons. The forges of Limousin, far from the Perigord mines, faced difficult roads impassable for five months of the year (Gille n.d., 105). An 1811 enquiry found that transport usually accounted for thirty to sixty per cent of the cost of ore to ironworks (Woronoff 1984, 224). Even worse, some deposits were not used at all due to the high cost of reaching the market.[26] In addition, there is much evidence that inefficient mining techniques were used, as they were with coal (Woronoff 1984, 219).

Nor was the cost of transport only large in terms of the cost of ore. In 1831, Perdonnet estimated that the cost of transporting raw materials was one third to one half the cost of fabrication; the completion of a canal network by 1835 improved matters considerably (Gille 1969, 56). The situation could only have been worse in the eighteenth century. Though I have spoken only of fuel and iron, there were other necessary raw materials as well. In England, one saw that transport improvements were essential to ironworks requiring large quantities of bricks and limestone. In France, obtaining these raw materials long remained a grave problem to ironmasters. Indeed, some furnaces were constructed of inferior materials because brick was unavailable (Woronoff 1984, 269).

Iron Output and Scale of Operation

Estimates of French iron output during the eighteenth century are more difficult to arrive at than estimates for England. Nevertheless, it is clear that Henderson's hypothesis (1956) that French output at the time of the French Revolution was at least equal to that of England was correct. In fact, the best evidence suggests that in the 1780s, when English iron output was between 60,000 and 80,000 tons, French output was 130,000 to 140,000 tons (Crouzet 1967, 152). Morineau, in Wilson (1977, 170), has estimated an output of 150,000 tons for 1789. Thus, the fact that the French iron industry did not undergo the same transformation as its English counterpart cannot be blamed on the size of national output. It would be a mistake to view the French iron industry as naturally inferior to the English.

It must, of course, be remembered that the French iron industry served the needs of a much greater population spread over an area nearly four times the size of England. On a national basis, the output of the French iron industry was great enough to have supported a modern, large-scale, technologically progressive industry such as emerged in England.[27] On a per-capita basis, French output was much lower. The high cost of moving this bulky material was an important factor in the lower per-capita use of iron.[28] While the national industry might have been capable of change, the individual entrepreneur saw little need or opportunity to alter his methods of production. In large part, this was due to the geographical diffusion and small scale of the French iron industry at the time. Once again, the French transport system was the main cause of this state of affairs.

The French iron industry was much more evenly distributed than the English (Pounds 1957a, 32). Very few regions were lacking in either ore or charcoal. There was universal demand for iron but the difficulties of transport meant that demand had to be satisfied locally. A Bureau of Commerce survey in 1788–89 found that only a few parts of France with no timber at all, such as Provence or the Paris area, were without an ironworks of some kind (Pounds 1957b, 3–5). This situation was to last well into the nineteenth century, at which time "the building of a network of railways and the improvement and extension of the system of canals permitted the concentration of raw materials at a few points and the distribution from them of the finished iron and steel" (Pounds 1957a, 152). Geographical concentration, much less integration, could scarcely have been achieved at an earlier date primarily because transport difficulties forced the use of local resources and dependence on local markets (Price 1981, 114). At least one French ironmaster was forced to build and maintain his own roads between his works and markets (Bamford 1988, 120); this could be a partial solution at best.

One result of the diffusion of iron production in the eighteenth century was that many ironworks were unable to produce a high-quality output. While French ores in general were of good quality, there were exceptions. "French ironmasters relied too much on native ores which were not of the best quality" (Henderson 1954, 37). The iron produced in Périgord, for example, was of very poor quality, but the market for local ironworks was protected by inadequate transport facilities (Pound 1957a, 39). Not only were some local ores poor, but the best results, as already noted, can often be achieved only by mixing ores with different qualities. As long as each ironworks was compelled to use only the ore close at hand, all ironworks would produce an inferior quality of iron. By producing poor iron, they limited the uses to which that iron could be put and thus reduced the potential market for their output.

For my purposes, a more important characteristic of this geographical dispersion is the lack of competition that went along with it. Not only were French ironmasters protected by tariffs from foreign competition, but "even between French ironmasters themselves there was relatively little competition. Most of them had their own little markets into which rival products hardly penetrated owing to the poor state of communications" (Henderson 1954, 37). "The insufficiency of the road network was a guarantee, in each province, against imports from abroad or the rest of France" (Levainville 1922, 50). I will describe later how this lack of competition created an environment in which technological change was unlikely. At present, my concern is the connection between the lack of competition among ironworks and smallness of scale in the French iron industry.

"The partition of the market, for want of developed transport, favoured equally the small local forges, with higher prices" (Gille 1969, 86). If ironworks were unable to send their output to a large market, they would be forced to produce at a small scale. Bamford analyzes the case of Chaussade, a naval contractor in France, to see why he does not have the commercial success that the Crowleys had in England; he concludes that it is because the Crowleys had access to a national market while France was composed of virtually autonomous regional markets (1988, 239–43). It is not surprising, then, that the 1788–89 Bureau of Commerce survey found the average size of French ironworks to be much smaller than in England (Pounds 1957a, 34). Even in 1815, small establishments with ten or fewer workers dominated the French iron industry (Dunham 1955, 119).[29]

Difficulties in obtaining raw materials and getting the finished good to a wide market were not the only difficulties preventing the expansion in scale of French ironworks. The iron industry also suffered from the unreliability of the French transport system and the lack of modern methods of distribution. In 1788, the forge of Dainville in Champagne was forced to close thanks to the difficulty of getting its inputs and exporting its output (Gille n.d., 105). Closures of smaller ironworks due to an inability to obtain adequate supplies of raw materials occurred often. Poor communications did not allow for regularity of supply which large ironworks needed unless they held large inventories (Price 1981, 115). Inventories of several weeks were held as a result, though both fuel and semi-finished goods had to be stored under cover (Woronoff 1984, 254–72). Even at Le Creusot in 1830, transport problems continued to shackle the development of a large modern works (Gille 1969, 123–4). Ironworks, more than other industrial enterprises, suffer if operations are irregular because of the high costs of blowing in and out. While continuous operation was often impossible in any case, especially if the furnace relied on water power, nevertheless it would be extremely costly to run out of supplies while the furnace was working. Thus, as long as transport was untrustworthy, there was great incentive for ironworks to remain small, relying as much as possible on raw materials that were very close at hand.

French ironworks also suffered from an antiquated distribution system. Middlemen between forges and consumers remained an important force well into the nineteenth century, and fairs remained important as well (Vial 1967, 34; Woronoff 1984, 440). One saw in England that the establishment of direct and regular links with heavy users of iron was of critical importance in encouraging ironmasters to set up large-scale works. In France, a few select ironworks were blessed with such connections, generally through military demand. English producers had a great advantage over their French counterparts in their ability to maintain steady sales (Woronoff 1984, 443). The French iron industry lived for the most part in a world where indirect irregular sales were the rule, and was thus much less likely to entertain the idea of radically expanding its operations.

IRON INDUSTRY TECHNOLOGY

There was little change in the technology of the French iron industry from the sixteenth century through the eighteenth. All of the major technological innovations of this period were made in England and only slowly adopted in France. Observers recognized that the French industry was backward and had to import technology from England (Woronoff 1984, 315). Given that the French iron industry was much larger than the English, this result might at first appear puzzling. The explanation is to be sought at the level of the individual firm. In the literature, there are two common explanations for the fact that French ironmasters were not technologically innovative:

The limits to demand were also the main limits to technical innovation. Few modern enterprises could be created before communications were improved, and even where the market potential existed it was often difficult to raise the necessary capital. Moreover, the whole spirit of the small enterprises, their inertia, routine, desire for security and independence served as barriers to further investment. (Price 1981, 114)

Transport as a direct cause must loom large in any explanation of the technological stagnation of the French iron industry. As long as ironmasters served only a small market, they had little opportunity or incentive to change their way of doing business. Not surprisingly, when changes did come, they occurred along rivers or near Paris where there was competition (Price 1981, 110). One can well imagine that ironmasters in a competitive environment would be actively searching for ways to gain an edge on opponents. Others with a small local monopoly would be little interested in change. Also, as I will show, a transport system which rendered difficult access to raw materials that were needed for particular technological innovations would make the adoption of such technologies very slow.

The role of transport does not end with these obvious effects, though, for in fact the "conservatism" of French ironmasters was itself due to the environment in which they lived. Each works was in its own world. In England, ironmasters commonly visited other works, and there was a considerable flow of detailed information on technology throughout the industry. If improvements were made in one place, they could easily be transferred to another. In France, interaction between ironworks was much more limited. There was less regional specialization, and information flowed much less freely. Thus, individual ironworks naturally developed their own methods of operation. Diversity in furnace design was the rule at the start of the nineteenth century (Woronoff 1984, 268–71). Technological knowledge was passed from generation to generation among the skilled workmen. Lacking information on operations elsewhere, ironworks were loathe to tamper with methods that had been successful for generations. Even ironmasters who used "modern" methods of economic calculation still relied on traditional production practices (Woronoff 1970, 571). As long as methods of distribution remained archaic, the time and energy of ironmasters would be devoted to selling their output rather than tampering with production processes.[30] It was not that French ironmasters were innately less innovative than their English counterparts. It was that their ironworks were isolated, not only from markets and raw materials, but also from information of all kinds.[31] When Jars visited Burgundy to explain better methods of coking, he found that people there had not known that there was a better way, and that prejudice could be destroyed by facts (F12 1300 IV). The various forces that create an environment conducive to technological innovation were either absent or much weakened in France. Not only were there no innovations in France but the country also proved very slow in adopting technology developed elsewhere.[32] Iron bellows, a very simple innovation, were only introduced from Germany in 1793, and even then they spread very slowly (Woronoff 1984, 270). In what follows, I will look more closely at the two major innovations of the eighteenth-century English iron industry, coke-smelting and puddling and rolling, and examine not only why France did not develop these first, but why France was so slow to borrow this technology.

Coke-Smelting

The French government had been sending agents to England to learn the secrets of coke-smelting, and from 1775 on the government increasingly recognized that English methods had to be copied if the French industry were to survive (Ballot 1923, 436–7). The most famous of these agents, Jars, was then dispatched on a tour of France to convert ironmasters to the new technology. While the French Revolution limited technological transfer, France had had ample access to English technology in the previous thirty years through the movements of Jars, Wilkinson, and many others; even after there was some contact: Dobson moved to France in 1790, and at least one English prisoner of war and many Germans were put to work in French ironworks (Woronoff 1984, 315–17). Nevertheless, in the eighteenth century, only the government-supported Le Creusot produced coke-smelted pig and even it failed a few years after opening. Woronoff attributes the failure of Creusot to its being too far from materials and markets (1984, 339). Other ironmasters appear to have experimented unsuccessfully with coke-smelting but their efforts are shrouded in secrecy. English ironmasters could not be secretive for discoveries spread quickly in their concentrated well-integrated industry. French ironmasters, in attempting to prevent others from learning their secrets, guaranteed that new technology would be developed or adopted slowly, if at all.

However, it was only a small number of ironmasters who even showed interest in the new technology. Most appear to have been quite content with charcoal and used it in their furnaces, with some exceptions, through the early nineteenth century. It was seen before that French slowness in adopting the use of coke in France cannot be blamed on the quality of either coal or iron. Phosphorus caused some experiments to fail; since it was not expedient to transport materials long distances, it was risky to try the new technique using local ores (Woronoff 1984, 340). Nor, it would seem, can slow adoption be blamed on the peculiarities of previous French technology. Pounds (1957a, 73, 108–10) champions the idea that France was unable to use coke because of the small size of French furnaces; he hypothesizes that they needed to switch over to larger, English-style blast furnaces first. This is a curious idea given that the first successful uses of coke in England were accomplished in charcoal furnaces. In France, as in England, the use of coke in founding would spread earlier than the use of coke for wrought iron, though not until the nineteenth century (Fohlen 1975, 56–7). Certainly, to produce iron suitable for casting, charcoal furnaces seem to have been adequate in England. Naturally, as coke use spread, new furnaces were designed specifically for its use, and these were more efficient. This is not to deny that it should have been possible for French ironmasters to smelt with coke. Though some French ironworks were extremely primitive, there is no reason to suppose that French furnaces on the whole were radically inferior to their English counterparts. Woronoff, in examining the Michel brothers' ironworks, discovered evidence of an apparently successful experiment with coke in their furnace in 1802–03 (1970, 562). Yet the Michel brothers returned to the use of charcoal. Woronoff suggests that this was probably due either to the high cost of transporting coal or the distrust among their customers of coke-smelted iron. These are indeed the two most likely explanations, and I will look at them in turn.

I noted earlier that coal and ore often occurred in close proximity to each other but that French transport made it impossible to bring the two together. Naturally, this greatly inhibited the adoption of coke. "The charges resulting from mineral transport largely exceeded the economy which the English methods gave concerning the use of fuel" (Gille 1969, 93). Though France could have benefitted by switching some of its iron industry over to the use of coal, its transport system was such that the costs of transport swamped the potential saving involved.[33] It is not surprising that the switch to coke had to wait for nineteenth-century transport improvements, in Commentry and Mont-lucon after the completion of the Canal du Berry, and in the Nord in 1835–40 after the completion of a network of canals (Gille 1969, 93). In the 1850s, with the construction of railways, there was a further dramatic increase in the use of coke (Price 1981, 116).

The problems of transport were aggravated by the location of furnaces near forests and water power. They had easy access to wood, but not necessarily to coal. In England, the changes that occurred in the metal trades encouraged the construction of new furnaces, whose location and scale were more appropriate for the new technology. In France, incentives for the construction of new works were not nearly as great. Thus, coal had to compete with charcoal in the latter's home park. This naturally tipped the balance in favour of the continued use of charcoal.

The second factor hindering the use of coke in France was the prejudice exhibited against it by forgemasters and metalworkers. This is another example of French conservatism which can be explained by poor transport. As Fohlen notes, forgemasters were able to hold on to their prejudice as long as poor transport meant that there was little internal competition (1975, 146–7). People are more likely to stick with tradition when they are geographically isolated. Ironmasters were even likelier to stick with tradition as long as transport costs meant that coal was expensive for them to obtain.[34] But this was only part of the story. As in England, use of coke for purposes other than founding could only become widespread after changes had been made in the technology of forges. Thus, to understand fully why coke-smelting was adopted so slowly, it is also necessary to look at the reasons for the late introduction of English technology into French forges.

Puddling and Rolling

Puddling and rolling may have been experimented with in the eighteenth century at Le Creusot but its successful adoption had to wait until two decades into the nineteenth century. In part, this can be blamed on the political turmoil of the time. Only a few years passed between the success of Cort and the onset of the French Revolution. However, Dobson introduced puddling and rolling to France in 1800 and 1803, though nobody copied him (Woronoff 1984, 343). Even if the French Revolution does explain, at least in part, the delayed acceptance of puddling and rolling in France, it cannot explain why there were no previous changes in French technology nor why earlier English improvements to the technology of forges were not adopted. As noted in the previous chapter, Cort's success was the culmination of decades of effort by numerous researchers. The competitive markets and interaction between ironmasters that stimulated this English inventiveness was lacking in France. Not only were French ironmasters unlikely to innovate on their own; they were unlikely to become acquainted enough with the innovations of others to consider their adoption. The reverberatory furnace, though experimented with in 1764, was virtually unknown in France (Gille n.d., 100). Rolling mills were almost as rare. In part, then, the slow adoption of puddling and rolling in France can be blamed on the failure to adopt earlier technologies which became constituent parts of puddling and rolling.

This is not to say that there was no pressure to change in France. I have already discussed the mistaken logic in the claim that England developed the use of coal earlier than France because she was running out of wood. France faced a similar situation with regard to wood supply. In some areas, there was considerable concern in government circles about the state of forests and pressure was put on ironmasters to economize. The difference in France was that, due to poor transport links, coal was not a readily accessible alternative. The location of forges in forested areas only exacerbated this problem. The Intendant of Bourges in 1783 asked if it would be possible for the forges of Danzy to use coal; he was told that it was possible to get coal to within four or five "lieues" of the forge but that the last stretch ran along bad roads impassable for much of the year (Gille n.d., 105). As long as transport made coal prohibitively expensive, any pressure resulting from problems with the wood supply would not lead to the investigation of alternative fuels. Foregemasters in the next century might recognize that the switch to coal was inevitable, but they also recognized that it would not happen until there was a significant cost advantage (Woronoff 1984, 348–9).

In sum, then, the failure to adopt or even investigate any of the technological improvements which would culminate in the puddling and rolling process cannot just be blamed on political instability or an abundance of wood. Instead, the answer is to be found in the isolation of French forges and the high cost of transporting coal. As transport improvements in the nineteenth century alleviated both problems, the way quickly opened for puddling and rolling to become predominant. In turn, the increased use of advanced technology in forges paved the way for the increased use of coke in smelting.

Steam Engines

France adopted the steam engine as slowly as she adopted other English technology. There were a few Newcomen engines in France, but the fact that in 1765 Jars included a careful description of a Newcomen pump seen in Newcastle in his account of a government-sponsored trip to England to study English technology indicates that the Newcomen engine could not have been widely used in France (Henderson 1954, 44). The Watt engine was imported to France in 1781, but its adoption was slow. The Periers set up a steam engine factory in the 1780s, but it was converted to the production of armaments during the war. The first good statistics on steam engine use date from 1835 (Payen, 1985), but some information is available for earlier periods. In 1810, Perier estimated that there were 200 steam engines in France, compared to 5000 in England (Henderson 1954, 45). The 200 were almost all in coal mines. Even in 1815, only 15 industrial establishments had steam engines (Fohlen 1970, 142). In the late 1830s the sectors which used steam engines the most were textiles and metals and mining (Payen 1986, 37), so these are the two whose development was potentially most delayed.

The main reason for this minimal use of the steam engine was the cost of obtaining coal.[35] In 1834, a Commission of Inquiry reported that the principal obstacle to the general use of the steam engine was the lack of canals and roads, and the resulting high cost of transporting coal (Fohlen 1970, 141). The Alsace cotton industry used very little steam power until the completion of the Rhône-Rhine canal in 1833 allowed easy access to the coal of the Loire (Fohlen 1970, 144). Before the transport improvements of the nineteenth century, steam engines were almost exclusively limited to mining areas. Also inhibiting the use of steam engines were, on the one hand, the isolation and small scale of French industry,[36] and on the other, the poor quality of French iron and engineering.[37] Nor was the cost of transporting the steam engine itself trivial. In 1825, it cost 12,000 fr to transport a steam engine costing 136,000 fr to Imphy, and another 260,000 fr for installation. (Price 1981, 19). Transport costs at an earlier date would have accounted for an even larger proportion of total cost.

It would be a mistake to ascribe too much importance to France's abundant supplies of water power in explaining the slowness to adopt steam power. England, after all, had been well provided with sources of water power. One of the problems with water power is that it severely limits choice of location. Given the nature of France's transport system, it would have been highly advantageous for French industry to locate near raw materials or markets. The need to seek out a location suitable for the use of water power often rendered access to both materials and markets difficult. In addition, differences in water power facilities contributed to the diversity observed in French ironworks (Woronoff 1984, 263–4).

It is instructive to consider the technology of water power. In 1824, Fourneyon followed the work of others and developed the hydraulic turbine which greatly increased the efficiency of water power. In the eighteenth century, though, Rees claimed that while the overshot wheel predominated in England, the less efficient undershot wheel was still in general use throughout the Continent ("Waterwheels"). In England, Smeaton and others had made a number of improvements to waterwheels. In France, again, isolated watermill operators proved uninterested in new technology, at least in the eighteenth century, and thus France could not fully capitalize on its water power resources.

SUMMARY

The poor quality of the French transport system hampered the modernization of the French iron industry in many ways. On the demand side, it prevented growth within the metal trades. While the total output of the French iron industry was quite respectable, the demand for iron remained localized and irregular. The only large scale purchaser of iron remained the government, and its demand was volatile. This situation was exacerbated by an archaic distribution system which relied on indirect links between producer and consumer. On the supply side, though France possessed both ore and coal, high transport costs prevented the two from being brought together. The continued reliance on charcoal limited the degree of concentration possible within the industry. Not only the high cost but also the unreliability of French transport limited the scale of French ironworks. The industry was thus characterized by small, isolated ironworks, and this, along with the high cost of obtaining the necessary raw materials, created an environment inhospitable to technological innovation. The slow adoption of the steam engine, itself due to similar circumstances, meant that industrial location decisions were severely constrained. This exacerbated the situation of the French iron industry, as well as of other industries.

CHAPTER FIVE

The English Textiles Industry

As with the iron industry, academic research on textiles has tended to concentrate on one or two stages of production – notably spinning and weaving – while other necessary stages on the path from raw material to finished good have been largely ignored. Technological and organizational change, however, occurred throughout the textile industry. The other stages of production did not simply react so as to rectify bottlenecks created by improvements in spinning and weaving: the timing of many improvements does not accord with a challenge and response framework.[1] Instead, a picture is created of pressures for change throughout the textile industry, and my task is to describe how improvements in English transport both allowed and induced these various changes.

A necessary first step is to give an overview of the whole process of production. I will concentrate mostly on the cotton industry throughout this chapter, for two reasons. First, the cotton industry undergoes by far the most dramatic transformation during this period, and is thus worthy of the closest scrutiny. Second, as the next chapter will show, the cotton industry allows for easier comparison of France and England than the other textiles do. Nevertheless, important changes occur in the other textile trades, and these will be discussed where appropriate. While falling cotton prices did cause problems for linen, silk, and wool, especially from 1790 (Edwards 1967, 32–4), they all had decent rates of growth through this period, and wool retained its predominance in English textile production until 1820. The growth rate of the cotton industry was phenomenal, "But the quantitative importance of cotton should not lead us to think that similar qualitative changes (in the organization of enterprises, or direct production of technologies) were not taking place elsewhere" (Brulard 1982, 112). Factories and new technology were not the exclusive privilege of cotton. Whether because of the suitability of the material for machinery, or because there was less agitation from workmen,[2] most new technology in this period was developed for cotton. The other textiles did adapt this technology to their own use, often quite rapidly. Moreover, they developed their own technology and cotton borrowed on occasion from its competitors. The failure to recognize the progress of wool and even linen is to miss the widespread nature of technological and organizational change during this period.

The cotton wool first had to be sorted into different qualities, and dirt and seeds had to be removed. The next step was batting, which opened up the cotton in preparation for the later stages. The other textiles had similar preparatory processes. Wool, after the picking out of extraneous objects, was scoured in running water and stale wine, then willeyed or beaten with rods to open up the staple, and then coated with grease to enable it to withstand manufacture.

Other important processes were necessary before spinning could commence, as well. Carding served to straighten the fibres out and place them side by side. Carding was often done in two stages. In the first stage, called scribbling, the cards used had very stout teeth. (In the worsted industry, the fibres were combed rather than carded.) Then, the fibres were drawn to create rovings of constant width, and to stretch the fibres and straighten them further. This stage was especially important for cotton, since the slivers had to be drawn out over and over before they were ready for spinning. If the slubbing created were not of consistent width – which could only be achieved by repeatedly joining slivers together and stretching them – then the result of mechanized spinning would be very uneven.

Spinning involved further drawing as well as the twisting together of the individual fibres in the slubbing so that they would form a strong thread. The spun yarn then had to be prepared either for warp or weft (unless it was destined for use as hosiery, lace, sewing thread, etc.) The yarn for warp had to be wound on spools, warped by being wound about two bars, sized to strengthen it by the addition of paste or glue, and then inserted in the loom carefully so that each thread had equal tension. The yarn for weft had to be wound on the spindle in such a way that it could be removed at a constant rate. It should be emphasized that the weaving process could not succeed for cotton or linen unless the warp was strengthened through dressing (being coated with a glutinous material).

After weaving, there was still much left to be done. Woolen cloth had to be fulled – the nap had to be raised – and sheared so that loose ends were removed and the cloth was smooth. Most cloth would then be bleached (in part to remove the grease and other substances put on earlier) and dyed. Often, wool was dyed before spinning (dyed in the wool), in which case the cloth was generally woven in a pattern, and bleaching and dying could be avoided. Rather than being simply dyed, much cloth was printed. Indeed, by 1792, sixty per cent of white cotton cloth was printed.

In the rest of this chapter, I will discuss first how improvements in transport did, in fact, lead to changes in methods of distribution, wider markets, and better access to raw materials for the textile industry. I will then describe the impact of these changes on regional specialization, division of labour, and the emergence of workshops. For the latter, it is important to show how widespread the phenomenon of the workshop was, not only in different textiles sectors, but at various stages of production.

I then move on to discuss technology. While my main aim is to relate technology to transport, it is important to establish that there were many independent technological advances in various stages of production. While some instances of challenge and response can be discerned, they cannot explain all of the developments I describe.[3] Instead, it is best to view the textile industry of the period as advancing on many fronts simultaneously. It must be remembered that the few great inventions that dominate most historical discussion in no way tell the whole story:

It is justly observed by Mr. Bannatyne that though it is in most cases possible to point out with tolerable precision the period when any considerable improvement was introduced into the spinning or weaving of cotton, it is not possible to exhibit in a similar manner the constant progress that has been going on in the better construction of the different parts of the machinery, and in the skill and dexterity of the workmen. But the operation of this gradual process is such that it has frequently been found that the quantity of work performed by a machine that had been considered perfect has in a few years been doubled or tripled. (McCulloch 1827, 18)

In turn, I will discuss carding, slubbing, spinning, dressing, weaving, fulling and shearing, bleaching, dyeing, and printing. I will also look at the hosiery industry and finally, the introduction of steam power.

CHANGES IN THE TEXTILE INDUSTRY

Methods of Distribution

Even though historical work tends to concentrate on production,[4] it is well documented that major changes took place in the methods by which textiles were distributed in the eighteenth century. Guest speaks of the Manchester trade in about 1740: "After the fustians were manufactured the merchants dyed them and then carried them to the principal towns in England on packhorses, opening their packs and selling to the shopkeepers as they went along" (1823, 8). Improvements in transport in the early part of the century gradually meant that, for the first time, correspondence with customers outside the main towns was possible; by the 1730s many West Country clothiers sold their whole output in rural areas (Mann 1971, 85). The Yorkshire wool industry functioned in much the same manner. Here, putting-out was much less common[5]; instead, merchants would travel about England with packhorses to sell their wares (Heaton 1965, 383).

The big transformation occurred in the middle of the century. "Instead of travelling with their goods on packhorses, the merchants or their travellers now rode from town to town, carrying with them patterns or samples, and on their return home the goods sold during the journey were forwarded by the carriers' wagons" (Guest 1823, 11). Smaller traders who could not afford their own rider "might entrust their pattern to a traveller who acted as an agent for other manufacturers of different commodities" (Mann 1971, 85). As noted in chapter 1, Aikin dated this transformation to between 1740 and 1770, and pointed out that it was due to turnpikes and professional carriers. Many other authors noted the transformation as well.[6] It is worth mentioning that the same changes that took place with finished goods also occurred in the marketing of intermediate goods. "A popular method of selling yarn was for the spinner to develop direct contacts with the weavers. Strutt sold a great deal of yarn direct to customers" (Edwards 1967, 132). He employed salesmen as far away as Scotland to obtain orders for this yarn.

London wholesalers had long played a role in the textile trade, buying from many manufacturers and then providing provincial drapers with a range of goods. While London retained this role for some time, inland trade separate from London traders became increasingly common as transport improved (Wilson 1973). Not only was it losing ground to salesmen operating directly for merchant-manufacturers, but it was also being eclipsed by a few large centres, especially in the north. Manufacturers in Manchester and a few other large towns would often hold auctions, or hold sale days on which provincial drapers could come and inspect products and place orders.[7] Such methods of sale could only exist if provincial drapers from a wide area could easily reach these towns. Warehousemen in other towns would send orders to textile manufacturers and then sell the goods in the same fashion. Often, this involved warehousemen asking manufacturers to produce particular types of goods, especially when it came to Lancashire printers

(Edwards, 156–9). London wholesalers retained their role as intermediary but no longer needed to handle the goods personally. Orders would be received from the provincial drapers and passed on to the manufacturer, who would dispatch the goods to the draper. At the tail-end of the eighteenth century a further change took place. Manufacturers over time ceased to involve themselves in retail marketing at all; that role fell increasingly to regional factors who would place orders with various manufacturers, and run their own local sales organization (Edwards, 171).

In many ways, then, transport improvements induced a number of changes in the way goods were sold. These all tended to reduce the cost of distribution and thus widen the market. They eased the pressure on manufacturers to devote so much time and effort to sales and allowed them to concentrate more on production. Also, face-to-face sales were replaced by sale by sample, which steadily increased the pressure to produce a standardized good. This last point is worth emphasizing.

In the later eighteenth century, "The manufacturers could standardize their main lines, and the drapers were able to take large orders at regular and stated intervals" (Edwards, 31).[8] This circumstance made it much easier for a manufacturer to set up a large-scale manufactury for he could contract in advance to sell his output. In order to do this, of course, he had to be able to produce many units of the same good, and this he could not accomplish unless he gathered his workers together. In weaving, it was difficult for one weaver to produce even cloth before the power loom: "The best hand weavers seldom produce a piece of uniform evenness; indeed it is next to impossible for them to do so, because a weaker or stronger blow with the lathe immediately alters the thickness of the cloth, and after an interruption of some hours the most experienced weaver finds it difficult to recommence with a blow of precisely the same force as the one with which he left off. In steam looms, the lathe gives a steady, certain blow, and when once regulated by the engineer, moves with the greatest precision from the beginning to the end of the piece" (Guest 1823, 46). It would be impossible for two weavers in different houses to produce cloth of equal thickness. Thus, the desire to standardize created pressure to gather workers together, and then to mechanize further. Both organization and technology would be required to change.

Weaving was not the only stage where standardization required concentration. The same was true of all stages of production. Heaton (1965, 339) discusses spinning: "it was well nigh impossible to secure uniformity of yarn. The clothier asked for a definite standard when giving out the wool to be spun, but the tendency would be for each house and each spinner to vary a little in the thickness and firmness of the yarn;

some sent in hard-twisted, others soft-twisted, and it was very difficult to reduce the work to one standard." In addition to allowing for standardization, gathering workers together also allowed for better quality control, and this became increasingly important as methods of distribution changed.[9]

There were limits to the degree of standardization that could occur. "Throughout these years cotton spinners found it necessary to produce a wide variety of counts" (Edwards, 121). Only as markets widened could firms come to specialize in a narrow range of goods. This process occurred slowly, but the expansion in production of finer yarns, which had been impracticable earlier in the century, provides some evidence that specialization increased as markets widened. As different counts required different qualities of cotton wool, the ability to specialize also lessened the inventory problem. Thus, while it might appear on the face of it that some merchant-manufacturers dealt with a very large market early in the century, the important issue is how large the market was for different types of output. The market-widening effects of improved transport had an important role to play.

Wider Markets

The transport improvements of the early eighteenth century greatly facilitated the trade of the textile producing regions, as historians writing in the later eighteenth century clearly recognized.[10] Improvements of this magnitude had to give individual manufacturers access to a wider market. As noted before, it had become possible in the early part of the century to serve the country market. On a national level, the fact that markets as far apart as London and Paisley reacted to price changes in the Manchester yarn market (Edwards, 138) is powerful evidence that manufacturers could deal with a national market.

The dramatic changes in cotton output would not have occurred had there been no potential market. Edwards ascribes a causal role to this: "At home a mass market for cottons emerged, which was the most stimulating influence on all sections of the trade" (7).[11] Yet it was seen that no dramatic increase in aggregate demand was possible. The only reasonable explanation is that the drop in the costs of transport and distribution was sufficient to increase the market for textiles greatly. This widening of the market allowed manufacturers to specialize while expanding their scale of operation, and opened the way for cost-saving measures which allowed output to expand even more.

In the nineteenth century, foreign markets would come to absorb most of the English cotton production but in the late eighteenth century, when major changes in organization and technology were introduced, this was not the case. Even as exports grew in importance over time, they suffered from the problem of instability. Thus, the national market was vital (Gregory 1982, 58). While exports may have been important to some manufacturers, the stable market necessary for supporting a large enterprise was found at home.[12] Furthermore, access to foreign markets was itself dependent on transport improvements. Watson described in detail how extending the Calder navigation would help the west Yorkshire woolen goods reach foreign markets.[13] Not only were the roads and waterways to Liverpool and Hull important, but it must be remembered that London remained the main port for exports, and most textiles for export were probably transported internally to London (Wadsworth 1965, 236–7).

Access to Raw Materials

By far the largest expense in textile manufacturing (after labour) was for the raw cotton, wool, silk, and flax, though a variety of other materials were far from insignificant. With cotton, it must be remembered that until technology developed to the point where all-cotton goods could be produced, the "cotton" industry produced a mixture of cotton and linen, and spent more on other fibres than on cotton.[14] In terms of cotton fibre, since the manufacturing areas were some distance from the ports, inland transport improvements could still have a significant impact on the price of cotton facing manufacturers, though it would be outweighed by the cost of international shipping.[15]

In the mid-eighteenth century, the bulk of imported cotton wool landed at London, and was then shipped internally to the manufacturing areas. "Until 1795, London remained the premier port for cotton ... In the winter months, bad roads and frozen canals often prevented cotton dispatched from London from reaching its destination in good time. This was fatal in a market which was subject to sudden price changes ... This is a recurrent theme in letters from Glasgow dealers to McConnel and Kennedy" (Edwards 1967, 107–8). If problems could arise late in the century on occasion, one can see that there must have been serious difficulties obtaining cotton supplies in Lancashire at a time when poor roads were the only connection with London.

In addition to major improvements in transport links to London, Lancashire benefitted from the rise of Liverpool. I showed earlier that the rise of new port facilities cannot be understood without reference to internal transport; Liverpool could not have grown so large had it not become closely connected with a vast hinterland.[16] The cost of obtaining cotton dropped further with the adoption of sales by sample, which removed the need for face-to-face meetings between manufacturer and broker.[17] "By 1800 Liverpool brokers were regularly sending samples of their stocks to the spinners" (Edwards, 123).[18]

Undoubtedly, similar progress was made with imports of linen and silk. For wool, most, though not all, of the basic raw material was supplied internally. It is important to recognize that Yorkshire itself produced very little wool, and this of very poor quality, and thus had to import most of its wool from the south of England, Scotland, Ireland, or the Continent (Heaton 1965, 329). Not only did transport improvements have a direct impact in lowering the cost of wool to manufacturers, but they may also have had an important indirect effect. The rapid growth of the West Riding wool industry would have been hampered if cross-breeding had not significantly improved wool output as well as quality (Jenkins 1982, 16). Cross-breeding is clearly an activity that would benefit from improved flows of information as well as of animals from one part of the country to another.

Other materials were necessary at various stages of production: soap for cleaning, grease to allow fibres to be handled by machinery, numerous materials for bleaching and dyeing. Especially with these last, the number of materials being used increased over the course of the century. Not surprisingly, they were often not to be found close to the place of manufacture. Fuller's earth, for example, a necessary material for the woolen manufacture, could only be obtained from Staffordshire, Kent, Surrey, Sussex, or Bedfordshire (Smith 1747, 475).

Some authors have suggested that the effect of the price of coal on the ultimate price of cloth was marginal (Jenkins 1982, 54) but there are reasons to believe this was far from the case. Certainly, once steam-powered machinery became important, the cost of coal loomed large for manufacturers, but even the cost of heating a factory was significant.[19] The activities of bleaching and dyeing required the use of fuel as well. Textile manufacturers could thus require considerable amounts of coal. Samuel Oldknow received at least 1300 tons of coal in the first six months of 1805 and was thus undoubtedly pleased to only pay 6s per ton (Oldknow Papers, 837). Beyond the direct expenses of employers, it must be remembered that coal was a large item in the budgets of workmen; hence inexpensive coal would lower the supply curve of labour and push down wage rates. Writers at the time certainly did not treat the question of coal lightly. In 1748, Morat, listing the advantages of Yorkshire, claimed that "provisions are cheaper, the poor more easily satisfied, and coals are very plentiful," while ten years later Massey confirmed that the cloth trades had moved "Northward where greater plenty of firing, and cheaper rates of other common necessities of life, or very small taxes, favour their increase much more than in our southern cities" (Gregory 1982, 48). Ure spoke of the Bridgewater Canal: "This is the most magnificent work of public utility ever executed by an individual ... The cotton trade of England is under peculiar obligation to this truly patriotic capitalist." The supply to Manchester of coal at 4d per cwt of 140 lbs. was "a circumstance which must have had an immense influence in expanding their industry during the last 75 years" (Ure 1836, 179).

Transport improvements allowed producers to obtain their various materials more reliably, as well. This would be of considerable importance in a world where the prices of some of these materials fluctuated greatly and where a number of different qualities of fibre might be required by one manufacturer. Potential factory owners would be much relieved to have close contact with their suppliers so that they could be confident of obtaining materials when needed, while better information flows would make them somewhat less subject to sudden price fluctuations.

Changes in Fashion

Over the course of the eighteenth century, England ceased to be a country where a few standard products dominated the market, and became a land where a wide range of products was produced to suit different tastes, and these tastes changed quickly.[20] On the broadest level there was a trend toward simplicity in clothing, and a shift away from silk and fustians toward muslins and calicoes. "Thus, from the late 1780s the fustian manufacturers were having to adapt themselves to the new conditions imposed by the market. Some of them went over to the production of calicoes and muslins; others had to reduce the scale of their undertakings or cut the wages paid to their workers" (Edwards 1967, 38).[21] While these trends were to spread to the Continent, they began in England.

More importantly, within the different types of textiles, a wide range of goods was produced. This change was well noted by contemporaries, though not always favourably. "Silks, cottons, and linens, combined in a thousand forms, and diversified by names without number, are now almost the universal wear, from her grace in the drawing room to the lowest scullion in the kitchen" (Tucker 1782, 9). One of the recurring themes in the *Annals of Manchester* (along with frequent mention of transport improvements) is the introduction of new textile trades to the area throughout the later part of the century. Aikin devotes eight pages to a description of various new textiles introduced over the years (1795, 157–65).

In the first chapter I discussed the beneficial effects of the introduction of new industries. Aikin describes how the introduction of new textiles involved and required various improvements in technique. The pressure to meet changes in taste would create great incentives to modify machinery,[22] and this inventive effort could easily have unforeseen effects on technology.

Along with the creation of new industries, the new world of fashion also had the effect of making industrialists sensitive to changes in tastes. Robert Peel, the Lancashire printer, took great pains to keep abreast of the London market. "Once a week he sat up all night with his pattern-drawer waiting to receive any new patterns which the London coach arriving at midnight might bring down" (Chapman 1981, 57). Items were printed with patriotic symbols and names to celebrate military victories during wartime. It was seen earlier that a desire to respond to fashion trends is one reason for centralized production. Beyond this it is also an incentive to the development of new technology. Hudson has described how worsted producers in the West Riding, catering to an increasingly fashion-conscious market at home and abroad, not only operated on a larger scale than their woolen counterparts, but invested more in tools and equipment so that they could respond more quickly to changes in demand (1981, 40).

Regional Specialization

The regional specialization of the textile trades, with the cotton industry centred on Lancashire and the woolen industry centred on the West Riding, is a commonly accepted characteristic of the Industrial Revolution period. It is important to emphasize that this specialization occurred, for the most part, before the age of great inventions.[23] Thus, the rise of the north cannot be attributed to the fortuitous occurrence of technological innovation there. Why, then, did it occur? Allen (1831 v.1, 186) pointed to the low cost of living, the industry of the inhabitants, and especially the low cost of coal. It was noted above that coal was much more important than might have been thought, even before the introduction of steam power. While one can see that Yorkshire had some advantages, the timing of the rise of Yorkshire has puzzled many historians. Only once it is recognized that the same process was occurring across industry in the mid-eighteenth century does the puzzle vanish. The slight advantage that Yorkshire possessed became of increasing importance as transport costs dropped. Yorkshire was able to invade markets previously served by others.[24]

Already by 1750 the fledgling cotton industry was concentrated in Lancashire and around Glasgow, though other areas had better access to the raw material (Wadsworth 1965, 171–2). The advantages of Lancashire included soft water, previous experience with linen, sources of water power, and abundant coal. Lancashire was able to take advantage of these due to transport improvements which allowed the raw materials to be obtained easily. She lacked iron, "but being at no great distance from the iron districts of Staffordshire, Warwickshire, Yorkshire, Furness, and Wales, with all of which it has ready communication by inland or coastal navigations, it is as abundantly and almost as cheaply supplied with this material as if the iron was got within its own boundaries" (Baines 1835, 85). Lancashire was able to add greatly to its own natural advantage by importing what it lacked from surrounding areas.[25] While this may not explain its success relative to the rest of England, it does point to why Lancashire was able to accomplish so much more than the Continental cotton industry.

Not only did particular counties come to dominate particular industries, but there was much specialization within industries. For example, "The Oldham, Ashton, and Stockport districts seem to have specialized in spinning – the last in reeled weft, the first two in harder spun cotton and twisted yarns for warps" (Wadsworth 1965, 275).

I showed earlier how regional specialization encouraged the centralization of work. It also aided technological development in a number of ways. It ensured that people within the region would turn their attention to technology. Thus, Ure describes Lancashire as a place "where the prospects of gain were most alluring, where the habits of this indoor occupation were mostly matured, and where the native spring of the mind had been long intensely bent upon it" (1836, 193). Regional specialization and urbanization also provided for the cross-fertilization of ideas essential to technological progress. "In the progress of these changes it was observed that much advantage was derived from the people associating together. Improvements in mechanism, and the means of putting these improvements to use, increased in proportion to the size of the village and its population" (Kennedy 1818, 11). In addition, technological advances flowed easily from one workplace to another, as shown by the spread of Wilson's improvement through the finishing trades: "The aversion of Lancashire manufacturers to publicity was hardly less than that of their French neighbours, and Wilson succeeded in keeping his dyeing and finishing processes secret for a time; but the concentration of the industry around a small centre tended much more to the diffusion of technical knowledge, in spite of efforts to confine the use of particular improvements to their inventors" (Wadsworth 1965, 202). Along with direct links to technology, regional specialization would also have an important indirect link through increasing the division of labour.

The Division of Labour

That many different tasks had to be performed to produce finished textiles was well recognized at the time: "Our manufacturing is divided into 50 distinct occupations, reckoning from the shearing of the fleece to the shipping the stuffs on board vessels for exportation, and the profit being thus divided into so many hands must be considered an essential advantage to this nation" (BL Add Ms 37889, 231).[26] As output expanded within particular regions, the degree to which labour was divided expanded. Increased division of labour was indeed the major factor in the growth of textile production before the Industrial Revolution (Coleman 1973, 8).

As the eighteenth century progressed, there was an increasingly wide market facing producers in Lancashire and Yorkshire, and this created an incentive to expand output. Naturally, there was a limit to the scope for division of labour within the family. "The next consideration was, could they get a neighbour to card or spin for them, they might be able to weave a still greater quantity" (Kennedy 1818, 5). As workers increasingly concentrated on one task, the scope for technological improvement was enhanced. Kennedy continues; "The attention of each being thus directed to fewer objects, they proceeded imperceptibly to improvements in the carding and spinning, by first introducing simple improvements in the hand instruments with which they performed these operations, till at length they arrived at a machine, which, though rude and ill constructed, enabled them to produce more in their respective families."[27]

Increasing division of labour also played a major role in bringing about the workshop. As it became necessary to transfer materials between a growing number of households, there was added incentive to gather workers together in one place. Baines recognized this:

The use of machinery was accompanied by a greater division of labour than existed in the primitive state of the manufacture; the material went through many more processes; and of course the loss of time and the risk of waste would have been much increased if its removal from house to house at every stage of production had been necessary. It became obvious that there were several important advantages in carrying on the numerous occupations of an extensive manufacture in the same building. Where water power was required it was economy to build one mill and put one water-wheel than several. This arrangement also enabled the master-spinner himself to superintend every stage of the manufacture; it gave him a greater security against the wasteful or fraudulent consumption of the material; it saved time in the transference of the work from hand to hand; and it prevented the extreme inconvenience which would have resulted from the failure of one class of workmen to perform their part when several other classes of workmen were dependent upon them. Another circumstance which made it advantageous to have a large number of machines in one manufactory was that mechanics must be employed on the spot to construct and repair the machinery, and that their time could not be fully occupied with only a few machines. (1835, 184–5)

A couple of points are worth emphasizing. As the work passed through a number of hands, it would become increasingly difficult to pinpoint responsibility for embezzlement or poor workmanship. The cost of closely inspecting the material at each stage could only be avoided if workers were gathered together and supervised. Supervision would also reduce the cost incurred when workers were left idle because others providing their inputs had not performed.

The significance of the need to repair machinery, especially in the early years of industrialization when wood and leather were the common building materials, has been neglected in the literature. Baines does not point out that the existence of specialized workers for repair and construction jobs was itself a further division of labour. Previously, spinners, weavers, and so on would often build and generally repair their own machinery. Only as an industry became concentrated in a particular locale would repairmen emerge. This would enhance the desirability of gathering machines together so the repairman could more easily perform his duties. This, in turn, would make it easier and more attractive to develop more complicated machinery that would be difficult for the average workman to repair.[28]

Of special significance is the emergence of machine-making firms during this period. As Lee has noted, the spectacular growth in the cotton trade could not have occurred without growth in engineering; machine makers are already listed in the Manchester Directory of 1772, and there was a great expansion in machine making by the end of the century (1972, 16–17). Newspapers in the 1770s provide evidence of many machine makers, and even of a tinplate worker specializing in rollers; a carding machine trade develops in Nottinghamshire from 1773, with sales to Yorkshire and Scotland (Wadsworth 1965, 493). While in the 1780s many machine makers were also manufacturers – indeed, this was the way some successful firms such as McConnell and Kennedy started – by the end of the century, most machine makers did only that.

Specialized machine makers could only emerge, of course, once regional specialization and transport improvements had occurred to the extent that a large number of firms could be served. These machine makers were able to make better machines at lower cost than could non-specialists. They were able to obtain the advantages of mass-production, while specializing in particular machines to suit different requirements of industry. Ure noted that the ability of English manufacturers to quickly and cheaply obtain quality machinery that would not break down was an important advantage over their counterparts on the Continent (1835, 37–8).[29] As machine making became increasingly specialized, special tools were designed for fashioning different parts,[30] which not only lowered the cost of production but increased the precision of the machinery.

Not only did it become possible to produce increasingly complex machines requiring even greater degrees of precision – and the advance of textile technology is more a story of tinkering until things worked than of brilliant insight – but the existence of competitive, specialized machine makers must have provided a powerful incentive for the development of new technology. Not only would this have served to inspire the major innovations of the period; it must be remembered that the number of small improvements of which virtually nothing is known had a greater effect on productivity than the handful of "great inventions." Engineering firms must continually have been trying to improve the machines they constructed in order to attract customers. The geographical concentration of the trade would make it impossible to monopolize the benefits of any improvement for long. In such an environment, technological advance is a natural occurrence.

Centralized Workshops

It is now increasingly recognized that centralized workplaces pre-dated the technological innovations that supposedly brought them forth. It is still worthwhile to note how widespread this phenomenon was within the textile industry. As Wadsworth and Mann put it, the mixed ancestry of the factory includes weaving sheds, the concentration of carding and weaving machines under one roof, and the growing size and complexity of finishing and printing works (1965, 303). This was not just the case in cotton; early workshops can easily be discerned in wool as well. Dyer, in 1757, appears to describe a workshop in Yorkshire in which scribbling, slubbing, and spinning were performed under one roof, perhaps for a parish workhouse (Bischoff 1842, 167). Jenkins and Ponting have found that large-scale workshops were less common, but not unknown, in the West Riding than in the West of England: "Unlike in the West of England there is not a great deal of evidence to suggest the widespread existence of large pre-machinery or machinery workshops. There is the occasional reference to quite large buildings housing hand processes but few clothiers seem to have been large enough to consider such investment necessary" (1982, 28–9).[31] Heaton is more generous in his appraisal: "Higher still in the industrial scale came the really big clothiers who were to be found in many parts, especially around Leeds, during the latter half of the eighteenth century. These men were large employers, and in the congregation of workpeople in their shops, they established miniature factories many years before the perfection of the power loom or the application of steam" (1985, 296). Whether one views the glass as half empty or half full is unimportant for my purposes; some manufacturers had clearly decided that it now made sense to gather their workmen under one roof throughout the textile industry. This trend is evidenced not only by these large establishments but by smaller ones as well. Whereas in the early eighteenth century one might find two looms together at most, it was no longer surprising, if still rare, to have five or six together in the late part of the century (Gregory, 90–6).[32]

Technological change did not produce these early workshops.[33] Indeed, it could be argued that some of the later innovations which supposedly required a factory were in fact applicable to the cottage setting as well. Arkwright's water frame could have been used domestically, but he only licensed it for large-scale use (Berg 1985, 236). This is not to say that there was no advantage in using the water frame in a centralized workplace. If, however, the factory system had not already shown its feasibility (and assuming, for the sake of argument, that Arkwright would still have developed the water frame), the new innovation could have been put to work in cottages.

If not for technology, then, why do these workshops emerge? Widening markets are part of the answer.[34] The need for standardization was clearly important. Chapman has noted that centralized production, where different processes were brought together for the purpose of supervision, was quite common before Arkwright in both the cotton and wool trades (1974, 470–2). Walker, interviewed by the Parliamentary Committee of 1806, noted that workers had been gathered together "on purpose to have [the work] near at hand, and to have it under our inspection every day, that we may see it spun to a proper length (*Report*, 1806)."

Atkinson considers that workshops emerged "principally to prevent embezzlement." This is a common explanation.[35] There is considerable evidence that the problem of embezzlement was becoming much worse in the eighteenth century. "The increase in the practice among spinners and weavers of defrauding their masters in new ways not employed, apparently, earlier in the century, prompted the Gloucester clothiers in 1774 to ask for renewed legislation with higher penalties" (Mann 1965, 114). The same occurred in the West Riding (Hudson 1981, 50). In some stages of production, part of the problem could be the use of more materials. Throughout the manufacture, however, the fact that larger markets were being served through new methods of distribution made it much more difficult to detect the frauds of individual workmen.

Hills has suggested that "From employing outworkers it was only a small step to placing these people under a common roof where they could be properly supervised and fraud detected" (1970, 26). It is worth remembering that this was not a simple step to take. Rural workers in cottages still had alternative employment which meant that they could be employed in a more flexible manner and paid somewhat lower wages than urban factory hands. Moreover, the vanguard of factory entrepreneurs had to solve problems of organization which had never arisen previously. Supervision to prevent fraud, achieve standardization, and ensure that material flowed efficiently from worker to worker was something new. Arkwright is often credited with being the first to solve the problem of workshop organization, "But many years of indefatigable effort passed over the inventor's head before the system was completed to his mind – scarcely a week being barren of some valuable improvement" (Ure 1835, 228).[36] While Arkwright was undoubtedly a leader in developing ideas of workshop management, it is a mistake to think that he had started from scratch. Workshops were an innovation just like new technology, and developed in a similar manner. Different entrepreneurs experimented with new methods of organization until gradually a system emerged by which workers could be supervised. The workshop did not spring to life in its mature form, but was gradually improved over the course of decades.

From their inception, workshops proved to be a powerful influence on technological progress.[37] To reiterate a point made in chapter 1, "Once the dutch looms and swivel looms were commonly to be found collected in loomhouses, the idea of connecting them and running them by power would naturally occur to an inventor acquainted with the use of water power for turning silk-throwing machinery or the machines of bleach works" (Wadsworth 1965, 301). There were numerous other ways in which factories would aid the development of technology:

... nor would it be difficult to prove that the factories, to a certain extent at least, and in the present day, seem absolutely necessary to the wellbeing of the domestic system, supplying those very particulars wherein the domestic system must be acknowledged to be inherently defective; for it is obvious that the little master-manufacturers cannot afford, like the man who possesses considerable capital, to try the experiments which are requisite, and incur the risks and even losses which almost always occur in inventing and perfecting new articles of manufacture, or in carrying to a state of greater perfection articles already established ... Diligence, economy, and prudence are the requisites of his character, not invention, taste, and enterprise, nor would he be warranted in hazarding the loss of any part of his small capital ... The owner of a factory, on the contrary, being commonly possessed of a large capital, and having all his workers employed under his own immediate superintendence, may make experiments, hazard speculation, invent shorter or better modes of performing old processes, may introduce new articles, and improve and perfect old ones, thus giving the range to his taste and fancy, and, thereby alone, enabling our manufacturers to stand the competition with their commercial rivals in other countries ... The history of almost all our other manufactures, in which great improvements have been made of late years, in some cases at an immense expense, and after numbers of unsuccessful experiments, strikingly illustrates and enforces the above remarks. (*Report* 1806, 12–13)

TECHNOLOGICAL DEVELOPMENTS

Carding

I shall begin this discussion by noting that the earliest preparatory processes were not without technical improvement in the eighteenth century. For example, "In the year 1797 a new machine for cleaning cotton was constructed by Mr. Snodgrass and first used at Johnston near Paisley by Messrs. Houston and Co." (Kennedy 1818, 18). In the early nineteenth century in Manchester, this machine was much improved upon. It could be used on all but the finest raw materials, and replaced the previous labour-intensive process of beating with switches.

"The carding engine was not invented at once nor by any particular individual but was the result of a succession of improvements made at various times and by different persons" (Guest 1823, 18). Rather than Arkwright's carding engine being a response to a challenge from improved spinning machinery, the development of better carding machinery, if anything, pre-dated the developments in spinning. "The first of these improvements was in the carding, by means of which one boy or girl could work two pairs of stock cards, so as to produce more than they did formerly. This continued for a short period when further improvements followed, until one person could work four or five pairs, by holding hand cards against stock cards fixed to a cylinder revolving on its axis, now called a carding machine, the inventor of which we have no account of. It was, however, partially in use, in this rude state about sixty years ago" (Kennedy 1818, 6–7).

Most of the elements of Arkwright's machine can be seen in Paul's patents of 1748, except for the mechanisms for feeding and taking off the wool after carding. Many small improvements over the years must greatly have improved the state of carding before Arkwright put the finishing touches on his machine.[38] His major contribution was the comb and crank for taking the cotton wool off the machine, so that the machine could work continuously. Even this improvement appears to have been in existence before Arkwright, however. Wadsworth and Mann think that it can be traced to Paul, that it had already undergone a number of improvements, and that it was in common use (1965, 486–7). The feeder had been developed by Lees of Manchester in 1772, though Arkwright improved it (Baines, 176).

Arkwright did not so much come up with a blinding new insight as bring together a number of previous insights in a new improved form: a less exciting but still essential task. The carding engine had evolved slowly for decades. Most of the various improvements took place in Lancashire, many in Manchester. The regional concentration of the cotton industry and the development of specialized machine-making interests must have aided the process immeasurably. The fact that carding had long taken place in centralized workshops must also have greatly stimulated the gradual development of machinery suited to such a setting.

Of importance as well was the fact that the making of cards had become concentrated in the Calder Valley with its centre at Brighouse. The makers of cards were in close contact with producers in both Lancashire and Yorkshire. Benjamin Gott received a letter from a cardmaker asking for orders and offering to visit Leeds to consult with Gott (Crump 1929, 202). As new types of cards were required, these cardmakers would endeavour to respond, and the proximity of cardmakers to each other would aid the process of improving the cards themselves. As well, this cardmaking district served as a major conduit through which developments in carding were transmitted between Yorkshire and Lancashire. It was indeed one of the main routes through which knowledge of Arkwright's machine spread quickly to Yorkshire (Crump 1929, 8). Earlier, it would have facilitated the combination of techniques used in wool and cotton.

While carding technology was quickly transmitted to the Yorkshire worsted industry, the woolen industry relied on combing, and here, too, improvements were made. Edmund Cartwright developed a combing machine in 1792 which was so successful that the woolcombers petitioned Parliament in 1794 for protection from the machine. Davison and Hawkley wrote to Cartwright in 1800, that "In answer to your favour of the 18th instant, we estimate our savings from the use of your patent combing machines at full £4500 per annum. This, if necessary, we would verify on oath. It is our opinion that the saving to the trade in general by the use of your machines, and the piracy of yours, now amounts to from £25,000 to £30,000 annually; and that, when they are universally adopted it will exceed £1,200,000 per annum" (Cartwright 1800, 46–7). Cartwright was not alone in making improvements. Rees describes a 1796 patent for making better combs from ivory ("Combing").

Slubbing

The 1770s saw not only improvements in carding, but major improvements in slubbing as well. Without improvements in slubbing, the mechanization of spinning would have been impossible, for unless an even roving was produced, spinning machinery would be unable to produce an even thread. The slubbing billy, when developed, in turn required that the carding engine produce continuous slivers suitable for the billy. Focusing on any one stage of the operation glosses over the fact that the machinery developed during this period had to be compatible with other machinery.

Since slubbing is a quite similar operation to spinning itself, it is not surprising that the two technologies developed together. The slubbing billy had similar parts to the jenny, "but they are differently arranged to adapt it to spin the wool as it comes from the carding machine, in the state of cardings, which are locks of wool drawn out to about the size of candles and from two to three feet in length. For this purpose, the spindles are made to travel on the carriage, and the clasps stand still, being the reverse of the jenny" (Rees, "Spinning").

The progression of slubbing machinery follows that of spinning machinery. Yet it must be recognized that many modifications had to be made to the spinning machinery to make it suitable for slubbing. These modifications, undertaken in general by different men than those who developed the spinning machinery, were essential for the spinning machinery itself to function.

Spinning

The many improvements in spinning technology seen in the late eighteenth century cannot simply be ascribed to the pressure created by improvements in weaving. While any drop in the cost of weaving would stimulate efforts to increase spinning output, so, too, would a drop in the cost of transport (of both raw materials and finished goods) and distribution. Master spinners had first responded to these influences by hiring more hand spinners, but the difficulties of supervising ever larger groups of workers led to centralization and the development of new technology.[39]

The resulting technological improvements were the product of more than a handful of inventors. "It should be recollected that thousands of ingenious contrivances have been tried and laid aside before spinning machines were brought to their present state of perfection" (Kennedy 1818, 20).[40] In the regions where textile trades were concentrated, news of these various attempts would reach other potential inventors and stimulate their efforts until eventually a workable improvement would be developed.

Among the early attempts that provided insight for later inventors was the machine associated with the names Paul and Wyatt. It is still unclear what the role of the two men was in the undertaking, though it would appear that Paul was the main contributor. The two were among the first to respond to the new environment facing the English textile trades from the middle of the eighteenth century. To their misfortune, they may have been slightly ahead of their time. They could not yet take advantage of new methods of distribution. Wyatt spent much of his time either in London or travelling about Lancashire to sell his yarn. "If Wyatt could have applied himself as closely to the perfecting and direction of his new machinery, and to the arrangements in his mill, as Arkwright afterwards did – finding someone to make known and dispose of his yarn – the great impetus to the cotton manufacture might have been given thirty years earlier ... The inventor soon after examined the state of the undertaking and found great deficiency and neglect in the management" (Baines 1835, ch. 8).

One of the advantages of the machine was that it would make a more standardized product, but this had not yet become a necessity. While tens of thousands of pounds were spent on the machine, it was not enough to make it workable. "No doubt the idea of roller spinning would have been developed as it was later by Arkwright had the demand for yarn been such as to induce people to sink capital into the enterprise; but it was not until about 1760 that the demand for more and better quality yarn grew really consistent" (Wells 1935, 60). If Paul and Wyatt had waited a decade or two, their names might well be as familiar to schoolchildren as Arkwright's is.

As they left it, the Wyatt-Paul machine was a long way from perfection.[41] It differed in important respects from later construction. One problem it possessed was that, whereas hand-spinners could regulate speed such that drawing and twisting could be accomplished simultaneously, machine-spinning required that they be done separately (Hills 1979, 118). Nevertheless, it did introduce the use of rollers to spinning. It cannot be proven without doubt that Arkwright knew of this previous attempt. However, it would be a great coincidence if two similar inventions were developed decades apart in the same part of the world.[42] Moreover, it is clear that there were people, such as Highs, who were in contact both with Wyatt and Paul and with Arkwright. The concentration of industry and ease of travel which characterize the mid-eighteenth century must have ensured that knowledge of Wyatt and Paul was widespread.[43]

"It was in these surroundings, in which improvements in methods of spinning were freely talked of, and the abortive experiments which have been described must have been known to many people, that Hargreaves and Arkwright produced their famous inventions" (Wadsworth 1965, 476). Compared to Arkwright or Crompton, very little is known of

Hargreaves' development of the jenny, so one can add little to the information that he lived in a time and place where many people were devoting considerable time and effort to spinning improvements. After his success, the efforts of others were intensified. "No sooner had it been seen what a simple mechanical contrivance could effect than the attention of the most ingenious men was immediately drawn to the subject; and the path was opened, by the following which so many splendid inventions and discoveries have been made" (McCulloch 1827, 5). The jenny spread fast – indeed, Hargreaves was unable to patent the innovation because it came so quickly into common use.[44] Not only was it common in Lancashire by the 1780s, but it passed to the Yorkshire woolen industry rapidly as well. A more diffuse textile industry would have seen neither the rapid diffusion of new technology nor the degree to which inventive activity was stimulated toward further innovation.

We know a bit more about the genesis of Arkwright's inventions. He had grown up in an area dominated by the linen manufacture and had thus naturally turned his attention to it (BL Add MS 6671). As a barber, he had travelled widely, and had thus likely been exposed to a variety of ideas concerning spinning machinery. He may have received inspiration from the use of rollers in the iron industry, as perhaps had Wyatt and Crompton (Ure 1836, 254). Even if he had no direct knowledge of Wyatt and Paul, he must have been aware of the widespread efforts to develop their ideas.[45]

Indeed, as with his carding engine, Arkwright performs the role of combining the ideas of others in a new and successful way. He may have been the first to place the rollers the appropriate distance apart, and to weight them so that the twist would not run through the rollers (Hills 1979, 121), but the other essentials of the machine can be traced to other sources. This does not mean that Arkwright's task was easy; the essence of innovation is to bring various ideas together in a workable manner. "The difficulty, delay, and expense which attended the completing of the invention, prove at the very least that Arkwright did not receive it from any other person a perfect machine" (Baines, 153). "The difficulties which Arkwright experienced before he could bring his machine into use, even after its construction was sufficiently perfect to demonstrate its value, would perhaps have forever retarded its completion" (BL Add MS 6671). The development of a workable water frame required a great deal of money, and would not have been possible if manufacturers such as Strutt had not seen the utility of such a machine to the extent of being willing to supply large sums of money.[46] Arkwright himself claimed that it had cost him and his partners £12,000 before they saw any return from the invention. Along with the need for capital, Arkwright required all along the aid of carpenters and other skilled craftsmen in fashioning his machines.[47] In Nottingham, "there had grown up with the framework knitting industry a class of skilled mechanics such as were generally difficult to obtain at a time when engineering as we know it was still in its infancy" (Wells 1935, 62).

As with the jenny, the water frame spread quickly. In the first few years, it was necessary for a couple of other people to use it successfully before more were willing to invest; there was also a need for improved carding machinery before the water frame could produce a decent output (Baines 1835, 170). By 1780, however, there were twenty water frame factories, and after Arkwright's patent expired in 1785, the number of such establishments reached 150 by 1790 (Guest 1823, 31).[48] In a country where manufacturers were not in such close contact with each other, this innovation would have spread much more slowly.

The water frame spun yarn suitable for the warp, but thread suitable for weft for fine goods could not have borne the pull of the rollers on the water frame. Crompton's mule never subjected the yarn to much stress and thus allowed for mechanized spinning of the weft for fine as well as coarse goods. "The twist and weft spun on the water frame and the jenny are coarse, and are chiefly used for strong goods, for thicksets, velveteens, fancy cards, and calicoes" (Guest 1823, 32).

The mule, as its name implies, was a hybrid of the jenny and the water frame. Though French (citing Kennedy) felt that the clumsiness of Crompton's roller construction was evidence that he did not know of the water frame, it would appear that the difference may be due to the fact that Arkwright had access to iron while Crompton worked with wood. Crompton might not perhaps have seen the water frame, but he must at least have been aware of the many attempts to use rollers for spinning.

The combining of these two ideas did not happen overnight. "It was in the year 1774, Samuel Crompton being then only 21 years of age, that he commenced the construction of the spinning machine that was ultimately called the mule ... and it took him five years to bring his improvement to maturity" (French 1859, 51). Crompton himself described the great deal of time and effort which he put into the mule, "having been four and a half years at least, wherein every moment of time and power of mind, as well as expense, which my other employment would permit, were devoted to this end, the having good wool to weave" (quoted in Baines 1835, 197).[49]

I noted earlier that a number of minor innovations of which little is known were of much greater importance than the handful of major inventions. This is clearly evidenced by the mule. Though in principle the mule was an excellent machine, the one produced by Crompton was a very rude piece of workmanship. Baines devotes several pages to a description of several improvements which greatly enhanced its efficiency (1835, 200–6). Replacing Crompton's wooden construction with iron was a major advance. Improved gearwork to control the rollers was another. The size of mules expanded dramatically, doubling or tripling the number of spindles per machine in the last decade of the century (Lee 1972, 19–20).[50] Strutt, as well as others, had begun work on the self-acting mule long before it was first made feasible in the 1790s – even then, it would take decades of advancement in engineering before the self-actor could become common.[51]

The advances discussed in this section were concentrated in the cotton industry. However, it would be a mistake to think that other textile sectors were uninterested in new technology. They showed their interest not only by developing technology suited to their own needs (as with woolcombing) but also by adapting cotton technology to suit their purposes. The short wool for making woolens could adapt cotton spinning technology fairly easily, whereas long wool for worsted and flax for linen, with longer and more irregular fibres, was less suitable to the new technology developed for cotton; "The spinning jenny, which was the same as that employed in the cotton manufacture, but somewhat larger, was introduced into Yorkshire from Lancashire about the year 1780 but did not become general till about three years afterward ... Before the year 1787 the old processes of carding by hand and spinning on the wheel were entirely discontinued in Yorkshire but it was some years before the new processes were generally introduced in the west of England" (Rees, "Wool").[52] In the 1790s, the cost of spinning in the Yorkshire woolen industry would drop from one and a half to two times that of weaving to only half of the cost (Von Tunzelman 1978, 244).

The jenny was poorly suited to worsted. The water frame was suitable to both woolens and worsteds, however, and modifications made soon after its invention allowed it to be applied to both trades (Allen 1831, v.1, 186). By the early 1800s, a satisfactory adaptation for worsted was available, the key modification being more widely spaced rollers. In the case of the mule, very nearly the same machine was used for woolens and, with some adaptations, for worsted as well (Rees, "Wool"). However, the jenny was generally thought to be better for woolens, and the water frame for worsteds, until decades into the nineteenth century.

Flax, by its nature, proved less amenable to machine-spinning. Nevertheless, in 1787, Kenfrew and Porthouse of Darlington invented a machine for spinning flax. Marshall of Leeds, seeing the advantages brought to the cotton industry by machinery, endeavoured to improve on this invention. Rimmer (1960) describes in detail the countless time-consuming and costly experiments that Marshall undertook. Interestingly, his success required that improvements be made to carding machines as well. He appears also to have visited scores of flax mills and a few cotton mills (Rimmer 1960, 57, 87), though we cannot know, of course, what useful information he may have gained on these visits. By 1792, Marshall was able to produce an acceptable yarn with his carding and spinning machines. A further great advance had to wait for the nineteenth century, when in 1825 Kay (following Girard) "showed that by steeping the flax for six hours the fibres were made more slippery and so could be drawn by machinery into finer threads" (Clow 1952, 169). However, a great deal had been accomplished in the eighteenth century.[53] By the end of the century, Leeds had become a centre of the flax-spinning industry and of the manufacture of the necessary machinery (Claphan 1963, 145). This machinery was steadily being improved.

The English silk industry fared less well than its competitors. Still, beyond a period in the 1780s and 1790s when it stagnated due to competition from cotton, the silk industry expanded through the late eighteenth and early nineteenth centuries, especially since it was able to replace Italian silk with imports from India. While the weaving of silk is the same as for other textiles, [54] it is spun quite differently. Indeed, the silkworm performs much of the necessary work, and silk-throwing becomes the easiest to mechanize. This had been accomplished centuries earlier in Italy. The story of Italian technology being brought covertly to England by Lombe in 1719 is well known. What is less well known is that silk-throwing mills were set up in other places, especially in the 1760s.[55] "Without the aid of these very curious and useful machines, it is not probable that half the number of people would ever have been employed in this country" (Bentley 1780, 3).

The silk industry, thus, was not entirely immune to technological change in the eighteenth century. However, beyond the introduction of silk-throwing, no other advances were made. In the second decade of the nineteenth century, many minor improvements would be made to the silk-throwing machine in England, but not in Italy or France (Porter 1831, 196). Until this late date, however, the English silk industry showed no tendency to innovate. Up to a point, this might have been expected, since the silk industry was much smaller than its rivals. There is more to the story however. The silk industry was centred in London, and it appears that producers there colluded to limit production[56] (foreign competition was severely limited by very high tariffs). The industry also suffered under regulations governing the wages of labour and the mode of production. The regulations ensured that there was no incentive to replace skilled with unskilled workers, and served as a "discouragement to all improvements in machinery" ("The Scotsman", 6 September 1823).

These regulations would have the tendency to "banish the trade from Spitalfields into the country where it may be carried on with freedom, and therefore with greater advantage and profit. Some branches of work are already done in the country at two thirds of the price for which they can be done under this act, and it is clear that there only for a time, or at least while this act continues in force, will every improvement in machinery be adopted" ("The Scotsman", 6 September 1823). The fact was that silk could have been far less expensively produced in the country than in London (see for example, A Citizen, 1765). Why, then, does one not see a greater movement of the industry into the country, where changes in methods of production would have been possible? Little research has been done on the silk industry, and our understanding of the eighteenth-century English textile industry would be much enhanced if an answer could be provided.

Dressing

Dressing involved coating the yarn with a glutinous material to cement the fibres and lay them close. For flax and cotton, but not wool or silk, it was necessary to give the yarn sufficient strength to bear the operation of weaving. Dressing had traditionally been applied on the loom, one portion at a time. This had meant that the loom had to be stopped often by the weaver, so that he could dress the next section. This clearly lowered the worker's productivity by forcing him to switch from one task to another. It also reduced the possibility of producing an even cloth, for the weaving was constantly interrupted. Without improvements in dressing, it is unlikely that cotton-weaving would have been automated, for it would be uneconomic to design a complex machine that would have to be turned off at regular intervals so that the dressing could be applied. Thus, the little noted innovations in dressing[57] – the development by Ratcliffe and Ross of a system whereby dressing could be done before weaving began, and Johnson's invention in 1803 of a machine for warping (winding the warp around two bars ready for the loom) and dressing – were of great importance. They allowed the production of better and less expensive cloth. Further, they paved the way for the later introduction of the power loom.

Weaving

Weaving did not see the same dramatic technological changes which are observed in spinning. Kennedy stated that, "With regard to the operation of weaving, I believe it will be admitted that it remains nearly the same as it was fifty or sixty years ago, or indeed at any period, or in any country where the people have been in the habit of weaving for subsistence; with the difference only of the application of the fly-shuttle" (1818, 4). This is an exaggeration.[58] The relative lack of inventiveness in the late eighteenth century would appear to fit poorly with a simple challenge and response view of the textile industry. First, we get an advance in weaving – the flying shuttle – at a time when one weaver already took the output of many spinners; then we see a series of spinning innovations which put increasing pressure on weaving; eventually we see slowly adopted a weaving innovation – the power loom, which could not process the fine yarn produced by the mule. The simple alternation of innovation at different stages which challenge and response would predict is not obvious.

Kay's flying shuttle, which allowed one man to operate a loom previously requiring two, was introduced in 1738. Though originating in Lancashire, it spread first in the woolen industry. It was widely used in the 1760s and 1770s and was certainly common in Leeds before 1780. In the 1760s, it was increasingly adapted to the cotton industry. Robert Kay added an important improvement in 1760. This was the drop box which allowed up to three shuttles (with different coloured yarn) to be used.

The idea of the power loom had attracted a great deal of interest. It was travelling through the manufacturing area and discussing with others the possibility of applying machinery to weaving as had been done with spinning, that first interested Cartwright in the scheme (Cartwright 1843, 54–6). Cartwright, like other inventors, went through a long period of difficulty in the early days. While partly due to managerial inexperience (see Cartwright, ch. 2), it must in large part have stemmed from the inherent difficulty of making practicable a complex piece of machinery. After the completion of the machine in 1787, there was a further long period during which it spread slowly. "This arose partly from the imperfections that originally attached to the machine, but chiefly from the circumstances of its being necessary to dress the webs from time to time after they were put into the loom, which made it impossible for one person to do more than attend to one loom" (McCulloch 1823, 17). Not only did the widespread adoption of the power loom[59] await improvements in dressing, but the loom underwent considerable revision itself. Baines (1835, 231) describes a number of improvements made by various people in the 1790s and early 1800s.

The weaving of textiles was not unchanged by technology in the late eighteenth century. The flying shuttle, though an earlier invention, became widespread during this period, and underwent at least one important improvement. The power loom, while not in common use until the nineteenth century, was the object of much effort in the last quarter of the eighteenth century. The insights gained into weaving and the preparation of yarn for the loom paved the way for a revolution in weaving in the nineteenth century.

Fulling and Shearing

After weaving, woolen cloth had to undergo the processes of fulling and shearing. Fulling involved submerging the cloth in a solution containing fullers earth (sometimes replaced with pig dung) and then beating it repeatedly to raise the nap. Loose threads and so on were then sheared off to leave a smooth cloth. Both of these tasks could be very labour intensive, but they also had the potential to be mechanized.

The gig mill appears to have been known of for centuries for use with coarse cloth. An expensive set-up capable of dealing with vast amounts of cloth, one would expect the gig mill to become common once regional specialization had advanced to a sufficient extent.[60] It is not surprising, then, to see gig mills spreading through Yorkshire from the 1750s on (Gregory 1982, 87). In Leeds, Lancashire, and the west of England, however, workers, by means of sabotage, succeeded in preventing widespread adoption of the gig mill for decades.[61] The gig mill seems to have undergone little change in the eighteenth century; in the nineteenth, wooden stocks were replaced by iron and attempts were made to pipe steam through the stocks to the cloth (Mann 1971, 293).

John Harner of Sheffield obtained patents in 1787 and 1794 for a shearing frame. Initially, the frame saved little time, but it could achieve as high a quality as all but the best of shearmen (Mann, 149). This machine, after the improvements wrought under the second patent, did come into wide use, proof in itself of its utility. Many minor improvements made in the next decade increased its labour-saving abilities. The outcome of these efforts would be the rotary shearing frame (forerunner of the lawnmower) which would cut costs significantly while improving the quality of the cloth. The shearing frame spread despite outcries from shearers.[62] The hostility encountered by both gig mill and shearing frame is evidence of the saving in labour effected by the two developments. Jenkins and Ponting argue that growth of the wool industry was limited in the 1780s and 1790s by a shortage of fulling mills (1982, 27). If labour-saving innovations had not been introduced in this stage of production as well, English textile output could not have expanded as it did in the eighteenth and nineteenth centuries.

Bleaching

Wolff has observed that, "While there are whole shelves of studies about the spinning machine, the loom, the steam engine, and everything associated with the revolutionary changes in the technology of textile making, there is very little indeed on the finishing of textiles to make them fit for the consumer" (1974, 144). Yet, especially once fashion markets emerged, good finishing – bleaching, dyeing, and printing – had a major impact on the saleability of goods. Further, the speed with which these tasks could be performed would determine how quickly changes in taste could be responded to. Changes within the finishing trades were of great importance in the eighteenth century. Their concentration in Manchester was the main reason for the town's rise as the commercial centre of the cotton industry. In terms of technology, "No sections displayed greater advances in the third quarter of the century than those of bleaching, dyeing, printing, and finishing" (Wadsworth 1965, 306).

In the early eighteenth century, bleaching suffered from two great drawbacks: it was slow and uneven. It took six to eight months to perform, and different bleachers – bleaching was a small-scale operation – would produce quite different outcomes.[63] Not surprisingly, pressures for standardization and speed would spur a search for technological improvements to the process.[64] As with other stages of production, technological answers were not to be found easily. "To cut through the traditional methods required capital and enterprise in experiment and research" (Wadsworth 1965, 306). While support was forthcoming from governments in Scotland, Ireland and on the Continent, progress in England depended on the entrepreneur's response to new incentives.

The first major change in bleaching occurred in the 1750s with the introduction of sulphuric acid. Without requiring modifications in the equipment of the industry, sulphuric acid reduced bleaching time from eight to four months. What allowed this change was an increase in output and a dramatic drop in the price of sulphuric acid itself. It is not clear whether the idea of obtaining acid from the combustion of sulphur originated in England or in France, but it was first employed successfully in England. Sulphuric acid was used by druggists, metal refiners, various metal trades, hatters, dyers, and printers, as well as bleachers. Whereas sulphuric acid had previously been produced in small amounts, in the 1740s large-scale production facilities emerge to serve this market. The Clows argue that, "Considering the state of the roads in England in the middle of the eighteenth century, sulphuric acid must have been a load only transported with considerable risk" (1952, 133). Knowing how much better roads had become by that period, one can see how conducive transport improvements must have been to the emergence of large-scale plants.[65] Associated with the increase in scale was a beneficial switch from glass to lead vessels, which further aided the drop in price to under one per cent of its previous level over a period of decades.

Another significant development occurred in about the middle of the century. After clothing had been bleached it was desirable to make the surface glossy so that it would be more attractive. Just before 1750, hot calendaring was introduced. This involved passing the cloth through heated iron rollers (yet another use of rollers). This, along with other advances in the finishing trades, greatly enhanced the quality of the product.

The next great improvement was the introduction of chlorine. This is one development which does owe much to the advance of science, though not, significantly, to English science. Chlorine had been discovered by Scheele of Sweden in 1774, and its usefulness for bleaching by Berthollet of France in 1785.[66] This second discovery was known within a year in England, where it would be greatly improved, much more so than in France. Gittins describes the costly process of early experimentation with chlorine (1979, 202). Bleachers continued to experiment because of the promise of huge savings in time as well as in labour. They were gradually successful in introducing chlorine into bleaching, for cotton at first, and for linen later. The process now took only a couple of days instead of months. Moreover, it could be done throughout the year. Such a system fit much better with new methods of distribution which were in place by this time. It also greatly decreased the cost of bleaching, which must have risen as the output of the various textiles increased. "Without this wonderful saving of time and capital, the quantity of cotton goods now manufactured could scarcely have been bleached" (Baines 1835, 249).

Chlorine was difficult to transport in its liquid state. One last improvement occurred at the very end of the century. Thanks at least to the efforts of Tennant and Mackintosh, an easily transported bleaching powder was developed by combining lime with chlorine. Individual bleachers no longer had to manufacture their own bleach.[67] Rees' description indicates not only how widespread the effort had been to develop such a powder, but how negative a role science had played: "Simple as the combination of the lime with the oxygenated muriatic acid [chlorine] may now appear, yet it was a long time attempted in vain; but this perhaps will not be such a matter of surprise when we reflect that the French chemists whose opinions were regarded generally as law by the common bleachers, and whose treatises on the subject were almost the only accounts published, considered lime as no farther useful in bleaching than in absorbing the carbonic acid or fixed air usually combined with alkalis or ashes" ("Bleaching").

Dyeing

Though frequently ignored in the literature, dyeing could often cost more than the production of the undyed cloth, take longer, and involve the use of more raw materials by weight (Fairlie 1964, 489). Wool and silk, as animal fibres, were easier to dye than cotton and linen. Thus, the dyeing of wool had earlier attained a degree of perfection. Cotton was quite different. In the early eighteenth century, blue was the only colour that could be achieved as well in England as it could in India. All other colours took poorly to the material. Dyeing was an art which over time had advanced through experimentation with local raw materials. Thus, many countries of the world excelled in the production of one or two colours. The task facing the English industry was to imitate dyes available to their competitors.

Though French science was more advanced, it was England and Scotland that excelled in the application of dyeing technology, thanks in part to Scottish government support and in part to extensive experimentation by manufacturers (Fairlie 1964, 507). In 1766–67, Dr. Williams of London successfully fulfilled a Society of Arts request for green and yellow dyes. The main challenge was to imitate the so-called "Turkey red" which remained a Levantine secret until late in the century. Its production in England was finally achieved by John Wilson of Manchester in 1786, after decades of effort.[68] Cudbear, another dyestuff suitable for a range of colours, was developed through a combination of traditional Scottish dyes.

In addition to developments in dyestuffs, Lancashire presided over the improvement of mordants – substances that would combine with the material and facilitate the adherence of the dye – during the late eighteenth century. The improvements were made through a process of trial and error, without knowledge of the chemical processes involved.[69] If patterns were to be produced on the cloth, it was necessary to protect some areas from the dye. This was done with citric acid in London and Scotland for some years, though it only caught on in Lancashire at the end of the century. Finally, Gott developed an improved method of applying dyes by making use of the steam engine. "Utilizing steam for heating, instead of individual fires, he carried out a long and expensive series of experiments in the dye house. Dyeing processes were, as has been just described, entirely empirical and extremely defective. Gott spent many thousands of pounds in research from which he evolved the most advantageous scheme of dyeing by steam instead of water" (Clow 1952, 220). In the last half of the century, then, a number of improvements had dramatically increased England's ability to produce attractively-coloured materials, especially cotton and linen. Such an accomplishment should not be ignored.

Printing

Cotton printing cost as much in 1787 as either spinning or weaving (Edwards 1967, 240). Beyond its role in the cost structure of the industry, printing was of major importance in determining the attractiveness of the final good. I discussed earlier in the chapter how the printing sector felt the pressure both to standardize and to be fashionable. Edwards attributes an important role to the latter. "This must have stimulated most of the manufacturers and printers to adopt new methods and designs, and to introduce improvements into their concerns ... The upper class market served as a constant challenge, and in responding to it the whole trade was able to mature rapidly" (1967, 47). It has been seen that more than just the upper class had become fashion conscious.

Printing had by its nature always involved a degree of specialization among its workers. Thus, even in the earlier eighteenth century, one saw large printworks, some with over a hundred employees, in England as well as on the Continent. Nevertheless, most printing was still being carried out in very small shops with only a handful of workers. The later eighteenth century would see the multiplication in England of large-scale printworks, within which labour would become highly specialized. This process was aided by regional concentration of the industry in Lancashire, and especially in Manchester. In the early eighteenth century, printing was carried out in London, but from mid-century on, as domestic cotton replaced imports, the industry was transferred. Manchester became the centre of the industry and a hotbed of technological change.[70]

There were a number of important technical developments in printing. "Calico printing has been the subject of modern improvements; which may be compared in importance with those in cotton spinning and bleaching; and most of these improvements have either originated or been improved and perfected in Lancashire" (Baines 1835, 264). Along with the better known innovations, the printers of Lancashire continually made minor modifications.[71] The first major development was picotage, a method of obtaining a pattern by inserting pins into the printing blocks. This was a quick and inexpensive way of responding to fashion changes, for new patterns could be produced without carving a new block. The next major improvement was the replacement of wooden blocks with copper plates. Copper plates may have been invented in Dublin, but Lancashire was where they were first widely used. They were a natural advance in an industry where large plants wished to produce large quantities of the same pattern. Wooden blocks wore quickly in use while copper plates could handle thousands of pieces. Copper plates were more expensive; they were only advantageous if a large market were served.

With copper plates as with wood, printing was a tedious task. A piece of calico twenty-eight yards long would require 448 applications of the block. "The grand improvement in the art was the invention of cylinder printing, which bears nearly the same relation in point of dispatch to block printing by hand, as throstle or mule spinning bears to the one-thread wheel" (Baines 1835, 265). One man and a boy could replace one hundred men.[72] This major improvement was not made overnight. It was patented by Bell of Scotland but first used successfully in Lancashire in 1785. "It cannot, however, be said that this was an absolutely new idea since the possibility of such a method of printing had been in the air for some time, and patents were taken out for machines" (Turnbull 1951, 50). "The cylinder printing machine was in fact the most spectacular breakthrough in a general innovative effort, which included other devices such as improved and mechanized blocks, and so on" (Bruland 1982, 109). Bell's machine was not immediately workable. The main problem was supplying an even flow of colour to the roller. The Peels experimented for years, and a couple of their workmen appear to have made the necessary modifications (Chapman 1981, 43). Later improvements would allow the printing of up to three different colours simultaneously.

The finishing trades were the only ones within textiles in which science might have been expected to play a major role. Yet it has been seen that almost all of the improvements were the result of trial and error, undertaken without knowledge of the chemical properties involved.[73] This was recognized by Thomas Henry, writing in 1785: "How few of the workmen employed in [the finishing trades] possess the least knowledge of the science to which their profession owes its origin and support! If random chance has stumbled on so many improvements, what might industry and experiences have effected, when guided by elementary knowledge? The misfortune is that few dyers are chemists and few chemists dyers. The chemist is often prevented from availing himself of the results of his experiments, by want of opportunities of repeating them at large; and the workman generally looks down with contempt on any proposals, the subject of which is new to him." He goes on to say, "Yet under all these disadvantages, I believe it will be confessed that the arts of dyeing and printing owe much of their recent progress to the improvements of men who have made chemistry their study" (Clow 1952, 198). However, outside of the introduction of chlorine itself, it is hard to see any important contribution made by chemistry to any of the finishing trades during the eighteenth century.

Hosiery

Not all textile production was aimed at producing woven cloth. A major outlet for yarn was the hosiery business. It is worth reviewing briefly some of the history of the hosiery industry, for the same changes visible elsewhere can be discerned here. The East Midlands counties of Nottingham, Leicester, and Derby became the centre of a trade previously focused in London, and accounted for seventy per cent of national output in 1750 and ninety per cent in 1770. This regional specialization having been accomplished by mid-century, the next decades witnessed concentration in fewer and fewer villages (Rogers 1981, 9). Transport improvements in the east Midlands enhanced the position of industry there as they had elsewhere.[74] Hosiery was changing from a luxury trade toward the mass production of standardized goods (Wells 1935, 54). The national market was gaining in importance over the foreign. Methods of distribution changed: goods were no longer sent through London; instead, manufacturers distributed goods themselves, sending riders with samples and receiving orders (Wells, 67). "As in all the domestic trades, particularly in those with valuable materials, embezzlement was the constant preoccupation of the employer"; Strutt helped found an association to punish embezzlers (Fitton 1958, 54).

Concentration of workers in workshops was common long before Arkwright's time, though most employers had only one workshop and most of their frames spread in groups of one to four in cottages (Chapman 1967, 34–7). "Hosiers contended that they got the work done better to their liking and were able to execute orders more promptly where the workers were under their supervision, which was particularly important in the higher quality trade and in the production of fancy goods where fashion changes were frequent and new lines were continually being introduced. There was also less chance of material being lost where it passed through fewer hands … there was always the question as to whether work brought in was up to the standard required by the hosier. A hose might be too small or too slack or perhaps soiled, for white silk was easily damaged in this way" (Wells 71, 81).

The environment was ripe for technological innovation. Over one hundred inventions are recorded in hosiery in the hundred years after 1730. The chief improvement was the invention of the stocking frame by Strutt, who had lived all his life in the hosiery-manufacturing area. The genesis of the invention is lost in legend but it appears that three or four people were involved at different stages (Fitton 1958, 24–5). Pilkington ascribes the idea of the frame to a worker named Roper, but credits Need and Strutt with the labour and ingenuity necessary for bringing it to maturity (1789, 173–4). He also notes that this innovation suggested improvements in the manufacture of mitts, lace, and a variety of figured goods. Several improvements to the stocking frame were rewarded by the Society of Arts in the 1760s.

The 1760s, 1770s, and 1780s witnessed a number of innovations in the hosiery industry (Wells 93; Chapman, 32). "In 1764 a device for making eyelet hole fabric was patented, and the first step taken towards a much more important achievement nearly twenty years later when print net was produced on the stocking frame. Velvet pile fabric and figured lace web came out in 1767 and 1769, followed by knotted work and twilled or plaited hose in 1776. An invention of a different kind, patented about the same time, was the warp machine, which, uniting the principles of the loom and the stocking frame, was superior to either in the range of patterns it made possible. It was still further improved in 1791 by the introduction of Dawson's wheels which made the working of the pattern automatic" (Wells, 92–3).[75]

Specialization, the introduction of new products, and technological innovation went hand in hand. "From the middle of the eighteenth century, major changes came over the industry in town and village alike. Technical changes on a small scale to the frames enabled increasing specialization of production; the machines were continually adapted to take new fibres and produce new designs, new meshes, and new garments. Fixed capital investment in the industry grew" (Rogers 1981, 10). "The constant introduction of new branches and new machinery stimulated a machine building industry which grew rapidly during the second half of the eighteenth century" (Chapman 1967, 29). Hosiers patronized those with the best machines, so framesmiths kept making improvements; hence technological progress was extraordinarily rapid from the middle of the eighteenth century. The vanguard of technological development was a small group of knitters and framesmiths living close to each other in Nottingham; those who left this circle ceased to contribute to the flow of ideas (Chapman, 29). The connection between regional specialization, machine-making firms, and technological innovation could not be clearer.

This burst of technological innovation could have little effect on the output of the industry until an adequate supply of suitable yarn could be obtained; the industry would expand greatly after there were improvements in spinning technology (Wells, 59). It is not just a coincidence that both Hargreaves and Arkwright spent a great deal of time in Nottingham. Earlier, I discussed the key role played by Strutt in supporting Arkwright. It is possible to trace a line of causation here similar to what was seen with the metal trades in chapter 3. Transport improvements stimulated changes in access to markets and methods of distribution, which in turn led to regional specialization, the emergence of new lines, the concentration of workers in workshops to respond to changes in fashion, the need for standardization, and the problem of embezzlement. These changes created an environment in which a number of important technological advances were made. This, in turn, meant that hosiers demanded both more and better yarn, and this clearly played a significant role in fostering improvements in spinning.

The Use of the Steam Engine

Where exactly does the steam engine fit into the story? Writers in the early nineteenth century credited it with great importance. "Had it not been for the accession of power and scientific mechanism, the cotton trade would have been stunted in its growth, and compared with its present state, must have become an object only of minor importance in a national view" (Kennedy 1818, 16–26). Ure further maintains that the steam engine "led those who were interested in the trade to make many and great improvements in their machines and apparatus for bleaching, dyeing, and printing, as well as spinning" (1936, 273–4). As shown in chapter 3, care must be taken not to exaggerate the shortage of water power. Newcomen engines were used to pump water above water wheels for textile mills. Moreover, it should be recognized that little power was required by the new machinery. McCulloch estimated that 350 spindles required only about one horsepower; few spinners were large enough to have need of a Watt engine of twelve or sixteen horsepower (Edwards 1967, 206). Nevertheless, it is clear that from about 1790, Watt's steam engine does start to play an important role. It did allow industrialists to locate near labour and materials rather than near water.[76] The regularity of motion attained in late eighteenth-century steam engines made them much better suited to driving machinery. Steam engines also heated plants so that fine yarn could be spun on the mule, thus increasing quality as well as quantity. It is clear that if this description of the textile industry was carried into the nineteenth century, the steam engine would play an important role.

Within the eighteenth century, however, the impact of Watt's invention was slight. From 1785, Watt rotation engines "began to be used in cotton mills in Nottinghamshire and Lancashire, though only at the rate of one or two a year until 1790" (Crump 1929, 13–14). Gott used one for wool in 1792, and Marshall had one for linen in 1794. "In summary, the steam engine had a belated effect on the spectacular expansion of the cotton industry in the last quarter of the eighteenth century, all the major technological breakthroughs in cotton spinning having been developed for other forms of power. The coupling of steam power to the major processes of cotton manufacture on a sizeable scale can be dated to the last few years of the eighteenth century" (Von Tunzelman 1978, 182–3).

Within the textile industry, I have shown how independent processes of innovation at different stages of production merged to form a unified system of mechanical production. The same occurred between textiles and other sectors. The greatest eighteenth-century innovations in textiles were designed for a world of water and Newcomen engines. The development of the Watt engine improved the capability of these inventions, and created potential for even further improvements in the next century. The same can be said of improvements in engineering which facilitated the construction of precision machinery. The merging of the advances discussed in chapter 3 with those outlined in this chapter set the stage for the nineteenth century.

SUMMARY

The textile industry benefitted from the various transport-induced changes outlined in the first chapter. New methods of distribution, wider markets, better access to raw materials, increased reliability and the emergence of new fashion markets affected all stages of production. Regional specialization, increasing division of labour, and centralized workshops were the result of these pressures in both the cotton and wool industries. Of particular importance was the emergence of specialized machine-making firms. Competition among such firms generated much of the technological innovation witnessed during the period. This point is best illustrated by the countless improvements that issued from firms in the hosiery trade. But it is also seen elsewhere, such as in cotton spinning.

The hosiery trade underwent many of the changes that affected textiles as a whole. There was regional concentration of the industry around mid-century, accompanied by division of labour and centralized workplaces. The industry faced pressures to standardize, but also to respond to changes in fashion. A large number of innovations were developed by Nottingham machine-makers to meet the needs of producers. The effects of improved transport on hosiery were transferred to other stages of production. Mechanized knitting required even yarn, and Nottingham hosiers played a substantial role in fostering the mechanization of carding and spinning.

Innovators in textiles, as elsewhere, did not leave detailed accounts of why they did what they did, and thus it is impossible to prove why particular innovations occurred. One can, however, still make a number of important points about the course of technological developments. The primary point must be that technological change occurred at various stages of production, in wool and linen as well as in cotton. These various innovations took decades to be developed. Thus, their development does not follow a single, sequential pattern; instead, they tend to occur simultaneously. This should eliminate the idea that one or two key innovations triggered everything else, especially when it is remembered that mechanization of one stage of production was often not feasible unless other stages were also mechanized. That is, spinning could not advance unless carding did, and the two developed simultaneously over a period of decades.

One can be confident, then, that England was not just lucky. There is one reason, or set of reasons, for the dramatic increase in the rate of technological innovation throughout the textile industry. The evidence that improved transport was the key is not conclusive – nothing can be. It is, however, much more convincing than the evidence favouring any alternative explanation.

I have already discussed the role played by machine-making firms in technological development. Such firms could only exist after a substantial degree of regional specialization had occurred. Regional specialization itself played a key role in providing incentives for innovation and increasing the contact between those interested in improvements. Growing division of labour enhanced the attractiveness of mechanization, made it easier to envision, and ensured that one set of workers would be devoted to one task. The centralization of workers was also key. It established a setting for which, and in which, new technology would be developed. People of the time noted the significance of these factors. One must recognize, moreover, that the aim of much of the new machinery was the production of standardized products, and I have shown why there were at exactly that time powerful incentives to achieve that goal. New technology also facilitated a quick response to changes in fashion. Proof of the role of these various forces cannot, of course, be found for every innovation. The fact that these positive factors clearly existed, and that people of the time commented on their importance, is powerful evidence that technological improvements in the eighteenth-century textile industry were to a large degree induced and allowed by previous transport improvements.

CHAPTER SIX

The French Textiles Industry

The relative importance of the four textile industries was different in France than in England. Silk was more important in France though its output was still much smaller than the output of the more common wool and linen. Cotton was much less important in France in the late eighteenth century than in England, but this difference is due to the incredible growth of the English cotton industry during the eighteenth century. It was seen in the last chapter that technological and organizational innovation occurred in wool and linen as well, though much more gradually than in cotton. The fact that these three sectors did not undergo the same changes provides more convincing evidence of a fundamental difference between France and England than the example of cotton alone. Still, as I will show, there is no obvious explanation, in terms of raw material access, for the slow growth (by English standards) of the French cotton industry. Nor is there any obvious reason why French tastes should have been less amenable to cotton. My purpose in this chapter is to show how the backwardness of French transport prevented all French textile industries from undergoing (or even borrowing) the changes that occurred in England. I will follow the same outline used in chapter 5, this time for the more difficult task of describing why something did not happen.

Methods of Distribution

Despite the relatively high value/bulk ratio of many textile products, the cost of transport still loomed large. Thus, methods of distribution that minimized necessary movement were chosen. "As long as transport was difficult, it was important to reduce the number of movements of people and goods necessary to the conclusion of exchanges" (Levy 1912, 257). The modern distribution system that had emerged at mid-century in England only started to appear in France late in the century. In Lyons, silk manufacturers were making trips to sell their wares in various parts of the Continent in the last days of the Ancien Régime (Mayet 1786, 14). Because of its reputation, buyers had previously been willing to undertake the expensive journey to and from Lyons to purchase goods. According to Mayet, it was only in the two decades before he wrote that Lyons manufacturers began to travel with their wares themselves. In both cases, he notes that the expense of distribution limited the market served by Lyons producers.

The Alsace cotton industry exhibits a similar pattern. It was seen in chapter 2 that fairs remained important in France long after they had become primarily social events in England. Throughout the Ancien Régime, Alsace manufacturers visited the fairs of France and of central Europe, (Levy 1912, 250). Only as transport improved in the nineteenth century would fairs lose their importance to the French cotton trade.[1] As in Lyons, one sees buyers visiting Alsace to purchase goods from local producers. Levy identified this as an intermediate stage between the primitive sales at fairs and the more advanced visits by sellers to buyers (Levy, 255–6). It is clearly quite different from the regular visits by some English drapers to the Peel warehouse to obtain the latest products. These buyers would make infrequent trips during which they might purchase goods to retail over the next year. It was a reaction to a world of high transport costs, the choice of distribution method being determined almost solely by the need to minimize these costs. The elimination of face-to-face selling was not to occur in the eighteenth-century Alsatian cotton industry.[2] Buyers either met producers at fairs or travelled to Alsace themselves.

The records of Oberkampf of Jouy provide a slightly more encouraging picture. Though customers still visited Jouy to make their choice, samples could also be sent to them for their perusal (Chapman and Chassagne 1981, 150). Still, even when the region they served was small (see below), firms would have difficulty corresponding with many of their customers. Thus, while there are some signs of change in the method of distributing French textiles, the bulk of the industry's output at century's end was distributed by means that had been obsolete in England for fifty years. This is evidenced by the fact that French producers generally continued to produce a wide range of goods. The important change in attitude observed in England, whereby producers ceased to concentrate on a high profit per unit and emphasized mass production instead, was not seen in eighteenth-century France (Léon 1976, 536–7). French producers did not face the same incentives to mass produce standardized goods as their English counterparts.

A Wider Market

As one might expect, the primitive distribution system, coupled with the backwardness of the transport system itself, imposed severe limits on the market area served by French textile producers. Despite the fact that the French internal market was more than three times larger than England's, and that France had easier access to most Continental markets, the French producer had a much smaller effective market than his English counterpart. "In aggregate no doubt the market for cheap textiles and household articles was large. The reason why this market was not tapped earlier and more rapidly by large scale producers is to be found primarily in the fragmentation of the market. Although thousands of kilometers of roads were built for the state during the century the rural population was still poorly served and transport of bulky goods of low value on the roads was prohibitively expensive over long distances" (Kemp 1971, 31). The situation was exacerbated in large parts of France by internal tariff barriers. Alsace, for example, had easier access to Germany than to France due to the high tariff wall separating it from the rest of the country (Levy 1912, 207).

Limited markets affected producers across the country. Even in the nineteenth century, the lack of good transport made it difficult for a factory to market any large quantity of silk (Dunham 1952, 173; he also speaks of credit scarcity). Mayet had complained in the late eighteenth century that high transport costs allowed high-cost producers to survive in many parts of Europe because lower cost Lyon producers could not advantageously reach those markets.[3] Though he speaks mainly of foreign markets, the same could be said of France. If silk could suffer in this way, the more common wool, linen, and cotton industries would be even more strongly affected. Butet described the efforts of an English company thirty years earlier to set up a factory in Bourges to produce printed cloth. They failed, and a handful of others had since followed and failed. He introduced the discussion by stating that "Bourges could be, if communications by land and water were made, an entrepôt which furnished to other lands a great number of goods" (an V, 18–19). He later said that the departement of Cher produced high-quality woolen goods and would be able to market them widely if there were good communications with other departments (37).

Limited market size may have contributed to the tendency in French industry to emphasize high-quality goods. A higher value/bulk ratio made it easier to bear the high costs of transportation. Even at this level there were problems. Oberkampf of Jouy had always produced higher quality goods and was unwilling to change this for fear of losing his good reputation. Despite its widespread reputation for quality, though, it appears that eighty per cent of the firm's sales in the 1790s were made to the north of a line from Rouen to Lyons (Chapman and Chassagne 1981, 150). While this is not a small area, it is noteworthy that three quarters of France remained almost untouched by one of the best-known manufacturers of the time.

Raw Materials

In France as in England, most wool and flax was obtained locally, though some was imported. There is no evidence that the French linen industry suffered from lower quality flax. French wool was better suited to some uses than English wool and worse suited to others.[4] One disadvantage for the French was their lesser ability to mix different types of wool, because of the higher cost of interregional transport. For the same reason, France could not benefit from closer access to Spanish wool. There is no clear climatic or geographic reason to suppose that French sheep may have been inferior to those of both England and Spain. Indeed, the fact that France spanned two climatic zones should have enabled it to cultivate and mix different types of wool. If French wool were in fact somewhat inferior, one would have to look beyond mere geography to such factors as insufficient information flows or a lack of cross-breeding.

In terms of silk, France should have had an advantage. For one thing, it was able to support silkworms itself, whereas England had to import all of its raw silk. Moreover, France was much closer to the major European producer, Italy. Lyons (and other silk processing centres) were not able to exploit these geographic advantages fully, however. "The rarety and excessive price of wagons influences in a very sensible manner the rarety and price of finished silk" (F12 1454, an III). Together with the costs of distribution discussed earlier, this must have hampered the development of the French silk industry severely.

Cotton had to be imported by both countries. As long as it was imported from the Levant, France should have had some advantage. Once Levantine cotton was replaced by Indian and American supplies, both countries had roughly equal access. Wadsworth and Mann (1965, 204) felt that the French cotton industry had access to better and cheaper raw materials than the English. Certainly, they should not have been at a disadvantage, at least during peacetime. The French industry suffered more from interruptions to supply during the Revolutionary–Napoleonic wars. They also were hurt by high tariffs imposed by the government (Chaptal 1819, 6). The main disadvantage suffered by France, though, occurred between port and producer. It was seen earlier that the development of Liverpool and of internal communications greatly aided the Lancashire cotton industry. Normandy lacked both a comparable port and comparable canals, rivers, and roads. Alsace suffered even more in this regard. Manufacturers there were forced by the government to import through French ports and could not, as a result, take advantage of shipping on the Rhine. This was not only expensive but it also introduced great delays and uncertainty because of the difficulty of transport along the Seine (Dunham 1952, 165–6). In the nineteenth century, the freight on a ton of cotton between Le Havre and Mulhouse ranged between ninety fr and 200 fr (Léon 1976, 255).

The textile producers needed other raw materials as well. Access to coal was poor compared to England,[5] as shown in chapter 4. In some districts near Montpelier, wool cloth was manufactured without the use of coal because of the expense of obtaining it (F12 2413, 1789). All regions of France suffered. Levy claimed that Alsace's relative success in copying English technology when compared to Normandy or Paris was due to the existence in Alsace of pure water, meadows, wood, coal, and access to the Rhine for transport. Yet he also noted that the biggest obstacles to the development of large-scale industry in Alsace were difficulty in getting raw materials, distance from markets, and the fertility of the soil (Levy 1912, 14–20). Even in the region most favoured by nature, textile producers had considerable difficulty in gathering the necessary materials.

Regional Specialization

It was earlier noted that there was some concentration of textiles manufacture in areas such as Alsace and Normandy, and the areas around Lyons for silk. This was much less than the degree of concentration achieved by English textiles during the eighteenth century. While the luxury end of the trade might be associated with particular centres, the production of common textiles was spread through the country, in thousands of villages and thousands of firms (Léon 1976, 544). Rees, in his article on wool, noted that "The circumstance of the coarse cloth manufacture being so widely spread over the country, tended also to prevent that degree of rivalry which promotes the spirit of improvement where manufactures are more concentrated." Roland attributed the backward state of the French cotton velvet manufacture to the distance between producers and to their deep suspicion of each other (Wadsworth 1965, 202). Only in the nineteenth century would the degree of regional specialization observed in England be achieved in France: Léon has described the eventual concentration of wool, linen, and cotton (1976, 557–8). While some regions gained, others would lose their textile industry; with the advent of railways, Languedoc came to specialize in wine, while the weak textile sector was overrun by competition from northern producers (Thomson 1982, 448–9).

Division of Labour

In England, it has been seen, one of the most important aspects of increasing division of labour was the emergence of specialized machine-making firms. The much slower emergence of similar operations in France is the most glaring evidence that division of labour could not proceed nearly as quickly in the geographically dispersed French textile industry as it had in England. As with technology in general, this lag occurred despite the presence of English machinemakers who had moved to France to set up shops (F12 2204). As late as the fall of Napoleon, France had only a few machine shops, and these were small and generally without power tools (Dunham 1955, 244). This, along with the slower development of the French iron industry, is responsible for the fact that the French were only beginning to switch to iron machinery decades after the English had done so. It also naturally con-tributed to the lack of innovation and the slow adoption of a variety of English machines.[6] There were close connections between English and French machinemakers and technology could potentially be transferred very quickly from one to the other (Dunham 1955, 247). However, the few French machinemakers did not deal with enough manufacturers to make the construction of various complex machines worthwhile. Nor did French manufacturers serve a wide enough market to make the use of such machinery attractive.[7]

Workshops

There were some large centralized workshops in late eighteenth-century France. "The industry was, however, far from having undergone any such transformation as had already taken place in England. The English workmen who were generally employed were not interested in training the French to succeed them, and the machines lacked the many small improvements which in England were continually being added by those who used them. The isolation of the French factories prevented com-petition from acting as a spur to greater efficiency, and the difficulties of obtaining capital, especially in the early days of the Revolution, con-tributed to restricting the number of machines" (Wadsworth 1965, 505). It would be a mistake to attribute organizational precocity to France because of the existence of a handful of factories. These workplaces could not and did not play a dynamic role in fostering technological innovation in France. Moreover, many were artificial creations of the

French government. The state helped in the development of several factories, where large numbers of weavers were gathered together, mainly to provide places for experiments with new machinery (Wadsworth, 202–3). These government efforts, it will be seen, were not successful in generating a technological revolution in French industry, and serve only to highlight the fact that most French entrepreneurs were uninterested in new technology.

Not only were there very few French textile workshops but the ones which did exist were inspired by the English precedent. That is, the problem was not simply that France was somewhat slower to develop than England. There is good reason to believe that, but for the English Industrial Revolution, French industry would have undergone no transformation at all. The provision of government aid bears this out. The state was determined that French industry keep pace with its English competitors. Private initiative also responded to the English example.[8] Visitors to England marvelled at the factories there, and some French entrepreneurs were induced to attempt to copy them. Since factories allowed English manufacturers to produce higher quality goods, the pressure on French manufacturers to duplicate the achievement was increased. Almost all of these early workshops relied on English supervision. In some cases, English managers and workers were imported by French manufacturers. I mentioned earlier that it took some time in England before managerial methods were devised to deal with large-scale works. Virtually every French workshop of the period relied on English expertise in organization as well as English familiarity with the latest technology. While the interaction between English and French workmen often proved to be fruitless in terms of transmitting either technological or organizational knowledge, it is nevertheless true that without access to English expertise the French transition to workshop production would have been much slower.

In the Alsace cotton industry, it was in the early nineteenth century that workers were first gathered together to any significant degree, to allow for supervision (Levy 1912, 156). The same is true of other regions and textiles.[9] While a few large works did emerge in the eighteenth century, most of the French textile industry slumbered on as before. Not only was it lagging far behind England but the small movement toward workshop production that one does observe had the English precedent to thank.

Technology

"The history of the introduction of machinery in the French cotton industry reduces itself almost exclusively to the introduction of English machinery" (Ballot 1923, 42). The same was true of wool and linen as well. French efforts at innovation generally proved unsuccessful during the period under study. The advantageous conditions for technological development in England were non-existent in France.[10] Inventors had little contact with each other; industry was widespread and small scale. Bruslé commented on the smallness of scale in the early nineteenth century: "The class of producers is composed entirely of workers without fortune; their position is an obstacle to the improvement of production because they cannot try the slightest experiments without ruining themselves" (Reddy 1984, 69). Undoubtedly some Frenchmen came up with good ideas during the eighteenth century. However, without assistance from others willing to put in the time and money[11] to translate an idea into a workable innovation, few of these ideas saw the light of day. Indeed, it will be seen that there was a significant degree of inventive effort in France. Lacking any reason to assume that French tinkerers were less competent than their English counterparts, one must conclude that the environment was less conducive to bringing new technology to fruition. The French problem went beyond an inability to develop new technology as fast as the English. The small-scale, dispersed French industry was hesitant to employ it.[12] Without the English example to guide them, French textiles producers were unlikely to come up with major innovations of their own at that time.

An alternative explanation of France's slowness in adopting English innovations would be that it simply took a long time to transmit these innovations to the Continent. It is true that workmen could not build the new machinery from drawings alone.[13] It was essential that machines and people familiar with their working move from England to France. Had England been successful in prohibiting such movements, this might be a convincing explanation. However, numerous Englishmen proved willing to move to France during the late eighteenth century, and often smuggled machinery with them. The lag between the emergence of a new machine in England and its introduction in France was usually a couple of years at most while the lag in widespread use would be counted in decades (Heywood, 1976).

Since mid-century, the French government had been sending agents to England to bring back English techniques. Englishmen such as the Holkers had moved to France in the same period to establish English methods of production. Clearly, the problem of French technological backwardness was widely recognized long before the French Revolution began.[14]

Preparatory Processes

I argued in chapter 5 that the introduction of mechanized spinning was dependent upon improvements in the preparatory processes. If carding and slubbing were not themselves mechanized, it would be impossible for spinning machines to produce an even thread. This fact was keenly felt by eighteenth-century French producers, who saw in it a major reason why so many efforts to mechanize spinning had failed. Holker recognized that existing methods of carding were incapable of supplying the new machines with uniform twist; mechanics would have to be trained to build carding machines before it could be hoped that spinning machines would spread (F12 2295, 1773). Bruslé also commented in 1778 on the critical role of carding: "When carding is well done, one gives to spinning a thread quite equal, solid, and proper to make good use of. On the other hand, if it is poorly made, one has a poor thread, unequal, and consequently little susceptible to forming a good cloth" (F12 2295). Modern English carding technology spread slowly in France,[15] and thus it is not at all surprising that the government's efforts to introduce mechanized spinning were largely unsuccessful.

The remaining question, of course, is why the preparatory processes remained backward for so long in France. The different relative weights of the various textiles in France cannot provide an answer. Wool was much more susceptible to the application of carding machines than to the application of spinning machines (Ballot 1923, 179). Thus, the smaller size of the French cotton industry cannot convincingly explain the slow adoption of carding machines in France. Nor is the transmission problem especially strong. Hay designed his new card-making machine in France, returned to England to perfect it, and then reintroduced the machine to France while living there from 1754–79 (Ballot, 480–1). Even the presence of the inventor could not hasten the spread of the machine. There were efforts in different parts of France to develop carding machinery. However, none of these resulted in a machine that compared well with English machines (F12 2195). One attempt is particularly instructive. Martin developed two simple machines to do the work of the complex Arkwright device. He did this because the Arkwright machine, despite its avowed success, often broke down (F12 2195, 1785). The French concern with this problem, which was not remarked on in England, suggests two possibilities. One is that French machine making was inferior to that in England.[16] As noted before, the process of division of labour in France was not as far advanced. Thus, specialized machine makers were relatively new. In England, a large number of machine makers were each able to concentrate on a narrow line of products. The French government reacted characteristically to this situation by paying to have machines built and sent to manufacturers around the country at government expense. This leads to the second possibility. Repair facilities would be nonexistent locally. Machine breakdown would be a much smaller problem in large-scale, regionally concentrated English industry than in the small-scale, dispersed industry of France. These two factors together go a long way toward explaining why Arkwright's machine was so slowly adopted south of the Channel. These same factors would hinder the development and spread of all types of machinery.

Spinning

In spinning, again, French attempts to develop machinery never achieved success, despite the claims of a number of Frenchmen that they had developed superior machinery. Barneville of Rouen developed a spinning machine in the 1750s. Ballot felt that the decades-long trials of this machine proved useless because it cost more than it was worth (1923, 63). L'Homond in 1787 complained bitterly that the French government had not supported his invention, and maintained that if the government had undertaken to send his machines to a few new establishments they would have been found superior to English machines. The government, however, concluded that his machine, while great in theory, functioned poorly in practice (F12 2413). Others with similar claims to superior machinery include Brison (F12 1412, 1774), Amanet (F12 2195, 1788), Maucel (F12 1340, 1786), and Millot (F12 1340, 1789). Some of these may simply have involved adaptations of English machines: Chaptal certainly felt that French technological efforts consisted of just such minor adjustments (1819, 16). While the government was supportive of these various efforts to some degree, it concluded in the end that French machines were inferior to English and devoted the bulk of its (still fairly unsuccessful) efforts to establishing English technology on French soil.

As noted in the first chapter, inventive effort is impossible to measure. Casual empiricism seems to indicate that relatively more English than French tinkerers gave their attention to new spinning technology, as the earlier theoretical discussion would lead one to expect. Unfortunately, one cannot be sure since unsuccessful tinkerers tend to be lost to history. The original efforts which we are aware of in France all failed. One is struck by the one-man nature of these efforts. The beneficial impact of interaction with other inventors, access to specialized craftsmen, and so on was severely limited in France. If one man could not take an idea through all of the stages leading to a commercially feasible machine almost exclusively under his own initiative, there was nobody else to pick up the pieces and carry on. English inventions were the result of many efforts over long periods of time. It is not surprising that the one-man efforts in France proved unsuccessful. French tinkerers were presumably as competent as the English, but operating in a vacuum they were almost doomed to failure. Such was the conclusion reached decades ago by Wadsworth and Mann:

It was not by accident that England led the way ... But the history of spinning machinery in France does not justify the belief that the machine would have met with anyone capable of improving it; and it is in the highest degree improbable that after it had been laid aside as useless the principle would have been taken up again and applied successfully by inventors drawn from the ranks of artisans and working manufacturers. One cannot avoid the conclusion that the new machinery spread quickly in England because the whole community was interested in it ... In France it was only the official class and the isolated and comparatively rich manufacturers of the *grande industrie* (many of whom were English) who were interested in foreign machines. (1965, 506)

The infertility of the French environment with respect to new technology is evidenced by the long delays in adopting English technology. In 1762 there were proposals to establish a works and school for wool spinning of the English type; similar proposals were made for cotton. It was noted that English superiority was only partly due to better English wool; with proper procedures the French could produce a good output. The English advantage was due in large part to the superiority of her tools (F12 1341). In 1773, it was observed in the *Mémoire Sur La Filature du Coton* that "Several years ago a cotton spinning machine was invented and put in use in England which had the advantage of greatly abridging the labour required and rendering the product more perfect than that of the ordinary spinning wheel" (F12 2295). Similar comments could be heard throughout the century.[17]

The spinning jenny, the first of the big three inventions in England, was also the first to be transmitted to France. "France had always managed to acquire successful English inventions; but their acclimatisation was a different matter"; the jenny was brought by Holker to France soon after its invention, but in 1776, "its use was confined to the workshops of the large and often state-aided manufactures" (Wadsworth 1965, 503). By 1787, there were still only 600 jennies in all of France, and most of these had been constructed at government expense (Reddy 1984, 52). Despite these government efforts, French industry continued to rely on hand processes; many manufactures supplied with jennies actually switched back (Ballot 1923, 45–9). The jenny was first applied to wool in about 1787. Contemporaries were aware of English successes such as Gott's mill and recognized that the French must adopt better carding and spinning machinery to compete in wool production. In 1790, the government paid for the translation of an English work on wool spinning (F12 1341). Still, only a few dozen machines existed in the wool industry by the end of the century (Ballot, 175–7). While French technology had been relatively backward before the jenny, the success of the English with this innovation, and the inability of the

French industry to adopt it, caused the French cotton and wool industries to fall far behind.[18]

Jacques-François Martin successfully smuggled Arkwright's water frame to France in 1783 (F12 2413). The Milnes soon after began constructing machines based on the Arkwright principle as well. Nevertheless, the machine crept slowly across France.[19] In the eighteenth century only a handful of works, all involving Englishmen in some capacity, employed the water frame. Only in the nineteenth century would it be used to a more significant extent.[20]

The mule was scarcely introduced at all to France within the eighteenth century. J.S. noted that while the mule had been known in France for a few years, its use had only begun to expand significantly five years earlier with the successful establishment of a mule factory by English workers (1803, 20–1). With all three famous inventions, then, France was decades behind in their adoption, though in each case the first machine was smuggled to France only a couple of years after its invention in England. At the start of the nineteenth century, both the cotton and wool spinning sectors were far behind.

As for linen, even the English had trouble in adopting the spinning machine to its use, but as earlier noted, they achieved some success before the last decade of the century. The last two decades saw a handful of unsuccessful attempts at producing machine-spun linen in France (Ballot 1923, 229). English machines were imported from an VI on but spread slowly.[21] While outside the scope of this study, it is instructive to follow the course of linen-spinning technology a bit farther into the nineteenth century. The breakthrough in flax spinning came in 1810 when the Frenchman Girard immersed the flax in a hot solution before spinning. His starting point was a desire to improve on the existing machinery imported from England (Ballot, 234). Over the next years he worked on improving his invention. One of the problems he faced in those years was that his establishment produced a wide variety of yarns so that his machine had to be continually adjusted (Dunham 1955, 296). He tried to sell his machines in 1815, but the government and others felt they were unfeasible. However, they were taken to England by a couple of his associates and quickly caught on there, with (according to Ballot) only a couple of minor adjustments. The invention was quickly claimed by Kay, and its success in England reinforced the idea that it was of English origin (Ballot, 214). Indeed, Girard's invention would not be successful in France until the late 1830s. Clearly, even in the early nineteenth century, and even in the linen industry, England provided more fertile ground for new technology than France. The question of what if Hargreaves or Crompton had been French could scarcely receive a better answer.

The many visits – often sponsored by the French government – of Englishmen to France, and Frenchmen to England,[22] ensured that English technology quickly became known across the Channel. Encouragement was also given to local inventors. Nonetheless, France was already decades behind England before the start of the French Revolution. The dispersed,[23] small-scale, unspecialized nature of French textiles was simply too hostile to technological innovation. The incentives to innovate were not as clear, the interaction between inventors nonexistent, access to specialized craftsmen difficult, and access to the financial support essential to critical revision almost impossible.

Weaving

France dragged its feet over English weaving improvements as well. The flying shuttle caught on very slowly indeed,[24] despite the fact that its inventor, Kay, brought the invention to France. "In England Kay met with jealousy and dislike, but the weavers after a good deal of preliminary grumbling pirated his invention. In France he was patronized by the government and given every facility for popularizing the fly shuttle but its use died out within a generation" (Wadsworth 1965, 465). The shuttle would have to be reintroduced in 1787 and would only become widespread during the Empire, over half a century later than in England. French weavers had a tendency to give up on the invention at the slightest problem, whereas weavers in England were willing to persevere with experiments until the machine worked (Wadsworth 1965, 469–70). Once again, it is clear that the efforts of one man are not sufficient to make an invention succeed. Others must be willing to improve upon the original idea. Even with government aid, the necessary interaction was lacking in France.

Cartwright's loom met the same fate. "In France, improvement of Cartwright's loom of 1785 began in 1804, the same year in which it was imported into Belgium, but progress was much slower than in England" (Dunham 1955, 270). In the cotton, wool, and linen sectors, France produced no new weaving apparatus during the eighteenth century. The net effect was that all three sectors entered the nineteenth century far behind England.

Some glimmer of success appears in the Lyons silk industry. Lyons was not the only centre of the French silk trade,[25] but silk was more concentrated than the production of other textiles. The convenient location of Lyons near France's better rivers led to the city's predominance within the industry.[26] There were of course other factors such as its supply of skilled labour which gave Lyons a comparative advantage, but reasonable access to transport facilities enabled the city to press its advantage over a wide area.[27] Earlier it was seen that the inefficiency of continental transport still served to limit market size. Nevertheless, natural advantages and the high value/bulk ratio of silk products combined to allow a large industry to emerge in Lyons. There was no comparison with Lancashire; but for France, this was an unusual concentration of a particular industry in a particular area. Lyons would thus present a somewhat more fertile environment for technological innovation than the rest of France.

Vaucanson developed a new machine in the 1770s after years of effort. Roland complained that this new machine was unfeasible. Ballot (1923, 322) notes that there is much merit in this accusation. Early attempts to use the machine failed; it was often replaced with Piedmontese machines. Still, others were willing to try to improve it. By the 1790s, the Jubies were successfully employing machines on the Vaucanson design in their business (Ballot, 327). This did not give the French an overwhelming technological advantage. Indeed, the English industry would be more technologically precocious in the nineteenth century.[28] Nevertheless, it does indicate that French craftsmen were capable of producing workable inventions given a conducive environment.

The most important French invention was the Jacquard loom, introduced in 1804, and it is worthwhile to venture briefly into the nineteenth century to discuss it. It shows again how the special circumstances of Lyons could produce a significant technological advance. Jacquard's loom was a machine that facilitated the operation of figure weaving – using different coloured threads to produce a design in the cloth. It was based in part on the previous machines of Vaucanson, Falcon, Bouchon, Ponson, and Verzier, and perhaps others (Ballot 1923, 371–2, 380–1). There is no evidence that any of these men were familiar with the English draw-loom, which accomplished the same task in a costlier manner.[29] However, given that information about other inventions reached France very quickly, it is certainly possible that the draw-loom was known. In any case, the first model produced by Jacquard, while astonishing those who saw it, was not ready for commercial use. The key to the loom was a series of cardboard cards with holes in them. In a manner similar to the reading of computer cards, the loom would respond to the holes in the cards by raising one thread over another, thus determining which colour would be prominent. Simple in theory, it required a great deal of precision in practice. Jacquard got down to it in a workshop in Lyons, where he was visited by prominent manufacturers with suggestions, and probably the necessary money (Ballot, 373). In the workshop itself he was never isolated, but always had two workmen to support him. In these special circumstances, it is not at all

surprising that a successful machine was produced. Even so, local manufacturers were unwilling to invest in developing minor improvements
to make the machine even better. "In the course of the very few years
during which the Jacquard machine had been known in England, it has
been thus materially simplified and improved, while in Lyons, the city
of its birth, it still remains unaltered, either in form or arrangement,
from the original conception of its first ingenious inventor" (Porter
1831, 256). Even at its best, France simply did not provide as encouraging a setting for new technology as England.

Bleaching

The story is repeated with respect to the various finishing processes.[30]
France led the world in the study of chemistry in the eighteenth century.
Moreover, French chemists were willing to devote their efforts to practical applications. Of the thirteen books which mark the technological
advance of bleaching between 1500 and 1856, ten were by Frenchmen,
one by a Venetian, one by an American, and one by a Scot (Chapman
1981, 196). Despite this scientific advantage, the commercial application
of new bleaching technology proceeded much more quickly in England
than in France.

As I mentioned earlier, the first breakthrough was the production and
application of sulphuric acid. At mid-century, English innovations and
large-scale production had reduced its price to less than one per cent of
its former level. According to Smith, attempts to follow the English
lead failed in France because of the small size of the national market for
bleach, until cotton took off after 1760 (1979, 6–7). At best, this begs
the question of why the French cotton industry was slow to expand.
Given that linen was bleached as well, arguments on the national level
are unconvincing, and one must recognize again the important role of
a poor transport system in limiting market size. Holker established a
sulphuric acid plant in 1769; despite his efforts at secrecy, a number of
others followed in various parts of France. "An obvious stimulus to
local production was the difficulty and cost of transport" (Smith, 15).
A bottle costing fifty to sixty livres at the factory gate cost seven to
eight to ship to Nantes, and fourteen to sixteen to Lyons. "Also significant was the risk of breakage en route, and indeed land carriers were
reluctant to take the acid at all because of its dangerous nature" (Smith,
16). The poor road conditions in France must have increased the danger
greatly, and made it difficult for many bleachers to obtain the acid.
Transport difficulties, to be sure, did not absolutely prohibit works like
Javel from obtaining a national reputation and market. However, they

must, especially in the early decades, have made it difficult for producers to achieve maximum economies of scale and deliver their output at reasonable prices to bleachers.

The history of sulphuric acid production in France illustrates a couple of points I have made before. Combustion of sulphur would only yield sulphuric acid if a catalyst such as saltpetre were used. French chemists such as Lavoisier continually questioned the importance of saltpetre and this led to much fruitless experimentation. Thus, the availability of skilled chemists interested in practical matters did not, at least in this case, facilitate the advance of sulphuric acid production, but rather hindered it. One of the reasons for trying to avoid the use of saltpetre was that it was more expensive than the sulphur itself. While this was largely due to government regulation of the use of the material, it still points up the importance of easy access to raw materials in the process of technological innovation.

Sulphuric acid was only the most conspicuous example of a French lag in both bleaching and chemical production[31] in the middle years of the eighteenth century. Both French industries appear to have been less interested in improvements than their English counterparts; minor improvements made in England were virtually ignored in France. Thus, it is not surprising that chlorine bleach, though developed in France, spread more quickly in England (Smith, 116–17).

In 1785 Berthollet described in principle the use of chlorine as bleach. He and several others then devised a method of applying chlorine to bleaching.[32] This method was far from perfect. It has been seen that English producers soon came up with improvements, especially the introduction of bleaching powder. Powder became known in France in the early nineteenth century but it spread slowly despite an immense cost saving. Liquid bleaches such as "eau de Javel" cost too much for industrial purposes and were basically used by washerwomen (Smith, 156–8). Bleachers either made their own or did without. The timing of the innovation suggests that the French Revolution was the culprit in the slow French response to this indigenous invention. However, even after the Restoration, France was slow to adopt the new technology. "The adoption of the new bleaching was clearly slower in France than in Britain, and for this the untimely intervention of the Revolution can only partly be blamed" (Smith, 178). Again, the small-scale, dispersed nature of French industry must be seen as a major barrier to technological change.

Chemicals would become one of France's most successful industries in the nineteenth century. Smith believes that by 1820, France had better technology in more chemicals than any other country. He points to the role of trained chemists in establishing new industrial works and products (1979, 312). Clearly, one must be careful not to denigrate the capabilities of French experimenters in chemistry. Chlorine was far from being the only discovery to be made in France in the late eighteenth or early nineteenth centuries. Nevertheless, at least in the period under study, development of chemicals with a great commercial potential would occur most rapidly in England. France's advantage in chemistry could be translated into new ideas, but it could often hinder their development as well. In any case, applying these ideas on a large scale was easier in England, and long into the nineteenth century, England would remain the low-cost producer of most major chemicals.[33]

Dyeing

In dyeing, as in bleaching, the French government encouraged research, and French chemists searched for improvements. Nevertheless, J.S. could write of Rouen cotton dyers that they did red well, that their blue and black were questionable, and that "All other colours are dyed in an indifferent manner, especially chemical colours in which they do not show superior skill, notwithstanding the French were always allowed to stand in the first rank of chemists" (1803, 14). While France was ahead in science, England and Scotland were ahead in practical application, partly, as noted earlier, because of support from the Scottish government, and partly thanks to experiments by manufacturers (Fairlie 1964, 507). Some French dyers, to be sure, did devote themselves to developing better dyes. As in England, workers from the Middle East were enticed to France that they might disclose the secret of Turkey red (Ballot 1923, 534–5). Other manufacturers experimented with a variety of other colours, and asked for government support (F12 2259). Again, isolated efforts by individuals seem rarely, if ever, to have produced the desired result. Frederick Breillat claimed to have developed a method of dyeing silk handkerchiefs in solid and durable colours. He noted that this was a branch of commerce that occupied many people in England. When examined, however, his product proved to be of lower quality than English versions. His attempts to dye cotton were even less successful (F12 2259, 1788). The government induced a number of English dyers to move to France. In 1761 Holker spoke of English dyers in Normandy; English blue was much preferred in the market to Normandy blue (F12 2259).[34] In the 1780s, the government tried to obtain certain secrets from the British Isles by dispatching agents there (Ballot 1923, 536). As with other movements of Englishmen to France, these did not result in widespread adoption of English dyes or dyeing techniques. At the end of the century, the English were able to produce better, more durable dyes for most colours. The success of English textiles in nineteenth-century export markets was only partly due to the fall in price resulting from labour-saving innovation. A number of innovations, especially those in the finishing trades, served also to enhance the quality of the final good.

Printing

Levy (1912, 150) and Ballot (1923, 280) both maintain that printing, for technological reasons, had always been centralized. To be sure, printing was ill-suited to a one-man cottage operation. Several distinct operations were required. Small workshops, similar to small-scale iron-works or potteries, had performed the task for centuries. In 1786, print-works in Alsace ranged from four tables to 186 (Levy 1912, 164). The large works that emerged in eighteenth-century Europe were a far cry from these early workshops.

I mentioned earlier that a number of large printworks emerged in England in the late eighteenth century. One or two large works appeared in France as well. Indeed, the largest factory in either country was the printworks built at Jouy in 1793. Chapman and Chassagne note that a student reading the standard textbooks on the Industrial Revolution would get the idea that eighteenth-century factories were confined to England and Scotland. The experience of Oberkampf of Jouy, they argue, shows that "this impression is little more than a caricature of the true situation" (1981, 202). It would be incorrect to treat workshops as non-existent in eighteenth-century France. A few examples, often attempts to imitate English methods, can be found in various industries. Along with Jouy, France possessed a couple of large print-works in Alsace. The simple fact is that England, though much smaller, had many times more printing "factories" than France. Moreover, a comparison of Jouy and the Peel works in Lancashire shows that the French firm placed much greater emphasis on the luxury end of the market. It is clear that the Peels had the advantage in price while Oberkampf emphasized quality (Chapman 1981, 205–8). The discussion of silk showed that in production of goods with a high value/bulk ratio a degree of concentration was possible notwithstanding poor transport links. It would be wrong to deduce from the existence of a few large works in France that France was undergoing the same transition as England. At best, France was decades behind.

The relative backwardness of French printworks is best indicated by the lag in technological innovation. A couple of isolated works simply could not provide as fertile an environment as the heavy concentration of printworks in Lancashire. The Peel-Oberkampf comparison is still instructive. "Although some allowance must be made for the fact that

Lancashire inclined towards the more popular products, the conclusion seems irresistible that the Peels' productivity was quite significantly above that of Oberkampf and their earlier Continental rivals. The data dramatically demonstrate the results of the Peels' drive for "long runs", economy of labour, and perhaps the beginning of mechanisation (roller printing)" (Chapman, 212).[35] In England, the concentration of a number of works in the same area had allowed (induced) each producer to produce a fairly narrow range of goods. Therefore, there was much greater incentive to develop mass production technology. While art historians may question English tastes in printing, the simple fact is that English producers were able to mass produce printed fabrics at a much lower average cost than their continental competitors.[36]

The general impression that France lagged behind in the technological improvement of printing is borne out by the history of the more important innovations of the period. "In 1766, when the use of the copper plate had for some time been general in England, they [the Continent] were still for the most part using the coarsely cut wooden block, and had long been deterred from competition in the finest varieties by the belief that the English manufacturers had secrets which they could not discover" (Wadsworth 1965, 143). Copper plates were advantageous in two ways. First, they could produce a somewhat sharper print since they wore less easily than wooden blocks. Second, while copper was more expensive to engrave than wood, copper plates could reap considerable savings on long product runs, for they lasted many times longer. For this reason, the innovation spread quickly in England where specialization and mass production were common. In France it spread very slowly. Oberkampf was the first to use copper plates. They were used only to supply the upper class market while wooden blocks were retained for the more common half of their market (Chapman 1981, 132–3). Since French printers were clearly aware of the potential of copper plates, one must assume that they simply did not produce enough of their commoner designs for the plates to represent a cost saving overall.

Not surprisingly, then, cylinder printing, used extensively in England from 1785 on, was hardly used in France during the eighteenth century. Oberkampf, who acquired the machine in 1793, was the only user in France until the nineteenth century (Ballot 1923, 290–1). It first appeared in Alsace in 1803 (Levy 1912, 163). Roland had developed a cylinder printing machine in France a couple of years before the English innovation. Given the response to the English machine, it is not surprising that he did not receive the support and encouragement that might have brought his machine into use. Ballot (1923, 293) suggests three possible explanations for the French reluctance to employ cylinder printing. The first is the low cost of labour. As Chapman and Chassagne (1981, 193–4) have pointed out, however, labour scarcity does not explain English technological superiority for skilled workmen were always difficult to find on the Continent.[37] Ballot's second explanation is the high cost of machinery. The third is the frequent need to replace rollers to respond to fashion. The difference between England and France was not that the French were more fashion conscious, but that French producers were unable to serve a large enough market to make mass production by cylinder printing feasible.[38]

Again, the French lag was not due to the fact that French industrialists were less interested than the English in technology. Oberkampf was keen to take advantage of any improvements introduced into the trade (Turnbull 1951, 54).[39] He undertook experiments into better methods of bleaching and dyeing, with some success. Still, the efforts of a couple of isolated firms could not, and did not, compare to the accomplishments of Lancashire. The fault lay not with the printers but with the world they lived in.

Hosiery

It was seen in the last chapter that the hosiery industry played an important, dynamic role in English technological development. The French hosiery industry, however, was in no way capable of playing such a role. Like other textile sectors, it was not anywhere near as regionally concentrated as in England. The market areas served by firms were highly localized.[40] Nor were workshops as common as across the Channel.[41] It is not surprising that technological advance was slow and difficult.

The stocking frame had spread more slowly in France than in England (Ballot 1923, 272), partly due to government regulation. Before 1754 the frames had been limited to certain French towns. Nevertheless, as Heywood has noted, the list of towns expanded as the frames spread elsewhere (1976, 91) so it does not seem that the restrictions were very binding. In England from mid-century on, a number of machines, starting with Strutt's, revolutionized the industry. These machines were only introduced into France at the end of the century; with a few exceptions, then, their adoption was basically a nineteenth-century phenomenon (Ballot 272–8).

France was not without its inventors. One of these was Leturc. After many long efforts at home, he eventually gave up and went to England for ten years "to learn their lessons, or to have my ideas developed by a great number of artists who know how to create useful establishments for themselves and for commerce in general" (in Ballot, 274). Leturc recognized the importance of interaction with a group of craftsmen interested in the same question, and realized that he could not find this at home. In 1787, after the trade treaty with England, English hosiery flooded the French market. The Academy of Science responded with attempts to attract English workers and machines. Leturc returned to England as a spy, noting that ninety per cent of what he saw there was unknown in France (Ballot, 276).

The Treaty of 1786 gave conclusive proof that English hosiery had become superior in both quality and price to its French competition. A similar message was imparted to other textiles.[42] Improvements in quality and price had allowed the output of various textiles to expand greatly in England. A transformation of the same magnitude did not happen in France. Neither in terms of output nor technology did hosiery have the effect in France that it had in England. The reason was that the hosiery industry, still largely based on putting-out and spread through the country, was not supportive of changes in organization and technology.

A Note on Steam Engines

In France, then, one has a textile industry characterized throughout by small units of production, antiquated technology, and poor access for most producers to raw materials such as coal. It is not at all surprising, therefore, that the steam engine was virtually unknown in French textiles during the eighteenth century. There was only one steam engine in use in textiles before 1789, and only a couple more by the end of the century (Ballot 1923, 412). Alsace did not get its first engine until 1812 (Levy 1912, 142). As earlier noted, steam engines came slowly into use in eighteenth-century England. Yet the stage was being set for them to play a more important role in the nineteenth century. France would fall far behind. We know that knowledge of steam engine developments spread quickly to France. French producers could indeed have gained an advantage over their English counterparts since they were not inhibited by English patents. Instead, the steam engine serves as a glaring example of French technological backwardness. As long as centralized work places were rare, so would be the steam engine. As long as coal was prohibitively expensive, the steam engine would spread slowly. And as long as manufacture was dispersed throughout the countryside, the creation or diffusion of new technology would be a painfully slow process.

SUMMARY

The development of the French textile industry was severely hampered in a number of ways by the backwardness of French transport. Until the end of the century, methods of distribution changed little; face-to-face sales predominated. Entrepreneurs still spent time travelling to fairs, and the pressure to standardize was minimal. The market area served by the individual firm, even for many "luxury" goods, was severely constrained by the cost of transport. On the supply side, France was not disadvantaged in its possession of raw materials. Nevertheless, the inadequacy of the transport network meant that French producers found themselves in a poor position with regard to obtaining a variety of materials. The results were as my theory would predict. The industry remained geographically dispersed with firms serving small local markets. Only a small number of firms moved to centralize their workers during the century. Not surprisingly, technological change was slow in coming. There were a good many Frenchmen tinkering with new technology (though seemingly far fewer than in England). However, they lacked the suggestions and support of others and were only rarely able to bring their ideas to completion on their own. More than one French inventor moved to England. Further evidence of the superiority of the English environment comes from the extremely slow diffusion of English technology in France. Despite government attempts to attract English workers and machines, the small scale and dispersed nature of the industry meant that it took decades for any English innovation to become widespread in France.

CHAPTER SEVEN

Pottery

As Berg points out (1985, 40), almost all works on the Industrial Revolution concentrate on the textile and iron industries. The lack of research on other industries means that general works tend to deal only with those two, and into this trap I, like Berg, have fallen so far in this work. There is a special reason to be concerned that major parts of eighteenth-century industry have been ignored. Berg notes that less dramatic but still impressive increases in productivity occurred in a wide variety of sectors and she quotes McCloskey approvingly: "ordinary inventiveness was widespread in the British economy 1780 to 1860 … the Industrial Revolution was not the age of cotton or of railways, or even of steam entirely; it was an age of improvement" (1985, 26). However, Berg recognizes that Crafts would disagree, maintaining that a small number of innovations in cotton and iron were the essence of technological change during the period. I discussed this criticism in the first chapter, and noted the importance of describing the breadth of technological innovation in late eighteenth-century England. This book has made headway in that direction: chapter 3 dealt with various innovations in the metal trades, coal mining, and the iron industry itself, and chapter 5 looked at innovations at various stages of production in wool, linen, and cotton. Still, it would be advantageous to show that the same phenomenon occurred in a totally different industry, and indeed, to show that my model can be applied to at least one industry outside of the iron and textiles complexes.

The overemphasis on iron and textiles is noticeable in the French as well as the English literature. The issue was taken up by Markovitch (1970), who maintained that this focus was due to a mistaken impression of the importance of various sectors in French industrial production.[1] For the 1780s in France, he provided the following breakdown of industrial production (I have changed the order):

iron, metals, mining	6.1%
textiles, chemicals	13.2%
fabric finishing, clothing	19.6%
construction, public works	25.6%
food processing	19.9%
wood and furniture	11%
leather	2%
paper	.7%
pottery	.5%
fats and oils	.6%
glass, tobacco, publishing, etc.	.7%

According to Markovitch, then, I have discussed less than forty per cent of industrial production (I have had little to say about clothing, and have discussed only certain types of mining and chemicals). Crafts' figures for England (1985, 22) are somewhat different. He does not include food industries, wood and furniture, or pottery. In 1770, he claims, textiles comprised 45.9 per cent of industrial production, and iron, copper and coal together 11.9 per cent (leather is an impressive 22.3 per cent). Even by Crafts' reckoning, then, I have still only covered about half of industrial production. It is worthwhile to consider the other elements of late eighteenth-century European industry.

Construction is clearly a special case, arguably less amenable to technological innovation, and certainly to workshop production. Food industries and wood and furniture involve a number of diverse products. We know extremely little about these industries. Mathias' work (1959) on the English brewing industry indicates an increase in scale of production from the mid-century on due in part to transport improvements and urbanization. The increase in scale, while not dependent upon any previous technological advance, does lead to the search for and application of new technology.[2] Research in other areas could disclose similar developments. Or, it could be that some sectors, due to the intrinsic nature of the products involved, were incapable of technological or organizational change in the eighteenth century. In the leather industry, attempts to improve the technology of production proved fruitless.[3]

Paper was one industry whose importance had been increasing for centuries and would continue to do so into the future.[4] Here again it appears that England was both technologically and organizationally more advanced than France in the late eighteenth century. In France, the industry was generally small scale with a couple of exceptions, and distributed throughout France (Ballot 1923, 554–61). In England, while few cities were without a paper mill by century's end, it was in the later eighteenth century that Kent and Buckinghamshire clinched their dominant position in the industry.[5] The average output of English print-works almost tripled between 1735 and 1800 (Coleman 1958, 111). While high-quality paper had to be imported in the first half of the century, the second half saw dramatic improvement in the English industry such that it surpassed the French (Coleman, 92–9).[6]

One reason for the improvement in quality of English paper was the introduction of woven molds at about mid-century. This was not the only technological improvement of the period. The "Hollander,", a Dutch machine for beating rags to pulp, was introduced to England in the 1730s. "In England there can be little doubt that its adoption was rapid and, in the course of the century complete; as new mills opened up most of them would install the Hollander, especially after the mid-century" (Coleman, 111). Ill-suited to the best quality paper, this defect was slightly felt in the manufacture of lesser grades. Though the English and Dutch adopted the invention readily, it was little used in Germany and Italy, and in France hardly at all (Coleman, 110). Near the end of the century, the Frenchman Robert developed a paper-making machine but neither the French government nor entrepreneurs had the desire or resources to undertake the costly development of the machine. Robert moved to England in 1801, where his invention was perfected and widely used, but it was some decades before it became known in France (Ballot 1923, 559–60).

Modern research on industries such as brewing and paper relies too much on the efforts of one or two scholars. Moreover, the primary sources are often sparse. It is thus impossible here to provide for each of these industries evidence of all the elements of my model. Yet one can see that the material available does coincide with various elements of my approach. One can be confident that continued research would further validate this approach. There is one industry, however, for which there is enough information available to sketch a more complete picture, at least for England. It is the pottery industry, to which the rest of this chapter is devoted.

In pottery, as in paper, it is clear that the French had fallen far behind their English counterparts by the late eighteenth century. Indeed, "as late as 1799, by which time the principal problems of pottery-making had been solved in England, the French national institute was offering prizes for earthenware which would not break with sudden changes in temperature" (Clow 1952, 299). French writers of the late eighteenth century noted the superiority of English pottery,[7] which was taking over the French market, and French potters – like French ironmasters and textile producers – were struggling to copy English innovations.[8] As with these other industries, it would take decades for French potters to adopt innovations introduced by the English in the eighteenth century. Again, this would occur despite the fact that English entrepreneurs moved to France and established English-style works.[9]

French writers observed that the English advantage was not due to a superiority in raw materials – France possessed all that was necessary.[10] Ease of access to these materials was another matter. One of the causes of the superiority of English ware was that higher temperatures could be obtained by the use of coal as a fuel. Chaptal (1819, 107) noted that the English had an advantage in this due to the accessibility of cheap and abundant coal. As I have shown, the reason for this advantage lay not in the coal reserves themselves but in the backwardness of the transport system. The same holds true for the other materials needed for pottery. Even in the nineteenth century, clay from the Indre was moved by land to Parisian porcelain works at exorbitant expense, because of inadequate water transport.[11] It will be seen that English potters made use of a wider range of inputs in the period under study. Their French counterparts would face great difficulties in doing the same. Transport difficulties not only hindered producers on the input side but also hurt their ability to serve large markets.[12] Indeed, a glance at Peuchet (1807) conveys the unmistakable impression of a small, localized industry, relying on local materials and markets.

The English pottery industry was similar to the French at the beginning of the eighteenth century. Staffordshire potters were content to dispose of their wares at Uttoxeter, but as transport charges dropped[13] these potters found other markets in Birmingham, and then in London and Liverpool (Thomas 1937, 411). McKendrick has dated this process of change. In 1730, Staffordshire potters made exclusively local sales, though pedlars occasionally travelled to Leicestershire, Liverpool or Manchester. Sales in London were rare, and in Europe unknown. By the 1750s the market had already grown such that most of John Wedgwood's sales were in London (McKendrick 1982, 103–4). Weatherill has also noted that, while some cheap goods like butterpots were sold locally for some time, many goods had achieved an England-wide market by the 1740s at least (1971, 70–80). While turnpikes and river improvements had greatly increased Staffordshire's access to a wide market by mid-century, the most important single improvement was the Trent and Mersey canal in the 1770s which brought water transport to the heart of the potteries.[14]

The changes in methods of distribution seen in other industries were duplicated in Staffordshire. By 1740 direct, on-the-spot sales by potters to craters were being displaced by direct trade with merchants in towns and the employment of riders-out (Weatherill 1971, 145).[15] By the 1760s, in the time of Josiah Wedgwood, the modern type of distribution previously discussed had emerged.[16] Wedgwood used pattern boxes, catalogues,[17] and samples, and followed in 1777 with travelling salesmen (McKendrick 1982, 126). By 1780 a national distribution network had emerged, wherein most provincial towns had at least one dealer in pottery and many towns far more (Weatherill, 145). This national market presented Wedgwood and other Staffordshire potters with the contradictory challenge of standardizing their product while at the same time responding to changes in fashion. McKendrick writes of a Newcastle woman demanding from her local shopkeeper a service that was much used in London, but of which he had not yet heard (1982, 120). "Though the correspondence of Wedgwood shows him alive to the advantages of standardization, the tendency was opposed by the character of the market, and the character of the process" (Bladen 1926, 125).

There were, of course, great changes on the input side of the pottery industry as well, for its manufacture required the transport of numerous bulky materials. Of key importance was the fact that in the second half of the eighteenth century, most of the clay used in Staffordshire was not local. On its own, local clay could not produce quality ware. Wedgwood looked as far afield as South Carolina for quality clay. However, Fothergill advised him in 1768 that with American clays, "unless they were restricted to the manufacture of highly-prized porcelain, the difficulties and expense connected with their transit from so remote a region would render them too dear to be available, to any remunerative extent, to either the importer or potter" (Meteyard 1866, v.2, 7–8). Though imports rose a little after 1776, "Internal navigation had by this time fully proved its capabilities; more was known of the Cornish clays; the roads were being sedulously improved in all the more populated districts of the country, and the spirit of industry animated the body of the people with a power hitherto unknown. As soon as clay ranked with other goods as an article of ordinary import, the potter had the ability to choose that which was best suited to his peculiar use" (Meteyard, 8). While Meteyard is somewhat late in her timing, the message is correct. Staffordshire potters needed a wide range of clay and the Cornwall clays were especially important. Imported clay was very expensive. Domestic clays became increasingly available as transport improvements opened the whole country to exploitation.[18]

Clay was far from the most important material in terms of total weight. Weatherill estimated that each ton of clay required five to twelve tons of coal for drying and firing (1971, 30). Indeed, Thomas (1937) attributed Staffordshire's pre-eminence to the availability of coal rather than clay. Nevertheless, transport costs could easily double the price of coal. In 1715 a Burslem pottery paid six shillings a ton for coal and eight shillings a ton to transport it (Weatherill 1971, 30). Shaw described an early eighteenth-century coal-carrier: coal was transported "on the backs of horses, the roads being then so bad that had a horse stumbled, or missed his step into the holes, he certainly would have fallen, and with difficulty would have been again raised" (1829, 156). Turnpikes and then canals dramatically increased the potters' access to coal. It must be remembered that different types of coal were used for different purposes; thus even if he were located close to a particular mine, a potter would require some coal from further afield.

There were other important raw materials.[19] Flint was brought from southeastern England to strengthen the ware and allow it to withstand high firing temperatures. Flint usually comprised between one quarter and one sixth of the mass of the final product (Shaw 1829, 159). Lead ore and salt were two other essential ingredients possessing a low value/ bulk ratio. "In addition ... a pottery created a great demand for oat and wheat straw for packing [paper was used later], and for hazel rods and coppice wood for crate-making" (Clow 1952, 295). Glazing required the use of various oxides, cobalt, antimony, silver, lead, gold, copper, iron, etc. (Clow, 320). As with other industries, the increased access to various materials stimulated innovation. Clow spoke of Wedgwood: "To the range of his products, he assiduously collected varied raw materials from all over the country; cobalt from Mr. Tolcher in Plymouth, growan clay from Redruth, soapstone from Lord Falmouth's property. He experimented with them and analyzed them insofar as he was able. Tests of their applicability to practical pottery then followed. At his death he left no less than 7000 specimens, classified according to utility" (1952, 310). In an earlier day, when travel about the country, carriage of materials, and transmission of information about local resources were all deficient, an effort on that scale would have been practically impossible.

Wedgwood was in fact highly conscious of the value of good transport. In chapter 1, I noted that many famous industrialists actively supported transport improvements. While on the one hand this is clear evidence of the importance of these improvements, on the other it must be emphasized that industrialists did not singlehandedly bring them about – transport improvements were not simply a result of industrialization. The Wedgwood case is illustrative. McKendrick writes that "the canals and turnpikes promoted by Wedgwood opened up the national market for all the Staffordshire potters" (1982, 143). He had actively participated in at least two turnpike trusts and fought long and hard for the Trent and Mersey canal. His 1795 "Gentleman's Magazine" obituary stated that, "At an early period of his life, seeing the impossibility of extending considerably the manufacture he was engaged in on the spot which gave him birth, without the advantages of inland navigation, he was the proposer of the Grand Trunk Canal, and the chief agent in obtaining the Act of Parliament for making it."[20] While he clearly devoted great efforts to transport, several points must be remembered. He offered little of his funds; the turnpikes and canals were largely financed by landowners, merchants, and others. Without previous pikes and river improvements these later improvements would have had a much smaller impact. French potters may have dreamed of good road and water transport, but they could not have achieved these goals.

The English pottery industry responded to the improvements in transport in a predictable manner. Weatherill (1983, 24) provides national employment estimates. In 1700 there were 1500 workers, in 1750 from 2000 to 2500, in 1800 more than 10,000, and by 1820 over 15,000. She estimates that output rose by 250 per cent between 1745 and 1780 (Weatherill, 27). Just as dramatic was the change in the composition of output. In 1740, sales of fine earthenware and china were negligible but by 1800–20 they comprised ninety per cent of sales. The growth in output was associated with a considerable improvement in the quality of the product.

Exports did play a role in this expansion. However, the growth in exports was erratic during the eighteenth century, and only after 1780 did exports start to rise faster than output (see Weatherill 1983, 24). Again, then, one must look to the domestic market for the central explanation. After speaking of a national increase in demand for all goods, Bladen, McKendrick, and Weatherill each refer to changing tastes in England. Increased consumption of tea (from the seventeenth century on) and beer perhaps caused some of the increase in the market for cups. The increased domestic market for plates is less easy to explain. Tastes, after all, are unlikely to change overnight in such a way. Perceived changes in taste are likely to be reactions to changes in prices. Lord spoke of the languishing state of the pottery industry in the early eighteenth century: "The probable explanation of this is that wooden platters for the very poor and metal utensils of baser or richer metal for the wealthier classes, sufficed in days when road transport was so bad as to endanger any frailer vessels" (1966, 47). The most promising explanation of increased sales of pottery, then, would be that transport improvements, acting on both the input and output sides, decreased the price of delivered ware to a point where many more people were willing to buy it.

While Staffordshire was not the only source of English pottery, the industry concentrated increasingly there throughout the seventeenth and eighteenth centuries (Weatherill 1971, 7–8). According to Shaw, its advantage lay not just in the possession of various coals and clays, but also in the air, water, and sunshine (1829, ch. 1). Whatever the case, contemporaries were conscious of the area's inexorable rise.[21]

Increased output, coupled with regional specialization, should lead to increased division of labour. It is clear that there was much division of labour in the later eighteenth century.[22] Shaw noted that in 1740, skilled workers commonly performed two or three different tasks at different manufacturies, but afterwards there was more specialization, which served to promote the manufacture by increasing the level of excellence and elegance (1829, 166). In 1761, Wedgwood expanded his works by adding buildings and labour – he began to insist on increased specialization (Meteyard 1866, v. 1, 260). This increase in the scale of operation was typical of the late eighteenth century. While total output rose by as much as 250 per cent between 1745 and 1780, the number of potteries increased only by twenty-five per cent (Weatherill 1983, 27). The potteries of 1700, employing about ten people, were similar to early ironworks – not exactly the textbook definition of domestic production but nevertheless a long way from modern factory production. Workers were often employed by more than one manufacturer. Some potters also had interests in other trades. As the century progressed potter-farmers became steadily less common (Weatherill 1971, 56). Establishments like Wedgwood's Etruria were very different from the small, early eighteenth-century potteries. A significant change in the organization of production had occurred.[23]

It was noted earlier that increased access to raw materials had encouraged Wedgwood at least to undertake many experiments. The process of technological innovation was also encouraged by increasing contact between potters.[24] Innovation of many types ensued. The experiments of Wedgwood and others were of great importance in making pottery considerably more attractive than it had been before.[25] A new method of printing pottery by transferring designs from copper plates was developed around 1760 at Worcester and spread to Staffordshire in about 1780 (Rees, "Printing"). Along with these and other improvements to the appearance of the ware, there were a number of innovations that saved labour in the production process. Rees describes several associated with Wedgwood including an improved lathe driven by a steam engine, and the use of iron cylinders with rotating knives to cut the clay into small pieces (Rees, "Pottery"). Wedgwood was not the only potter interested in technological advance and his improvements, inventions, and new products were quickly copied (McKendrick 1982, 107).[26]

One indication of the organizational and technological development of the pottery industry is the application of the Watt steam engine. The first industrial works to use this engine were Staffordshire potteries.

Only after they proved successful in the potteries were they used in textile production. "In 1782, Wedgwood ordered his first engine from Boulton and Watt. This was fortunate for Watt, since after he had displaced many Newcomen engines in Cornwall, Staffordshire was ripe for mechanization. It was only after the general adoption of mechanical power in the potteries that the market for engines developed in the mills of Lancashire and Yorkshire" (Thomas 1938, 407). For this service alone, the pottery industry deserves greater attention than it usually receives.

I have described, then, much the same developments that were seen in iron and textiles. Transport improvements had the same impact. Regional specialization, division of labour, increased scale of production, and technological innovation occurred at the same time in pottery as in the other industries. The Industrial Revolution was more than iron and textiles, and transport improvements are capable of explaining change across a variety of industries.

CHAPTER EIGHT

Conclusion

A close look at the eighteenth-century English and French economies does show that improved transport had an important impact on the process of industrialization in many ways. The appearance in England of the four phenomena which characterize the Industrial Revolution – regional specialization, increasing scale of production, the emergence of new industries, and a dramatic increase in the rate of technological innovation – can be explained in terms of the improvements in England's transport network during the eighteenth century. The non-occurrence of the same phenomena in France can be seen as a natural result of the fact that her transport system remained of very poor quality throughout the century.

This work has bridged the gap between the literature on transport and the literature on industrialization. To be sure, the connection between transport and the Industrial Revolution has been suggested before, though never in as much detail as here. I have gone beyond the necessary first step of showing that England had the best transport system in the world to show how she was thus enabled to experience the Industrial Revolution. The key to this analysis was an ability to show that various technological innovations could indeed flow from the environment created by transport improvements.

This argument would have been less convincing had I looked at England alone. Comparative studies are too little used in economic history. In claiming that early modern transport was a necessary condition if the Industrial Revolution was to occur, one must show not only how the possession of such a network could facilitate industrialization, but how the absence of such a network would make the Industrial Revolution impossible. By looking at French industries, one could see that their development was hobbled by an inadequate transport network. Especially noteworthy is the degree to which the small-scale, geographically dispersed nature of French industry made it difficult not only to develop new technology but also to borrow technology developed elsewhere.

Recent writings on methodology in economics have concluded that there is no one correct procedure. Rather, the profession must weigh various types of evidence and use its collective judgement in order to decide which ideas are likely to be correct.[1] I have been able to provide some evidence, from two countries and several industries, to support each element of my model. The anecdotal evidence assembled here represents the views of contemporaries on what was happening around them. Though none could see the big picture, several grasped each piece of the puzzle. I find this approach more persuasive than some high-powered mathematical exercise grounded in dubious data and restrictive assumptions.

I have tried not only to provide an explanation of why the Industrial Revolution occurred when and where it did but also to reassert the importance of the Revolution. Much of modern research in economic history serves a smoothing role. Gross National Product (GNP) never increases by more than a few per cent a year. Structural change does not happen overnight. There is an inherent danger of imagining that important transformations never occurred, simply because these transformations occurred only gradually over time. Yet the main purpose of economic history must be to determine why some economies perform differently from others over long periods of time. And England from about 1750 began to undergo changes that did not occur elsewhere for decades. The English Industrial Revolution ushered in the modern world of technological change, factories, new products, and industrial concentration. It happened, it was important, and there are reasons why it happened when and where it did. The fact that per-capita GNP grew slowly, or that labour was only gradually transferred from one sector to another changes this not at all.

A work such as this, while shedding light on a number of important questions, also raises some new ones. If my main thesis is accepted, a number of directions are open to future research. There are two approaches to economic history: one is to select one's favourite analytical tools and hunt around for a place to apply them; the other is to look at interesting historical questions and then choose the most suitable tools for analysing them. Both, perhaps, have their place. I am decidedly in favour of the second approach. In what follows, then, I will raise questions and only rarely suggest what might be the best means of analysing them.

The first question, and one which I discussed at some length in chapter 2, is why England was able to develop the best transport system in the world. A comparative study of various European countries could make considerable headway on this matter and lead to a much deeper understanding of why the Industrial Revolution occurred when and where it did. The geographical capabilities of different countries could be better explored by scholars familiar with the requirements of civil engineering. A related question is why western Europe as a whole was so far ahead of the rest of the world in terms of transport development. Not only is this issue important in its own right for shedding light on Europe's eventual rise to world dominance, but it could also provide insight into the role of imperialism in European economic development. The coincidental occurrence of colonialism and industrialism has led many scholars to imagine that there must be some line of causation from one to the other. However, it would seem that both could be traced back to an early time when Smithian growth encouraged the expansion of both internal and external transport links.

The role of political instability in retarding French development could also be studied by looking at the evolution of the French transport system. To what extent was the failure to develop a canal network in the eighteenth century due to political instability? What exactly were the effects of the Revolutionary and Imperial periods on transport development? This book has shown that France was incapable of having an industrial revolution in the late eighteenth century. Thus, the contention that France and England would have industrialized similarly but for the French Revolution must be mistaken. An in-depth analysis of the course of transport development in the late eighteenth and early nineteenth centuries could illuminate the degree to which France's development suffered from its political troubles.

It is possible that even with a good transport network French development might have been sluggish. I have never claimed that transport improvements were sufficient for development, only necessary. Social attitudes may have been less conducive to change in France,[2] and political institutions less amenable. Furthermore, both contemporary and modern writers may have underestimated the importance of government regulation.[3] Harris (1986, 55) notes that while the French mint insisted on licensing the use of stamps and other equipment to avoid counterfeiting, and the English mint ignored evidence of counterfeiting in Birmingham, writers on stamping have ignored the different governmental attitudes in the two countries. Yet even Thomson (1982, 455) who himself has claimed that the importance of regulation has been downplayed, disagrees with Heckscher's argument that it was the main reason for the divergence between France and England. England, after all, had regulations on the books that simply were not enforced. French regulations were often evaded, though manufacturers paid a price for doing so. Restrictions on cotton cloth production, for example, were repealed in 1759, because the French government realized that they were not being enforced (Levy 1912, 207). The difference between the two countries is clearly one of degree. Moreover, it is likely that French regulation was more a symptom than a cause of French backwardness (Heywood 1977, 26). As the French economy developed, regulations were overcome and eventually abolished. It is possible that future research might show that this and other seeming explanations of French backwardness were in fact its results.

While my work has focused on England and France, there are other countries that merit attention, especially at a later period. I mentioned earlier the interesting case of early nineteenth-century Belgium, but of course there are many nineteenth-century success stories that could be addressed. Such research should not focus solely on one mode of transport but should recognize instead the complimentary interrelatedness of a transport network and seek to describe the role played by transport improvements of every sort. Nor, of course, should attention be paid only to countries that succeeded in industrializing. It is as profitable to discern the role of transport in preventing industrialization. One interesting line of inquiry was raised in a footnote in chapter 2. Poland (and similar arguments could be made for other countries) possessed in its rivers good transport links for the export of its raw materials. However, east-west links were exceedingly poor. To what extent did the nature of the transport network encourage the export of raw materials to the detriment of local industry?

It should be recognized that many parts of the world to this day do not have transport networks equal to that of eighteenth-century England. By understanding more clearly the dynamic effects of transport improvements in the eighteenth and nineteenth centuries, one can perhaps shed light on the importance that should attach to transport development in present-day less-developed countries.[4]

Even within eighteenth-century France and England, there is a great deal more that could be done. While much has been written on the iron and textile industries, most other industries have received scant attention. Continued study of these two industries is, of course, in order, if we are to understand them as fully as possible. However, they need not be the only focus of economic historians. There is as much or more to be gained by extensive, rather than intensive, research. The Industrial Revolution was a widespread phenomenon which undoubtedly had effects on many industries. Yet our knowledge of most other eighteenth-century industries is too scanty to allow for discussion of their development at that time.[5]

There is also a strong connection between transport and agriculture. Crafts has maintained that productivity growth in agriculture was high during the period of the Industrial Revolution, and that the agricultural sector was able to increase output while releasing labour to the industrial sector. Mokyr and Williamson have questioned both the rate of productivity growth and its importance, noting that Britain could have imported food as she eventually did. While the role of agriculture will undoubtedly be debated far into the future, it is clear that there were some agricultural improvements during the period of this study. It is clear from the primary literature that the transport boosters of the time emphasized transport's potential for agriculture almost as much as its importance to industry. One might quibble, of course, by noting that many canal projects in the agricultural south of England failed miserably. Nevertheless, there was a widespread view both in England and France that transport improvements could unleash a dramatic transformation in agriculture. It is difficult to quantify the importance of these linkages without further research, but it is worth noting here that contemporary comment upon them was extensive.

Most often mentioned was the role of transport in expanding the market area served by farmers. Agricultural produce generally has a low value/bulk ratio and therefore the effective market available to individual farmers is greatly dependent on the availability of low-cost transport, by road or water. "Landed property in particular improves with the road. If a farmer cannot bring his produce to market, he cannot give much for his land, neither can that land well be improved or the market properly supplied" (Hutton 1791, 261). "That inland navigation benefits greatly the landed gentleman can not be denied as in many instances their lands have been improved to tenfold value. Without this artificial communication, corn, timber, iron, coals, stones etc. would be of little use to the landowner which the cheapness of carriage now will enable him to transport to a profitable market" (Brindley 1766; quoted also in Phillips 1785). One must remember how costly transport could be before early modern transport was established.[6] Even late in the century, there were still agricultural areas in England that were very poorly attached to markets, so that "large tracts of land, for want of such an easy conveyance of manure, and for the carrying off of the products thereof, are rendered of very little value to the owners and occupiers of them, and if any industrious labourer in such a district makes any improvements in his farm he beholds the fruits of his daily toil almost confined to his own consumption" (Leach 1790, 4). In France, wide areas of the country were virtually unconnected with good markets until well into the nineteenth century. One writer in 1777 did calculations to show how much better off French farmers would be if transport costs were lowered. Citing previous writers, he noted that away from the big towns and the main routes, a great deal of land went uncultivated for lack of markets (De L'importance, 20, 34). Later authors commented on the conditions endured by the inhabitants of these areas. "How many Departments in France are there, for example, where wine and wood are at a base price? Their inhabitants live always poor and unhappy in the middle of this abundance of two objects of the first importance, which it would be possible, by canals, to advantageously carry to the extremities of the Republic" (Lequinio, an I, 4). Another writer observed that the inhabitants of such areas were not as productive as they could be "because, lacking an outlet, all surplus serves for them as pure loss" (F12 1513, 1791). Lacking any market incentive to produce a surplus, farmers supplied only their own subsistence.

Market access was only one of the benefits provided by improved transport. Many writers noted the importance of better access to fertilizer. According to Homer, poor roads were accountable for the earlier slow advance of agriculture. "Discouraged by the expense of procuring manure, and the uncertain returns which arose from such confined markets, the farmer wanted both spirit and ability to exert himself in the cultivation of his lands" (1767, 5). Many promoters of transport improvements touted their ability to supply lime or manure to agriculturists.[7] Hey has recently described the role of lime in agriculture and notes that Yorkshire limestone was not quarried on a large scale until the Aire and Calder, followed by the Don, were made navigable into the heart of the coalfield (1980, 147).

Transport improvements naturally also facilitated increased regional specialization. Thus, Pilkington spoke in 1789 (ch. 7) of the shift in Derby agriculture from arable to dairy over the past few decades. Derbyshire now exported cheese and imported grain. Certain river improvements and canals also played a positive role in draining lands.[8] Finally, there is the common assertion that canals would free horses for agricultural work (see for example, Vallancey, 1763, iv), a benefit that was in fact outweighed by the increased usage brought on by lower transport charges. Clearly, one ought not to take the opinions of these people as gospel truth.[9] Nevertheless, the fact that so many commented on the potential benefits of transport improvement to agricultural development suggests that one should further examine the importance of these links.

Along with these specific suggestions for future research, it is necessary to make one general comment. I have noted a number of times that most historical works pay too little attention to the role of transportation. This problem is not exclusive to eighteenth-century historiography. There is too great a temptation, especially among economists, to ignore the spatial dimension of economic activity when looking at any time or place. Economic activity requires the movement of materials and people from one place to another. The workings of an economy can only be understood with reference to the ability of that economy to move goods and people around. The importance of transport cannot be overemphasized – there are too many souls to be saved. And there are too many social scientists who continue to ignore its importance. Integrating the spatial dimension into one's work is not an easy task but it is a necessary one.

Notes

1 Most students of the Industrial Revolution would agree that we have yet to isolate a causal factor which meets three criteria: England was clearly superior to her major Continental rival – France – in terms of this factor; there is some change in the factor itself in the immediate pre-industrial era which could explain the timing of the Industrial Revolution; and there are strong causal links connecting this factor to the phenomena that characterize the Industrial Revolution. This book will show that the transport system meets these three criteria admirably and should thus play a major role in explanation of the Industrial Revolution.

2 The word "factory" tends to bring forth the idea of a works using much powered machinery. One of my main contentions is that the earliest factories used the same technology as that previously used in people's homes. Throughout, I will use the word workshop, which more closely describes the true character of these early centralized work places.

3 Kemp (1971, 37) spoke of these state-sponsored factories: "They were examples of a general practice in the absolutist states of the time and were in no real sense precursors of modern capitalist industry." This was recognized at the time. "The experience of centuries, and of all countries has proved that national or royal enterprises ... have never had the success of private enterprise. One could state in principle that the love of private property, the desire to augment this a little, the fear of losing it are the only forces which stimulate vigilance and assure success" (*Rapport*, an III, F12 1454).

4 Mumford (1934) claims that the shift from the eotechnic phase of technology based on water and wood to the paleotechnic phase of coal and iron occurred around 1750 (see Clow 1952, xiv).

5 While Schumpeterian growth has been continuous to this day, and, one hopes, will continue well into the future, the centre of technological activity has shifted between various countries in the modern era. For a discussion of modern technological development see Mokyr (1990). To many Englishmen, it seemed that their head start would last forever. "Yet we see no ground for apprehending that England will lose her present manufacturing pre-eminence. All the natural and political causes which originally made this a great manufacturing and commercial nation remain unimpaired. The exhaustless beds of coal and ironstone, the abundance of streams with an available fall of water, the inland navigation and well situated seaports, the national tranquility, the security for person and property, the maritime superiority – all these advantages in the happiest combination, contribute to place England at the head of manufacturing countries" (Baines 1835, 505–6).

6 The above suggests that one way around this difficulty would be to locate industrial establishments in London, itself surely a large enough market to support modern workshops. While London was the largest manufacturing centre in the country, it suffered, like all large capitals, from high costs of labour and materials, and for the most part remained a centre of production only for luxuries or for goods like beer which could not easily be transported. Tatham (1797, 418) noted that producers faced a choice of manufacturing in the country and shipping to London or producing in London and having to import food and supplies; transport improvements would facilitate either option.

7 If it were, then the whole story of the Industrial Revolution would be easier to tell. I discussed earlier how the Industrial Revolution marks the transformation from Smithian to Schumpeterian growth (using Prof. Parker's terminology). If one led naturally to the other, the analysis would be simple.

8 In analyzing the individual entrepreneur's decision making, it should be kept in mind that the larger the potential market, the more attractive would seem the risky undertaking of establishing a workshop. Moreover, one must never forget that any advantage possessed by workshops (see below) lay in the production of large quantities of a few goods. The large putting-out firms produced a wide range of goods; the potential workshop owner had to worry about the size of market for a handful of very narrowly-defined goods.

9 "It must be evident that whatever tended to reduce the expense and to facilitate the mode of conveyance from one place to another, must tend to remove the manufacture from districts where the proximity to the growth of the raw material had formerly been important, and to fix them where they had other advantages. The first circumstance which led to the transference of the manufacturers from detached districts, spread over the whole surface of the island, and their concentration in towns and populous

neighbourhoods, were the improvements in the public roads, and the introduction of canals, affording cheap and easy carriage ... These modes of conveyance materially tended to remove manufactures, and fix them in the South of Lancashire and in the West Riding of the County of York; which, by means of those canals, had cheap access to Liverpool and Hull, for obtaining the raw materials from distant parts of the world by means of our mercantile navy, and opening both domestic and foreign markets for their fabrics" (Bischoff, 1842).

10 "This practice, far more commodious than the rude and inconvenient mode of carrying their merchandise from town to town, has become general, not only in this but in every other business; and it may now be asserted that the whole of the internal wholesale trade of England is carried on by common travellers – they pervade every town, village, and hamlet in the kingdom, carrying their samples and patterns, and taking orders from the retail tradesmen, and afterwards forwarding the goods by wagons or canal barges to their destination" (Guest 1823, 11).

11 As Chartres has noted, wagon haulage over long distances only became profitable when there were roads passable year-round and a regular demand for back-carriage. Before turnpikes, wagons were only used over short and medium distances (see Hey 1980, 98). Horses could pull about five times as much in a wagon as they could carry on their backs. Only with the creation of a nation-wide network of all-weather roads was it profitable for a nation-wide network of professional carriers providing regular service to emerge.

12 As Whitworth put it, "the more hands any good or merchandise go through, the dearer they are to the consumer, as every person through whose shop they go must have a profit" (1766, 28).

13 "At a time when the bulk of capital was tied up in debts, wages, inventories, and goods in transit, any innovation which speeded up the time it took for goods to pass through the various stages of production, to be transported, and to come to market was crucial. Innovation in transport and communications, retailing, and market institutions, all reduced the cost of circulating capital, and these just as much as actual technical innovations increased profitability" (Berg 1983, 12–13). This is especially important given the role of retained earnings in financing both workshops and new technology.

14 A factory that quickly processed materials into finished goods and did not need to hold large inventories of either inputs or output could in fact be less capital intensive than domestic production, due to the greater importance of circulating relative to fixed capital. See Field's analysis (1985) of a much later period.

15 O'Brien notes that in nineteenth-century Russia, one quarter of the social savings of railways came from decreased inventories, but in England, the

greater efficiency of road and water transport meant that railways only had a small effect on inventories (1983, 13). In the same volume, Hawke and Higgins suggest that the inventory effect of canal improvements was probably greater than that found later for railways (196–8).

16 One must be careful not to exaggerate the difference. There were implicit contracts within domestic industry which limited the arbitrary behaviour of entrepreneurs. Nevertheless, it should be clear that a centralized work force with only one source of income required the maintenance of regular employment to a much greater extent than domestic industry. Pollard (1964) noted that many factories were set up in smaller towns so that employers could exercise greater control over their workers; this meant that they had to be provided with regular employment or else they would starve or leave.

17 "Dispatch which is the very life and soul of business, becomes daily more attainable" (Homer 1767, 7). London merchant Thomas Nath corresponded with a Dutch counterpart in the 1750s; "quick sales being infinitely most agreeable, though with small profits ... we are exceedingly sorry to see that your charges are not modern, but according to the old fashion where little business was attended with great profits ... a quick sale ... is the very life of trade" (Chapman 1979, 208).

18 As late as 1735–36, Richard Dalton had to arrange for his incoming goods to be left at Bawtry till the following summer for the highway was impassable (Hey 1980, 113).

19 For example, Dent of Kirkby Stephen noted in 1784 that knitting in the area was done between September and February when no other work was available. See Thirsk in Harte and Ponting, 1973.

20 This is certainly Aikin's opinion (1795, 548): "The roads began to be greatly improved ... The fairs in different parts of the kingdom annually decreased in their importance, because shopkeepers could be supplied with goods at any time of year." In the next chapter I will show that fairs remain important much longer in France.

21 The key role of transport was better recognized at the time. "Do the materials of manufacture lie dispersed? Canals unite them, and at the same time supply the persons employed in it with every necessary at the cheapest rate" (Phillips 1792, 4). "Susceptible of high cultivation as the soil of England is, and abounding in different parts with various materials requisite for our manufactures and commerce, of what avail would these be comparatively, were it not for the expediting advantages of canal navigation, by which internal traffic can be carried on and intercourse with the most embosomed districts maintained at the cheapest possible rate. By this medium all ports may be connected through the interior; the raw material can be brought cheap from a distant quarter to the place where there are local advantages for manufacturing; and we may convey the

manufactured article from thence to the maritime towns for exportation" (Oddy 1810, 25).

22 "Inland navigation will encourage old manufactures to work with fresh vigour, now their materials come cheap to them, and will give opportunity to set up new trades and manufactures, as they can convey the produce or materials to any part whatsoever" (Whitworth 1766, 35).

23 Bentley includes the following among the necessary conditions for a successful manufactory: "It should have a great variety and plenty of raw materials at a moderate price, either in the neighbourhood or if possible within the limits of the same government, that it may not be liable to frequent interruptions from the difficulty of coming at materials" (1779, 28). The Staffordshire pottery industry, by way of example, increasingly used clay from various regions rather than relying on local resources, imported flint from southeastern England, and used a growing variety of materials from all over the world for decorative purposes.

24 There are many examples of transport improvements that halved the price of coal. In Birmingham itself, the completion of a canal to Wednesbury in 1767 caused the price of coal to drop from thirteen to seven shillings per ton (Hutton 1791, 266).

25 Schumpeter's distinction leaves open the question of why people develop the original invention. While some tinkerers may try to develop new technology for the same reasons one does crossword puzzles, one would expect that most inventors do so only with an eye toward the employment of this technology in the economy.

26 Some claims for a separation of the processes of invention and innovation are based on the seeming existence of a temporal gap between a particular invention and its commercial application. The average time span between patent and diffusion was five to six years, though in some cases such as Watt's steam engine it was as long as ten (Von Tunzelman 1978, 297). This is because it often takes a number of minor improvements before any given invention becomes practicable. This matter will be returned to below, when I discuss the period of critical revision as an essential component of the process of innovation.

27 MacLeod (1989) did find that patents were concentrated in areas near water – a result similar to Sokoloff's findings in nineteenth-century America – but attributes it to a greater propensity to patent. Sullivan has questioned MacLeod's conclusion in his review of her book (*Journal of Economic History*, December 1989).

28 This is discussed elsewhere when I talk about Crafts' critique of attempts at answering the question, "Why England First?"

29 Baines (1835, 114) quoted approvingly from "A Treatise on Taxes and Contributions" (1679), maintaining that every stage in the improvement of the cotton manufacture illustrated the truth of these remarks: "when a

new invention is first propounded, in the beginning every man objects, and the poor inventor runs the gantloop of all petulant wits; every man finding his several flaw, no man approving it unless mended according to his own device. Now not one of a hundred outlives this torture, and those that do are at length so changed by the contrivances of others, that not any one man can pretend to the invention of the whole, nor will agree about their respective shares in the parts." Ironically, it was only during the Industrial Revolution that the idea of the heroic inventor became popular (Basalla 1988, 59).

30 The link between transport improvements and technological advance was not lost to all minds of the time. "Indeed, no train of consequence in reason, in nature, or mathematical demonstration, can be more evident than this. That buyers and sellers will desire to meet for the supply of their wants and the disposal of their redundancies. That, where a ready and cheap passage is opened for the purpose, their commerce will be frequent and mutually beneficial. That such a beneficial communication will necessarily incite the laborious to industry, and the ingenious to improvement, by further study and invention" (Brooke 1759, 88–9).

31 Urbanization, naturally, worked hand in hand with regional specialization to foster the process of technological innovation. As Pawson notes, "It was the big towns that were the centres of innovation in production" due to "competition and collaboration within and between firms" (1979, 186). I discuss the role of transport in fostering urbanization below.

32 An important aspect of mechanization is that manufacturers were steadily changing from a concentration on high profit per unit to small per unit profit on a large output. Mechanization (and factory production) increased their ability to do this. "Now by machinery he not only increases his ability but comes to an exact estimate of that ability; can come to a tolerable certainty whether the orders offered him will yield him any sure profit, in which case he will engage, though a small one; this he could not do in the old way where, from the irregularity and disappointment of spinners etc. he is obliged to calculate for a larger profit" (Wansey 1791, 68).

33 "I shall only observe, therefore, that the invention of all those machines by which labour is so much facilitated and abridged, seems to have been originally owing to the division of labour. Men are much more likely to discover easier and readier methods of attaining any object, than when it is dissipated among a great variety of things. But in consequence of the division of labour, the whole of every man's attention comes naturally to be directed toward some one very simple object. It is naturally to be expected, therefore, that some one or other of those who are employed in each particular branch of labour should soon find out easier and readier methods of performing their own particular work whenever the nature of it permits of such improvement." Asserting that many inventions

occurred in precisely this way, he added, "Whoever has been much accustomed to visit such manufactures must frequently have been shewn very pretty machines, which were the invention of such workmen, in order to facilitate and quicken their own particular part of the works" (Tatham 1797, 436–7).

34 A case in point is the dressing machine, a necessary development for machine-weaving to be successful. "Great however as its advantages are some time must necessarily elapse before it can be accommodated to general use. In large establishments, where the different processes of the manufacture are carried on together ... it has been adopted with the happiest success, but the weaving in this country is chiefly done in the cottages of the poor, and to their use the costly and bulky apparatus of Messrs Ratcliffe and Ross is not adapted" (Rees, "Cotton").

35 "But even under the same government, or in the same province, it is some time before a combination of knowledge can take place, but in proportion as the difficulty of communications is removed, the spirit of enterprise increases, and neighbouring associations begin to mingle, their habits and customs assimilate, each transmits its improvements to the other, and each feels the beneficial effects resulting from the union" (Fulton 1796, 12). Research on nineteenth century religious communes (Cowan 1983, 116) and twentieth-century research and development laboratories (Nelson 1962) has shown the great importance for the rate of innovation of interaction between people with similar interests but diverse viewpoints and experiences.

36 "The discoveries and improvements made in one art, and even its common processes, are generally little known to those who are employed in another, so that the workman can seldom avail himself of the advantages which he might receive from the correlative arts, and an effect wanting to the perfection of his own art may be actually produced in another" (Lewis 1763, xii). Even as he was writing, this circumstance was changing in England.

37 It would be a mistake to exaggerate the ties between scientists and industrialists. "There are no two classes of men in society that are more distinct, or that are separated from each other by a more marked line, than philosophers and those who are engaged in arts and manufactures. The distance of their stations – the difference of their education, and of their habits – the marked difference of the objects of their pursuits in life – all tend to keep them at a distance from each other, and to prevent all connection and intercourse between them ... Anxious only to make new discoveries, and to establish his reputation among philosophers, whom he considers as the only competent judges of his merit, and whose suffrages alone can bestow that fame which he is ambitious to acquire; he has seldom either leisure or inclination to interest himself in those busy scenes in

which the great mass of mankind are employed, and which he is perhaps but too apt to consider as being unworthy of his attention" (*Proposals* 1799, 7). While perhaps unduly harsh, the modern academic might recognize the basic truth involved.

38 The idea that English scientists were more practical than their French counterparts does not bear close scrutiny. The French Royal Academy of Sciences published a lengthy series under the title, *Description des Arts et Métiers*, mostly during the eighteenth century (a description of this source and the circumstances of its publication are found in Cole and Watts, 1952). This series is the earliest comprehensive description published anywhere of the technology used in industry. Its publication was due to the interest shown by the great scientists of the day, such as Réaumur, in the completion of the project. The English Royal Academy had also shown an interest in the study of handicrafts during the seventeenth century, but while the French were pushing ahead with their practical work the English academy was becoming more theoretical (Cole and Watts 1952, 13–14). One of the aims of the French Academy was to bring industrial techniques out of the jealous obscurity in which they were held by the skilled craftsmen so that they could be improved upon through observation and the application of science. In terms of spreading knowledge of industrial technology, the accomplishments of England's Royal Academy were negligible compared to the success in France (Cole and Watts, 14). Hundreds of volumes covering different trades were published under the authority of the French Royal Acadamy. Many of these were so authoritative that they were individually translated into other languages. During the years 1760–80, an average of four to six volumes per year were published. In the words of Cole and Watts, "The volumes of the *Description des Arts et Métiers* remain nevertheless a monument to the "gentlemen" of the Académie Royale des Sciences, and to the age in France when arts and skills were not only well regarded, but stood still long enough for an all inclusive portrayal of their methods to be contemplated and carried well towards completion" (23). Ure (1835, viii) felt that French manufacturers had derived great benefit from these works, and that the English should do the same.

39 That these forces were stronger in England than elsewhere is evidenced by the fact that a number of outside "inventions" were first applied successfully in England. As Bentley complained at the time, this sometimes led foreigners to make the "common but erroneous remark that the French excelled most in invention and the English most in improvement" (1780, 14).

40 "Workmen must see the thing they are to imitate; bare descriptions of it will not answer to give them such precise ideas of what is to be done, as to prevent their being liable to mistakes in the execution of the work"

(Proposals 1799, 5). Even Rolt, in the preface to *A New Dictionary of Trade and Commerce* (1761) shared this opinion: "Of every artificial commodity the manner in which it is made is in some measure described, though it must be remembered that manual operations are scarce to be conveyed by any words to him that has not seen them."

41 See for example my discussion in chapter 5 of Wilson's attempts to keep new dyeing technology a secret.

42 Duckham (1983, 134) states that "Inland navigation complemented enclosure and other agricultural improvement." Chartres and Turnbull (1983, 81) note, "There was also an important connection between turnpikes and enclosures although the exact nature of the relationship is not completely clear, as so many factors influenced both." In Leicestershire, for example, enclosure followed turnpikes and most enclosures were within one to three miles of those roads.

43 "As the vicarage [of Halifax] is thus far extended and so populous, what must the market be which supplies this vast number of inhabitants? And yet these are all brought from other parts of the country. For as to corn they sow little and they feed very few oxen or sheep; and as they are surrounded with large manufacturing towns on every side; all of them employed like themselves in the clothing trade, they must necessarily have their provisions from other more distant parts ... The consequence then is plain, their corn comes in great quantities out of Lincolnshire and Nottinghamshire and the East Riding, the black cattle from thence and from Lancashire, sheep and mutton from the adjacent counties every way, butter from the north and east Ridings, and cheese out of Warwickshire ...
Thus, one trading manufacturing part of the country in a barren soil gives and receives support from all the countries around it" (Anderson 1777, 195, quoting another author from 1748).

44 The price of food was naturally a matter of great importance to workers and employers alike. As late as 1758, there were riots in Manchester over the prices charged by the local flour monopoly. "Since that time, the demand for corn has been increased to a vast amount, and new sources of supply had been opened from different parts by the navigations, so that monopoly or scarcity cannot be apprehended, though the price of these articles must always be high in a district which produces so little and consumes so much" (Aikin 1795, 203).

45 Homer's analysis was simpler: the population of trading towns increased as trade increased as transport improved (1767, 8).

46 Urbanization also increased demand for such materials as paving stones, bricks, lumber, and iron pipes.

47 The effect, of course, goes beyond any one industry. "It would seem that once industrial activity (of any sort) had begun to develop in a certain locality, it attracted to itself other forms of industry" (Rogers 1981,

19). Thus, an even larger pool of labour and so on would be available locally.

48 The drawing together of various workmen in one locality also aided the process of technological development. It is no surprise that most innovations occurred in an urban setting. Kennedy described the behaviour of potential inventors as follows: "Exercising however great labour and ingenuity in carrying into execution their various inventions, they soon found that if they could readily get a blacksmith's or a carpenter's assistance, they would be able to get their little apparatus more substantially made. This induced them to remove to villages where such men were to be found, and receiving from them the assistance so much wanted, the improvements made more rapid progress" (1818, 8). Though oversimplified, this description does indicate some of the advantages held by the urban-based inventor.

49 "We need not convey our enquiries into the state of England more than half a century backward before we shall be able to trace the dull marches of our ancestors through mire and clay" (Homer 1767, 3). Homer goes on to describe how people were fearful of taking long journeys at that time, adding that this was no longer the case.

50 J.B. Say in the nineteenth century described the necessity of transport for the development of new ideas: "I tell you only, gentlemen, that it is in vain that men have the ability to understand by speaking or writing, if they are deprived of the ability to move, some to others, because it is necessary to meet to speak, and it is necessary for someone to be able to travel from one place to another to carry our letters and our books" (1852, v.2, 302).

51 Not everyone was pleased by this trend. John Byng, in the 1770s, wished "with all my heart that half the turnpike roads of the kingdom were ploughed up, which have imported London manners – I meet milkmaids on the road with the dress and looks of Strand misses" (cited in Pawson 1979, 196). "These stage coaches make gentlemen come to London on every small occasion, which otherwise they would not do but on urgent necessity; nay, the convenience of the passage makes their wives come, who, rather than come such long journeys on horseback would stay at home. Here when they have come to town, they must presently be in the mode, get fine clothes, go to plays and treats, and by these means get such a habit of idleness and love of pleasure that they are uneasy ever after" (John Cresset 1762, quoted in Add MS 27828, 17).

52 "But still we know far too little of the actual working of markets in the eighteenth century, and of the microeconomic impact of improvements in transport and the breakdown of monopolies which clogged the circulation of commodities" (Berg 1983, 13).

53 Hoppit (1990) has recently highlighted the shaky bases of eighteenth-century aggregate output estimates, and particularly Crafts' 1985 estimates of English national income. He asserts that it is a mistake to rely too much on such quantitative evidence, when there is much qualitative evidence of important transformation in the late eighteenth and early nineteenth centuries. Williamson (1984) has argued that the wars between England and France in the period between the French Revolution and 1815 had a significant impact in slowing the growth of the English economy. Other authors, including Mokyr, have questioned the importance of the crowding-out effects of these wars on the English economy.

54 Crafts had argued that previous writers such as McCloskey and Von Tunzelman had overemphasized the role of technology and underestimated the role of capital formation in the Industrial Revolution (1985, 71–2). Williamson has reasserted the traditional textbook wisdom that most of the increase in per worker output (ninety per cent) during the Industrial Revolution was due to total factor productivity growth rather than capital deepening, noting that Crafts' latest estimates agree with this conclusion (1987, 272). This result separates the English experience from that of all other early industrializers. Sullivan (1989) has found that increased inventive activity preceded, and thus likely caused, increased total factor productivity.

55 "Few Countries are equal, perhaps none excel, the English in the number of contrivances of their Machines to abridge Labour. Indeed the Dutch are superior to them in the use and application of Wind Mills for sawing timber, expressing Oil, making Paper & the like. But in regard to Mines and Metals of all sorts, the English are uncommonly dexterous in their contrivance of the mechanic Powers; some being calculated for landing the Ores out of the Pits, such as Cranes and Horse Engines; others for draining off superfluous Water, such as Water Wheels and Steam Engines; others again for easing the Expense of Carriage such as Machines to run on inclined Planes or Roads downhill with wooden frames, in order to carry many tons of Material at a Time. And to these must be added the various sorts of Levers used in different processes; also the Brass Battery Works, the Slitting Mills, Plate and Flatting Mills, and those for making Wire of different Fineness. Yet all these, curious as they may seem, are little more than Preparations or Introductions for further Operations. Therefore when we still consider that at Birmingham, Wolverhampton, Sheffield and other manufacturing Places, almost every Master Manufacturer hath a new Invention of his own, and is daily improving on those of others; we may aver with some confidence that those parts of England in which these things are seen exhibit a specimen of practical Mechanics scarce to be paralleled in any part of the World" (1757, 20, on iron and related industries).

56 This idea, of course, has been extant in the literature for some time. One potential counter-argument involves the fact that transmission of technology at the time required the movement of workers or supervisors familiar with the new technology; this might explain the lengthy lag in French adoption. However, the French government in the eighteenth century devoted considerable effort to attracting English workers cognizant of new technology, so this factor alone cannot explain the slowness of French industry to adopt English technology.

57 Bruland (1982, 91–2) noted the importance of explaining technological innovation in understanding the Industrial Revolution: "This is a serious problem because although technical change can and should be rejected as an autonomous determining factor in the social and economic transformations of the period, it did happen and requires explanation."

58 Mokyr also questions whether changes in aggregate demand would induce technological innovation, and wonders whether there were economies of scale which could be realized by expanding the size of the market. As this is not the major thrust of his article, and as it would merely repeat what I have discussed before, I need not deal with these matters here.

59 This is certainly Fishlow's opinion. He stated that "What made railroad carrying services ultimately dispensable was the prior development of two other innovations, the canal and the steamboat. These lowered transport costs far more than the railroad in its turn" (1972, 471).

60 The opinion of Hawke and Higgins on this was noted earlier. Albert, claiming first that "The lack of even the most basic statistical data for the period of this study precludes any attempt at quantification similar to that undertaken by Fishlow," then states that a lower bound for the social rate of return on turnpike construction is provided by the private return of forty per cent (with the social rate likely much higher), and he hypothesizes that the social return on canals was probably higher still due to the greater drop in transport costs involved (1967, 193–6).

61 Williamson has found that there were profound forward linkages in the American Midwest in the nineteenth century – important effects on market size, competition and specialization. This is discussed by O'Brien (1983, 14–20), who also notes that beyond social savings transport improvements have a dynamic effect on savings and investment, location, markets, product mix, scale, technology, urbanization, flows of capital and labour, etc., for which quantification is impossible.

62 Many contemporary writers did recognize the greater importance of internal trade. Thermopilae noted that the mercantilist claim that wealth was only created through foreign trade was nonsense, and continued, "In that country [Scotland], the opinion is, that the foreign trade of this and every other great nation is trifling, both in point of extent and advantage to the state and the individual, when compared with its internal trade" (1774,

22–3). Adam Smith noted that "The freedom of interior commerce is certainly one of the principal causes of the prosperity of Great Britain, every country being necessarily the best and most extensive market for the greater part of the production of its industry" (1776, Book V, ch.2).

63 Not only was the internal market larger but it was more stable as well, and this was of great importance to entrepreneurs considering risky investments in large-scale production or expensive new technology. Foreign trade fluctuated much more than internal trade during the eighteenth century. A further problem with foreign trade is that manufacturers had much greater difficulty collecting funds owed them by foreign merchants than from domestic merchants (who could be pursued through the courts if necessary). Indeed, many manufacturers refused to sell abroad without the guarantee of a merchant based in England (Chapman 1979, 211).

64 As modern product-cycle theory would suggest, new industries only emerge and go through their early growth in response to the home market. Wallace (1798, 74–8) recognized various advantages of the home market for a new industry: a quicker and more certain return could be obtained and thus less capital required, the potential market for various products could be more adequately gauged, etc. To the extent, then, that the emergence of new industries was a key element in the Industrial Revolution, a healthy home market was absolutely essential.

65 "The wholesale trader and merchant are ... enabled to extend their commerce by means of canals, as they can thus export greater quantities and varieties of goods from places remote from the sea, and easily supply a wider extent of inland country with the commodities that are imported from foreign countries" (Rees, "Canals", borrowing from Phillips 1792; similar comments could be made for rivers and roads).

66 Ballot (1923), indeed, treated the period 1780–1815 as the age of machinism in France, when for the first time, the new technology was employed on a significant (though still small, relative to England) scale. He applauded the roles played by the various governments of the time in encouraging industrial innovation. He recognized that the necessary impetus for this behaviour was the example set by England and the fear that English industry would invade the French market (9). He quoted the 1795 report of the Bureau of Commerce, which concluded, "We cannot permit or leave to England her superiority of invention" (25).

CHAPTER TWO

1 Speaking in favour of the Trent and Mersey canal, Bentley suggested that once completed, it would save at least two thirds of the land carriage cost along the route, noting that the canal between Liverpool and Manchester had saved three quarters of the previous land carriage cost. He was correct

in predicting that various raw materials along the canal would be exploited for the first time due to this drop in cost of transport (in *Correspondence* 1906, 293).

2 William Stout, for one, sent goods by land to avoid privateers at sea (Albert 1967, 6).

3 In general, canals were more reliable than rivers. Garbett wrote to Darwin that promoters of the Trent and Mersey Canal should emphasize the "certainty of arrival" by canal as this was a major problem with rivers and many goods were thus sent by land even at double the price (*Correspondence* 1906, 265). Publicola had the same attitude toward the advantages of the Birmingham and Worcester Canal over the Severn: "The delays and damage incidental to such a navigation have induced the manufacturers of Birmingham to employ land carriage at a great expense ... to convey goods or manufactures which cannot await the delay or damage to which in the present navigation they are necessarily exposed" (1798, 15). Andreossey (an VIII, 10) agreed that canals were more reliable than rivers or coasting, as they were less vulnerable to nature.

4 Bourn was far from alone. Hutton (1791, 70) stated that, "According as a country is improved in her roads, so will she stand in the scale of civilization." The relationship between transport and civilization was remarked on by Say as well: "One could say that a nation is not civilized except to the extent of the means of communication one finds there" (1852, 302).

5 Major Rennell noted that Africa was peculiarly disadvantaged with respect to transport over two centuries ago: "But Africa stands alone in a geographical view. Penetrated by no inland seas like the Mediterranean, Baltic, or Hudson's Bay, nor overspread with extensive lakes like those of North America; nor having in common with the other continents rivers running from the centre to the extremities but on the contrary its regions separated from each other by the least practicable of all boundaries, arid deserts of such extent as to threaten those who traverse them with the most horrible of deaths, that arising from thirst. Placed in such circumstances, can we be surprised either by our ignorance of its interior part, or of the tardy progress of civilization in it" (Phillips 1792, x-xi).

6 Eighteenth-century knowledge of China was quite rudimentary. It was often considered a land of immense wealth, and stories of the great roads and canals had reached western ears. Thus Brooke (1759) and other authors of the time saw in China an example of a country that had achieved wealth through having a superior transport system.

7 It is worth noting that English roads were also better than any that had gone before. Roman roads have justifiably earned much praise but they were not the equal of eighteenth-century construction. Like the Chinese roads, they had been built primarily for military and administrative purposes. They often, for example, lacked bridges since armies or messengers

on horseback could ford streams. There were few wagons in Roman times, thus Roman roads would not likely have supported eighteenth-century traffic. (*De L'Importance* 1777, 50). Couderc (1829, 23–4), noted that Roman and modern roads were so different that they could not be compared.

8 In the Polish areas, for example, the wide rivers flowing into the Baltic provided a good link to foreign markets. There was, however, little linkage between different areas. The Poles had, in effect, better access to foreign markets than to their own. They thus were able to export large amounts of agricultural produce while lacking the internal integration capable of fostering industry. The situation can be compared to nineteenth- and twentieth-century colonies where the European powers established rail lines only from mine to market. One of the first priorities of independent governments was to attempt to integrate their transport systems.

9 "Let us further consider that Holland, the most populous and opulent country in the world (of its dimensions) owes much of its prosperity to its numerous canals, and would soon fall almost into desolation if deprived of them" (Phillips 1785, 29). De Vries (1981), however, has noted that many Dutch canals were restricted to the transport of passengers and thus did not play the role that they might have.

10 It is worth noting that Belgium, the second country in Europe to industrialize, had a road-building boom in the mid-eighteenth century and then in the nineteenth adopted the English turnpike system and greatly expanded its road network (Pollard 1981, 125–7).

11 Brooke could see the advantages accruing to England from inland navigation. He bemoaned the lack of similar improvements in Ireland. "As I have already observed that Ireland is of all countries the best situated and by nature made the most susceptible of an inland navigation, I shall further take notice that of all countries it is in the greatest want thereof ... Hence it is that the inner parts of this island resemble a desert, or, at best, are a stock farm for the propagation of cattle ... So that Ireland lies like a carcass whose exterior parts are kept warm by outward application, while the heart and vitals are inanimate, that should naturally communicate both action and nourishment to the whole system" (1759, 64–6). Burkitt (1755) decried the poor workmanship of the Boyne navigation. A Parliamentary Report of 1805 discussed the many failed efforts to improve Irish navigation in the eighteenth century. Those few projects which had succeeded – such as the Grand Canal – were deemed to charge excessive tolls. These high tolls had reduced the incentive to construct other navigation to connect with those in existence. It was felt again that the failure to construct adequate waterways was responsible for the backwardness of the Irish interior.

12 This was bemoaned by numerous contemporary authors. One spoke in 1792 of the potential gains from the unfinished Picardy canal, and added, "Many other canals in France, of a lesser extent and a less difficult execution, rest also with their creator" (F12 1515). In most of these cases, it does not appear that the problem was insurmountable geographical obstacles, as evidenced by the fact that many projects would be completed in the nineteenth century.

13 The emphasis on canals in France was also misguided – canals were projected, and occasionally finished, between rivers that were hardly navigable. Members of the Royal Academy of Sciences advised the supporters of canal construction in Brittany that they should first concentrate on simple and less expensive river improvements, after which it would be easier to determine if and where canals were needed (Bossut 1786, 18–19). Butet found it necessary to advise the Departmental Assembly of Cher of the simple idea that canals should only be built where it was not possible to make rivers navigable (Butet, an 5, 14). In England, canal construction only came after river improvements were basically complete.

14 Pillet-Will (1837, 204–6) still found much to criticize in French waterways. The upper Loire was little better than a torrent, and the lower Loire was dangerous in a number of places. Boats were stranded on the Canal du Centre for months for lack of water (207). The upper Saône, which was the endpoint for the Rhône and Rhine and Burgundy canals, was slow and difficult and stopped in places for months (276). Pillet-Will suggested that one had only to look at the effect of the canals linking Liverpool and London for an idea of what canals linking Paris with Lyon or Marseilles might achieve (ch. 8).

15 It even appears that some navigable rivers had become unnavigable in France. In the seventeenth century, the Seine was navigable to Bar-sur-Seine; in the eighteenth only to Troyes (Sée 1939, 295). Dutens (1829, Intro., 37n) invoked other historians to show that many previously navigable rivers throughout the country could no longer be so described. As for efforts at improvement, even Tucker, who generally praised French transport, was aware that French rivers remained largely the products of nature (1762, 10).

16 Since I am concerned here with the provision of sufficient transport links for an industrial revolution, I need not dwell on the fact that some English waterways proved to have insufficient capacity once the Industrial Revolution was underway.

17 "It was natural that extending and improving the navigation of rivers should be the first expedient thought of for this purpose, and many projects of this kind were brought to effect in this kingdom before the more expensive and artificial construction of canals was ventured upon" (Aikin

1831, 105). That this "natural" order was not followed in France is perhaps indicative of the impact of centralized bureaucratic decision making,
and of an emphasis on impressive achievements in civil engineering rather
than on what was best for the economy.

18 Du Lac de La Tour D'Aurec wrote of a dangerous, rocky passage on the
Loire (1807, 180). Dutens agreed with many on the need for a lateral
canal between Briare and Dijon but no progress was made on this stretch
during the eighteenth century (1829, 220).

19 Bernard was especially critical of the situation at the mouth of the Rhône.
The sandbars shifted so much that they were daily marked by buoys
(1779, 73). Still, currents there and elsewhere on the river often pushed
boats into rocks or sand (15–17). Bernard felt that while the Romans had
managed to improve the mouth of the Rhône, the French had allowed it
to become very dangerous (4–5). Though funds had been allotted for
improvements, they had not been spent (1779, 43).

20 This was, perhaps, even more true of the lesser rivers. In 1813, merchants
from all ports along the Allier complained of the poor state of the river
thanks to rocks, trees, etc. (F14 589).

21 That the overall picture was quite bad was noted by contemporaries.
Raup-Baptestin spoke of river navigation in 1789 as "hindered almost everywhere, and necessarily slow, troublesome, I could also say very dangerous at a number of points" (an IX, 13).

22 Dutens (1829, 37) concurred that extremes in water levels rendered many of
France's great rivers unnavigable for part of the year. Salt merchants complained in 1813 of their inability to reach the Paris market at the correct time
due to the closure of the Orleans and Loing canals and low water in the
Loire river (F12 1515). The author of a Report to the Minister of the Interior in an 12 noted that many French canals were dry part of the year "less
because they lack water than because they are not built wisely" (F12 1515).

23 When discussing ice, it must be remembered that climatic conditions in
northwestern Europe during much of the eighteenth century were quite
different than they are today. De Vries, using data on Dutch canal closures and French grape harvests, deduced that the period from 1634 to the
present could be divided into five climatic eras. The years from 1698 to
1758 generally saw much colder winters than we do – more like the climate of the so-called little ice age of 1840 to 1939. From 1758 to 1839,
the climate was closer to today's (1977, 214). The transition points
between periods are rough estimates. De Vries unfortunately lacks data on
canal closures for the period between 1758 and 1813. It would appear,
then, that the actual date of transition from cold to warm climate may
have occurred later in the century. De Vries' data on the number of days
the Haarlem-Leiden Canal was closed due to ice are of interest to us in

their own right. Of the years 1700–57, only eight saw no closure due to ice. The average for this period was about twenty-three days with seven years in which over fifty days were lost.

24 Bentley noted that speed of water transport was of special importance as it reduced the possibility of pilferage or adulteration *en route*. Potters had often sent their goods by road at three times the cost to protect their reputation (*Correspondence* 1906, 288–9). "The expedition in conveying goods by inland navigation being a matter of great importance to traders, it is worthy of remark that goods are frequently carried coastwise from London to Gainsborough, and from thence into Staffordshire, by means of the River Trent and the Grand Trunk Canal, from fourteen to twenty days, and from Hull to Manchester in ten days, a distance of nearly 250 miles" (Cary 1795, 28).

25 French waterways suffered in other ways from government interference. The need to collect tolls and enforce various regulations meant that government officers often stopped and searched boats. There was also an increased amount of paperwork (F12 1512C d.6). A curious example of the prevailing attitude toward commerce was Bruguière's suggestion (an III) that Paris was not correctly provisioned because there not enough boats; hence the government should subsidize boat construction.

26 Liverpool received its first act for building docks in 1708 and expanded its port facilities greatly over the next decades. Hull's first act for dock-building came in 1774 and London waited till the 1790s to expand its facilities (Rees, "Docks"). However, much work in dredging, building retaining walls, etc., was carried on in various English ports in the eighteenth century. In France, far less was accomplished. Rouen remained unchanged. It was impractical for a quarter of the year (F12 1515). Le Havre was rarely accessible to larger ships and protection from shifting sandbars was only achieved in the nineteenth century (Montalivet 1813, 43). It also was in its original state (Noël de la Morinière 1795, 83–6). Marseilles required much work in the nineteenth century thanks to sand accumulation in the previous century (Montalivet 1813, 43–4).

27 "The merchants who reside at the ports where they [canals] terminate must also derive very considerable advantages from them, as they are enabled by them to export greater quantities of goods from places at a distance from the sea, and to supply with ease a greater extent of inland country with the commodities they import from foreign nations" (Phillips 1792, iii). "To the beneficial effects of these canals Liverpool has to attribute much of her present greatness" (Rees, "Liverpool"). Aikin (1831, 338–42) and Brindley (1766, 68–9) describe the role of transport improvements in fostering the growth of Liverpool. Brindley notes that the Trent and Mersey Canal was first surveyed at the expense of the Liverpool Corporation (55–6). Elsewhere, Priestley (1831, 681) describes the extent of the

hinterland that came to be serviced by the port of Hull. Nor was all the expansion to serve foreign trade. There had been fears that canal construction would replace the coasting trade but instead, coasting tonnage rose dramatically between 1760 and 1790 (Ure 1836, 180).

28 "On the Channel, nature has done everything for England; she has done everything against us. During the reign of Louis XVI, we had perceived the importance of having a port on that sea" (Montalivet 1813, 60). Not only was France slow in providing good port facilities but it was slow in construction of lighthouses as well. Rees ("Lighthouses") describes with approval the efforts from 1690 to 1750 to build one on the Eddystone rock off Plymouth. In 1785, French authorities were still trying to raise enough money to build four lighthouses along the coast of Normandy, a project that had been underway for at least twelve years (F12 1512 d.12).

29 Beyond the problem with port facilities, the French coasting trade was also hampered by regulation. Say decried the fact that French captains had to take exams, unlike their English counterparts, but that there were no fewer accidents as a result. Other obstacles to coasting were furnished by military, customs, and health authorities (1852, v.1, 332).

30 Noël de la Morinière (an VII, 39) cited England as a country France should look to, for there the advantages of canals were fully understood and the system was rapidly being perfected. Of course, one can also find English writers who were impressed by such French achievements as the Languedoc Canal. The best evidence of English superiority is the efforts of people such as Becquey (1820) in the nineteenth century to induce drastic changes in French internal navigation. Lequinio noted that the English network had already progressed to the point where there were small canals between the large ones which still were useful for carrying heavy objects (an III, 11).

31 "Before carriages of burden were in use, little more was required than a path upon hard ground, that would bear horses. All marshy grounds were therefore shunned, the fords of rivers were resorted to, and the inequality or circuit of the road was of much less consequence than when carriages instead of packhorses began to be employed" (Edgeworth 1817, 3).

32 Packhorses may have been fed as much as 40 per cent less than wagon horses, so that the cost differential may be exaggerated by these figures (I am indebted on this point, and other horse-related matters, to a private conversation with Dorian Gerhold). The quality of road made a huge difference to the size of a load and the speed at which it could be pulled. "It is proven, by the experience of workers, that a wagon, on old roads, in a season which is neither the driest nor the worst, could not carry but one third of the cargo which it can carry on a new road, and that it can cover three lieues on the new roads in the same time it covered two on the old" (De L'Importance 1777, 18–19).

33 Pawson (1979, 141) provides a brief description of turnpike development in the early eighteenth century: "They were empowered to levy tolls on road users (according to prescribed schedules), and to borrow money on the security of the tolls, for the maintenance and improvement of their roads. Turnpike Acts were readily granted from the 1690s, as parishes petitioned Westminster, often with evidence of considerable extra contributions to road repair over preceding years. By 1750, there were 143 trusts in existence, repairing at least 3,400 miles of road. [Buchanan (1986), looking at the original acts for many trusts that were expanded in size, points out that the rate of growth of turnpike mileage is underestimated.] Although they were local bodies, often controlling only twenty miles of road or so, they had combined to form a coherent network of improving roads. Lines of turnpike road radiated from London, particularly to the north and west, and into the Midlands. There was an extensive network of trusts in the industrialising and rich agricultural counties of the West Midlands, as well as several links over the Pennines between the growing economies of Lancashire and Yorkshire, and some important coal routes further north. The line of trusts on the Great North Road was almost unbroken to the Scottish Border."

34 Albert looked at thirteen main routes emanating from London and found that they were virtually completely turnpiked by 1750. Those sections with the most traffic, and those with the worst natural conditions, had been turnpiked first.

35 "[S]ince the erection of turnpikes in England, the roads have received such improvement as to abate the price of land carriage generally thirty per cent (Rolt 1761, "Roads"). "There never was a more astonishing revolution accomplished in the internal system of any country than has been within the compass of a few years in England" (Homer 1767, 8).

36 "The introduction of turnpikes turned the attention of gentlemen to the improvement of crossroads; but for many years in some places, and in some to this very day, the crossroads of England continue in a wretched state of repair" (Edgeworth 1817, 4).

37 Languedoc roads benefitted from two factors: provincial Estates willing to expend vast sums on main routes, as well as hot warm weather which made maintenance easier.

38 "Add that most of our crossroads are in so pitiful a state that it is necessary to wait for a favourable season" (Ornay 1776, 11). "Leave a route of the post or messagerie, you are no longer walking on a road, you are on a narrow footpath, tortuous, of four or five feet in width, often as well you think with reason you are in a ditch destined to receive the water which flows across the fields. A perpetual mud, caused by the height of the banks and the thickness of the hedges" (De Vitry 1777, 64).

39 English roads likely had an edge in 1700. Still, areas of backwardness in England can be found till mid-century. Andrew Thompson travelled from

Glasgow to London on horseback in 1739. There was no turnpike until Grantham. Before then, he travelled on a narrow causeway with soft road on each side. He had to get off the causeway for at least one packhorse train and had difficulty getting back on (Add MS 27828, 10). Hey (1980, 66) has noted that this type of "road" was quite common before the eighteenth-century road improvements. As late as 1769, an Englishman drowned in a roadside ditch, a mishap more common in earlier days (Copeland 1968, 11).

40 Though turnpike trusts suffered from waste and inefficiency due in part to inexperience, they did regularly repair the roads. "Despite these shortcomings ... the repairs undertaken by these trusts proved to be fairly effective and provided benefits for both the road user and the economy" (Albert 1967, 167). From the records of a Warwickshire trust, Homer (1767, 78) calculated that it took at least £84 a year to properly maintain one mile of road properly, and suggested that other roads could be more expensive.

41 "After a road has been made, it will for some time require the attention of the maker; ruts will be continually formed in the loose materials, these must be sedulously filled up, and a small sprinkling of river gravel should be added. All stones larger than the rest should be removed and broken smaller, and no pain should be spared to render the whole as compact and smooth as possible" (Edgeworth 1817, 29).

42 "Technically well conceived and constructed, many of the French highways carried little commercial traffic, having been built for political and strategic reasons and having only poor connections with the villages and small towns in which the majority of the population lived. Local roads remained poor and bridges were often falling in ruin; little was done to remedy the situation. As a result each area was bound to be highly self-sufficient; it could not sell its produce far afield and consequently it could exert little pull on distant producers" (Kemp 1971, 52).

43 This paucity of royal roads meant that there were huge gaps in the system. "The mail carriers, post wagons, diligences, and wagons which leave departments situated to the south, southeast, or east of the department of Allier, to reach those which are situated in the northwest of France, and those which border the Loire, cannot do so except by going through Paris; whereas if a route were opened from Moulins to Tours or Blois by Bourget, one could save 66 lieues both going and returning" (Butet, an V, 9).

44 Petot provides a lengthy discussion of differing regional effects, noting for example how Languedoc and Bourgogne had considerable success in road-building, while Bretagne and Provence put little effort into roads.

45 Sée (1939, 298–9) provides some examples of freight speeds and prices. He concludes that roulage was both slow and expensive and was little improved in the second half of the eighteenth century.

46 Léon describes diligences as heavy, unstable, slow, and uncomfortable, and notes that writers such as Hugo and Balzac described them as horrible

(1976, 251). Edgeworth (1817, 103) agreed that the diligence was "a most uncommodious uncouth uneasy vehicle." He felt that the English stage-coach was certainly better though there were limits on its speed until springs were introduced "in the last few years". There was a natural connection between improvements in roads and improvements to the carriages which travelled upon them (Add MS 27828, 14). Better English coaches, then, are themselves symbolic of superior English roads.

47 This does not mean that there was no regular coach service on lesser routes in England. Jackman (1916), for example, lists a regular coach from Oxford to Southampton in 1790. These have just not shown up in my sample. Though many English interprovincial routes saw coaching services only in the last quarter of the eighteenth century, regular carrying services had long existed. In France, regular services occurred only on main routes. For France, Léon (1976, 177) cites evidence from primary sources that speeds on many French routes did not improve over the course of the century. Toulouse to Marseille took twenty days at the start and end of the century. He notes that the many gaps in the French road system made apparent gains in speed illusory.

48 When speaking of payment, one must consider the existence of highway-men. Calonne (1801), formerly the chief of the French Maréchaussée (horse patrol), felt that Ancien Régime France had been adequately protected from such crime and recommended the formation of a similar force in England. This call was echoed by at least one other author (*Proposal*, 1764). Whitehead (1834) felt that highwaymen had been eliminated by the establishment of the patrol, as well as the increased use of paper currency and other forms of credit. Yet his book makes no reference to the existence of highwaymen after 1750. Beattie (1986) indicates that the incidence of highway robbery had dropped steadily over the eighteenth century as traffic on the roads increased.

49 Pawson (1979, 154) discusses the role of improved information flows due to better transport in the English Industrial Revolution: "Speedier and more reliable information flow was a central characteristic of the Industrial Revolution: indeed, it was essential for it. It was through the postal system that firms kept in touch with their suppliers, buyers, and customers. The mail was the only effective means by which the new, large firms of the eighteenth century could coordinate their various parts: Abraham Crowley showed the way, but Wedgwood, Boulton, Arkwright, Wilkinson, all depended on the letter-post as did the smaller manufacturer and tradesman, the merchant and farmer."

50 Boislandry (1815) still spoke of the need to eliminate abuses of monopoly power. Another way to reduce the cost of mail service would be to borrow the English idea of sending some mail on coaches that would travel day and night and only carry small packages (136).

51 "Many persons now living must remember that it was not uncommon formerly for a rich Birmingham manufacturer to make his will before he took his departure for London" (Edgeworth 1817, 103). The safety of coaches was still an issue in the nineteenth century thanks in large part to increased ridership (Milton, 1810), but the risk associated with a lengthy trip had dropped considerably in the previous century.

52 Meuvret (1988, v.3, 57) agrees that dispersion was so great that it would be inappropriate to speak of an average. Price (1983, 43–5) describes difficulties in estimating French transport costs even in the nineteenth century. This in itself is evidence of a more haphazard, less reliable, less integrated system.

53 Albert noted that government regulations in England reduced the maximum number of horses per wagon between 1662 and 1751 while increasing the maximum allowed load from between twenty and thirty cwt. in 1662 to sixty cwt in 1741. "This lends support to the view that the significance of trust development before the Turnpike Mania has been seriously underestimated" (1967, 181). Rolt asserted that "a team of six horses can now draw 50 or 60 cwt. with more ease than 30 cwt was drawn before the establishing of turnpikes" (1761, "Roads"). Wrigley has noted in addition that France had only sixty-two per cent of the horses and two thirds of the oxen per square mile of England, and this could have been of great advantage to the English system (1988, 41).

54 This point was sometimes lost on contemporaries. One writer felt in 1756 that, while pikes had done much good, tolls would be a great drag on trade; hence he recommended that the army maintain the roads (Add MS 27966, 281).

55 On top of these were the effects of government regulation, which limited markets and the quality of service. (Boislandry 1815, 126). Boislandry goes on to recommend that the diligence monopoly be ended, the tax on places and *paquets* be removed, and the law forcing operators to pay the post for horses they did not use repealed.

56 Frequent tolls caused a doubling or tripling of the price of water transport (Letaconneux 1908–09, 287). Whereas English tolls were payments for efforts to improve waterways, most French tolls were simply payments to local landowners or authorities, or the crown, for the right to pass (though the right to charge tolls had often originally been attached to a responsibility for dredging etc.). Added to the unnecessary expense of such tolls was the cost of the delay and inconvenience associated with stopping to pay them. In 1774, it was estimated there were still more than seventy tolls on the Loire below Saint-Rambert. Each time, the boat had to stop to pay, and this meant arriving during office hours, and often waiting in long lines. Moreover illiterate boatmen could easily be abused by toll-takers for the tolls varied with the goods carried (F12 1512A).

57 Pilfering was not, of course, unknown in England. The raiding of brandy barrels by boatmen was legendary. Baxendale was sure that this was exaggerated and the actual amount of pilfering was trivial (see Turnbull 1979, 95).

58 Léon (1976, 544) concurs with this judgment: "At the start of the nineteenth century, in effect, the industrial geography of France ... was characterized essentially by its dispersion."

59 It is, of course, possible to disentangle the two effects using the methodology applied by Weir (1984). While capable of showing that integration increased over time, studies based on one country can only provide limited insight into the questions I am concerned with. Comparative studies along these lines, while difficult, could potentially provide great insight into the relative degrees of market integration in different countries.

60 "There exist in France thousands of situations where wine, fruit, coal, and iron ore are abundant and inexpensive, if they could be sold, but the charge it is necessary to pay to carry these goods from their localities raises the price above that which consumers can afford" (Say 1852, v.2, 309).

61 Evidence of the emphasis on local consumption can be found in the number of different weights and measures used throughout France. In the Eure et Loire, the basic unit of measure was the *minot*, but at each of eight different markets in this area the *minot* meant something different, ranging from 24,000 to 40,000 cubic centilitres (Peuchet, 1807). The story was the same in many departments. Increased trade would naturally increase the benefits of a unified system of weights and measures.

62 Only in the late nineteenth century did many village communities overcome their isolation. Weber's excellent work describes how cut off from French national society villagers were through most of the century. They rarely left their villages because of the difficulty and expense of travel (1976, 198–9). Many areas saw no wheeled carts until the late nineteenth century (200). Weber quotes Marcel Lachiver: "It was not the railroads that changed the countryside in the second half of the nineteenth century; it was the creation of roads that could be used in all seasons" (200). Eighteenth-century efforts on main highways had had little effect on rural villages. "A system built to serve the government and cities and lacking a supporting network of secondary thoroughfares had little to do with popular habit or need" (195).

63 Braudel's discussion of peddling (1982, 79) provides further evidence of inferior French transport. Braudel makes two points: that peddling occurs when alternative local methods of distribution are absent, and that pedlars are supposed to have disappeared in eighteenth-century England while remaining important well into the next century in France.

64 Unfortunately, most French regional histories ignore the state of transport services. Price (1983, 24) comments on the lack of space given to communications in regional works by both historians and geographers. Those that do address transport generally speak only of state expenditures, with no indication of what they resulted in. Primary works provide a greater insight into the state of eighteenth-century transport.

65 "This departement, in spite of the numerous reservoirs and the immense amount of water on its surface, has no navigation ... People have been occupied at various times with means to open to the province of Berry, of which this department is part, a navigation which could put it in communication with other parts of France" (Peuchet 1807, "Indre"). The provincial assembly had devised many projects. Some at least – such as making the Creuse navigable – were clearly possible, but nothing came of them.

66 Peuchet saw this unfinished canal as more important than the Saône et Loire or Languedoc canals. "It suffices to glance at a map to recognize the importance of the canal du Bourgogne, it joins the two seas, facilitates the transport of the goods of Burgundy to the south of France, and those of the south to the interior, it allows wine, iron, grain, hemp to avoid the long passage by the canal du Charolais, or du Centre, and the canal d'Auxerre, in order to reach Paris and the navigable rivers of the Seine basin" (1807, "Côte d'Or"). Construction of the canal, suspended in 1792, had recently begun again.

67 The roads in the Aube were also bad. Many of the main roads were incomplete, though "The expenses necessary to finish the roads are not large" (Bruslé, an 10, 28). "Complaints are general of the poor state of the roads" (30). The reason for this predated the Revolutionary period. "If, at the start, they had made a solid base and followed the principles of the art, roads repaired with care would be good. But the embankment was never made" (29).

68 The only navigation in the Haut-Marne was the Marne itself to St-Dizier. It was hoped in the early nineteenth century that the government would devote funds from its recently imposed tax on navigation to extend the navigation to Vitry, as had been demanded for some time (Annuaire 1804, 119–20).

69 The Aisne had only three first-class roads, ten third-class roads and one departmental road. "The other departmental roads are only projected" (Miroy-Detournelles 1813, 185–6). The intensive network of good roads seen in England was still in the planning stages here.

70 Important improvements to water transport, as to roads, awaited the nineteenth century. "To give more movement to the commercial enterprises of Mulhouse, people are impatient that the new canal become navigable" (Mieg 1823, xvii). The Haut-Rhine had no significant internal navigation

though few countries possessed such potential due to the great number of watercourses (Peuchet 1807, "Haut-Rhine").

71 "The necessary provisioning of Paris has always excited the vigilance of the government on the means to make navigable the rivers which could carry it. This is why we have opened the canals of Briaire and Orleans, and consider countless others" (*Memoir of Brullée* 1786, F12 1513). Brullée goes on to note that these rivers and canals are often interrupted by flood, drought, ice, and maintenance work. The water level was often too low at Paris for boats to arrive.

72 Quillebeuf, near the mouth of the Seine, was famous for shipwrecks; the sandbanks were caused at least in part by the sinuosity of the river (Noël de la Morinière 1795, 62–3). The government had long recognized the need to clear the riverbed but had done nothing; "We have, in that, followed a direction entirely different from that of our neighbours, the English: we lack ports, refuges, canals etc., and those islanders possess all of these" (64). "All the world knows that the navigation of the Seine, below Paris, is long, expensive, often, and sometimes for half the year, interrupted by flood, drought, ice etc., exposed to these dangers, these losses, and to great delays, who would not prefer, most often, passage by roadway" (Lemoyne 1791. *Précis Historique Sur Le Canal de Paris à Dieppe et à Roven*. F12 1513).

73 Of the district of Gournay Noël de la Morinière wrote, "People have complained for a long time that the riches of this territory lack outlets, the butter, cheese, cider, and eggs have only a limited consumption, and the only way to make the land more valuable is to open roads and canals which will allow communication with large centres in distant districts" (1795, 11).

74 Becquey (1820, 11) spoke of the Nord as the one example in France of how a region could develop economically when supplied with good communication. Peuchet (1807) listed about twenty small canals in the Nord and said the area had long been provided with a good network. The Pas du Calais also had many canals for navigation, irrigation, and flood control. "But these canals do not form everwhere a perfectly combined hydraulic system" (Peuchet, "Pas de Calais"). Nevertheless, it is clear that these two departments possessed the best water network in eighteenth-century France.

75 In chapter 4, I discuss in some detail the problems faced by the Anzin coal company in getting its output to consumers through the transport network of the Nord.

76 It should be noted that many of the canal schemes carried out after the Duke of Bridgwaters' had been proposed over a century earlier. See Cunningham (1921, 532).

77 Sée has noted that the Ponts et Chaussées budget rose from 700,000 livres under Louis XIV to seven million by 1789 (1939, 294). Still, many authors maintained that this budget was far too small to look after French roads, especially after the end of the corvée (*De L'Importance* 1777, 113, Couderc 1829, 8).

78 Hawke and Higgins (1983) suggested that one sees private social overhead capital in England for two reasons: because development occurred slowly and because England was relatively rich. If France was in fact as rich as England one is still left with the question of why slow but steady transport improvement (private or public) did not occur to the same extent as in England. Once France (and the rest of Europe) had fallen far behind England in terms of transport, it would take massive government expenditures, as well as private investment, to catch up.

79 Contemporaries were also divided on the issue. Dutens argued that France had the advantage with its many great rivers flowing in all directions, while England was divided by a chain of mountains. He even thought that this explained the English advantage in canals, for which they had a greater need (1829, 76–7). Raup-Baptestin also saw French geography as advantageous. "Of all the parts of Europe, France is perhaps the most favoured by nature for water transport ... but feudal privileges are an often fatal barrier to useful projects" (an IX, 9). Noël de la Morinière, however, felt that nature had given England "the lakes, the volumes of water which most French departments lack, without vast forests and snowcapped mountains: this gives them over us and all lands of dry plains, an incontestable superiority" (an VII, 39). Yet elsewhere he noted that the English, unlike the French, had not been satisfied with the natural state and had devoted much effort to improvement (1795, 64–5).

80 Any geographical advantage England possessed may have increased the marginal return on any project by tying it to a larger existing network. This appears to be part of the explanation offered by Say, though he also writes of the important effects of good legislation in England (1852, v.2, 316). Many French authors spoke of one advantage that France may have had with respect to returns on transport investment. This was the fact that France alone spanned two distinct climatic zones and thus possessed greater potential for internal trade than any other country in Europe (Andreossey an VIII, 7; Becquey 1820, 7; Dutens 1829, 2).

81 If Englishmen were better disposed toward transport improvement, the feeling was far from unanimous. "I beg leave to call your attention however engaged to a matter which appears to be pregnant with much public mischief – you are not ignorant that a rage for canals has long prevailed and is at length become, if I may so speak, epidemical. The inconvenience and even injury which frequently arise from them to the owners and

occupiers of land are too well known to need being set out by me. Equally unnecessary is it that I should attempt to describe the effect they have on the general appearance of the countries through which they pass. Every traveller of taste sees and laments it" (letter to Pitt 1793, HO 42/24).

82 A writer in the 1790s asserted that publicly funded works always cost much more than privately funded: "the canals of Picardy, Burgundy, Charolais, Givors, Berry, etc. are good examples, many were started over fifty years ago, if not undertaken by companies aided by the government they would have been long since in operation" (F12 1515). Louis XIV bought the necessary land for a Eure-Loir canal and work was near completion but Louis XV sold the land (Peuchet, "Eure et Loir"). The Canal de Bourgogne was completed in 1793 by a private company under government supervision. This, Dutens noted, had by his time become an acceptable way of proceeding, but was not so thought of in the eighteenth century (1829, 207).

83 "Already we have public roads from one end to the other of the Kingdom, and of obvious beauty. Unfortunately their merit is only on the outside, on the surface. They are noble, wide (too much so, no doubt), built at great cost, rigorously straight, but poorly made, much too flat" (Ornay 1776, 7). The best evidence of the extent of eighteenth-century waste is nineteenth-century determination to end it. D'Haussez felt that it was necessary to renounce ostentation to achieve good roads (1828, 6), and noted that canals were often designed by engineers in new and expensive ways; some projects were delayed or stopped as a result while others were never begun (D'Haussez, 24, 30–1). Becquey tried to instill a new spirit among engineers: "Solidity, economy, and celerity, these are the principal obligations we must fulfill ... Never forget that these are not monuments which . we are to build, but essentially useful works ... I can not insist too much on the observation that, in navigation work, the glory of the engineer consists above all in attaining the goal with the least expense" (*Rapport*, 1820, 15–8).

84 D'Haussez asserted that the reason why England had succeeded in building roads where needed while France had not was that the English relied on local initiative. Local people would recognize the utility of a road or canal (1828, 40). He neglects the important ability to charge tolls, in the absence of which local people in both countries had displayed unwillingness to repair roads used by others.

85 "Engineers would visit a particular stretch of road only twice a year, creating a possibility for great abuse (D'Haussez 1828, 7–8). Mahuet (an VIII, 5) recommended the establishment across France of locally based groups of workers. He stated that it had been proven that small, regular repairs were less expensive than large-scale efforts. Say (1852, v.2, 302)

agreed that decentralized, regular inspection and maintenance were needed.

86 "It is incontestable that the attitude of power with respect to roads never varied. They were and remained an instrument of the state" (Léon 1976, 244). The attitude toward waterways was somewhat less close-minded. In the nineteenth century, the government would be more willing to compromise.

87 Lequinio made the point that people will only pay the toll if they are better off doing so (an I, 19–20). Mahuet (an VIII, 9) noted that good turnpikes would allow travel time to drop enough to more than compensate for the toll charged. A toll was established on French roads in 1797 but it was considered unfair given the poor state of French roads and was withdrawn in 1806 (Couderc 1829, 13–17). In 1828, D'Haussez calls for tolls on selected roads (not on all roads as during the Revolution) and reasserted that those who used the road should pay (1828, 43–4).

88 It would be too easy to define the difference between England and France as one between public and private initiative. Nevertheless, there is some truth in the notion. Later chapters will show that industrial enterprises run by eighteenth-century governments were horribly inefficient. However, one must remember that English turnpikes and river improvements were made by non-profit companies. The overriding dichotomy is between centralized and decentralized decision making.

89 "But as no extensive work, however generally desired, could be executed without interruption, from the perverseness of some individuals, or the inability of others to contract (where the estate belongs to a minor, or is fettered by family settlements), the intervention of Parliament becomes necessary. The authority of the legislature compels a sale, securing a liberal compensation by the same means which protect all our rights, the decision of a jury, where the parties cannot agree" (Publicola 1798, 3–4).

90 Corbière, the Secretary of the Interior, complained that despite new laws, some landowners were holding out for exorbitant prices for their land, and it was often necessary to take lengthy legal action in order to force them to do what was in the public interest. Interruptions to construction were the result (*Rapport* 1824, 8–9). D'Haussez suggested that to avoid arbitrary seizure, the English rules for expropriation should be adopted (1828, 60).

CHAPTER THREE

1 The reader is referred to Raistrick (1970, 9–11) for examples of such trips and the customers dealt with.

2 Lloyd echoes Hunter (1819, 168) who stated that in the middle of the eighteenth century, "The cutler himself had to rely for custom on the factor,

or chapman, who periodically visited the town; whilst some of the more affluent manufacturers carried their articles to the country fairs, and a few to London."

3 Hutton (1791, 70) claimed that the chief cause of Birmingham's rapid increase was the replacement of face-to-face sales by merchants riding out through England and into foreign parts. Like many authors of the time, he overemphasizes the importance of foreign markets.

4 Again, Lloyd echoes Hunter speaking of the early eighteenth century: "Even the home consumption was principally supplied by means of the London houses, the manufacturers of Sheffield scarcely doing more than sending small ventures to Chester, Bristol, and some other places at the time of their annual fairs" (1819, 153).

5 Aikin, at the time, had a keener insight into the reasons for Sheffield's rise from an unpromising state in the seventeenth and early eighteenth centuries: "Their trade was inconsiderable, confined, and precarious. None presumed to extend their traffic beyond the bounds of this island, and most were content to await the coming of a casual trader rather than to carry their goods, with much labour and expense, to an uncertain market. Old persons still remember that the produce of the manufactury was conveyed weekly by pack horse to the metropolis ... In 1751 the River Don was made navigable up to within three miles of the town, which greatly facilitated the conveyance of goods abroad. A stage-wagon was set up by Mr. Wright which was soon succeeded by others. Master-manufacturers began to visit London in search of orders with good success ... The roads began to be greatly improved, and Britain and Ireland were thoroughly explored in search of trade. The fairs in different parts of the kingdom annually decreased in their importance, because shopkeepers could be easily supplied with goods at any time of year" (1795, 547–8).

6 Bentley, advocating further canal construction, notes that transport charges are so important for guns, nails, etc., that it is impossible to estimate the gain to those trades from transport improvements (1906, p. 305). Priestley speaks of the role of such canals as the Staffordshire and Worcestershire in giving the Black Country metal trades access to the national market (1831, 618).

7 Hutton said of the 1767 canal to Birmingham that "This watery passage ... tends greatly to the improvement of some branches of trade, by introducing heavy materials at a small expense, such as pig-iron for the foundries, limestone, articles for the manufacture of brass and steel, also stone, brick, slate, timber, etc." (1791, 267). The Soho foundry alone in 1798 needed almost 3000 tons of coal, 900 tons of copper, sixty tons of lime, 300 of engine materials, thirty of timber, and forty of sundries; not surprisingly the major concern in planning a new foundry was that it be on the banks of a canal (Boulton and Watt Records, Box 37). Among Soho's

other requirements was sulphuric acid: 13,333 lbs were used in 1792–94 (Clow, 1952, 144).

8   Boulton alone produced eighty tons of buttons in 1798 (Boulton and Watt Records, Box 37.) A more complete list of raw materials is supplied by Rees ("Buttons"): "The number of substances of which they are made is almost inconceivable, and each requires a distinct set of manipulation. Amongst them are gold, silver, plated copper, white metal, pinchbeck, steel, japanned tin, glass, soil stones, mother of pearl, ivory, bone, horn, tortoise-shell, jet, cannel, coal, paper, leather, and a thousand others."

9   In 1756, William Anderson estimated that making muskets involved twenty-one separate employments (Add MS 27966, 282).

10   Also, putting out to geographically dispersed workers would become exceedingly difficult as division of labour increased in degree. There would be an incentive to gather workers together to reduce the cost of moving semi-finished goods from one to another.

11   It would be impossible, without actually performing a variety of obsolete functions, to judge the level of skill involved in each. Mastering seemingly simple tasks could require much dexterity and practice. Berg (1981, 265–75) provides many examples of the continuing importance of certain skills despite substantial division of labour. However, some other strands of evidence seem to indicate a low level of skill in many early workshops. Rowlands describes how, at about mid-century, there was increasing social concern about the comparatively low wages being paid in the emerging workshops (1975, 157). If all else were equal, this would indicate that the level of skill required inside the workshops was lower than that required outside. Other explanations are, of course, plausible once it is recognized that in this historical case all else was not equal. The use of a substantial amount of child labour also points to a lack of skill in workshop labour. Lord Shelburne, commenting on the many steps involved in the button trade (see above), continued, "the work becomes so simple that 5 times in 6 children of 6 to 8 years old do it as well as men" (Court 1946, 96). In fact, one of the main reasons for the high level of child labour employment in England during the Industrial Revolution may be that workshops were built for those functions demanding the least skill and their main purpose was to employ labour more cheaply by dividing formerly skilled occupations into a series of simple tasks.

12   Here I have described only how transport-induced changes made the idea of centralizing work more attractive. The other side of the coin is that transport improvements simultaneously made centralization less costly by ensuring reliable supplies of material inputs and food, and allowing access to a wide market.

13   I am not, of course, implying that the later introduction of new machinery did not hasten the transition of whole industries to workshop produc-

tion, but merely asserting that the transformation to workshops began some time before the emergence of such technology, and thus must be explained in some other fashion.

14 When I look at the much better documented iron industry later, it will be seen that a number of minor innovations have been virtually ignored as attention focuses on Darby, Cort and other "major" inventors. It is not difficult to see, then, that a number of advances we do not know of could have occurred in various metal trades.

15 She goes on to say that historians have ignored how technology fit into organization structures because of the mistaken idea that these were determined by technology. Elsewhere, however, she (with others) writes that "these new tools also provided the opportunity for extensive subdivision of process and extreme specialization of production' (1983, 11). The new technology was, rather, designed to fit a world in which increased division of labour already existed.

16 "Technical change took the form of small improvements and adaptations of basic machines and handtools ... Many such innovations went unpatented and some were lost to the world when their products went out of fashion" (Berg 1983, 11).

17 See entries on buttons, nails, pipes and locks. Rees also noted that there were numerous attempts to devise machines for cutting files but none were successful ("Files"). Indeed, the precision required for a number of tasks in the metal trades rendered mechanization extremely difficult. Cutting a groove on the side of a needle was beyond the capability of the machines of the time. I will show later in this chapter that the ability to produce better machinery of many types was one of the key results of the changes in the iron industry in the eighteenth century. Thus, while much inventive effort late in the century produced no immediate success, the stage was being set for increased mechanization in the next.

18 Taking patent activity in Birmingham as a kind of proxy for innovative activity, one finds only one patent before 1738, then a slow increase until 1770 after which the increase in patents becomes more marked (Court 1938, 246). This fits well with the idea that the move toward workshops would promote innovative behaviour. While undoubtedly many of these patented "inventions" were never of any practical use, they still give evidence of increasing inventive activity and one must remember that workable inventions are more likely to emerge when a number of people are experimenting.

19 The application of stamping and pressing also depended on the previous development of new alloys of zinc and copper (Berg 1981, 298–9). Harris (1986) indicates that the use of stamps must predate 1755, for Alcock tried to introduce then to France in that year.

20 In addition, these machines were forerunners of increasingly automatic machines in the next century. See Musson and Robinson (1969, 430) for a

discussion of the role of two of the metal trades, watchmaking and buttonmaking, in the development of machine tools during the Industrial Revolution.

21 There were one or two slitting mills in England before 1750 but they only became widespread after that date. Hunter cites *Trade and Manufactury of Iron* (1750) as evidence that rolling and slitting mills existed, just like coke-smelting, but notes that "These details show some little progress in the iron trade but no approach to its present condition" (1819, 168).

22 "Rolling mills were not very generally used in the iron manufacture till within these sixty years" (Rees, "Rolling Mill"). While noting that "The operation of the rolling mill is so simple as scarcely to require any description," he discusses the difficulty of getting the rollers to move at the same speed: "if one roller moves quicker than the other, the metal becomes more extended on that side than on the other, and it is thus rendered convex." Various improvements were made to this rolling technology.

23 Though he does not mention Cort, Rees discusses Wilkinson's application of rollers to puddle iron in his section on the rolling mill.

24 Berthollet only proved in 1786 that the difference between wrought iron and steel was due to carbon content (Clow 1952, 341). The superiority of French science in the analysis of steel making had been evidenced earlier in the century. Savigny, in 1771, felt it necessary to translate Réaumur's work on tempering steel into English for the use of English mechanics, as there was no English author who could explain the process as well.

25 "The great difficulties which he [Huntsman] had to overcome were finding proper clay for his melting crucibles, which had to resist an intense heat, and obtaining a sufficient degree of heat, which he effected by the use of coke" (Hunter 1819, 170–1). "It has been lately found in the cast-steel works at Sheffield, that the best crucibles for their purpose are formed of the Stourbridge clay, worked up with powdered coke of pit-coal. This enables the crucibles to bear sudden changes of temperature, and at the same time to bear the greatest heat of our best airfurnaces" (Rees, "Pottery").

26 Nor was Huntsman's the only successful innovation. The process of tempering steel was improved by Hartley in 1789 by use of a thermometer and heated oil (Rees, "Tempering").

27 The author of *A Brief State of Facts* (1787) maintained that English output was restricted due to the poor quality of the product "for the raw materials are in a manner inexhaustible." Undoubtedly, puddling and rolling's ability to produce a homogeneous output made English iron much more attractive to customers.

28 In letters to Goldney in 1736, Richard Ford complains of the difficulty in finding buyers for all of the pots produced at Willay furnace (Coalbrookdale MS 3190).

29 Johnson (1951) describes how as the metal trades concentrated in Birmingham, the iron industry concentrated in rings around the town.

30 A writer in the 1780s noted that one of the factors delaying the establishment of new ironworks was that "it would be necessary to make many contracts for materials, and with workmen" (Add MS 38354). The weekly accounts of the Horsehay iron works for 1798 show weekly deliveries of ironstone, clod coal, and limestone. If anything, the furnace both receives and sells more in winter than in summer (Coalbrookdale MS 335).

31 In 1661, visitors to London complained to the king of the awful smell of coal in the city, an indication that the use of coal was uncommon in the English countryside. By the end of the eighteenth century, it could be claimed that almost the whole island was accustomed to the smell of coal (Add MS 5866, 222). Though he does no calculation, Flinn notes that by the end of the century, the proportion of the population that could not get coal except at prohibitive cost was exceedingly low (1985, 231).

32 Nevertheless, Scrivenor (1841, 56) did blame some of the problems of the early eighteenth-century iron industry (he believed output had fallen) on the fact that agriculture was encroaching on forest land. On the other hand, Thomas had described successful efforts to encourage government and landowners to replant trees in the seventeenth century, which helped make timber supply less of a problem in the eighteenth. (1986, 138).

33 Thomas (1986, 139–40) noted that the ability to use forest resources in the seventeenth century was restricted by the availability of transport links. Transport improvements in the next century, then, would add to the effective supply of timber.

34 Flinn correctly notes that the expansion of the iron industry in the late eighteenth and early nineteenth centuries would not have been possible if there had been continued reliance on domestic wood resources. However, there was no really damaging increase in the price of wood until long after the discovery of coke-smelting (1984, 452).

35 Indeed, Flinn notes that a number of innovations occurred in the early eighteenth century. Coal, the first industry to be significantly affected by transport improvements, was perhaps the first to respond technologically. Concentrations of large works could be seen on a number of coalfields in the first half of the century.

36 Not all coalfields could use the longwall method. It is not surprising, however, that the technique was being adopted where possible as mines gained increasing access to information on mining practices in other coalfields. In the seventeenth century, inland coal mines had been quite isolated.

37 Improvements in industrial organization may also have reduced cost (Flinn, 448). Flinn also concludes that transport improvements gave more consumers access to coal. While new technology allowed the pithead price

to remain relatively static (in part, perhaps, due to the breakup of monopoly power discussed later), it will be seen below that transport improvements meant a dramatic drop in price to most inland consumers.

38 "There are always certain expenses, called on-cost, attending every colliery, which is much the same whatever is the output ... Whether you raise 10 or 20,000 tons, the expenses of these engines are the same; the pay of the manager, oversman, wrights, smiths; the making roads below ground, sinking pits, and an infinite number of other things, must go on at the same expense whatever is the output of the colliery" (Johnson, 1793, 16–17). Perhaps exaggerating the importance of these costs, he computes that more profit can be made on 40,000 tons at four shillings per ton than on 10,000 at six shillings per ton.

39 In 1962, Davis listed thirty-six commodities by value per ton from Customs records of 1756. Wrought silk was highest at £3920 per ton; coal was lowest at less than £1 per ton (Flinn, 1984, 146).

40 "Before coals were brought here by water, they were at double the present price, owing to a badness of the roads by frequent carting, and on some roads no coals could be brought but on sacks upon horses: add to this there was a combination among the getters of coal, not to be broken by any force or law or reason" (Ogden 1783, 5–6). He credited to this change the tremendous increase in the size of Manchester since that time.

41 The geographical spread of the use of coal was quite extensive. Duckham (1983, 128–9) gives examples of coal moving halfway across England internally as a result of transport improvements. Staffordshire coal reached Reading, while Yorkshire coal reached Peterborough. I noted earlier that by the end of the century, almost all of England had access to reasonably priced coal.

42 In some cases, transport improvements allowed coal to be obtained from sites with lower extraction costs. "In [some] coalfields the coming of the canals permitted an extension of the developed area within the coalfields, often towards more easily mined, or better quality seams" (Flinn, 447).

43 Flinn, naturally, did not miss this phenomenon. He also notes the efforts of monopolists to prevent canal construction, and, citing Ardayfio, recognizes that after canal construction competitive pressures did push prices down, especially in the Midlands (1984, 185–7).

44 Long-distance travel was generally required for the appropriate mixture. Ironstone from the Midlands was shipped to Cumberland, as it was found that mixing two ores produced the best tough iron (Aikin 1831, 121). Cumberland ore was shipped to the Midlands for the same reason. Bentley felt that one of the benefits of improved inland navigation would be to facilitate the mixture of northern and Staffordshire ores; ironmakers would thus be able to make better and cheaper iron (1780, 304). Whitworth, years earlier, said of Shropshire furnaces that "Cumberland ore alone is a

very important article ... a very small furnace will use at least one thousand one hundred ton of it in a year, which comes now entirely from Winsford Bridge in the county of Chester at 6 shillings per ton for a very small distance" (1766, 39).

45 In the Horsehay Weekly Accounts, for every dozen tons of ironstone, about 1.5 tons of limestone were brought in (Coalbrookdale MS 335).

46 Brindley – somewhat biased as a promoter of canals – recognized the various benefits of inland navigation for Staffordshire ironmasters: "We have already mentioned the important circumstance of bringing ores out of the north to mix with those in Staffordshire; by which the iron of that country must be rendered better and cheaper; and to this we may add the great advantages of having charcoal, lime, and other fluxes, brought to the furnace at a small expense, and likewise the great saving there may be in conveying this heavy article from the forge to the manufacturer by water; all which circumstances must contribute to increase the consumption of English iron, and enable the ironmasters in that neighbourhood to come upon a competition with foreigners so far as to reduce the price of foreign iron, and upon the whole greatly to benefit both themselves and the manufacturers: and certainly the first object in the encouragement of any manufactury is to furnish it with its raw materials at the lowest price, to which nothing in general contributes so much as inland navigation" (1786, 68).

47 I noted earlier that in the late eighteenth century, the Coalbrookdale company received supplies weekly. On the other hand, in the largest ironworks in the early eighteenth century, the Crowleys in their Law Book instructed their managers to order in May enough coal to supply all requirements for twelve months, and deliveries of coal were to be restricted to the utmost when carriage costs were high (Flinn 1957, 43).

48 Allan (1983) has noted the great importance of numerous other unpatentable innovations in the iron industry in the nineteenth century. Significantly, he found that innovators, unable to protect their discovery, would freely disclose the new information, and would benefit by receiving in turn the discoveries of others. One of the reasons for this behaviour was that with interaction of many types between ironworks, it would be impossible to maintain a secret. The following pages will show that such interaction played a key role in the development of the major eighteenth-century innovations.

49 The contract taking Thomas Luckock into the Darby employ in 1714 stipulated that he was not to disclose secrets of casting to other ironworks (Norris MS, 82–4). Whereas in the later part of the century ironmasters abandoned secrecy, in the early part of the century they still considered it possible.

50 The development of closed vessels for coking not only allowed production of more and better coke but also allowed the recovery of a number of by-products; the recovery of tar helped pay for the cost of the closed vessels (Rees, "Coke"). The perfection of the process for recovering tar in 1781 by the Earl of Dundonald followed numerous other efforts. "Many trials for extracting tar from coal had been made by the late Marquis of Rockingham, near Sheffield, and by various persons at Coalbrookdale and at Newcastle" (Dalrymple 1785, 1). Dundonald himself made many experiments, and had to borrow hundreds of pounds before he achieved success. "At first sight the opinion expressed by a contemporary writer that the patent granted in 1781 to Archibald Cochrane, 9th Earl of Dundonald, for producing tar, was of greater national importance than Watt's engine patent may seem extravagant. But the primary position now occupied by coal tar derivatives, with their wholesale displacement of natural by made products, signalises visionary rather than imprudent thinking" (Clow 1952, 389). At the time coal tar was used for shipping, wagon wheels, iron objects including guns, steam engine cylinders etc. (Dalrymple, 1785). There were two other by-products as well. Salammoniac – formerly derived from soot – was used for tinning iron, brass, and copper, by pharmacists, and textile printers (Clow, 419–20). The role of coal gas in illumination was recognized by Dundonald and communicated to others (Clow, 417). After the work of many others, gas lighting would become a great innovation in the nineteenth century.

51 Scrivenor noted that Cort had made numerous experiments over the years. He emphasized that these were doomed to failure until the idea of the separate refinery was firmly established (1841, 118). Watt maintained in a letter to Black in 1784 that all that was new in Cort's process was the rollers (Muirhead 1854, 188–9).

52 The author of *A Brief State of Facts Relative to the New Method of Making Bar Iron* (1787), speaking of puddling and rolling, noted that there are always additional costs incurred in the early stages of a new invention.

53 When asked by the Committee on Trade and Colonies in 1786 whether English iron would be able to compete in quality with the best Swedish oreground, Crawshay replied that "metallurgy is almost a new science here and will improve greatly under its present leaders who set a noble example by their liberal expenditures on new improvements and erections, which serve to diffuse a spirit of emulation throughout the kingdom, from which still greater discoveries may reasonably be expected" (Add MS 38347).

54 Since it was difficult to transport charcoal long distances, its use as a fuel did serve to tether scale of operation to the size of nearby charcoal resources.

55 Scrivenor attributed the first use of iron cylinders for blowing to Smeaton at Carron in about 1760. He asserted that this was a response to the difficulty of creating a sufficient blast when coke was used (1841, 82–3).

56 This was the effect of steam engines emphasized by Dalrymple (1784, 6): "By means of their improvements, almost all the gross articles of the iron manufacture, which have hitherto, from the want of a sufficiency of water, or of waterfall, been almost always conducted in separate places, and by separate systems of expense, may now be made parts of one common work." He spoke of furnace, forge, slitting, and rolling mills and the manufacture of various articles.

57 Rochefoucault-Liancourt of France in 1786 admired the English for "their skill in working iron – the great advantage it gives them as it regards the motion, lastingness, and accuracy of machinery. All driving wheels and in fact almost all things are made of cast iron, of such a fine and hard quality that when rubbed up it polishes just like steel. There is no doubt but that the working of iron is one of the most essential of trades and the one in which we are the most deficient" (Berg 1981, 266).

58 Hicks emphasized the importance of second-generation machines – those that could only be built by machines (1969, 147). The late eighteenth-century saw the development of machines (for planing, drilling, etc.) that allowed the construction of precision machinery. In his article on the lathe, Rees wrote, "To the mechanic the lathe is an invaluable machine, as a very great proportion of all the parts of machines is formed in it, and it is the only method of working metal which may be considered as perfect. All things which can be turned are made in the lathe, both for accuracy and expedition."

59 The change from wooden to iron frames was evident before the end of the century (Lee 1972, 19). Andelle, visiting from France in 1819, was impressed that all the English spinning machines he saw were made of iron (F12 2295). Rees, in his article on manufacture, noted that all cotton machinery had in recent years switched from wood to iron. Of carding machines, he wrote "These circumstances, though they do not alter the parts of the machine are great improvements to it, as the steadiness of such framing, and the stability of their figure, enables the cylinders to run much closer together, without the danger of the teeth of the cylinder coming in contact at times, as they will sometimes do in wooden frames, and thus destroy the card teeth very soon, as well as produce less perfect work." Significantly, he noted that cast iron parts could be cast from the same mould. As the cotton industry become concentrated, ironfounders could cast machine parts for a large market.

60 Of great importance also was the introduction of iron-framed buildings. Early wood-framed workshops, poorly ventilated, full of wooden machinery, dust, and oil stains, lit by oil lamps and candles, and protected

by poor fire-fighting equipment, had been prone to heavy loss by fire; few firms escaped loss at one time or another (see Fitton 1958, 200). Strutt built the first fireproof building of iron and brick in 1792–93. Rees noted that, "when the mill is built fireproof, the safety from fire is not a trifling advantage, it saves the manufacturer the heavy cost of insurance, or what of course is nearly equal, the risk of losing his property by fire ("Manu-facture").

61 "On the score of invention, Newcomen does not appear to have much claim. The agency of the atmospheric pressure was long known; the for-mation of a vacuum by the condensation of steam was Savary's discovery; the elastic force of steam used to balance the atmosphere in the ascent was the discovery of Lord Worcester; the construction of the boiler, gauge-pipes, regulator etc. were similar to those in Savary's engines ... Never-theless, very considerable credit must be acknowledged to be due to Newcomen for the judicious combination of these scattered principles, so as to form the atmospheric engine" (Lardner 1828, 53). Von Tunzelman reaches the same conclusion (1978, 17).

62 Again, the role of science was minimal. "An ironmonger, a glazier, and a country boy brought to perfection the lever fire engine which all the uni-versities and academics of Europe had not the least notion of before these ingenious mortals appeared" (Blakely 1793, 3–4). The scientific principles had been long understood; the difficulty was in engineering.

63 He is somewhat too severe. Smeaton had improved the Newcomen engine by "proportioning its parts, but without altering anything in its principle" (Rees, "Steam Engine"). His modifications were so successful that Boulton and Watt insisted on having the fuel economy of their engine tested against pre-Smeaton Newcomen engines as this made their engines look much better (letter from Watt to Smeaton 1778, quoted in Roll 1968, 31).

64 Boulton and Watt always produced some of the more important small parts such as nozzles. Due to a shortage of capital resulting from the heavy expense of developing the engine, they did not produce the larger engine parts for the first two decades. These they subcontracted to iron-masters such as Wilkinson. "The greatest problems (with subcontracting) were the lack of standardization and quality control" (Tann 1981, 9). Eventually Boulton and Watt came to produce all the engine parts them-selves.

65 It must be emphasized that the difficulty of transporting large engine parts was not trivial. Even in 1792 local production of the less demanding engine parts was advisable: "We have yours desiring us to procure you your two boilers, but since we first proposed the question to you whether you or we should get them, we have found that to transport them either from the district of Bersham (near Wrexham) or here, especially such large ones as yours, is attended with much danger of breaking the joints,

and that to send them in a few parts is likewise unadvisable, when gentle-men can get them made near the place of erection" (Southern of Boulton and Watt to Gott 1792, in Crump 1929, 200–1). Roll noted canals faci-liated the movement of steam engine parts, but that there were still minor problems in the 1770s which obviated the advantage; transhipment was always problematic, the road journey from Bersham to Chester difficult for bulky cylinders, and the hatchways on boats sailing to the all-impor-tant Cornish market were generally too small for the cylinders (1968, 58). Without the improvements of the previous decades, transport of the unwieldy cylinders would have been extremely slow and costly. Landes describes how the first completely German-built steam engine in 1792 took so long to reach its destination by river and carting that the mine no longer wanted it and it remained in storage for eight years (1969, 142).

66 Watt ordered a cylinder from the Carron works in 1765. "This cylinder was never used but came to Soho where it lay long; it was very ill bored, and thereby useless, though the best Carron could make." (Muirhead 1854, v.1, 11). Improvements in boring technique were not the whole story. In the early eighteenth century, cast iron was of poor quality: "By degree the ironfounders improved so much as to be able to cast cylinders for the atmospheric engines" (Farney 1827, 271).

67 It would be a mistake to draw a strong link between English science and the development of the Watt steam engine. Von Tunzelman (1978, 11), cit-ing Cardwell and Watt himself, notes that Watt did not learn of latent heat from Black, and that Watt was guided mainly by economic considerations. "We know not, therefore, how the remark was originated, or what philos-ophers first claimed for theoretical men any part of the honour of being instrumental, even indirectly, in the perfecting of the steam engine ... The fact is that science or scientific men never had anything to do with it ... Indeed there is no machine or mechanism in which the little that theorists have done is more useless. The honour of bringing it to its present state of perfection, therefore, belongs to a different and more useful class. It arose, was improved and perfected, by working mechanics – and by them only" (Stuart 1825, v).

68 It is interesting to note that Boulton and Watt were interested from the beginning in the application of steam to transport. Watt wrote of using engines to move carriages in 1769 while Boulton in 1770 spoke of the potential to move canal boats by steam as well as supplying locks with water by use of the steam engine (Muirhead 1854, v.1, 53).

69 He wrote to Boulton, "By several unsuccessful projects and experiments I had involved myself in a considerable debt before I had brought the the-ory of the fire engine to its present state" (Muirhead 1854, v. 1, 30).

70 This is according to Boulton himself in "Proceedings of the Public Meeting For Erecting A Monument to the late James Watt" (Watt, 1824). He boasts

of the assemblage of workmen familiar with various branches of the mechanical arts. His remarks not only underlie the type of collective effort required for the development of the Watt engine but serve also to emphasize again the need for centralized manufacture of a number of parts.

71 This is the estimate of Lardner (1828). Stuart (1825) estimates £47,000.

72 "After-sales service became increasingly important from the early 1790's and in this the agents and senior mechanics performed an important role. Moreover, when any of the partners were away from Birmingham, they took the opportunity of visiting customers in the area, realizing that efficient machines and satisfied customers were the best advertisements for their engines" (Tann 1981, 15). Watt, especially in the early days, used to grumble about being always on the road responding to customer complaints. Roll noted that "the lack of skilled and reliable engineers and erectors who could be sent out on the firm's business was very keenly felt as soon as the business was started" (1968, 60).

73 The Hornblower engine of 1781 was the first compound engine. It was abandoned because it infringed on Watt's patent (Lilley 1965, 106). After the patent expired, Woolf would improve upon Hornblower's design and produce an engine preferable to Watt's for some purposes (Rees, "Steam Engine").

74 Von Tunzelman agrees with Farey and Ashton that Watt's patent lasted too long and that it hindered further technological development for decades. As future developments all required the separate condenser, they could all be viewed as infringements (1978, 292–3). Rees noted at the time that in the nineteenth century major changes occurred in steam engine manufacture with large works relying on substantial division of labour. "Since the expiration of the patent, there has been a total change in the manner of constructing and putting together every part of the engine, and many advantageous improvements have been made, as far as respects the durability and accurate performance of the machine" ("Steam Engine").

75 Watt had considered the possibility of an engine which used steam to move the piston. "But I soon relinquished the idea of constructing an engine upon this principle, from being sensible it would be liable to some of the objections against Savary's engine; namely from the danger of bursting the boiler, and the difficulty of making the joints tight" (Galloway 1831, 49). Galloway goes on to note that making the joints tight is no longer a problem.

CHAPTER FOUR

1 For example, the poor state of the mines of the Vallée de Vercours in Dauphiné was attributed to the unnecessarily high cost of moving first the raw materials and then the final product (F12 1421).

2 Boislandry (1815, 233–4) recognized the superiority of English iron products. While the difference may have been due in part to superior ore, climate, or water, it was mainly due to better tools and machines, and the overwhelming explanation was division of labour: "this admirable division of labour, which simplifies the work, augments the competence and speed of each worker to such a degree that, by this combination, each piece of manufacture, in iron and in steel, is able to attain an almost unlimited perfection, and with much less expense than if this division of labour was not employed."

3 One of these was de Mornay. His letter to the government in 1792 indicates that he had been sent to spy on the metal trades. He speaks of his accomplices; he has visited a scythemaker, and is trying to get admitted to Baron Durkheim's operation (F12 2470).

4 "Fine cutlery rests inferior to that of England because of the difficulty in manufacturing it without as good a steel as English cast steel" (Chaptal 1819, 93).

5 Several manufacturers in the half-century after 1770 claimed to be able to produce steel as good as the English if they received government support. Support they sometimes achieved; success they did not (see F12 1300, 2230). The Conseil d'État du Roi noted in 1787 that despite considerable funds devoted to the royal steel works at Amboise, the result was still not of English quality.

6 Holker was told in 1771 to attract English workers to establish a steel manufacture. In 1786, De Laplace noted that the French were forced to buy good steel from England or Germany; a man was sent to England with a promise of 12,000 livres if he could learn the secret (F12 1300 I). Coing, in an VI, speaks of training people in the English methods (F12 2230). An 1830 report speaks of an inspector visiting French steelworks to explain methods he had observed in England (F12 1300 I). The government also supported experiments by Réaumur, Duhamel, and others (Woronoff 1984, 351–2).

7 Ballot speaks of the English monopolizing the trade with Sweden, but also notes that Amboise was using Swedish ore in 1786 (1923, 489–93). Certainly England dominated the trade, but why?

8 As I am arguing here only that a better transport system could have fostered dramatic improvements in the French iron industry, not necessarily would have, one need not be overly concerned with the fact that France levied high tariffs on iron imports. Naturally, if French iron output had been booming as in England, one would expect there to have been some pressure to lower tariffs.

9 A 1785 Arrêt of the Conseil d'État du Roi stated that the king felt the use of coal was becoming increasingly necessary due to the shortage of wood; tolls were to be removed (it never happened) on the shipment of coal,

especially on the Rhone (F12 1512 B). In 1786, there were suggestions for reforestation as Paris faced difficulty in obtaining enough fuel for heating (F12 653).

10 Other industries were similarly affected. In 1782, a glassworks in Provence was allowed to begin operation only on the condition that it use coal rather than charcoal (F12 1514). Guiraudet (1802, 24) was still complaining that charcoal shortages stemmed from its use in glassmaking and other luxuries, and that these should be forced to use coal.

11 Bruné, of Sorel in Eure-et-Loir, asked for government aid in an IX due to the high and rising price of wood he had faced for twenty years (F12 2455).

12 The Indre had vast wood resources which remained unused because the simple transport improvements needed to gain access to them were not undertaken (Peuchet 1807, "Indre").

13 Complaints of inferior quality concerned such matters as the coal being poor for coking or forging, the pieces of coal being too small, or the coal possessing impurities. Complaints were not unanimous. M. Maréchaud visited England in 1773 to see if English success in coke-smelting was due to superior coal. "He had had the satisfaction of seeing that English coal and iron mines were not superior to our own fine coals" (F12 1300 II).

14 To be sure, France had considerable deposits of anthracite coal not suited to coking. However, she also had great quantities of bituminous coal which was.

15 Pounds (1957a, 110–11) describes the differences in coking technology. Coke had first been made in small rounded heaps as charcoal had before it. Then, the beehive oven, a closed retort-like vessel came into use. However, continental coal was less suited to either the heap or the beehive than English coal. A number of ovens, variants on the English beehive, were designed for use on the Continent. In some of these, the heat for coking was supplied from outside, with the hot gases from combustion drawn around the oven. The ovens produced coke more quickly than English ovens, which suited the different compositions of the two coals.

16 Leducq (1834, 30) speaks of coal and iron deposits in the northwest which were only fifty lieues apart and could easily be joined by a canal. In 1814, it was noted that fifteen of forty departments with ore also had known deposits of coal, "and by rivers and canals, many other departments could easily and inexpensively supply themselves with coal" (F12 2223).

17 The mines of Creusot had coal of the best quality but possessed no other outlet. Le Creusot received half the output of the Blanzy coalfield (F12 2455, 1815).

18 There appears to have been some ironstone, but with a low ore content, in the coalfield. The Anzin Company experimented unsuccessfully with smelting in the early nineteenth century (Geiger 1974, 212).

19 The poor quality of transport links often meant that known reserves were scarcely exploited. "Coal is not so widespread in the Côte-d'Or, its transport some distance too expensive, for us to be able to count this fuel among our resources" (Guiraudet 1802, 24–5).

20 The government received innumerable complaints from merchants and manufacturers in the north about the exactions of the Bateliers de Condé, a government-enforced monopoly. Dunkirk imported English coal only because of the exorbitant prices charged to move Valenciennes coal (F12 1514). A writer in the 1770s estimated that the actual cost of the round trip from Anzin was 38fl but the Bateliers charged 157fl (F12 1512A).

21 " ... it's the cost of transport which comprises the major part of the price of coal" (Say 1852, 313). "However, the distance, or more exactly the cost of carriage is the greatest obstacle to the use of coal in works" (Woronoff 1984, 333).

22 Morineaux (in Wilson 1977) suggests figures of 750,000 metric tons for France in 1789 and 10.3 million for England in 1800. The English figures are lower than Flinn's. Further research may inflate the French figures but the result that English output was ten times larger is likely to be maintained.

23 Dufaud, in his *Mémoire sur les forges de l'Empire*, noted, "It is perhaps to the great abundance of this mineral is due the little perfection which exists in the methods people use for its reduction" (F12 2223, 1814).

24 1,287,452 tons of iron ore were produced in Lorraine on the eve of Gilchrist-Thomas (Pounds 1957a, 191).

25 Guiraudet's description of furnaces and forges in the Côte-d'Or shows each forge obtaining its pig iron from only one furnace (1802, 13). This is quite different from the common English practice.

26 "A multitude of iron mines, and of coal, placed in the interior, rest useless, which could be exploited with great profit by the state and individuals, if canals existed to facilitate their transport" (Lequinio, an 1, 5).

27 Size of output is far from being the whole story, of course. With England, it was seen that a steady growth in demand was of great importance. Earlier it was shown that the French metal trades were incapable of supplying the French iron industry with this and thus the industry remained too dependent on fluctuating government demand.

28 Leducq (1834) discussed the possibility of dropping the tariff on English iron in the future without hurting French producers. "In truth, before arriving at this result, it is necessary that, like our neighbours, the iron industry assists or achieves first economical means of transport" (23).

29 Leducq (1834, 6) recognized the key role of transportation in determining the scale of production: "The only condition of prosperity for furnaces established with economy and discernment, depends on nothing more than the low price of raw materials rendered to the works, possessing

convenient facilities for their products to reach with profit the greatest number of consumers possible."

30 Guiraudet (1802, 28–9) complained that forgemasters only concerned themselves with buying and selling, rather than production. He recommends that a school be established to teach the children of forgemasters the new theories of metallurgy.

31 "All the forgemasters of the Haut-Marne complain, with reason, of the great number of works, and of the infinite abuses of abandoning the art and routine of the forges to the caprices of the workers. These forgemasters have proposed the creation of a school ... The practical lessons have for their object to diminish the amount of fuel, to substitute some coal for charcoal, and to improve the amount of iron (*Annuaire* 1804, 119–20). Woronoff (1984, 196–7) notes that schools were viewed as a possible solution by masters wishing to overcome the secretiveness and routine of the workers. Workers were often accused of hostility to new ideas (330).

32 Dobson complained in 1811 of the difficulty of getting French ironmasters to adopt English methods: "Isolated in their forests, they are of an incurable ignorance, deaf to all appeals, blind to the evidence, invidious toward innovators" (Ballot 1923, 524). One visit from a government representative could not have the same effect that constant interaction and competition among English ironmasters created.

33 Leducq, in 1834, noted that despite the prevalence of both coal and ore, coke-smelting was still in its infancy; it would be necessary to develop transport to meet the needs of this industry (5). Masters at least used the high price of coal as an excuse for not switching to it (Woronoff 1984, 335).

34 Charcoal was expensive in the Haut-Marne but ironmasters were so suspicious of coal they were unwilling to mix the two. "Besides, nobody forgets that the work of forges is one of those in which routine exercises its empire the most. The first point, the essential object, is to have abundant coal at low price" (Peuchet 1807, "Haut-Marne"). If coal were cheap, the authors were confident that tradition would be overcome.

35 Von Tunzelman has argued that the major reason for the slow adoption of the steam engine in most parts of the Continent was the high cost of coal, though he attributes the high costs in France to narrow inclined seams (1981, 277–9).

36 Andelle reported to the Minister of the Interior after his trip to England in 1819. He asserted that the steam engine had not been widely adopted in France because works served only small local markets protected by internal tariffs (F12 2295).

37 In England, as iron quality and engineering skills developed over the course of the eighteenth century, the iron industry was able to produce sophisticated machinery to service the needs of other industries. In France,

the development of machine making was hindered along with the development of steam engines.

1 There are some problems with the challenge and response approach in any case. These were discussed in chapter one.

2 Rees takes the latter view: "In considering the processes of the woollen manufacture as they were practised 40 or 50 years ago and comparing them with the present practices, we find great changes and improvements, but they are by no means carried to so great an extent as in the cotton manufacture … The reduction of labour, or the substitution of ordinary hands for experienced workmen was in this case all that machinery of the most perfect kind could effect; both these were advantages to the public and the manufacturer but were so directly opposite to the inclination and interest of the able workmen that we find they have made greater and more effectual opposition to the introduction of improvements in the woollen than in any other of our great manufactures" ("Wool").

3 It should be noted that proper functioning of machinery at one stage of production generally required machine-produced inputs; i.e., slubbing machinery required an even sliver, which required an improved carding machine. The simultaneous developments occurring in the different stages of production were mutually supportive. This important relationship is missed if one concentrates only on one or two stages. It goes a long way toward explaining why the Continent had such difficulty borrowing English technology.

4 "All this means that the traditional theories about the industry's development put too much stress on the technological changes, and their effects on the structure and organization of the trade. The greater emphasis should be placed on the commercial aspects of the trade; on the ways in which manufacturers held and then disposed of their stocks, the methods of settling debts, the credit mechanism, and the payment of wages. These are the really vital characteristics of the trade's development during this period" (Edwards 1967, 215).

5 As Gregory (1982) notes, however, much of the cloth did not go through the cloth halls; increasingly, workers made goods of the sort particular merchants desired and delivered them directly to the merchants.

6 Timperley's *Annals of Manchester* for the year 1764 states, "At this time the trade of Manchester was greatly pushed by the practice of sending out riders for orders all over the kingdom, carrying with them patterns in bags" (1839). In 1775, Henry Warrall, a Manchester cotton manufacturer, testified that it was common practice for manufacturers to employ riders-out in travelling into various parts of the kingdom for the purpose of get-

ting orders for, and vending and disposing of goods and wares (Edwards 1967, 165).

7 Thus, in the later eighteenth century, the Peels' sales occurred partly through drapers making frequent visits to their Manchester warehouse, and partly through the efforts of four constantly employed travelling salesmen (Chapman 1981, 85).

8 While anxious to respond to changes in fashion, the Peels' printing works in Manchester in the 1780s produced a few simple one-colour patterns which could justify production of 20,000 pieces per year and they seem not to have changed these patterns much from year to year. Three or four patterns could account for the bulk of their annual production (Chapman 1981, 78).

9 The Strutts were always very concerned with the quality of their yarn, and received many complaints from their agents of the difficulty of selling it (Fitton 1958, 307–9).

10 "Until this improvement [Aire and Calder Navigation] took place it will be difficult for a mind accustomed only to modern ideas and appearance to conceive the impediments which lay in the way of commerce and manufactures. The roads were sloughs almost impassable by single carts, surmounted at the height of several feet by narrow horsetracks, where travellers who encountered each other sometimes tried to wear out each others patience rather than either would risk a deviation. Carriage of raw wool and manufactured goods was performed on the backs of single horses, at a disadvantage of nearly 200 to 1 compared to carriage by water. At the same time and long after, the situation of a merchant was toilsome and perilous" (Whitaker 1771–75, 80–1). "It is amazing to think under what disadvantages the trade of this country must formerly have been carried on, before the roads were repaired and widened by the different Acts of Parliament which have lately been obtained" (Watson 1775, 7–8).

11 A similar point is made by Heaton who notes that, even without technological advance, the cotton trade would have expanded quickly in the late eighteenth century due to the developments in industrial and commercial organization and communications (1965, 66).

12 Military demand naturally suffered from the same problems of instability. Wars generally led to a major redistribution between textiles, with linen output expanding dramatically, and other sectors perhaps contracting (Ashton 1959, 76–8). Given that the linen industry was slow to develop during this period, it would be hard to ascribe a very positive role to military demand.

13 "For the merchants and tradesmen concerned in the woollen manufacture of this city at that time sent all their goods by land carriage, and on horseback too, to Leeds, where they were all unpacked and made up into

bales, and then put on board boats or lighters down to Hull; but if the navigation was continued to Sowerby-bridge, these goods would be baled up at home, and go to Sowerby-bridge from places adjacent on wheel carriages and back again in one day; and a packhorse could only go from those parts to Leeds and back again twice in a week; the goods also being baled at home would go much neater and cleaner, as well as cheaper, to foreign markets" (Watson 1775, 15–16). Before the completion of the Calder and Hebble Navigation (1769), 'A considerable portion of the manufactures of Manchester and Rochdale were brought by land carriage across the grand ridge to the navigation at Sowerby (Priestley 1831, 132).

14 One estimate in 1776 was that £1,200,000 worth of cotton goods were produced, broken down as follows (BL Add MS 38342): 250,000 linen yarn from Britain, Ireland, Baltic; 250,000 cotton, half from French or Turkish territory; 60,000 worsted, silk, wool, furs; 40,000 dyeing materials; 20,000 bleaching materials; 580,000 wages and profits.

15 Baines (1835, 519) estimated that in the early nineteenth century, cotton wool was ten per cent more expensive at Havre than Liverpool, and England gained another one per cent advantage in the cost of carriage to the place of manufacture. This may be an underestimate (see chapter 5).

16 A letter from the Liverpool Collector of Customs to the Privy Council in 1806 explains why Liverpool had gained dominance of cotton exports: "the principal cotton factories are within 60 to 80 miles of Liverpool in the counties of Lancashire, Yorkshire, Cheshire, Derbyshire, Nottinghamshire, Staffordshire, and Flint, and there is good communication between those places and Liverpool by inland navigation" (Edwards 1967, 107).

17 The largest cotton manufacturers only began to import their own cotton wool in the nineteenth century.

18 Edwards maintains this would have been impossible for London brokers, as they needed a quick reply in a market subject to sudden price fluctuations. This seems odd, given how quick travel between London and Lancashire had become by the late eighteenth century.

19 Turnbull (1987, 555) discusses how important access to coal was for the success of cotton, wool, and linen manufacturers. Baines, comparing the cost of manufacturing in France and England, found the largest difference was in fuel. Fuel for the steam engine cost 33,750fr in Essonne but only 4875fr in Manchester. Fuel for heating cost 8000fr in Essonne but only 1200fr in Manchester (1835, 519).

20 Edwards dates this transformation very late: "Until 1785 at least, before the expansion of the muslin trade, most firms were producing standard lines; fashion and the subtleties of taste, colour, and design, played a relatively small part in output decisions" (1967, 163). Rather than imagine a sudden break in behaviour, it would be better to see a gradual shift as

transport improvements allowed increasingly rapid changes in taste across the country.

21 The rise of the cotton industry cannot be understood without reference to changes in fashion. "Fashion changes inevitably played an important role also; calicoes and fustians were particularly in demand for working class and middle class male clothing, but the market for cotton stockings, handkerchiefs, cotton dress materials, and muslins greatly developed, and at a faster rate" (Butt 1977, 116).

22 Thus, the Scottish Chamber of Commerce encouraged innovations in finishing and weaving, "a vital component in any textile sector where fashion was a critical element in the structure of demand' (Butt 1977, 117).

23 This is the consensus in the literature on wool. Heaton writes, "In conclusion, therefore, the West Riding had reached a position of pre-eminence even before the great inventions came into operation" (1965, 281). Jenkins and Ponting note that already by 1770 Yorkshire possessed one third of the English wool industry and one half of the exports, a result of decades of expansion; in the third quarter of the century, Lancashire and Yorkshire expanded while there was stagnation elsewhere (1982, 1–2). Rees noted in the early nineteenth century, "Until the middle of the last century, worsted goods were manufactured in considerable quantities in Warwickshire, Oxfordshire, and Northamptonshire, but about that time the extension of the worsted trade in the West Riding of Yorkshire, particularly at Halifax, Bradford, and Wakefield, gradually drew this trade in a great measure away from those counties" ("Worsted").

24 This is something of a simplification. One is acting as if only one good, "wool," were produced, when there was a variety of different goods, requiring slightly different techniques and skills. Thus, the West County industry survived by specializing in superfines (Mann 1971, ch. 2). Part of the explanation for decline in East Anglia may be a shift in tastes away from the goods produced there (see Jenkins 1982, 75–6).

25 "To the above natural advantages, we must add the acquired advantage of a canal communication, which ramifies itself through all the populous parts of this country, and connects it with the inland cities, the seats of other flourishing manufactures, and the sources whence iron, lime, salt, stone, and other articles in which Lancashire is deficient are obtained. By this means, Lancashire being already possessed of the primary requirements for manufactures is enabled at very small expense to command things of secondary importance, and to appropriate to its use the natural advantages of the whole kingdom" (Baines, 78). "With all these advantages derived from water carriage to so many places and more particularly to Liverpool, the second seaport in the kingdom, no wonder that Manchester has consequence in the modern world" (*The Manchester Guide*

1804, 3). "This land owes its superiority in large part to the advantages it obtains from the richness of its coal mines and the many canals which render transport as easy and economical as possible" (report by Andelle to Minister of Interior on trip to England, 1819, F12 2295).

26 This is a very low estimate of the number of occupations. Another writer claimed that weaving stuffs alone involved thirty different employments (BL Add MS 27966, 282).

27 Even as tasks became simpler and were given to unskilled labour, techno-logical change still occurred as long as labour was specialized. "Those who have been in the habit of superintending their labour have noticed that the observations of even the least of the children have often led to important improvements by pointing out what to them was an inconven-ience. Sometimes, the children themselves succeed in applying the rem-edy" (Kennedy 1818, 14).

28 Again one sees that new technology did not create the earliest workshops. Rather, the existence of centralized workplaces with on-site repair special-ists increased the probability that machinery suitable to such a setting would be developed.

29 Machine making was a difficult industry to transplant, as Mr. Brooke found in Ireland when trying to establish the cotton industry there: "it was with infinite labour and expense Mr. Kirchoffer arrived at perfection, as making any part of these machines is a trade in itself, and any one part ill-made or imperfect rendered the whole useless. At length he collected the different artists under his own eye, and the differences with respect to machinery were surmounted, which had impeded Mr. Brooke's progress as well as many others in the cotton business' (Brooke 1783, 16).

30 "The tools and implements employed in constructing the different machines are very curious; for as there are such immense numbers of each part of every machine to be made, it becomes in the same manner as with the clock-maker, worth the machine-makers' trouble to construct compli-cated tools and engines to expedite the manufacture of the parts; thus cut-ting engines for forming the teeth of the numerous wheels" (Rees, "Manufacture").

31 As Hudson (1983) has noted, the type of organization previously found (putting out or not) will influence the rate at which factories emerge.

32 Even in the nineteenth century, small factories would remain common. "In many cases private dwelling houses were converted to cotton mills and printing works. In Oldham, many mills were made from cottages, 'a steam engine attached to them, and the rooms laid together'" (Edwards 187, quoting Fitton and Wadsworth).

33 "What then of Gott's great factory at Bean Ing? Could it not show new machinery, even if not power, applied to the weaving and finishing of cloth? The answer must be that in neither branch did it dispose with the

traditional hand processes. Neither in name nor in methods did the weaving shops, the burling chamber, and the cropping shops at Bean Ing mark any new departure. What was new was the factory organization, and in the weaving a division of labour in place of the old system of apprenticeship" (Crump 1929, 25–6). "There are, incidentally, many examples of jennies and hand looms being used in Yorkshire mills before the spinning and weaving processes were mechanized" (Jenkins 1982, 29).

34 Edwards describes how master weavers, faced with much greater markets as the cost of spinning dropped, first employed middlemen to deal with a geographically dispersed group of weavers (a difficult endeavour, as I have shown, in an age before middle management was common) but, "A small but growing number of master weavers, like the jenny spinners, were finding it convenient to move their workers into weaving sheds" (1967, 9). Mann also speaks of the role of increasing demand in encouraging both workers and employers to move to factories (1965, 135).

35 "It is proved by accurate experiments made between cloths woven under the master's eye at home or in the weavers' houses abroad that the former have invariably produced better, longer, and heavier cloths for a less quantity of wool" (BL Add MS 33110, 390). Mann (1971, 143) describes the setting up of loomshops in the 1780s; "The motive for establishing them was to prevent the embezzlement almost universally practiced by weavers who worked in their own homes." Embezzling was done in many ways: by adding oil or water to the material to increase its weight, switching low for high-quality materials, and by spinners producing different levels of fineness throughout (see Styles, 1983). Though widespread, it would be facile to think that employers could treat it as part of the wage – they clearly felt otherwise. Many of the workers' practices, it should be noted, made it even more difficult to produce a standardized product.

36 Bannatyne took this point of view. "His plan of management, which must have been entirely his own as no establishment of a similar nature then existed" (*Supplement to Encyclopaedia Britannica*, vol. 3, 395, quoted by McCulloch, 1827 14–15).

37 Coleman (1973, 2–7) notes that textiles had seen very little technological change since the Middle Ages, and posits that domestic industry was simply unconducive to technological change.

38 "Arkwright adopted the invention and improvements in the preparatory processes which were now being made by many poor practical men who could not protect their right by patents in consequence of the enormous expense attending these. He combined, altered, and improved" (French 1859, 60).

39 Guest astutely notes that increased output could not have been achieved as easily at an earlier date. "In the then state of manners and prejudices, when the facilities of communication between places were less, and the

population generally possessed with much greater antipathy to leaving their natural place than at present, this inducement would have failed to bring together a sufficient number of hand spinners, and a further rise in the price of spinning must have been the consequence" (1823, 12). What then would have been the effect on technology? Output would have stagnated, perhaps, and resources would have been transferred from weaving to spinning.

40 The Society For the Encouragement of Arts, Manufactures and Commerce in 1783 possessed models of six different spinning machines invented during the 1760s, none of which proved commercially successful, but all of which involved some new ideas. It is interesting to note that the Society had, between 1754 and 1783, distributed £544 in premiums, "for improving several machines used in manufactures, viz the comb-pot, cards for wool and cotton, stocking frame, loom, machines for winding and doubling, and spinning wheels" (Baines 1835, 154).

41 This is the opinion of Wyatt's son: "To pretend, however, that the original machinery, without addition or improvement, would alone have produced the prodigious effects which we now behold, would be claiming improbable merit for the inventor, and degrading the talents and sagacity of his successors in the same field of enterprise; for it cannot be denied that a great fund of ingenuity must have been expended in bringing the spinning works to their present degree of perfection" (quoted in Baines 1835, 135–6).

42 Such a coincidence is not impossible, given the circumstances of the time. "Two persons may invent machines, acting upon very different principles, the design of which is to produce the same effect. But the circumstances of time and place contribute no little to give an extraordinary stimulus to genius and a perseverance to overcome those obstacles which are in the way of a first effort to obtain some desirable object" (Kennedy 1818, 25).

43 Wadsworth and Mann note that the Wyatt-Paul machine was the subject of much experimentation in Lancashire (1965, ch. 21).

44 The jenny could easily be used in cottages. However, they were often employed in centralized workplaces. "Jenny spinning reached its peak in the 1780s, and machines with 80 or more spindles had become fairly common. Many jenny spinners were combining carding with spinning, and moving into workshops, usually converted cottages, as the size of their machines increased. But there was nothing new about this; it was merely the continuation of a trend well marked in the previous decade" (Edwards, 8).

45 "In the whole series of inventors who gradually evolved [the water frame], only one had a novel idea of the first importance, and he was probably of French extraction. The rest, or at any rate those who contributed anything to the final solution spent their time in the endeavour to utilize that

brilliant thought of Lewis Paul's that spinning might be performed by means of rollers. All their additions were secondary to the main principle but the machine would never have worked satisfactorily without them. It may be doubted whether in any other country so much experimentation, extending, though not in unbroken sequence, over a period of more than thirty years, would have been bestowed on an idea so difficult of realization" (Wadsworth, 413).

46 "When Sir Richard had constructed his machine he found that he had many difficulties to encounter and surmount before he could derive any benefit from his invention. Being in very low circumstances, it was necessary in the first place to look out for some persons of property who were able and willing to encourage his project" (Pilkington 1789, 304).

47 Arkwright's ability to accomplish what he did would also have been greatly hampered had communications not improved so much. "Arkwright was a severe economist of time; and that he might not waste a moment, he generally travelled with four horses and at a very rapid speed" (Baines 1835, 196). This was especially important as he developed concerns in Derbyshire, Lancashire, and Scotland.

48 Writers such as Clapham have assumed that water frames were only used in large factories like Arkwright's, but they were often used in comparatively small rooms (Edwards 1967, 182).

49 Elsewhere, Crompton wrote of the mule, "which machine to complete to my satisfaction cost me years of study and personal labour, and at the expense of every shilling I had in the world" (BL, Egerton MS, 2409, 27).

50 The development of increasingly complex mules must have been aided by the emergence of factories in the preceding period. It should, however, be noted that the original mule was for years used mainly in the dwelling houses of spinners (Guest 1823, 32).

51 The "Derby Mercury", 12 Jan. 1831, said of Strutts' role, "but we believe that the inferior workmanship of that day prevented the success of an invention which all the skill and improvements in the construction of machinery in the present day has barely accomplished" (Fitton 1958, 198). As the Industrial Revolution progressed, increasing degrees of precision in machine making would be necessary for technological improvement.

52 Slow adoption of the jenny in the west of England was partly due to worker antagonism and partly as the jenny was less suited to fine cloths (Mann 1971, 126). The geographical proximity of Yorkshire and Lancashire may also have helped.

53 As evidenced by carding, developments were not limited to the spinning stage. Mills for scutching flax had been developed in the middle decades of the century. An ingenious mechanic had developed a machine for splitting straw in six or eight parts so that chip hats could be made lighter and less expensively; the quantity demanded increased both at home and

abroad as a result (Anstie 1803, 26n). The biggest advances in the finishing trades were made with the rubbing mill and drying house which did substitute machinery for labour (Drurie 1977, 91). While the linen industry grows slowly relative to cotton during this period, it is clear that even here there were important efforts to develop better technology.

54 It had long been thought that silk was too delicate for power weaving but this was not so (Porter, 1831, 267).

55 Fitton (1958, 64) notes this, and suggests that Strutt, a silk-manufacturer himself, may have been motivated to set up a cotton mill because of his experience in silk. While the precedent of silk may have been of some importance, a direct transfer of technology was impossible as "silk throwing consisted merely of twisting together almost continuous strands of silk filaments" (Hills 1979, 114).

56 This is the opinion advanced in "The case of the silk-weavers and of the silk-manufacturers stated and considered" (PRO T1440 1765,173–4). A small number of manufacturers located in one place found it easy to do so.

57 Von Tunzelman notes that Ratcliffe's dressing methods required more imagination than Cartwright's loom (1978, 295) but most modern works devote relatively little attention to the operation of dressing relative to weaving. Yet Rees ("Cotton") asserted that Ratcliffe and Ross had achieved the greatest improvement in this area. Kennedy spoke of Johnson's machine as a precursor of the power loom (1818, 19).

58 Along with the improvements in dressing noted above, Rees spoke of recent improvements in winding, reeling, and sizing, the other preparatory processes required by weaving ("Cotton"). The draw loom had been improved so that one worker replaced two ("Draw Loom").

59 It was adopted much more rapidly in cotton than in wool. We see the first power loom in worsted in the early 1800s and in wool somewhat later, but, as Clapham asserts, the use of power weaving in the wool industry was experimental until 1830 (1963, 145). Baines feels that the slow adoption by the wool, linen, and silk industries cannot be explained on technological grounds (1835, 239).

60 Both fulling and shearing were often done on commission for other manufacturers (see Heaton 1965, 298–9).

61 It was discovered that there were centuries-old statutes prohibiting the use of gig mills, and workers appealed to Parliament for their enforcement. This led to a debate on whether the gig mills referred to were the same as those presently in use. It was discovered that there were over 200 statutes regulating the woolen manufacture that had fallen into disuse (see BL Add MS 33110, 250–66, 388). This is an interesting example of the fact that England had as many regulations as countries on the Continent, but often did not enforce them.

62 Again, Leeds would lag behind the rest of Yorkshire thanks to successful opposition from workers.

63 "It [bleaching] consisted of steeping the cloth in alkaline leys for several days, washing it clean, and spreading it upon the grass for some weeks. The steeping in alkaline leys, called bucking, and the bleaching on the grass, called crofting, were repeated alternately for 5 or 6 times. The cloth was then steeped for some days in sour milk, washed clean, and crofted. These processes were repeated, diminishing every time the strength of the alkaline ley, till the linen had acquired the requisite whiteness" (Baines 1835, 246). White cotton required somewhat less bleaching than green linen. "At the present the cloth bleached by every private hand differs so much from one piece to another, that scarce one pack of goods of the same fineness is to be had of the same colour" (Patrick Lindsay 1733, in Clow 1952, 173).

64 Wolff (1974) speaks of improvements in bleaching as a result of a bottle-neck due to limited supply of bleaching grounds as productivity increased in spinning and weaving. However, again we see a decades-long series of improvements, many of which pre-dated the major discoveries in spinning. The introduction of sulphuric acid at mid-century significantly reduced the need for bleaching grounds. In any case, linen had often been transported long distances, and thus the more valuable cotton could have been treated in the same way. Bleaching did not respond to changes in spinning but developed at the same time as a result of the same pressures.

65 Access to raw materials was also important. Along with imports of sulphur and nitre, the Prestonpans works needed sixty tons of local coal per week in the late eighteenth century (Clow 1952, 138).

66 This is an indication that French scientists were indeed interested in the application of science to industry.

67 Clow (1952, 194) quotes from J. Liebig's *Familiar Letters on Chemistry* (1844, 28): "By the combination of chlorine with lime it could be transported to distances without inconvenience. Therefore it was used for bleaching cotton and but for this new bleaching process it would scarcely have been possible for cotton manufacturers in Great Britain to have attained the enormous extent which it did during the nineteenth century, nor could it have competed in price with France and Germany."

68 "This valuable colour (Turkey Red) cost me several hundred pounds. In the year 1753 I sent a young man to Turkey on purpose to learn to dye it ... He executed the business I sent him about, and I rewarded him for his trouble; but when I got it, to my great disappointment, it would not suit my purpose, that is, for cotton velvets, nor any other sort of piece work I then made. The tediousness of so many operations and the exactness required every time, rendered it of no more value to me than madder red

... which is so easily dyed, whereas the Turkey Red requires 12 or 13 operations in repeated steepings, dryings, washings, and dyeings" (Wilson 1786, in Clow 1952, 215).

69 "The most valuable of all mordants is the acetated aluminous mordant, first employed by the calico printers of this country, and the discovery of which would have been worthy to form an era in the art, if it were not that its application was the result of accident rather than of science, and that it was long used empirically and ignorantly, together with several other ingredients which were perfectly useless. Alum was employed by the English calico printers ... and guess seems to have led some of them to put in sugar of lead together with the other materials; by the combination of these two, acetate of ammonium was formed, but amidst the number of ingredients employed the printers did not know which produced the effect. By degrees they found out that sugar of lead and alum were the most important, and they discarded first one and then another of the ingredients they had been accustomed to mix them with, though without the aid of any chemical reasoning" (Baines 1835, 274).

70 "and hence there was a communication of nostrums and chemical secrets between printers and dyers, to the advantage of both branches in the farther perfecting of grounds and giving a firmness with a clearness to colours" (Ogden 1783, 86). Chapman notes that the 1780s saw great improvements in bleaching, dyeing and printing: "All these innovations took place in Manchester, Bolton, and Stockport, reasserting their position as the major centre of technical innovation as well as the commercial hub of the cotton manufacturing region" (1981, 49).

71 As Baines said of the Peels: "They eagerly adopted every improvement suggested by others, and many improvements originated in their own extensive establishments" (1835, 262).

72 This is Baines' opinion. Rees states that "A piece of calico which would take a man and a boy three hours to print with one colour, or six hours to finish with two colours, may by this means be done in three minutes, or three minutes and a half, and this much more completely than could even have been imagined before the introduction of this innovation" ("Printing Calico").

73 Cameron (1989, 181) is one author who suspects that in the eighteenth century scientific chemists learned as much from industrial users as industrial users learned from them.

74 I discussed earlier the importance of coal. "It is asserted that the poor manufacturers of Nottingham are under a necessity of purchasing coals in the winter season at the price of ten pence, eleven pence, or twelve pence per hundredweight. This hardship they can no longer labour under ... as a communication is now opened and opening to five collieries upon a road already established by Parliament, from whence both the town of Not-

tingham and the whole country can and will be supplied with whatever quantity of coals they shall demand, either in winter or in summer, delivered at the town of Nottingham or the navigation there, under six pence per hundred" (*Answer to the Case* ...).

75 The mechanization of lace manufacture began in 1768, and would be greatly furthered in 1809 by Heatcast of Nottingham – after years of effort by the manufacturers of Nottingham (Rees, "Lace") – and this would almost eliminate the hand lace manufacture in England, France, and Belgium (Baines 1835, 340). Neither the lace nor the velvet manufacturers have received much attention from historians, as Wadsworth and Mann point out: "The place of velvet in the history of the cotton industry has been neglected, probably because there is little information to be found about it in English sources. Foreign observers placed it high" (1965, 175). As will be seen below for hosiery in general, the requirements of these trades for well-spun yarn was a significant encouragement for the improvement of spinning machinery.

76 Manufacturers, without the option of steam, would have been forced to move ever further afield. Baines notes that this would have been unfavourable to the division of labour, the perfection of machine making, and the cheapness of conveyance (1835, 220).

CHAPTER SIX

1 "The perfecting of means of transport has killed the fair in general, and the establishment of railways has dealt a mortal blow to the Beaucaire fair" (Levy 1912, 252).

2 Levy notes that indirect sales are only possible when buyer and seller can communicate by letter, while the Mulhouse post office only had one employee as late as 1830 (1912, 261). The imperfect network of postal service, and of regular passenger and freight service, made it virtually impossible for indirect sales to be conducted with a large number of customers.

3 "... a great distance ... overloads the goods of Lyons with transport costs, and these fall in competition, with regard to the high price, with cloth which many foreign monarchs can manufacture at great cost in their states" (Mayet 1786, 14). Mayet goes on to criticize the quality of many of these foreign products as well.

4 "Prior to this [French] revolution the superfine cloths of France were superior to those of England in texture, colours, and softness. In the finer articles of worsted goods, and in the mixed worsted goods made partly with long combing wool, and partly with silk or goat's wool from the Levant, they surpassed the manufactures of this country, but the manufacturers of the commoner kinds of worsted goods, as tammies and shalloons, could

not rival us in foreign markets for want of a proper supply of wool suited to the purpose" (Rees, "Wool"). It has been seen that there are other potential explanations for the French emphasis on higher quality goods.

5 "Coal, which is so necessary to the advancement of the manufactures, and which is there both scarce and dear, becomes a very material as well as natural objection, for notwithstanding the country produces this valuable article, yet is either too far from the centre of trade or the quality so inferior that they can procure it from England in peaceable times at a more reasonable rate. Their usual fuel, which is wood, becomes doubly expensive, its consumption being as rapid" (S.J. 1803, 48).

6 "We are far from having in France the profusion of machines which one sees in England" (Chaptal 1819, 31). Chaptal went on to note that machine making was not as well done in France as in England (33). This does not appear to have resulted from any inherent lack of engineering skill. Not only did France have schools to train engineers but Chaptal notes that France did excel in at least one art, clockmaking (33–4).

7 The English manufacturer Fairbairn was asked by a parliamentary enquiry in 1824 if France could adopt English machinery. He responded that the French had against them many disadvantages, notably the high price of transport (Say 1852, v.1, 332).

8 "In this very visible evolution, the influence of Great Britain appears no less essential than in the properly technical domain. Numerous visitors to that "paradise" carefully toured the vast mills of Lancashire, and the Midlands; they admired the grandiose and methodical arrangement, the strict division of workers, the central organization which facilitated decision and the conception of policies. They spoke of the idea of the "rationalized" firm" (Léon 1976, 504).

9 Inspector Bruyard in 1781 described a quite traditional woolen industry in Provence. There were no real manufactories. Work was performed only in the agricultural off-season. Producers took their cloths to market on particular days for sale. Instead of commenting on a need for modernization, Bruyard suggests ways of strengthening regulations to support the existing manufacture (F12 677A).

10 Léon outlined the conditions necessary for technological development in the nineteenth century. After discussing the foreign market, he concludes, "Singularly more important is the impulse of the internal market, both unified and enlarged by the effect of many modern transport networks, and the commercial institutions adopted" (1976, 478).

11 It could be conjectured that the problem confronting French producers was poorly developed capital markets. Heywood, however, provides examples of capital being available when needed by industry, and suggests that capital markets would develop in France only as the demand for such services expanded (1977, 21–2).

12 Heywood notes that while the cost of land and buildings was lower in France, the cost of machines was higher (1977, 22). The dispersed nature of industry and the high level of transport costs must have contributed to the high price of machinery. The government spent hundreds of francs transporting some carding and spinning machines from Paris to Lyons in the early nineteenth century (the machines had cost thousands to construct – F12 2322).

13 This point was made by A.D.F. in 1786, translated by J.S. (42–3). He maintained that one of England's main advantages at the time was that she possessed workmen familiar with the new machines. Nevertheless, it could be noted that machine technology was more readily transmitted than that which had gone before. "It is indeed in the opinion of many an uncomfortable reflection that our trade lies now much more open to the designs of other nations than it ever did before. Machines, say they, have had this bad tendency. They have made it a much more easy matter to take it from us if we are so simple as to give them leave. Whilst a manufacture lies chiefly in the ingenuity and dexterity of the hands employed, this dexterity depends on education and early habit, you can not take it away without taking away the people. But machines belong to no place or country. They are commoners of nature. They will work as well in France or Spain as in England, and as well in one part of England as another" (Friend 1780, 18).

14 A letter of an VII about a new machine for carding and spinning being designed in Rouen begins: "we cannot deny that it is to the aid of machines that England owes for some time its preponderance in commerce" (F12 2322).

15 "Carding is an operation which requires the greatest attention, it requires much practice, experience, and skill. The regularity of spinning depends on this first premise. To card, it is necessary to have two parallel cards" (*Mémoire of Lajeune* 1786, F12 1412). While recognizing the importance of proper carding, Lajeune appears unaware of any of the improvements that had occurred in England in the previous decades.

16 One contributing factor would be that the English moved to the use of iron in machine making earlier than the French. The reasons for this were discussed earlier.

17 "The astonishing prosperity of the cotton manufacture in England has only occurred in the last thirty years. The English owe this to the discovery of new spinning technology" (F12 2195, an IX). The writer notes further that jennies have only in the last couple of years begun to spread widely, while the mule, necessary for finer threads, is rare and those that exist do not function well.

18 The *Mémoire Sur L'État actuel de la filature des cotons* (1790, F12 1341) asserted that the English industry had only had an edge on the French

since the introduction of the jenny two decades earlier. The author continued that carding machines were even less prevalent in France than spinning machines, and spoke of the need to attract slubbing billies which had only recently been introduced to France.

19 "But it was still a long time before it could be brought to any tolerable degree of perfection; perhaps from the incompetency of the undertakers; perhaps from the ill execution of the workmanship, the different artisans being employed therein being altogether not acquainted with the work, and proper tools not being procurable at that time; or from the difficulties arising from the inexperience of the people and children occupied in the carding, spinning etc. all being totally ignorant of this process" (S.J. 1803, 15). Some such delay was inevitable. In a world almost without specialized machine shops, it was considerably exacerbated.

20 The wife of Jacques-François Martin asked for government aid in 1811, stating, "It is to the introduction of these machines, Sire, that many of the most important towns in France owe today for new types of industry, and the flourishing state of their commerce" (F12 2322). Government rewards for successful smuggling of foreign technology were not unusual.

21 For some years, machine-spinning of linen was unable to compete with hand-spinning. Ballot suggests that this may be due to lower wages of rural French spinners. Wages appear to have been lower in France than England. For some machines this could be a significant factor in slowing adoption. For machines that could potentially save enormously on labour requirements, however, there must be a further explanation.

22 A few examples from the later part of the century: 1783 found the English mechanic Hall at Sens building a variety of machines for different works, and the Englishwoman Law asking for government assistance to set up a school to teach English spinning methods (F12 1340). Macleod also offered to teach French workers to use the new spinning machines in 1789 (F12 2195). Wood claimed a pension from the government in an X for smuggling in spinning secrets in 1784 (F12 2195). Le Turc was ordered by the government to bring over English spinners in 1785 (F12 2204). In 1788 Douglas, a Manchester machinemaker, approached the French ambassador in London, who arranged support so that he could move to France and construct a variety of machines (F12 2195). Other English machinemakers – notably the Milnes and Pickford – also moved to France. Bauwens made thirty-two trips to England, returning with the flying shuttle, printing technology, and the mule (Ballot 1923, 100–6). The list goes on.

23 Léon notes, not surprisingly, that in the nineteenth century, new technology spread more quickly in the relatively concentrated cotton industry than in the dispersed wool and linen sectors (1976, 496).

24 "Whereas in England the flying shuttle spread rapidly and transformed weaving to the point possible, of its adoption, the departure point for the Industrial Revolution, there had been no success in everyday France" (Ballot 1923, 248). While Ballot exaggerates the importance of this one innovation, it is nevertheless true that the slowness to adopt this innovation is a glaring example of French backwardness during the period.

25 Silk was also manufactured in Nimes, Tours, the Loire region, and Avignon (Chaptal 1819, 113–17).

26 This is, at least, the opinion of Mayet. His first answer to the question of why the manufactures of Lyon have prospered is, "This town is placed at the confluence of two great rivers, and in the neighbourhood of two others, which facilitate prodigiously the transport of goods within and without the Kingdom" (1786, 12).

27 Lyons possessed a reputation for quality, as, interestingly, did the English (Boislandry 1815, 227). Other countries viewed France and England as producing the best quality.

28 Porter (1831, 209) attributed this to the different wage rates. "Our French rivals are fully aware how greatly the English throwsters are in advance of them in this particular, but they have not the same inducement that exists in this country to incur a heavy first expense in alterations, that they may secure a prospective advantage. From the lower wages paid for labour in that country, such advantage would not be in any proportion to that realized by our manufacturers." I discussed earlier the shortcomings of this argument.

29 "It detracts nothing from the merit of the inventors and improvers of [the draw loom] which removed so many of the disadvantages attendant upon the system of figure weaving, as then usually practised, that another and a better system has since been imported from a neighbouring country, which has occasioned the laying aside of the draw loom and its attendant draw-boy for the production of figured silk goods" (Porter 1831, 238).

30 The government had tried to attract calendars and workers familiar with them since the 1740s, recognizing they were essential for certain quality products (Ballot 1923, 294–6). The handful of calendars established by the Ancien Régime all appear to have fallen out of use by the end of the century (F12 2246). Emard in 1806 speaks of it as a machine virtually unknown in France but common in England for a long time. He had smuggled one out of England and wished to set it up in France (F12 2246).

31 When Demachy wrote his volume for the Academy of Sciences in the 1770s, nitric acid was the main product and it was not really industrially produced but could be thought of as domestic production (Smith 1979, ch. 1).

32 According to Ballot (1923, 529) these others were really responsible for this development. Berthollet's role becomes even more questionable when it is found that from 1787 on, he argued against the use of alkalis in bleaching liquors. Like Lavoisier's invocation against saltpetre decades earlier, this would lead to many misguided experiments.

33 Chamberlain complained to the king in 1822, for example, that France had been importing iron sulfate from England for decades at great expense, despite processing all the necessary materials for its manufacture. He, along with a number of other manufacturers of various chemicals, wanted government support of various types, in order to compete with the English (F12 2234).

34 It is worth noting that Holker had first moved to France with technology for the finishing processes such as calendars and methods of dyeing. He kept an eye on England for further inventions, and thus knew of the inventions in spinning as they occurred (Ballot 1923, 44).

35 Chapman and Chassagne raise the possibility that their comparison turns out this way because they are comparing Lancashire with Paris and suggest that Alsatian producers might be more similar to the Peels. They have no evidence to support this suggestion.

36 On top of this, English producers had the advantage of being able to obtain the unprinted cloth more cheaply due to the greater efficiency of the preceding stages of production in England. The cloth was generally seventy to ninety per cent of the final cost. The inability of French producers to produce the type of cotton cloth Oberkampf wanted caused him to take two months off every year to visit London sales (Chapman 1981, 157).

37 They do however feel that English trade unionism may have been a major factor inducing labour-saving innovation.

38 French adoption of cylinder printing was also delayed by problems in obtaining well-cast copper cylinders and then engraving them (Dunham 1955, 264). The mechanization of French industry would naturally be delayed by the slower development of metal production and engineering.

39 Turnbull also speaks of Oberkampf travelling a great deal and members of the firm did often visit other establishments. Yet these visits appear always to have been part of trips to visit family or transact business (Chapman 1981, ch. 10). While open to new ideas, the Oberkampfs still did not undertake long trips lightly.

40 Despite its reputation, the Valenciennes lace industry produced almost exclusively for Paris and Brussels. There was some slight contact with the German and Italian markets, but almost none with southern France (Guignet, 1979). Such a limited market for a good with a high value/bulk ratio is amazing.

41 Heywood (1976), while maintaining that hosiery was slow to concentrate in England as well, paints an interesting picture of the Champagne hosiery industry. Putting out predominates. The higher quality goods, at least late in the century, are produced in workshops so that workers could be supervised. Still this is only one fifth of output in 1810. Even by 1826, while fifteen to eighteen merchants have established workshops of 300 frames, most merchants in the trade were still putting out.

42 In 1784, an Englishman approached the French ambassador with an offer to establish in France a manufacture of silk gauze for the ladies "which might be made equally as good in France as they are here" (F12 1453). Blondel, in a 1783 memoir, noted that "The English manufacture of bars, cloths, and velveteen, have over those of France a superiority which excludes all competition on price as well as quality" (F12 2413).

CHAPTER SEVEN

1 Much of the disagreement between Markovitch and previous authors revolves around the use of the word "industry". Should small-scale handicraft production be considered industrial? In this work, I have taken a broad view similar to Markovitch's. However, different industries may have widely different potential for undergoing the Industrial Revolution.

2 "Developments in the industrial structure of brewing were largely a product of rising demand, given by the unprecedented increase in numbers after 1750, supported by cheaper land transport and progressive urbanization" (Mathias 1959, xxvi–xxvii). The development of porter may have been necessary for large-scale works to emerge; once they were in place they led to improvements in thermometers, hydrometers, and the eventual application of the steam engine (63, 81), innovations which improved the regularity of production in terms of both quality and quantity. Urbanization was especially important in brewing. Not only did beer have a low value/bulk ratio but most types of beer went bad quickly and thus tended to be consumed locally. Still, as transport speed improved (and as longer lasting beer was developed) wider markets were exploited. By 1809, at least one of the London brewers had one third of its output going to the country (141). Foreign markets were unimportant; total exports, excluding Ireland, throughout the eighteenth century were equivalent to the output of one second-rate London brewery (171). There was a nation-wide trade in hops and barley. The makers of fine ale searched all England for the best barley (448). By 1789, the Stourbridge fair had declined as a clearing point for hops replaced by a more continuous form of commercial organization (497–8). Clearly, many of the elements of my model can be found in the brewing industry. Further research might provide greater detail.

3 "Though there has been no radical alteration or any great practical improvements in the art of tanning, yet for the last 20 or 30 years it has attracted the attention of many celebrated chemists and philosophers in all countries, who have investigated the subject with great accuracy and precision" (Rees, "Tanning"). He lists six English patents between 1790 and 1799, but notes that none of the methods described has ever been widely practised.

4 The English paper industry was relatively stagnant in the first third of the eighteenth century but output quadrupled between 1735 and 1800 (Coleman 1958, 90). Coleman believes growth was even faster in the late seventeenth, but again it must be remembered that one would be speaking of growth from a very small base. The long-term reason for the rise of the importance of paper is due to the spread of literacy and printing, but there seems to have been no radical change in the printing industry during the eighteenth century (102). The imperfect statistical evidence "points to the English industry's growth as resting more upon successful capture and consolidation of the home market than upon any striking venture overseas" (104–5). Coleman's explanation for the growth of the national market relies, beyond remarks on the growth of income and population, on the requirements of increased trade for wrapping paper, bills of exchange, bank notes, and commercial correspondence (101).

5 The paper industry might have been expected to be less subject to the forces of regional specialization than others. Before the nineteenth-century use of wood pulp, the paper industry relied on rags for the raw material. Thus, each urban setting provided both raw material (presumably of much the same quality everywhere) and market for the potential paper mill if a source of clear water could be found nearby. One might expect, then, few strong local advantages to arise. Nevertheless, as the century progressed, the industry increasingly produced a variety of goods, with particular types of paper requiring a national market (see Coleman 1958, 97). This encouraged concentration in the Home Counties around London, the biggest source of raw material as well as the largest market. (A port was especially important – one third of English rags were imported, and used ropes and sails were also a valuable source of supply.)

6 Only in 1787 was it possible to duplicate the finest quality French paper for engraving (Coleman, 98–9). In 1815, Boislandry admitted that English (and Dutch) paper was better than French, but claimed that it was more expensive (1815, 242).

7 Already in 1756, the French are conscious of the advantages gained by the English in applying Chester salt to pottery. In 1785 there are comments that English methods of making better and stronger pottery are now available to France as skilled English workmen are willing to move to France

(F12 2380I). The Institut National des Sciences et des Arts in an VI noted that there had been many improvements in pottery making abroad. The English had developed many machines which they used to great advantage. While France could compete in high-quality porcelain, it could not in common pottery (F12 2381 II).

8 Chaptal complained that French pottery "has been replaced by English pottery. We have known nothing for many years but the products of foreign manufacture" (1819, 106). During the Republic the Rapport au Comité d'Agriculture et des Arts stated that, "For a long time, we have desired the establishment in France of a manufacture of pottery of the genre called "à l'Anglaise," remarkable for their properties, their lightness, and their ability to withstand fire. The style of this pottery is well known, and since the treaty of commerce, enormous quantities have spread over France" (F12 2381 III). Efforts to duplicate English pottery are clear from at least 1783 (F12 2380 I). Peuchet (1807) speaks of work in the English style in Aisne and Seine-et-Oise.

9 An Englishman fittingly named Potter became a naturalized French citizen and established a works in Pontoise to produce pottery like that of Wedgwood. In an II he asked for government funding (F12 2381 III).

10 The fact that France possessed all of the necessary materials was affirmed by government reports of 1756 (F12 2380 I) and recognized by the Institut National des Sciences et des Arts in an 6. The Institute also noted that part of the English advantage was in their access to cheap coal, lead, and other materials (F12 2381 II).

11 "The lands of the Haut-Vienne have exported at great cost to Paris for the manufacture of porcelain: they could do this by the navigation of the Creuse and Loire with a considerable dimunition in price" (Peuchet 1807, "Indre").

12 An optimistic entrepreneur of 1783 wanted to set up a porcelain works in Poitou. While feeling that the poor state of local transport was not an insurmountable obstacle, he did recognize that substantial improvements would be necessary to fortify the position (F12 2380 I).

13 Weatherill describes the use of packhorses to carry raw materials and finished goods in the early eighteenth century but notes that carts and wagons may have appeared from the 1750s (1971, 89). Josiah Wedgwood was active in promoting turnpikes which enhanced still further the ability to send goods by wheeled transport. Even after the Trent and Mersey Canal was completed, many Staffordshire producers preferred to send goods as far as London by road (Weatherill 1983, 29–30). Shaw (1829, 148–9) interviewed eighty-three-year-old Ralph Leigh in 1813. He recalled the use of packhorses to carry coal, flint, and pottery. Later, he was able to use a cart and horses, though the roads were still bad. Finally, he would be replaced

by regular carriers. Shaw is unclear on the timing, though he does speak of the Act of 1760 for repairing the roads then made and opening new ones, and the fears this aroused among local workmen (169).

14 Brindley, promoting the canal, spoke of the advantages which would accrue to the potteries: "the ware which is sent to Hull is now carried by land upwards of 30 miles, to Wellington, and that for Liverpool 20 miles to Winsford. The burthen of so expensive a land carriage to Winford and Willington, and the uncertainty of the navigation from those places … occasioned by the floods in winter and the numerous shallows in summer, are more than these low-priced manufactures can bear, and without some such relief as this under consideration, must concur, with their newly established competitors in France, and our American colonies to bring these potteries to speedy decay and ruin" (1759, 67). Land carriage to Birmingham alone was still five to ten per cent of the final price (*Correspondence* 1906, 261). Afterwards, Aikin noted that "the consequence of a water conveyance to and from the pottery, in such bulky and heavy articles as the raw materials used in this country, and the goods when manufactured, must be obvious to everyone" (1831, 521). "Without this new method of bringing in their bulky materials and sending out their fragile ware the potteries could not have developed as they did" (Bladen 1926, 128).

15 The earliest riders carried goods with them and received cash on the spot. "The practice customary then was, not to take out invoices, or on returning to render an account of the sales; but merely to empty their pockets; after which they received their wages, for the time of the journey; their expenses having been paid out of the cash received" (Shaw 1829, 155). One can well imagine the potential for abuse in such a system. As communications improved, it was natural that producers would move to a system where payment was received afterwards by carrier.

16 Shaw (1829, 169) described the situation in about 1740: "The chapmen or dealers kept a gang of horses which carried small crates that were filled with wares, then driven to different parts, and there opened for the inspection of purchasers. The expense of carriage necessarily impeded the extension of the manufacture …. Afterwards [after turnpikes] carts and wagons were substituted for packhorses, persons were sent to the different places for orders; business was extended, and the district benefited."

17 According to Meteyard (1866, 355), the first Wedgwood catalogue appeared in 1773.

18 Clay had been imported from Cornwall in the early eighteenth century but at such expense that Staffordshire potters went to great lengths to economize on its use (Clow 1952, 301–2). The import from Cornwall of ball clay to make white ware increased dramatically after the Weaver Nav-

igation of 1733 (Weatherill 1971, 17). Kaolin, previously imported from North America, was discovered in Cornwall in 1755 (Clow, 308).

19 Among the advantages to the potteries of the new canal was the ability to import food into a poor agricultural area (Shaw 1829, 10).

20 At one point, Wedgwood wrote that he was "so hurryed up and down and allmost off my life with this Navigation" (*Correspondence* 1906, 269).

21 "English porcelain, in imitation of foreign china, has long been manufactured in this town, and formerly not without success. But of late this branch has been much upon the decline, partly because the Liverpool artists have not kept pace in their improvements with some others in the same way, but chiefly because the Staffordshire ware has had, and still continues to have, so general a demand as almost to supersede the use of other English porcelain" (Enfield 1774, 90).

22 There was certainly much scope for it. Aikin described how a common enamel tea pot would pass through fourteen hands in production and then added, "Several more are required to the completion of such pieces of ware, but are in inferior capacities, such as turners of the wheel, turners of the lathe, etc." (1831, 534).

23 Though Weatherill emphasizes gradual change, earlier writers were sure that an important transformation had occurred after mid-century. Thomas (1937, 403) castigated others for not recognizing that an Industrial Revolution of factories and technological change had occurred in pottery. The Hammonds spoke of the emergence of the factory system and felt that this was a necessary reaction to increased demand and the use of clay from far afield (1925, 168).

24 "The Burslem potters often rambled to other places where there were potteries, as Derby, and Worcester, acquiring information concerning the porcelain of these places, and afterwards on returning made trials of various kinds" (Shaw 1829, 204).

25 This point will be brought home in any museum where the best of Josiah Wedgwood can be compared with early eighteenth-century pottery. Wedgwood developed his products through a process of trial and error. Though he corresponded with scientists such as Priestley, he owed them nothing but encouragement (Bladen 1926, 124–5). After all, even in modern times scientific precision has been lacking in pottery creation, recipes rather than formulae determining composition (Clow 1952, 293).

26 Weatherill maintains that most of the major eighteenth-century innovations were developed in the first half of the century. While these had no effect on output then, they were responsible for the growth in output later in the century (1971, 26). Two points must be made. Many innovations which I have discussed have no clear precedent from early in the century. Moreover, it appears that the developments Weatherill describes were nei-

ther perfected nor widespread until much later in the century. One should not be surprised that the early part of the century witnessed efforts toward change in the potteries. This should not blind one to the fact that the victory of new technology and organization occurred after mid-century.

CHAPTER EIGHT

1   "In the study of eighteenth-century economic history, it is seldom safe to accept a generalization based on figures alone, unless it can be supported by some confirmatory, non-quantitative evidence" (M.W. Flinn, quoted favourably in Hoppit, 1990).

2   Chaptal complained that children of French manufacturers did not want to continue in the same line of work as it was not respected. Thus, manufactures were wound up rather than transferred from one generation to another. Chaptal noted that political and social attitudes were more favourable in England and urged the government to set a precedent by showing increased respect to manufacturers (1819, 220–4).

3   "The regulations on manufacture have kept our industry captive for over a century, she has rested stationary, whereas that of our neighbours, released from all fetters, marches quickly toward perfection." (Chaptal 1819, 1–2)

4   We must be careful, of course, to recognize the differences between the capabilities of countries then and now. The British succeeded largely through private (mainly non-profit) efforts, and it does appear that the French government was incapable of creating such a system itself. The governments of modern developing countries may be able to succeed where their eighteenth-century predecessors could not. Interestingly, many writers suggest the use of tolls to finance road maintenance in less-developed countries.

5   It would, for example, be very interesting to know to what degree development in industries such as brewing and paper were due to the increasing urbanization of the period.

6   "Before the establishment of turnpike roads in England, many parts of that kingdom, like the highlands of Scotland, were scarcely accessible. Coal, manure, grain, etc., as is still the case in many parts of Cornwall, were carried on horse's backs. Where wagons were used, 7 or 8 horses were necessary to draw two tons, and seldom were able to proceed above 20 miles a day." After pikes, those horses could pull five tons and travel twice as far (Rees, "Roads").

7   Bentley predicted that by increasing access to marl and manure, the Trent and Mersey Canal would double the produce and value of many farms along the route (*Correspondence* ... 1906, 293). Priestley notes that one of

the main purposes of the aptly named Tamar Manure Navigation of 1796 was to supply lime to farmers (1831, 650).

8   Aikin claimed this role for the Leeds and Liverpool Canal (1795, 381) while Priestly noted that the Market Weighton Canal of 1771 drained "the low lands and fens which abound in its vicinity" (1831, 473).

9   Phillips follows many writers, for example, in suggesting that canals will play an important role in watering the surrounding lands through the accumulation of dew (1785, v-x). Promoters, in particular, could sometimes heavily overestimate the value of canals.

Bibliography

MANUSCRIPT SOURCES

ARCHIVES NATIONALES, PARIS
Series F12 Commerce et Industrie
Series F14 Travaux Publics
Series F20 Statistique

BRITISH LIBRARY, LONDON
Additional Manuscripts
Egerton Manuscripts

PUBLIC RECORD OFFICE, LONDON
Treasury Papers
Home Office Papers

LIBRARY OF THE SOCIETY OF FRIENDS, LONDON
Norris Manuscripts

SHREWSBURY PUBLIC LIBRARY
Coalbrookdale Manuscripts

BIRMINGHAM CENTRAL LIBRARY
Boulton and Watt Papers
Matthew Boulton Papers

JOHN RYLANDS LIBRARY, MANCHESTER
Oldknow Papers

EIGHTEENTH- AND
NINETEENTH-CENTURY WORKS

Aikin, John. 1795. *Description of the Country ... From Thirty to Forty Miles Around Manchester.*
Allen, Thomas. 1831. *A New and Complete History of the City of York.*
Allnutt, Z. 1810. *Useful and Correct Accounts ... Canals.*

Anderson, James. 1777. *Observations on the Means of Exciting a Spirit of National Industry*.

Andreossey, F. An VIII. *Histoire du Canal du Midi*.

Annuaire du Département de la Haute-Marne. 1804.

Anstie, John. 1803. *Observations on the Importance and Necessity of Introducing Improved Machinery Into the Woollen Manufactury*.

Answer to the Case Relating to the Intended Road from Nottingham to Belper-Lane-End, n.d..

Baines, Sir Edward. 1835. *History of the Cotton Manufacture*.

Beaumont, Charles. 1789. *Treatise on the Coal Trade*.

Becquey, Francois. 1820. *Rapport au Roi Sur La Navigation Intérieure de la France*.

Beilby, et al. 1830. *An Historical and Descriptive Sketch of Birmingham*.

Bentley, Thomas. 1780. *Letters on the Utility and Policy of Employing Machines to Shorten Labour* (also attributed to John Kay).

Bernard, M. 1779. *Premier (Second) Discours Sur Les Moyens les Plus Propres à Vaincre Les Obstacles que le Rhône oppose au Cabotage entre Arles et Marseille*.

Bischoff, James. 1842. *A Comprehensive History of the Woollen and Worsted Manufactures*.

Blakey, W. 1793. *A Short Historical Account of the Invention, Theory, and Practice of Fire Machinery*.

Boislandry, Louis de. 1815. *Examen des Principes les plus Favorables aux Progrès*.

Bossut, et al. 1786. *Rapport ... sur la Navigation Interieure de la Bretagne*.

Boucqueau, P. An XII. *Mémoire Statistique du Département du Rhin-et-Moselle*.

Bourn, Daniel. 1763. *A Treatise Upon Wheel Carriages*.

Bowen, Emmanuel. 1761. *New Dictionary of Trade and Commerce*.

A Brief State of Facts Relative to the New Method of Making Bar Iron. 1787.

Brindley, James. 1766. *The History of Inland Navigation*.

Brooke, Henry. 1759. *The Interests of Ireland Considered, Stated and Recommended, Particularly with Respect to Inland Navigation*.

Brooke, Robert. 1783. *Thoughts on the Establishment of New Manufacture in Ireland*.

Bruguière. An III. *Moyens D'Approvisionnement Pour La Commune de Paris*.

Bruslé, Claude-Louis. An X. *Tableau Statistique du Département de L'Aube*.

Burkitt, R. 1755. *Observations on the Inland Navigation*.

Butet. An V. *Mémoire Sur Le Département du Cher*.

Calonne, M de. 1801. *Proposal for Preventing Highway Robberies in the Environs of London*.

Cartwright, Edmund. 1800. *A Memorial*.

– 1843. *Memoir of Edmund Cartwright*.

Cary, J. 1795. *Inland Navigation*.

Chambers, Abraham. 1820. *Observations on the Formation, State, and Condition of Turnpike Roads and Other Highways*.

Chaptal, M. 1819. *De L'Industrie Française*.

A Citizen. 1765. *Thoughts on the Times and the Silk Manufacture*.

Couderc, J. 1829. *Essai Sur L'Administration et le Corps Royale des Ponts et Chaussées.*

Dalrymple, Sir John. 1784. *Address and Proposals ...*

– 1785. *Account of the Qualities and Uses of Coal Tar and Coal Varnish.*

Defoe, Daniel. 1748. *A Tour Through the Whole Island of Great Britain.* 4th Ed.

D'Haussez, M. 1828. *Des Routes et Des Canaux.*

De L'Importance et de la Nécessité Des Chemins Publics en France. 1777.

De Vitry. 1777. *Mémoire Qui a Remporté le Prix Pour L'Année 1777.*

Du Lac de La Tour D'Aurec. 1807. *Précis Historique et Statistique de Département du Loire.*

Dutens, J. 1829. *Histoire de la Navigation Intérieure de la France.*

Edgeworth, Richard. 1817. *An Essay on the Construction of Roads and Carriages.*

Edington, Robert. 1813. *Treatise on the Coal Trade.*

Enfield, William. 1774. *Essay Toward the History of Liverpool.*

Farey, John. 1827. *A Treatise on the Steam Engine.*

French, Gilbert J. 1859. *The Life and Times of Samuel Crompton.*

A Friend of the Poor. 1780. *Thoughts on the Use of Machines in the Cotton Manufacture.*

Fulton, Robert. 1796. *A Treatise on the Improvement of Canal Navigation.*

Galloway, Elijah. 1831. *History and Progress of the Steam Engine.*

Guest, Richard. 1823, 1968. *Compendious History of the Cotton Manufacture.*

A Guide to Stagecoaches. 1793.

Guiraudet, T. (Préfet). 1802. *Mémoire Sur Les Forges Du Département de la Côte D'Or.*

Hawkins, John. 1763. *Observations on the State of the Highways.*

History of Leeds. 1797.

Homer, Henry. 1767. *An Enquiry Into the Means of Preserving ... Public Roads.*

The Humble Petition of the Iron Manufacturers In and Near the Town of Birmingham in the City of Warwick. 30 Geo II.

Hunter, Joseph. 1819, 1869. *History of Hallamshire.*

Hutton, William. 1791, 1976. *An History of Birmingham.*

Johnson. 1793. *Consideration on the Present High Price and Scarcity of Coals in Scotland.*

J.S. See S., J.

Jordan, S. 1878. "Notes on the Resources For Iron Manufacture in France." *Journal of the Iron and Steel Institute.*

Kennedy, John. 1818. *Observations on the Rise and Progress of the Cotton Trade in Great Britain.*

Lardner, Dyonisius. 1828. *Popular Lectures on the Steam Engine.*

Larroque-Labecede. 1792. *Rapport et Projet de Décret ....*

Laumond, J-C-J. An X. *Statistique du Département du Bas-Rhin.*

Leach, Edmund. 1790. *Treatise on Universal Inland Navigation.*

Leducq, M. 1834. *Du Développement de la Production du Fer dans le Nord-Ouest de la France.*

Lequinio, J.M. An III. *Richesse de L'État.*

Lewis, William. 1763. *Commercium Philosophico – Technicum.*

Mahuet. An VIII. *Observations sur le Droit de Passe.*

Meteyard, Eliza. 1865. *Life of Josiah Wedgewood.*

Milton, William. 1810. *The Danger of Travelling in Stagecoaches.*

Miroy-Detournelles. 1813. *Annuaire du Département de l'Aisne.*

Montalivet, J-P-B. 1813. *Exposé de la Situation de l'Empire.*

Moore, Francis. 1783. *The Contrast; Or a Comparison Between our Woollen, Linen, Cotton, and Silk Manufactures.*

Moreau, Cesar. 1826. *Rise and Progress of the Silk Trade in England.*

Muirhead, J.P. 1854. *Origin and Progress of the Mechanical Inventions of John Wilkinson.*

Noël de la Morinière, S.B.J. 1795. *Premier (Second) Essai Sur le Département de la Seine-Inférieure.*

– An VII. *Mémoire Contre le Canal de Navigation Intérieure depuis Dieppe jusqu'à Paris.*

O'Brien, Lucius. 1785. *Letters Concerning the Trade and Manufacture of Ireland.*

Oddy, J. Jepson. 1810. *A Sketch for the Improvement of the Political, Commercial, and Local Interests of Britain.*

Ogden, James. 1783, 1887. *A Description of Manchester.*

Opinion des Ingénieurs Composant La Minorité de L'Assemblée des Ponts et Chaussées ... An X.

Ornay. 1776. *Mémoire Qui a Remporté le Prix Pour L'Année 1776.*

P.M. 1806. *Annuaire du Départment du Loir et Cher.*

Paterson, Daniel. 1776. *A New and Accurate Description ... Roads.*

Peuchet, J. and P.G. Chamlaire. 1807. *Description Topographique et Statistique de la France.*

Phillips, John. 1785. *A Treatise on Inland Navigation.*

– 1792. *A General History of Inland Navigation.*

Phillips, Robert. 1737. *A Dissertation Concerning the Present State of the High Roads of England.*

Pilkington, James. 1789. *A View of the Present State of Derbyshire.*

Pillet-Will, M-F. 1837. *De la Dépense et du Produit des Canaux.*

Porter, G. 1831. *Treatise on the Origin, Progressive Improvement, andPresent State of the Silk Manufacture.*

Priestley, Joseph. 1831, 1967. *Historical Account of the NavigableRivers, Canals, and Railways Throughout Great Britain.*

Proposal For a Horse Patrol Through All the Great Roads of the Kingdom. 1764.

Proposals for Forming by Subscription ... A Public Institute for Diffusing the Knowledge and Facilitate the General Introduction of Useful Mechanical Inventions and Improvements. 1799.

Publicola. 1798. *Reflections on the General Utility of Inland Navigation.*

Radcliffe, William. 1828. *Origin of the New System of Manufacture Commonly Called Power-Loom Weaving.*

Rapport au Roi Sur La Situation Des Canaux. 1823, 1824.

Raup-Baptestin, A.J. An IX. *Mémoire Historique Sur La Navigation Intérieure.*

Rees, Abraham. 1802–20. *The Cyclopaedia, or Universal Dictionary of Arts, Sciences, and Literature.*

Report From the Committee on the Woolen Manufacture of England. 1806.

Rolt. 1761. *A New Dictionary of Trade and Commerce.*

S., J. 1803. *A View of the Cotton Manufacturies of France.*

Savigny, J. 1771. *Extracts from Réaumur; An Essay on the Mystery of Tempering Steel.*

Say, Jean-Baptiste. 1852. *Cours Complet d'Économie Politique.* (Compilation of earlier writings).

Scrivenor, Henry. 1841. *A Comprehensive History of the Iron Trade.*

Shaw, Simeon. 1829, 1900. *History ... Staffordshire Potteries.*

Smiles, Samuel. 1862. *Lives of the Engineers.*

Smith, Adam. 1776. *The Wealth of Nations.*

Smith, John. 1747. *Memoirs of Wool.*

The State of the Trade and Manufactury of Iron in Great Britain Considered. 1750.

Stuart, Robert. 1825. *A Descriptive History of the Steam Engine.* 3rd ed.

Tatham, William. 1799. *The Political Economy of Inland Navigation.*

Thermopilae. 1774. *The Speech of a Scots Weaver.*

Timperley, Charles. 1839. *Annals of Manchester.*

Tucker, Josiah. 1757. *Instructions to Travellers.*

– 1762. *A Brief Essay on the Advantages and Disadvantages Which Respectively Attend France and England With Regard to Trade.*

– 1782. *Reflections on the Present Low Price of Coarse Wools.*

Ure, Andrew. 1835. *Philosophy of Manufactures.*

– 1836. *The Cotton Manufacture of Great Britain.*

Vallancey, Charles. 1763. *A Treatise on Inland Navigation.*

Wallace, Thomas. 1798. *An Essay on the Manufactures of Ireland.*

Wansey, Henry. 1791. *Wool Encouraged Without Exportation.*

Watson, John. 1775. *The History and Antiquities of the Parish of Halifax in Yorkshire.*

Watt, James. 1809. *Memoir of Matthew Boulton.*

– 1824. *Memoir of James Watt.*

Whitaker, John. 1771–75. *The History of Manchester.*

Whitaker, Thomas. 1816. *Loidis and Elmete.*

Whitehead, C. 1834. *Lives and Exploits of English Highwaymen, Pirates and Robbers.*

Whitworth, Richard. 1766. *The Advantages of Inland Navigation.*

Young, Arthur. 1771. *A Farmers Tour Through the North of England.*

– 1900. *Travels in France During the Years 1787, 1788, and 1789,* edited by Betham-Edwards.

TWENTIETH CENTURY WORKS

Addis, J.P. 1957. *The Crawshay Dynasty*. Cardiff: University of Wales Press.

Albert, William. 1967. *The Turnpike Road System in England, 1663–1840*. Cambridge: Cambridge University Press.

Aldcroft, Derek and M.J. Freeman, eds. 1983. *Transport in the Industrial Revolution*. Manchester: Manchester University Press.

Allan, Robert C. 1983. "Collective Invention." *Journal of Economic Behaviour and Organization* 4: 1–24.

Arbellot, G. 1973. "La Grande Mutation des Routes de France au Milieu du XVIIIème Siècle." *Annales: Économies, Sociétés, Civilisations* 28: 765–91.

Ashton, T.S. 1939. *An Eighteenth Century Industrialist: Peter Stubs*. Manchester: Manchester University Press.

– 1951. *Iron and Steel in the Industrial Revolution*. Manchester: Manchester University Press.

– 1959. *Economic Fluctuations in England 1700–1800*. Oxford: Oxford University Press.

– 1966. *Economic History of England*. London: Methuen.

– and J. Sykes. 1964. *The Coal Industry in the Eighteenth Century*. Manchester: Manchester University Press.

Bagwell, Philip S. 1974. *The Transportation Revolution From 1770*, London: Batsford B.T. Ltd.

Ballot, Charles. 1923. *L'Introduction du Machinisme dans l'Industrie Française*. Paris: F. Rieder.

Bamford, P.W. 1988. *Privilege and Profit*. Philadelphia: University of Pennsylvania Press.

Barker, T.C. and C.I. Savage. 1974. *An Economic History of Transport in Britain*. London: Hutchinson.

Basalla, G. 1988. *The Evolution of Technology*. Cambridge: Cambridge University Press.

Beattie, J.M. 1986. *Crime and the Courts in England*. Princeton NJ: Princeton University Press.

Berg, Maxine. 1985. *The Age of Manufactures*. Oxford: Basil Blackwell.

– 1983. "Manufacture in Town and Country Before the Factory." In *Manufacture in Town and Country Before the Factory*, edited by M. Berg, P. Hudson, and M. Sonenscher. Cambridge: Cambridge University Press.

Birch, Alan. 1967. *The Economic History of the British Iron and Steel Industry, 1784–1879*. London: F. Cass.

Birnie, Arthur. 1933. *An Economic History of Europe 1760–1930*. London: Methuen.

Bladen, V. 1926. "The Potteries in the Industrial Revolution." Economic History Supplement to *Economic Journal*.

Borchardt, Knut. 1975. "Germany, 1700–1914." *The Fontana Economic History of Europe* vol. 4, London: Collins.

Braudel, Fernand. 1973. *Capitalism and Material Life*. London: Weidenfeld and Nicholson.

Braudel, Fernand. 1982. *The Wheels of Commerce*. London: Collins.

Brelot, Claude. 1977. "Un Équilibre Dans La Tension: Économie et Société Franc-Comtoises Traditionnelles (1789–1870)." In *Histoire de la Franche-Comté*, edited by Roland Fietier.

Bruland, J. 1982. "Industrial Conflict as a Source of Technical Innovation." *Economy and Society* 11, no. 2: 91–121.

Buchanan, B.J. 1986. "The Evolution of the English Turnpike Trusts: Lessons From a Case Study." *Economic History Review* 39: 223–43.

Butt, John. 1977. "The Scottish Cotton Industry During the Industrial Revolution 1780–1840." In *Comparative Aspects of Scottish and Irish Economic and Social History 1600–1900*, edited by L.M. Cullen and T.C. Smout. Edinburgh: J. Donald.

Buyst, Eric, and Joel Mokyr. 1990. "Dutch Manufacturing and Trade during the French Period (1795-1814) in a Long Term Prespective." In *Economic Effects of the French Revolutionary and Napoleonic Wars*, Proceedings, Tenth International Economic History Congress, Session B-1, edited by Erik Aerts and François Crouzet. Leuven: Leuven University Press.

Cameron, Rondo. 1989. *A Concise Economic History of the World: From Paleolithic Times to the Present*. New York: Oxford University Press.

Caron, François, 1983. "France." In *Railways and the Economic Development of Europe 1830–1914*, edited by P. O'Brien. London: MacMillan.

Cavailles, Henri. 1946. *La Route Française*. Paris.

Chalkin, G.W. 1974. *The Provincial Towns of Georgian England*. London: Edward Arnold.

Chandler, Alfred D. 1977. *The Visible Hand*. Cambridge MA: Belknap.

Chapman, S.D. 1967. *The Early Factory Masters*. Newton Abbot: David and Charles Publishers.

– 1974. "The Textile Factory Before Arkwright, A Typology of Factory Development." *Business History Review* 48: 451–78.

– 1979a. "British Marketing Enterprise." *Business History Review* 53, no. 2: 205–34.

– 1979b. "Financial Constraints on the Growth of Firms in the Cotton Industry, 1790–1850." *Economic History Review* 32: 50–69.

– and S. Chassange. 1981. *European Textile Printers in the Eighteenth Century*. London: Heinemann.

Chartres, J.A. 1977a. *Internal Trade in England, 1500–1700*. London: MacMillan.

– 1977b. "Road Carrying in England in the Seventeenth Century: Myth and Reality." *Economic History Review* 30: 73–94.

Chartres, J.A. and Gerard Turnbull. 1983. "Road Transport." In *Transport in the Industrial Revolution*, edited by Derek Aldcroft and M.J. Freeman. Manchester: Manchester University Press.

Clapham, J.H. 1921. *The Economic Development of France and Germany 1815–1914*. Cambridge: Cambridge University Press.

– 1963. *An Economic History of Modern Britain*. 2nd ed. Cambridge: Cambridge University Press.

Clarkson, L.A. 1971. *The Pre-industrial Economy in England 1500–1750*. New York: Schocken Books.

Clough, Shephard Bancroft and C. W. Cole. 1946. *Economic History of Europe*. Boston: D.C. Heath Co.

Clout, Hugh. 1977. "Industrial Development in the 18th and 19th Centuries." In *Themes in the Historical Geography of France*, edited by Hugh Clout. London: Academic Press.

Clow, Archibald and Nan Clow. 1952. *The Chemical Revolution*. London: Batchworth Press.

Cohen, Jon S. 1981. "Managers and Machinery: An Analysis of the Rise of Factory Production." *Australian Economic Papers* 20: 24–41.

Cole, Arthur and George Watts. 1952. *The Handicrafts of France 1761–1788*.

Coleman, D.C. 1958. *The British Paper Industry 1495–1860*. Oxford: Clarendon.

– 1973. "Textile Growth." In *Textile History and Economic History*, edited by N.B. Harte and K.G. Ponting. Manchester: Manchester University Press.

– 1977. "The Coal Industry, A Rejoinder." *Economic History Review* 30: 343–5.

Coornaert, Emile. 1970. *La Flandre Française de Langue Flamande*. Paris: Éditions Ouvrières.

Copeland, John. 1968. *Roads and Their Traffic 1750–1850*. New York: A. M. Kelley.

Corfield, Penelope. 1982. *The Impact of English Towns 1700–1800*. Oxford: Oxford University Press.

Correspondence of Josiah Wedgwood 1781–1794. 1906.

Court, W.H.B. 1938. *The Rise of the Midland Industries, 1600–1838*. London: Oxford University Press.

– 1946. "Industrial Organization and Economic Progress in the Eighteenth Century Midlands." In *Transactions of the Royal Historical Society*, Series 4, 28: 85–100.

Cowan, Ruth. 1983. *More Work For Mother*. New York: Basic Books.

Crafts, N.F.R. 1977. "Industrial Revolution in England and France, Some Thoughts on the Question, 'Why Was England First?'." *Economic History Review* 30: 429–41.

– 1984. "Economic Growth in France and Britain, 1830–1910: A Review of the Evidence." *Journal of Economic History* 44: 49–67.

– 1985. *British Economic Growth During the Industrial Revolution*. Oxford: Clarendon.

– 1987. "British Economic Growth 1700–1850; Some Difficulties of Interpretation," *Explorations in Economic History* 24: 245–68.

Crouzet, François. 1967. "England and France in the Eighteenth Century: A Comparative Analysis of Two Economic Growths." In *The Causes of the Industrial Revolution in England*, edited by R.M. Hartwell. London: Methuen.

Crump, W.B. 1929. *The Leeds Woollen Industry 1780–1820*. Leeds: Thoresby Society.

Cule, J.E. 1938–40. "Finance and Industry in the Eighteenth Century, the Firm of Boulton and Watt." Economic History Supplement to *Economic Journal*.

Cunningham, William. 1921. *The Growth of English Industry and Commerce in Modern Times*. Cambridge: Cambridge University Press.

Daniels, George W. 1920. *The Early English Cotton Industry*. Manchester: Manchester University Press.

David, Paul. 1975. *Technical Choice, Innovation, and Economic Growth*. London: Cambridge University Press.

Deane, Phyllis. 1965. *The First Industrial Revolution*. Cambridge: Cambridge University Press.

Dechesne, Laurent. 1932. *Histoire Économique et Sociale de la Belgique*. Liège: J. Wykmans.

De Vries, Jan. 1977. "Histoire du Climat et Économie." *Annales; Économies, Sociétés, Civilisations* 32: 198–226.

– 1981. *Barges and Capitalism*. Utrecht: HES Publishers.

– 1983. *Urbanization in Europe 1500–1800*. Cambridge MA: Harvard University Press.

Donald, J. 1971. "The Crendon Needlemakers." *Records of Buckinghamshire*.

Duckham, Baron F. 1970. *A History of the Scottish Coal Industry, 1700–1815*. Newton Abbot: David and Charles Publishers.

– 1983. "Canals and River Navigations." In *Transport in the Industrial Revolution*, edited by Derek Aldcroft and M.J. Freeman. Manchester: Manchester University Press.

Dunham, Arthur Louis. 1955. *The Industrial Revolution in France 1815–1848*. New York: Exposition Press.

Durie, Alistair J. 1977. "The Scottish Linen Industry in the Eighteenth Century: Some Aspects of Expansion." In *Comparative Aspects ... 1600–1900*, edited by L.M. Cullen and T.C. Smout, Edinburgh: J. Donald.

Dyos, H. J. and Derek Aldcroft. 1969. *British Transportation, An Economic Survey From The Seventeenth to the Twentieth Century*. Leicester: Leicester University Press.

East, W.G. 1935. *An Historical Geography of Europe*. London: Methuen.

– 1969. "England in the Eighteenth Century." In *An Historical Geography of England Before 1800*, edited by H.C. Darby. Cambridge: Cambridge University Press.

Edwards, Michael M. 1967. *The Growth of the British Cotton Trade 1780–1815.* Manchester: Manchester University Press.

Enos, J. 1962. "The Rate and Direction of Inventive Activity; Economic and Social Factors." *N.B.E.R. Special Conference Series* no. 13.

Evans, F. T. 1982. "Wood Since the Industrial Revolution: A Strategic Retreat?" *History of Technology* vii, 37–56.

Fairlie, Susan. 1964. "Dyestuffs in the Eighteenth Century." *Economic History Review* 17: 488–510.

Field, Alexander. 1985. "On the Unimportance of Machinery." *Explorations in Economic History* 22: 378–401.

Fishlow, Albert. 1972. "Internal Transportation." Lance Davis et al. *American Economic Growth: An Economist's History of the United States.* New York: Harper and Row.

Fitton, R.S. and A.P. Wadsworth. 1958. *The Strutts and the Arkwrights 1758–1830.* New York: Augustus M. Kelley Publishers.

Flinn, M. 1962. *Men of Iron.* Edinburgh: Edinburgh University Press.

– 1985. *The History of the British Coal Industry, v. 2. 1700–1830.* Oxford: Clarendon.

– ed. 1957. *The Law Book of the Crowley Ironworks.* Durham: Andrews.

– and A. Birch. 1954. "The English Steel Industry Before 1856 With Special Reference to the Development of the Yorkshire Steel Industry." In *Yorkshire Bulletin of Economic and Social Research.*

Fogel, Robert. 1964. *Railroads and American Economic Growth, Essays in Econometric History.* Baltimore: Johns Hopkins Press.

Fohlen, Claude. 1966. "Charbon et Révolution Industrielle en France (1815–1850)." In *Charbon et Sciences Humaines,* edited by Louis Trenard. Paris: Mouton.

– 1970. "The Industrial Revolution in France." *Essays in French Economic History,* edited by Rondo Cameron. Homewood, IL: R.D. Irwin.

– 1975. "France, 1700–1914." *The Fontana Economic History of Europe* vol. 4. London: Collins.

Freeman, M.J. 1980. "Road Transport in the English Industrial Revolution." *Journal of Historical Geography* 6, no. 1: 17–25.

– 1983. "Introduction." In *Transport in the Industrial Revolution,* edited by Derek Aldcroft and M.J. Freeman. Manchester: Manchester University Press.

Gaski, J. 1982. "The Cause of the Industrial Revolution: A Brief 'Single Factor' Argument." *Journal of European Economic History* 11, no. 2: 227–34.

Gay, Edwin F. 1927. "Arthur Young on English Roads." *Quarterly Journal of Economics* 41: 545–55.

Geiger, Reed. 1974. *The Anzin Coal Company 1800–1833.* Newark DE: University of Delaware.

Gibbs, F.W. 1951. "The Rise of the Tinplate Industry." In *Annals of Science* 7: 25–61.

– 1953. "Historical Survey of the Japanning Trade." In *Annals of Science* 9: 88–95, 197–232.

Gilfillan, S.C. 1935. *The Sociology of Invention.* Cambridge MA: MIT Press.

Gille, Bertrand. 1969. *La Sidérurgie Française au XIXe Siècle.* Geneva: Librairie Droz.

– n.d. *Les Origines de la Grande Industrie Métallurgique en France.* Paris: Éditions Domat Montchrestien.

Gillet, Marcel. 1969. "The Coal Age and the Rise of Coalfields in the North and the Pas de Calais." In *Essays in European Economic History,* edited by F. Crouzet et al. London: Edward Arnold.

Ginarlis, J.E. 1971. "Capital Formation in Road and Canal Transport." In *Aspects of Capital Formation in Great Britain, 1750–1850,* edited by J.P.P. Higgins and S. Pollard. London: Methuen.

Girard, L. 1965. "Transport." *The Cambridge Economic History of Europe* vol. 6. Cambridge: Cambridge University Press.

Gittins, L. 1979. "Innovation in Textile Bleaching in Britain in the Eighteenth Century." *Business History Review* v. 53, no. 2.

Goodman, J. and K. Honeyman. 1988. *Gainful Pursuits: The Making of Industrial Europe 1600–1914.* London: Edward Arnold.

Gould, J.D. 1972. *Economic Growth in History.* London: Methuen.

Gregory, D. 1982. *The Transformation of Yorkshire.* London: Methuen.

Gregory, John Walter. 1938. *The Story of the Road from the Beginning Down to AD1931.* London: Maclehose.

Griffin, C.P. 1978. "Transport Change and the Development of the Leicester Coalfield in the Canal Age: A Re-interpretation," *Journal of Transport History* 4, no. 4: 227–38.

Griliches, Zvi. 1957. "Hybrid Corn: An Exploration in the Economics of Technological Change." *Econometrica* 25: 501–22.

Guignet, P. 1979. "The Lacemakers of Valenciennes in the Eighteenth Century." *Textile History* 10: 96–113.

Gutmann, Myron. 1988. *Toward the Modern Economy: Early Industry in Europe: 1500–1800.* Philadelphia: Temple University Press.

Habakkuk, H.J. 1955. "The Historical Experience on the Basic Conditions of Economic Progress." In *Economic Progress,* edited by P. Dupriez and D. Hague. New York: St. Martins Press.

Hadfield, Charles. 1950. *British Canals, An Illustrated History.* Newton Abbot: David and Charles Publishers.

Hammersley, G. 1979. "Did it Fall or Was it Pushed: The Foleys and the End of the Charcoal Iron Industry in the Eighteenth Century." In *The Search For Wealth and Stability,* edited by L.C. Smout. London: MacMillan.

Hammond, J.L. and B. 1925. *The Rise of Modern Industry.* London: Methuen.

Harris, J.R. 1978. "Attempts to Transfer English Steelmaking Techniques to France in the Eighteenth Century." In *Business and Businessmen,* edited by S. Marriner. Liverpool: Liverpool University Press.

– 1986. "Michael Alcock and the Transfer of Birmingham Technology to France Before the Revolution." *Journal of European Economic History* 15, no. 1: 7–57.

Harte, N.B. and K.G. Ponting. 1973. *Textile History and Economic History*. Manchester: Manchester University Press.

Hatley, V.A. 1980–81. "Locks, Lords, and Coal: A Study in Eighteenth Century Northamptonshire History." *Northamptonshire Past and Present* 6: 207–18.

Hausman, W.J. 1984. "London Coal Prices and the Vend." *Journal of Economic History* 45: 675–82.

Hawke, G.R. and J. Higgins. 1983. "Britain." In *Railways and the Economic Development of Europe 1830–1914*, edited by P. O'Brien. London: MacMillan.

Heaton, Herbert. 1948. *Economic History of Europe*. New York: Harper and Row.

– 1965. *The Yorkshire Woollen and Worsted Industries*. Oxford: Clarendon.

Henderson, W.O. 1954. *Britain and Industrial Europe 1750–1870*. Liverpool: Liverpool University Press.

– 1956. "The Genesis of the Industrial Revolution in France and Germany." *Kyklos* 9: 190–207.

– 1967. *The Industrial Revolution on the Continent 1800–1914*. London: F. Cass.

Hey, D. 1972. *The Rural Metalworkers of the Sheffield Region*. Leicester: Leicester University Press.

– 1980. *Packmen, Carriers, and Packhorse Roads*. Leicester: Leicester University Press.

Heywood, Colin. 1976. "The Rural Hosiery Industry of the Lower Champagne Region 1750–1850." *Textile History* 7: 90–111.

– 1977. *The Cotton Industry in France 1750–1850*. Loughborough: Department of Economics, Loughborough University.

Hicks, J. 1969. *A Theory of Economic History*. Oxford: Oxford University Press.

Hills, R.L. 1970. *Power in the Industrial Revolution*. Manchester: Manchester University Press.

– 1979. "Hargreaves, Arkwright, and Crompton: Why Three Inventors." *Textile History* 10: 114–26.

Hoppit, Julian. 1986. "Financial Crises in Eighteenth Century England." *Economic History Review* 39: 39–58.

– 1990. "Counting the Industrial Revolution." *Economic History Review* 43: 173–93.

Hudson, P. 1981. "Proto-Industrialization: The Case of the West Riding Wool Textile Industry in the eighteenth and early nineteenth centuries." *History Workshop Journal* 12: 34–61.

– 1983. "From Manor to Mill; The West Riding in Transition." In *Manufacture in Town and Country Before the Factory*, edited by M. Berg, P. Hudson, and M. Sonenscher. Cambridge: Cambridge University Press.

Hunt, E.H. and F.W. Botham. 1987. "Wages in Britain During The Industrial Revolution." *Economic History Review* 40: 380–99.

Hyde, Charles K. 1977. *Technological Change and the British Iron Industry 1700–1870*. Princeton NJ: Princeton University Press.

Jackman, W.T. 1916. *The Development of Modern Transportation in England*. Cambridge: Cambridge University Press.

Jackson, Gordon. 1983. "The Ports." In *Transport in the Industrial Revolution*, edited by Derek Aldcroft and M.J. Freeman. Manchester: Manchester University Press.

Jenkins, J.G. and K.G. Ponting. 1982. *The British Wool Textile Industry 1770–1914*. London: Heinemann.

Jenn, Françoise. 1980. "Partager Le Sort Commun (XVIIe–XVIIIe Siècle)." In *Histoire du Berry*, edited by Guy Devailley. Toulouse: Privat.

John, A.H. 1943. "Coal and Iron on a Glamorgan Estate." *Economic History Review* 13: 93–101.

Johnson, B.L.C. 1951. "The Charcoal Iron Industry in the Early Eighteenth Century." *Geographical Journal*.

Jones, Eric. 1985. "Disasters and Economic Differentiation Across Eurasia: A Reply." *Journal of Economic History* 44: 321–8.

– 1988. *Growth Recurring: Economic Change in World History*. Cambridge: Clarendon.

– and G.E. Mingay. 1967. *Land, Labour, and Population in the Industrial Revolution*. London: Edward Arnold.

Jones, S.R.H. 1978. "The Development of Needle Manufacture in the West Midlands Before 1750." *Economic History Review* 31: 354–68.

– 1984. "The Country Trade and the Marketing and Distribution of Birmingham Hardware 1750–1810." *Business History* 26, no. 1: 24–42.

Kaldor, Nicholas. 1972. "The Irrelevance of Equilibrium Economics." *Economic Journal* 82: 1237–55.

Kanefsky, J. and J. Robey. 1980. "Steam Engines in Eighteenth Century Britain: A Quantitative Assessment." *Technology and Culture* 21: 161–86.

Kaplan, Steven Lawrence. 1984. *Provisioning Paris*. Ithaca: Cornell University Press.

Kemp, Tom. 1971. *Economic Forces in French History*. London: Dobson.

Kenwood, A.G. and A.L. Lougheed. 1982. *Technological Diffusion and Industrialization Before 1914*. New York: St. Martins Press.

Kerridge, Eric. 1977. "The Coal Industry in Tudor and Stuart England: A Comment." *Economic History Review* 30: 340–2.

Kleinklausz, Arthur. 1976. *Histoire du Bourgogne*.

Kriedte, Peter, Hans Medich, and Jurgen Schlumbohn. 1981. *Industrialization Before Industrialization*. Cambridge: Cambridge Univerity Press.

Landes, David. 1969. *The Unbound Prometheus*. Cambridge: Cambridge University Press.

– 1986. "What Do Bosses Really Do?" *Journal of Economic History* 46: 585–624.

Lee, C.H. 1972. *A Cotton Enterprise 1795–1840; A History of McConnel and Kennedy Fine Cotton Spinners*. Manchester: Manchester University Press.

Léon, Pierre. 1976. "La Conquête de L'Espace National." "Les Nouvelles Répartitions." "L'Impulsion Technique." "Le Moteur de l'Industrialisation." In *Histoire Économique et Sociale de la France*, edited by P. Léon et al. Paris: Presses Universitaires de France.

Lepetit, Bernard. 1984. *Chemins de Terre et Voies d'Eau*. Paris: Éditions de l'École des Hautes Études en Sciences Sociales.

Letaconneux, J. 1908–09. "Les Transports en France au XVIIIème Siècle." *Revue d'Histoire Moderne et Contemporaine*.

Leuillout, P. 1959. *L'Alsace au Début du XIXe Siècle*. Paris: Sevpen.

Levainville, J. 1922. *L'Industrie du Fer en France*. Paris: A. Colin.

Levesque, Pierre. 1965. "D'Un Empire à l'Autre: Permanences et Changements (1814–1860)." In *Histoire de la Bourgogne*, edited by Jean Richard. Toulouse: Privat.

Levy, Robert. 1912. *Histoire Économique de l'Industrie Cotonnière en Alsace*. Paris: F. Alcan.

Lilley, Samuel. 1965. *Men, Machines, and History*. New York: International Publishers.

– 1976. "Technological Progress and the Industrial Revolution, 1700–1914." *The Fontana Economic History of Europe* vol. 3. London: Collins.

Livet, G. 1970. "Le XVIIIe Siècle et l'Esprit Des Lumières." In *Histoire de l'Alsace*, edited by Philippe Dollinger. Toulouse: Private.

Lloyd, Godfrey. 1913. *The Cutlery Trades*. New York: Longmans, Green, and Co.

Locke, Robert L. 1981. "French Industrialization: The Roehl Thesis Revisited." *Explorations in Economic History* 18: 415–33.

Lord, J. 1966. *Capital and Steam Power*. London: Frank Cass.

MacLeod, Christine. 1989. *Inventing the Industrial Revolution: The English Patent System 1660–1800*. New York: Cambridge University Press.

Mann, J de L. 1971. *The Cloth Industry in the West of England from 1640 to 1880*. Oxford: Clarendon.

Mantoux, Paul. [1905] 1961. *The Industrial Revolution in the Eighteenth Century*. New York: Harper and Row.

Marglin, S.A. 1974. "What Do Bosses Do? The Origins and Function of Hierarchy in Capitalist Production." *Review of Radical Political Economy* 6, no. 2: 60–112.

Markovitch, T.J. 1970. "The Dominant Sectors of French Industry." In *Essays in French Economic History*, edited by R. Cameron. Homewood, IL: R.D. Irwin.

Mathias, P. 1959. *The Brewing Industry in England*. Cambridge: Cambridge University Press.

McCloy, Shelby Thomas. 1952. *French Inventions of the Eighteenth Century*. Lexington KY: University of Kentucky Press.

McKendrick, Neil. 1982. *The Birth of a Consumer Society; The Commercialization of Eighteenth Century England*. London: Europa Publications.

Meuvret, Jean. 1971. *Études d'Histoire Économique*. Paris: A. Colin.

Meuvret, Jean. 1988. *Le Problème des Subsistances à l'époque Louis XIV*. Paris: L' École des Hautes Études en Sciences Sociales.

Moffit, L.W. 1925. *England on the Eve of the Industrial Revolution*. London: Frank Cass.

Mokyr, Joel. 1977. "Demand vs. Supply in the Industrial Revolution." *Journal of Economic History* 37: 981–1008.

– 1987. "Has the Industrial Revolution Been Crowded Out? Some Reflections on Crafts and Williamson." *Explorations in Economic History* 24: 268–92.

– 1990. *The Lever of Riches: Technological Creativity and Economic Progress*. New York: Oxford University Press.

– ed. 1985. *The Economics of the Industrial Revolution*. Totowa NJ: Rowman and Allenheld.

Morton, C.R., and N. Mutton. 1967. "The Transition to Cort's Puddling Process." *Journal of the Iron and Steel Institute* 205, no. 6: 722–8.

Mott, Reginald Arthur. 1936. *The History of Cokemaking*. Cambridge: W. Heffen and Sons.

Mumford, Lewis. 1934. *Technics and Civilization*. New York: Harcourt, Brace, Jovanovich.

Musson, A.E. and Eric Robinson. 1959. "The Early Growth of Steam Power." *Economic History Review* 11: 418–39.

– 1969. *Science and Technology in the Industrial Revolution*. Manchester: Manchester University Press.

Nef, J.U. 1932. *The Rise of the British Coal Industry*. London: Routledge Kegan Paul.

Nelson, Richard. 1962. "The Link Between Science and Invention: The Case of the Transistor." In *The Rate and Direction of Inventive Activity: Economic and Social Factors*. National Bureau of Economic Research.

North, Douglass. 1981. *Structure and Change in Economic History*. New York: W.W. Norton.

Nussbaum, Frederick L. 1968. *A History of the Economic Institutions of Modern Europe*. New York: F. S. Crofts.

O'Brien, George. 1977. *The Economic History of Ireland in the Eighteenth Century*. Philadelphia: Porcupine Press.

O'Brien, Patrick. 1983. "Transport and Economic Development in Europe 1789–1914." In *Railways and the Economic Development of Western Europe*, edited by P. O'Brien. London: MacMillan.

O'Brien, Patrick and Caglar Keyder. 1978. *Economic Growth in Britain and France 1780–1914*. London: George Allen and Unwin.

Parker, W.N. 1982. "European Development in Millenial Perspective." In *Economics in the Long View*, edited by C. Kindleberger and G. DiTella. New York: New York University Press.

Pawson, Eric. 1977. *Transport and Economy; The Turnpike Roads of Eighteenth Century Britain*. London: Academic Press.

– 1979. *The Early Industrial Revolution*. New York: Barnes and Noble.

Payen, Jacques. 1985. *La Machine à Vapeur Fixe en France*. Paris: Comité des travaux historiques et scientifiques.

Pelham, R.A. 1963–64. "The Water Power Crisis in Birmingham in the Eighteen Century." *University of Birmingham Historical Journal*.

Petot, Jean. 1958. *Histoire de L'Administration des Ponts et Chaussées*. Paris: Librairie M. Rivière.

Pollard, Sidney. 1964. "The Factory Village." *English Historical Review* 79: 513–31.

– 1965. *The Genesis of Modern Management*. London: E. Arnold.

– 1980. "A New Estimate of British Coal Production 1750–1850." *Economic History Review* 33: 212–35.

– 1981. *Peaceful Conquest: The Industrialization of Europe 1760–1970*. Oxford: Oxford University Press.

Pounds, N.J.G. and W.N. Parker. 1957a. *Coal and Steel in Western Europe*. London: Faber and Faber.

Pounds, N.J.G. 1957b. "Historical Geography of the Iron and Steel Industry of France." *Annals of the Association of American Geographers* 47: 3–14.

– 1979. *Historical Geography of Europe 1500–1800*. Cambridge: Cambridge University Press.

Pratt, E.A. 1912. *A History of Inland Transport and Commerce in England*. London: K. Paul, Trench, Trübner and Co.

Prêcheur, Claude. 1959. *La Lorraine Sidérurgie*. Paris: S.A.B.R.I.

Price, Roger. 1981. *The Economic Modernization of France, 1730–1880*. London: Croom Helm.

Price, Roger. 1983. *The Modernization of Rural France*. London: Hutchinson.

Raistrick, A. 1970. *Dynasty of Ironfounders*. London: Longmans, Green and Co.

Riden, P. 1977. "The Output of the British Iron Industry Before 1870." *Economic History Review* 30: 442–59.

Rimmer, W.G. 1960. *Marshalls of Leeds Flax-Spinners*. Cambridge: Cambridge University Press.

Ringrose, David. 1970. *Transportation and Economic Stagnation in Spain 1750–1850*. Durham NC: Duke University Press.

Rioux, Pierre. 1971. *La Révolution Industrielle*. Paris: Éditions du Seuil.

Roehl, R. 1976. "French Industrialization: A Reconsideration." *Explorations in Economic History* 12: 230–81.

Roepke, Howard G. 1970. *Movements of the British Iron and Steel Industry 1720–1850*. Urbana IL: University of Illinois Press.

Rogers, Alan. 1981. "Rural Industries and Social Structure: The Framework Knitting Industry of South Nottinghamshire." *Textile History* 12: 7–36.

Roll, Eric. 1968. *An Early Experiment in Industrial Organization*. London: Longmans, Green, and Co.

Rolt, L.T.C. 1968. *Tools for the Job*. London: B.T. Batsford Ltd.

Rosenberg, Nathan. 1976. *Perspectives on Technology*. Cambridge: Cambridge University Press.

Rouff, M. 1922. *Les Mines de Charbon en France au XVIIIe Siècle 1744–91*. Paris: F. Rieder.

Rousseau, P. 1961. *Histoire des Transports*. Paris: Fayard.

Rowland, K.T. 1974. *Eighteenth Century Inventions*. Newton Abbot: David and Charles Publishers.

Rowlands, Marie B. 1975. *Masters and Men in the West Midlands Metalware Trades Before the Industrial Revolution*. Manchester: Manchester University Press.

Rule, John. 1981. *The Experience of Labour in Eighteenth Century English Industry*. London: Croom Helm.

Saussure, Cesar de. 1902. *A Foreign View of England in the Reigns of George I and George II*. Mme. Van Muyden, ed. and trans.

Schumpeter, Joseph. 1939. *Business Cycles*. New York: McGraw-Hill.

Scitovsky, T. 1986. *Human Desire and Economic Satisfaction: Essays on the Frontiers of Economics*. New York: New York University Press.

Sée, Henri. 1939. *Histoire Économique de la France*. Paris: A. Colin.

Singer, C. et al. 1958. *A History of Technology*. Vol. 4. New York: Oxford University Press.

Smith, John. 1979. *The Origins and Early Development of The Heavy Chemical Industry in France*. Oxford: Clarendon.

Sokoloff, Kenneth. 1984. "Was the Transition From the Artisanal Shop to the Factory Associated With Gains in Efficiency?: Evidence From the U.S. Manufacturing Censuses of 1820 and 1850." *Explorations in Economic History* 21: 351–82.

Styles, John. 1983. "Embezzlement, Industry, and the Law in England 1500–1800." In Berg, Hudson, and Sonenscher. *Manufacture in Town and Country Before the Industrial Revolution*. Cambridge: Cambridge University Press.

Sullivan, Richard J. 1989. "England's 'Age of Invention': The Acceleration of Patents and Patentable Invention during the Indutrial Revolution" *Explorations in Economic History* 26: 424–52.

Szostak, Rick. 1989. "The Organization of Work: The Emergence of the Factory Revisited." *Journal of Economic Behavior and Organization* 11: 343–58.

– 1991. "Institutional Inheritance and Early American Industrialization." In *The Vital One: Essays Presented to Jonathan R.T. Hughes*, edited by Joel Mokyr 289–309. Greenwich: JAI Press.

Tann, Jennifer. 1981. *The Selected Papers of Boulton and Watt*. Cambridge MA: MIT Press.

Thbaut, Louis. 1961. "Les Voies Navigables et L'Industrie du Nord de la France." *Revue du Nord*.

Thomas, Brinley. 1986. "Was There an Energy Crisis in Great Britain in the Seventeenth Century?" *Explorations in Economic History* 23: 124–52.

Thomas, J. 1937. "The Pottery Industry and the Industrial Revolution." Economic History Supplement to *Economic Journal*.

Thomson, J.K.J. 1982. *Clermont-de-Lodève 1633–1789*. Cambridge: Cambridge University Press.

Trenard, Louis. 1950. "De La Route Royale à L'Âge D'Or Des Diligences." In *Les Routes de France Depuis Les Origines Jusqu'à Nos Jours*, edited by G. Michaud. Paris: Association Pour La Diffusion de La Pensée Française.

Tresse, René. 1955. "Le Développement de la Fabrication des Faux en France de 1785 à 1827." *Annales: Économies, Sociétés, Civilisations* 10: 341–58.

Trinder, B.S. 1973. *The Industrial Revolution in Shropshire*. Chichester: Phillimore.

Turnbull, Geoffrey. 1951. *A History of the Calico Printing Industry of Great Britain*. Altrincham: J. Sheratt.

Turnbull, Gerard. 1979. *Traffic and Transport: An Economic History of Pickfords*. London: George Allen and Unwin.

– 1982. "Scotch Linen, Stores, Wars, and Privateers." *Journal of Transport History* 3rd series, 3, no. 1.

– 1987. "Canals, Coal, and Regional Growth During The Industrial Revolution." *Economic History Review* 40: 537–60.

Usher, A.P. 1920. *An Introduction to the Industrial History of England*. Boston: Houghton Mifflin.

– 1954. *A History of Mechanical Inventions*. Cambridge MA: Harvard University Press.

Vial, Jean. 1967. *L'Industrialisation de la Sidérurgie Française 1814–1864*. Paris-La Haye: Mouton.

Von Tunzelman, Knick. 1978. *Steam Power and British Industrialization to 1860*. Oxford: Oxford University Press.

Wadsworth, A.P. and Julia deLacy Mann. 1965. *The Cotton Trade and Industrial Lancashire 1600–1780*. Manchester: Manchester University Press.

Ward, J.R. 1974. *The Finance of Canal Building in Eighteenth Century England*. London: Oxford University Press.

Weatherill, Lorna. 1971. *The Pottery Trade and North Staffordshire 1660–1760*. New York: Augustus M. Kelley Publishers.

– 1983. "The Growth of the Pottery Industry in England 1660–1815: Some New Estimates and Evidence." *Post-Medieval Archaeology*.

Webb, Sidney and Beatrice. 1963. *The Story of the King's Highway*. London: Longmans, Green, and Co.

Weber, Eugen. 1976. *Peasants Into Frenchmen: The Modernization of Rural France*. Stanford: Stanford University Press.

Weir, David. 1984. "Life Under Pressure: France and England 1670–1870." *Journal of Economic History* 44: 27–47.

Wells, F.A. 1935. *The British Hosiery Trade*. London: George Allen and Unwin.

Westerfield, R.B. 1920. *Middlemen in English History*. New York: Augustus M. Kelley Publishers.

White, D.P. 1977. "The Birmingham Button Industry." *Post-Medieval Archaeology.*

Willan, T.S. 1964. *River Navigation in England.* London: F. Cass.

– 1967. *The English Coasting Trade.* Manchester: Manchester University Press.

Williamson, J. 1984. "Why Was British Growth So Slow During the Industrial Revolution?" *Journal of Economic History* 44: 687–712.

– 1987. "Debating the British Industrial Revolution." *Explorations in Economic History* 24: 293–319.

Williamson, Oliver. 1980. "The Organization of Work: A Comparative Institutional Assessment." *Journal of Economic Behavior and Organization* 1: 5–38.

Wilson, Charles and Geoffrey Parker. 1977. *An Introduction to the Sources of European Economic History 1500–1800.* London: Weidenfeld and Nicolson.

Wilson, R.G. 1973. "The Supremacy of the Yorkshire Cloth Industry in the Eighteenth Century." In *Textile History and Economic History*, edited by M.B. Harte and K.G. Ponting. Manchester: Manchester University Press.

Wolff, K.H. 1974. "Textile Bleaching and the Birth of the Chemical Industry," *Business History Review* 48, no. 2: 143–63.

Wolkowitsch, M. 1960. *L'Économie Des Transports Dans Le Centre et le Centre-Ouest De La France.* Paris: Société d'Édition d'Enseignement Supérieur.

Woronoff, D. 1970. "Tradition et Innovation Dans la Sidérurgie; Un Exemple de Gestion d'Enterprise en Haute-Marne Sous le Consulat et l'Empire." *Revue d'Histoire Moderne et Contemporaine* 17: 559–73.

– 1984. *L'Industrie Sidérurgique en France Pendant la Révolution et l'Empire.*

Wrigley, E.A. 1988. *Continuity, Chance, and Change.* Cambridge: Cambridge University Press.

Youngson, A.J. 1967. *Overhead Capital: A Study in Development Economics.* Edinburgh: Edinburgh University Press.

Index